Poppies, Politics, and Power

Poppies, Politics, and Power

Afghanistan and the Global History of Drugs and Diplomacy

James Tharin Bradford

Cornell University Press
Ithaca and London

First published 2019 by Cornell University Press

Library of Congress Cataloging-in-Publication Data

Names: Bradford, James Tharin, 1982– author.
Title: Poppies, politics, and power : Afghanistan and the global history of drugs and diplomacy / by James Tharin Bradford.
Description: Ithaca : Cornell University Press, 2019. | Includes bibliographical references and index.
Identifiers: LCCN 2018047979 (print) | LCCN 2018053979 (ebook) | ISBN 9781501738340 (e-book pdf) | ISBN 9781501738357 (e-book epub/mobi) | ISBN 9781501738333 | ISBN 9781501738333 (hardcover) | ISBN 9781501739767 (pbk.)
Subjects: LCSH: Opium trade—Afghanistan—History. | Drug traffic—Afghanistan—History. | Drug control—Afghanistan—History.
Classification: LCC HV5840.A3 (ebook) | LCC HV5840.A3 B73 2019 (print) | DDC 364.1/336509581—dc23
LC record available at https://lccn.loc.gov/2018047979

This book is dedicated to my children, Winston, Lewis, and Beatrice, and especially to my wife, Cara, whose patience, love, and support helped see this project through

Contents

Acknowledgments ix

Introduction 1

1. Colonial and Global Engagements: Afghan Opium on the Periphery of the Global Drug Market 16

2. The Politics of Prohibition: How Diplomacy with the United States Shifted the Drug Control Paradigm in Afghanistan 44

3. The Consequences of Coercion in Badakhshan: The 1958 Prohibition of Opium and the Issue of Culture in Drug Control Policy 85

4. East Meets West: Hippies, Hash, and the Globalization of the Afghan Drug Trade 116

5. The Afghan Connection: Smuggling, Heroin, and Nixon's War on Drugs in Afghanistan 145

6. All Goods Are Dangerous Goods: Development, the Global Market, and Opium in the Helmand Valley, Afghanistan 180

Epilogue 214

Notes 223

Bibliography 261

Index 273

Acknowledgments

I'm sure many of my undergraduate professors would be astonished to know that not only did I get a PhD but published a book. Needless to say, I was not a great student during my first few years of undergraduate studies. Much like the poppy plant, however, I matured in time, and let us hope this book can be as powerful, effective, and maybe even as addictive (figuratively), as opium itself.

During graduate school, there were times when I was at a total loss as to the direction of my doctoral research. For that, a special thanks goes to the late Dr. Christina Gilmartin. Before her passing, Chris was one of the few professors who believed in my work. She not only convinced me to pursue my doctorate, despite having entirely different geographic and topic specialties, but she spent the time to learn the literature of drugs and Afghanistan to accommodate my needs. If not for Chris, I would never have pursued a doctoral degree, and for that I am forever grateful. After her passing, I was fortunate to have many wonderful academics in the Northeastern History Department who helped guide me to the finish line. My adviser, Heather

Streets-Salter, provided me with keen insights and critiques that helped guide my project and facilitated its focus and completion. I am especially grateful for her willingness to take the chair after Professor Gilmartin's passing. Dr. Tom Havens also gave so much of his time and energy to my intellectual and professional development. He is the role model for everything I hope to become.

But none of this would have happened without Dr. Thomas Barfield in the Anthropology Department at Boston University. It was his class that first introduced me to Afghanistan. More important, however, was his incredible patience in dealing with the many variations of the project. I once sat in his office for an hour, lamenting whether this was a project that could even be done. Although he was probably quite annoyed, he remained kind, and more important, patient, and ultimately offered keen insights that took my project into a broader and more attainable direction. For his personal and professional insights, I offer my tremendous gratitude.

I was fortunate to work with tremendous doctoral students at Northeastern who could be counted on not only for their intellectual insights but also for an important pint at Punters. Thank you to Andrew Jarboe, Zachary Scarlett, Samantha Christiansen, Malcolm Purinton, Stephanie Boyle, and Stacy Farenthold. A very special note of appreciation and thanks goes to my brilliant friend Burleigh Hendrickson, who read this entire manuscript and provided a great deal of healthy criticism. I cannot imagine how much time you took to edit this book, but you offered such valuable critiques for which I am forever indebted.

I met many wonderful and stimulating colleagues on my travels for research and conferences. I want to thank Alfie Paul at the National Archives in College Park for his time and patience in helping me figure out just what exactly I was doing. I would also like to thank Hirad Dinavari at the Library of Congress, who was the model of helpfulness and responsiveness. Masuma Naziri was most supportive in helping navigate the National Archives in Kabul, Afghanistan. For taking the time out of their hectic schedules to talk about their work from many years ago, many thanks to Terry Burke, Doug Wankel, Joe Keefe, and Elizabeth Jones. To the staff at the American Institute of Afghanistan Studies in Kabul, Dr. Rohullah Amin, Sultan Barakzai, and Zafar Daqiq: thank you. And to Jebrael Amin, you are a wonderful representative of the love, sincerity, and hospitality of the Afghan people. For your help doing research, thank you.

A great thanks goes to my editor Jim Lance, who encouraged me to follow through with this book. I would also like to thank the rest of the team at Cornell University Press, especially Carmen Adriana Torrado Gonzalez, Jennifer Savran Kelly, and Ellen Murphy, as well as Sandy Aitken for indexing, and Mary Ribesky at Westchester Publishing Services. Thank you all for your patience in helping me finish this book. And most importantly, thank you for giving me the opportunity to publish my first book. I have presented various excerpts of this book at conferences and workshops over the last several years. At the Alcohol and Drug History Society, I would like to thank Professors James Mills, Patricia Barton, Paul Gootenberg, Stephen Snelders, and Miriam Kingsberg for their keen insights. To Mario Del Pero and Andrew Preston, and the participants of the SHAFR (Society for Historians of American Foreign Relations) summer workshop at the University of Cambridge, thank you for your criticisms and suggestions. To John Buchanan, who introduced me to iconic figures in the study of drugs in Southeast Asia such as Alfred McCoy and Bertil Lintner, thank you, and may we eat royally again soon. I have also been fortunate enough to meet researchers who risk both life and limb to study the contemporary drug trade in Afghanistan, and took the time to help in my own historical inquiry. I would also like to thank the two readers of this manuscript for the attention and detail paid to my project. In that regard, a special thank you to Pierre-Arnaud Chouvy, who helped guide this project into much needed new territory. And to David Mansfield, thank you most of all. I have the utmost respect for all that you do and am truly grateful for your ideas about my work and conducting research in Afghanistan. If only more people in the drug field shared your empathy and understanding.

I am also grateful for the following sources of financial support. I was fortunate to receive the John F. Richards Fellowship and the John F. Richards Travel Grant from the American Institute of Afghanistan Studies for archival research and travel abroad. I also received a tremendous amount of financial support from Berklee College of Music, where I teach primarily, as well as from Babson College, where I teach as an adjunct. Both schools helped fund my research, and I feel fortunate to work at both institutions.

And to my students, a tremendous thank you. The millennial generation gets its fair share of criticisms, much of it justified, but many of my students inspire me with their willingness to engage and interact with a topic (drugs) that is both universal and relevant, yet remains taboo. Fortunately, we don't have that problem in my classroom. Thank you for your honesty, desire to learn, and your willingness to engage with me and the academic world of illicit drugs. You give me hope for the future. To my colleagues, thank you as well. Your support in both writing and teaching has gone a long way in helping me finish this book.

Last and most important, I wish to express a great deal of love and appreciation for my family. I offer thanks to my siblings, Will, Leslie, and Marion, for their unyielding support; to my grandparents, who gave up on me becoming a lawyer and accepted me as a historian; to my in-laws, Bob and Ann Marie, who treat me as one of their own; and most important, to my parents, John and Marjorie—I'm not sure you ever imagined it would be me publishing a book. I could not have done it without you.

It is to my wife and kids that I dedicate this book. To Beatrice, Lewis, and Winston, you are the inspiration of my life. Your love, energy, and support push me to be the best I can be. And to my wife, Cara, who took care of our three kids when I was away from home and who spent countless hours listening to me talk about my project, I love you and thank you with all of my heart.

Poppies, Politics, and Power

Introduction

Opium holds a special place in the contemporary story about Afghanistan. Unlike hashish (*charse*), or bhang, which have been used, and in some cases venerated, for centuries, opium is a relatively new character in the Afghan drama. Nonetheless, opium has become an omnipresent piece of the contemporary Afghan narrative: in Afghanistan, opiates, particularly heroin, run rampant in the streets of Kabul; during the late spring, poppies dominate much of the Afghan countryside; in Afghanistan's political economy, opium remains a primary source of revenue for many antistate groups and a pervasive source of corruption for many of the countries' politicians; and for many observers, opium is seen as one of, if not the major, impediment to a stable Afghanistan.

In essence, opium has come to define Afghanistan. If we are to think solely about the contemporary situation, this is mostly true. In 2007, Afghanistan produced an estimated 8,200 metric tons of opium, at that time, the largest single-year output ever;[1] it surpassed 9,000 tons in 2017.[2] Opium has become so important to the Afghan economy that it currently exports roughly

80 percent of the world's illicit opium and is estimated to be roughly 4 percent of Afghanistan's GDP.[3] The depth, influence, and impact of the drug trade in Afghanistan is unprecedented, and not just in Afghan history, but possibly in the history of the world. More significant is that opium thrives amidst an ongoing conflict: Afghanistan has been at war for the better of four decades. And since 2001, with the US invasion and seventeen years of US support and aid, the Afghan government has struggled to deal with an incessant Taliban insurgency. Opium is thus tied to the political and social problems, especially the insurgency, that continue to plague the country.[4] As a result, opium is perceived as the major impediment to the reconstruction of the Afghan state; it thrives because of the conditions of statelessness and lawlessness that now characterize Afghanistan.

The story of the Afghan drug trade wasn't always like this, however. Opium was not associated with terrorism, or addiction, or even political instability. There was little concept of counternarcotics or its association with counterinsurgency.[5] Rather, opium was part of a larger story about political power, state development, diplomacy, and even health care. It embodied an image of modernity, transformation, and growth. In other words, it was tied to the formation of the Afghan state. This connection, between state formation and both the licit and illicit drug trades, has largely been lost in the contemporary narrative; this, in turn, limits our understanding of how the contemporary illicit drug trade is not merely juxtaposed to governance but entangled and enmeshed within it. As David Mansfield states, "It is impossible to isolate illicit drugs from the wider issue of governance in Afghanistan; the two are intrinsically linked and, as such, will require a clear and coherent strategy to address them."[6] In other words, opium is not entirely the cause of, or exacerbating force to, the conditions of instability and chaos, but rather exists and thrives as a symptom of deeper issues of governance, culture, and even diplomacy.

What has changed in recent decades to shape the role opium plays in Afghanistan? Opium, for the past century, was a quasi-legal commodity, traded in regional or global markets. It was sometimes taxed, and to some extent, regulated. And while addicts, smugglers, and corrupt politicians certainly existed during the past century, they were only part of the picture, not *the* picture. This book aims to recast this image to reflect the nuances of opium and its historical legacy in the country. For example, and as you will soon see, the farmer would likely be followed by government officials trying to buy the crop for the government-run joint stock companies (*shirkat*); or dealing with American pharmaceutical agents keen to buy the cheap but potent Afghan opium; or foreign antinarcotics agents nervously watching the harvest, fearful of the almost certain reality that Afghanistan may well become *the* major illicit drug producer for the world; or (what is often familiar to many rural Afghans), government and police officials descending on their fields to eradicate their only livelihood. In essence, the picture would be far more complex and constantly evolving; this would better reflect the historical reality of this commodity, both in Afghanistan and in its relationship to the world.

One of the major impediments to demystifying the Afghan opium trade has been the lack of historical analysis. Most, if not all, of the contemporary analyses of the drug trade start with the Afghan-Soviet War as their genesis. This, of course, has been part of the much broader trend of political and economic analyses that have focused overwhelmingly on the last forty years of Afghan history. The clear need to understand why and how opium endures despite the continued US presence is fundamental to assessing the larger aim of US policy in Afghanistan to build a functional and stable state. As a result, a massive body of work has emerged that explores the profound impact of illicit opium on the social, political, and economic dynamics of contemporary Afghanistan.[7] The breadth and depth of the contemporary analysis is impressive. Anyone interested in drugs or Afghanistan can now easily dissect almost any aspect of the contemporary drug trade. One can examine opium's role in providing a form of labor or credit, or analyze the root causes of its persistence or its relation to the United States' "War on Terror."[8] International organizations, such as the United Nations and NATO (North Atlantic Treaty Organization), produce yearly summaries of the Afghan opium trade.[9] Reporters and scholars have produced valuable and insightful books that bring to life the deeper, more personal dimensions of the contemporary drug trade.[10] Yet despite all of the valuable contributions to understanding the contemporary drug trade, there remains one significant flaw: the focus remains on the current situation and omits the historical antecedents.

Unfortunately, the overwhelming emphasis on the contemporary Afghan drug trade relegates the features of previous events and processes to obscurity.

By the beginning of the twentieth century, opium (and other drugs) from Afghanistan were actively and increasingly being traded on the global market. The growing presence of Afghan drugs in the regional and global economic systems, in both licit and illicit forms, also coincided with the beginning of international drug control regimes, which ultimately led the Afghan government to participate, to varying degrees, in international drug control. Thus, the history of drugs in Afghanistan is, in many ways, entangled with the history of the global drug trade and international drug control. Understanding Afghanistan's role in this dynamic helps explain how and why the drug trade, and domestic drug policy, changed and evolved over time. This is mostly because international drug control did not stop the global drug trade; rather, it forced it to evolve and grow. In fact, international drug diplomacy did little more than to push the drug trade to new markets, prompting traffickers and distributors to search for new sources, and consequently, catalyzing an evolution in the global illicit drug trade, of which Afghanistan would play an increasingly important role.

For many governments, participation in the international drug control system was not only part of an effort to stop drugs but was also used to bolster other, broader state-building ambitions. Producer countries in particular were influenced tremendously by the pressures and attractions of international drug diplomacy. For them, to suppress the production of drugs brought potential for new trade deals, increased military support, or infrastructural developments. In effect, for most producer and consumer nations, embracing international drug control was not really part of a moral crusade, but rather, as Kathleen Frydl states, stemmed from the recognition that drug control was "a valued tool of statecraft," one that over time, developed "into less of a specific mission and more of a modality, a way to exercise state power."[11]

Although drug control was an important tool in the state craft armory, it carried with it a cultural weight that reflected the perspectives of a rather small contingent of antidrug crusaders. As a result, it was not only a projection of state power but a reflection of the cultural influences at the root of that projection.[12] The impact of international drug control was most acute at the local and national levels of producer nations, in which the international norms guiding the principles of drug control were shaped primarily by the context of local and national political culture. As Itty Abraham and Willem van Schendel state, drug laws are

> relational, culturally inflected, and act asymmetrically along the contours of power and social mores. Legal restrictions often come up against socially sanctioned practices, and while this may have the effect of driving these practices into the sphere of criminality, it does not eliminate them nor does it necessarily force them into hiding.[13]

Thus, to examine the history of drug control is to analyze not only how it fits into the history of the formation of the state but also how it factored into the state's impacts, fissures, schisms, fractures, and failures. Furthermore, it raises important questions about the persistence of illicit drug trades. Are they simply products of the global market? Or do they also reflect forms of political resistance, or the power of non- or antistate actors? And if that is the case, is the perseverance of the illicit drug trade a deeper indictment against the failure of the national and international political systems?

In Paul Gootenberg's seminal work, *Andean Cocaine*, he analyzed how drugs were "made" into or "constructed" as global commodities;[14] in a similar vein, this book explores how drugs and drug policy, too, were "made" and "constructed" in Afghanistan. Analyzing these features reveals the ways Afghanistan used drug control not only as a "modality" of state growth, but perhaps more important, how drug control fit into the deeper mores of governance in Afghanistan. In this vein, drug control was not simply a reaction to the drug trade but also served to catalyze and shape its very future.

My research considers the relationship between the Afghan government and its various state-building projects, Afghan society, and the emergence of opium within a longer historical analysis. In sketching the historical roots of the contemporary opium trade, scholars have presented opium's emergence in Afghanistan as a consequence primarily of the Afghan-Soviet War (1979–89). This has created a mutual dependence between historical and contemporary sources about the narrative of the Afghan opium trade and its origins in the Afghan-Soviet War. For these writers, the history of opium in Afghanistan begins with the war in Afghanistan and pegs its emergence to when the country became a stateless place as the principal engine driving their story. While these explanations certainly contribute to the understanding of why opium expanded in Afghanistan, they do not explain how the contemporary opium industry began. Ultimately, the lack of deeper historical analysis obfuscates how the contemporary Afghan opium industry is tied to longer historical narratives involving opium, the formation of the Afghan state, and the conflicts of governance in Afghan society.

Examining the history of opium and other drugs in Afghanistan during the twentieth century (the late 1800s–1979), reveals that drugs and drug policy were active features in the formation of the Afghan state. In particular, by analyzing why and how the Afghan government gradually embraced antiopium policies, we see that it was not simply a straightforward response to the threat of the growing illicit drug industry. Rather, drug control, particularly total prohibition, was largely shaped by international diplomacy. As a result, Afghan drug policy largely reflected ambitions of foreign states, especially the United States, which envisioned drug control through the suppression of supply, regardless of how such policies would manifest in local situations far from their shores. More important, the conflicts that surrounded these policies not only served to delegitimize the building of the state, but in turn, also stimulated the illicit drug trade. Thus, opium's emergence in the illicit market occurs not as a by-product of lawlessness, statelessness, and war but as a consequence of the conflict surrounding the process of state formation in Afghanistan during the twentieth century.[15]

Analyzing the history of opium in Afghanistan before the Afghan-Soviet War unearths a mutually constitutive relationship between state formation and the production and trade of opium, one that fundamentally alters the conventional historical narrative. On the one hand, opium policy was an important aspect of the state's attempt to project its authority throughout the country.[16] After abandoning efforts to become a legal opium producer, the Afghan state embraced the prohibition of opium production and trade as a means of expanding state control. The attempts to use drug control as a conduit for the expansion of the state were ultimately inhibited by the government's goals, however. The Afghan state, especially under Musahiban leadership (1929–78), was designed to limit interactions with rural Afghanistan, which in turn created a structural dependence on foreign aid to finance the state. As a result, during the late 1960s and 1970s, when the state needed to enforce drug control laws to maintain access to the foreign aid on which it was so dependent, the state did not have the ability to impose effective drug control policy. Thus, analyzing Afghan drug control policy reveals how the historical antecedents, particularly the growing social, political, and economic uncertainty of the late Musahiban dynasty, were fundamental to the emergence of the contemporary drug trade. This is critical not only to understand the historic dimensions of the drug trade and drug control but how drugs fit into the landscape of governance in Afghanistan today.

The roots of drug policy as a consequence of state design, in this case, the dependence on foreign money, led the Afghan state to establish and enforce laws that ultimately went against cultural, political, and economic norms. As a result, drug policy had the effect of reinforcing the profound disconnect between the government and much of Afghan society. In particular, the extent to which state policy was enforced or ignored, complied with or resisted, largely revolved around tribal, ethnic, familial, or local needs, or some combination of the aforementioned, i.e., the *qawm*.[17] In fact, *qawm* influenced every level of drug policy and the drug trade. Consequently, the Afghan government's continued and expanded pursuit of antinarcotics policy contributed to the deepening fragmentation of Afghanistan as individuals opted to enforce or ignore laws based on the needs of the *qawm*. Inevitably, as drug policy proved increasingly invasive to conventional ways of life, it contributed to the greater illegitimacy of the state, all but reinforcing, if not stimulating, the expansion of drug production and trade in subsequent years.

As a historical analysis of the emergence of the illicit drug trade in Afghanistan, this study recognizes the limitations of the state as an analytical framework. By adopting analytic perspectives that highlight the participants in the international narcotics trade (farmers, traders, smugglers, and international crime organizations), we come to very different conclusions about the "causes, meanings, and processes" that shaped the contemporary opium situation.[18] Fragmentation, in particular, is not just a consequence of Afghan drug policy but also a product of Afghan peoples' response and reaction to state policy. Drug smuggling across borders, the manipulation of prohibitions, and the otherwise ambivalence toward drug control symbolize the ways individuals and groups respond to and influence the creation and implementation of government drug policy, ultimately contributing to this process of fragmentation.[19] The history I hope to convey is not only one of the state's actions and impact but also one in which people respond to and influence state actions.

Ultimately, this study examines how drug control policy and the resistance to it reflected deeper political, social, and cultural tensions between the state and Afghan society. I attempt to recast the history of opium in Afghanistan to demonstrate that drug control, as a reflection of the ambitions, desires, and needs of the Afghan state, were fundamental in shaping the conditions of statelessness and lawlessness that are commonly thought to characterize the Afghan opium industry today. The flourishing opium trade, then, is not simply the *result* of a fragmented state but rather a critical component of the historical *process* of state formation, social resistance, and fragmentation in the region.

A survey of existing scholarship on Afghanistan and opium reveals a gap between the two fields. Although Afghan history and the history of opium have well-established bodies of scholarly consideration, the history of opium as a component of nation building in Afghanistan before the events of the 1970s, although significant, has generated little scholarship. Louis Dupree, Vartan Gregorian, Stephen Fry, Barnett Rubin, Leon and Leila Poullada, Larry Goodson, Richard Newell, Thomas Barfield, Olivier Roy, Ahmed Rashid, and Ashraf Ghani have all published extensively on various aspects of the history of Afghanistan in the twentieth century. Their work has dealt extensively with the building of the Afghan state and the role of political culture in shaping the nation-building process. They emphasize how the political culture led to government policies constructed around the state's conscious recognition of its limitations, weaknesses, and fears of tribal insurrections, ultimately manifested in the state's increasing reliance on foreign patrons for state revenue. Yet opium remains largely absent from these histories.

The connection between drugs and political culture has been a major focus in histories of other drug-producing nations and regions. William McAllister, Francisco Thoumi, William Walker, Andrew Bagley, Patrick Clawson, and Alfred McCoy have all published books on the history of drugs in various countries around the world during the twentieth century. Their work has examined how the political and cultural history of those nations provided necessary conditions for narcotic economies to emerge and thrive. And yet, paralleling the dearth of literature on the history of Afghanistan and on the history of drugs in other nations, the history of opium in Afghanistan remains remarkably incomplete. McCoy,[20] M. Emdad-ul Haq,[21] David MacDonald,[22] Pierre-Arnaud Chouvy, Nigel Allan,[23] Amir Zada Asad,[24] Catherine Lamour and Michael Lamberti,[25] Ikramul Haq,[26] and Alan Labrousse have all written on the history of opium in Afghanistan. Their focus centers primarily on the 1970s, however, particularly the prohibitions in Iran and Pakistan and the Afghan-Soviet War. Although their work is essential to understanding the contemporary opium trade in Afghanistan, earlier periods remain relatively unexplored. In fact, this is the first historical monograph to address the history of drugs in Afghanistan.

The overarching narrative that emerges from the histories of Afghan opium focuses on global and regional factors, which are undoubtedly important. Yet they inevitably produce a story in which Afghanistan emerges as a victim of these global and regional processes and events. In other words, the history of opium in Afghanistan is essentially marginalized within the country's own history. Why has such an important factor in the history of opium in Afghanistan remained so understudied? Sources are partially to blame. The study of drugs, particularly during the twentieth century, is difficult in and of itself. Many of the more recent documents have remained classified or are heavily redacted. Nonetheless, the United States has the most substantial historical record of narcotics matters, primarily because of its significant presence in leading antinarcotic regulation. In other words, since it was an issue to the United States, the issue generated an archive. Thus, my approach is rooted in archival records collected at the National Archives at Kew in the United Kingdom, the British Library, the Hoover Institution Library at Stanford University, the United Nations Archive in New York, and the National Archives II in College Park, Maryland.

Afghanistan has never been a place conducive to historical inquiry. The cultural indifference to record keeping, reinforced by the fact that Afghanistan was never formally colonized, has made Afghan records difficult to find. As a result, this study undoubtedly lacks a strong Afghan voice. The shortage of Afghan sources certainly contributes to this dilemma, and as a result, some of what I analyze here should not be read as conclusive. Despite such limitations, documents from the Arshaf-e Milli (National Archives), Afghanistan Research and Evaluation Unit (AREU), and the Afghanistan Center at Kabul University (ACKU) in Kabul, Afghanistan, do supplement this study. The Library of Congress also provided some of the Dari language newspapers and publications that reinforce this study. Much remains to be discovered, particularly further examination of Afghan voices, such as farmers, smugglers, and lower-level government officials. However, the records

I found shed important light on the role opium played in the building of and resistance to the Afghan state during the twentieth century.

Analyzing the history of drug control in Afghanistan provides a unique lens for refracting the design of the Afghan state and the character of Afghan political culture. It brings particular attention to the dimensions of law and diplomacy, and how such forces were integral to both the growth of the state and its limitations. In this sense, the establishment of laws defining the legal parameters of drug use and trade provide an important lens for examining the ways drugs were incorporated into the design of the Afghan government. Chapter 1 analyzes how the use of drugs by Afghans was discouraged by both Abdur Rahman Khan and Amanullah Khan through the implementation of draconian criminal penalties, but conversely, the export of drugs into British India and China was encouraged by the augmentation of customs levies. Chapters 2, 3, and 5, through analysis of the antiopium laws of 1945, 1956, and 1972, reveal how the creation of more specific laws were deeply entangled with the diplomatic engagements between Afghanistan and the international antidrug community, particularly the United States. Most important, during the later years of the Musahiban state antiopium laws were also followed by structural changes to the drug control apparatus, often employing more coercive means to eradicate the growing drug trade.

Afghan drug policy was shaped by the conditions of political culture. Especially under Musahiban leadership (1929–78), the state was constructed around the conscious recognition of its limitations and weaknesses, which led to a policy of "gradual modernization."[27] The policy was a direct recognition of the threat tribal authorities posed to the state in rural Afghanistan. In particular, the state feared resistance from Pashtun tribes and consciously designed policies either to benefit Pashtuns or reduce the negative impact on them.[28] Furthermore, to decrease the need to interact with the rural population, the government relied increasingly on trade and investment with foreign powers for revenue to build the country, ultimately developing into a rentier state.[29] The Afghan state's dependence on foreign money meant that it never had to legitimize itself among the rural population.[30] Opium contributed to this process. As both chapter 1 and 2 describe, before World War II, opium was an important export commodity for the government. It allowed the state to generate revenue through foreign trade rather than domestic taxation. As described in chapters 2 and 3, when the state launched prohibitions in 1945 and 1957, it was trying to appeal to foreign ambitions for narcotic control to gain access to more foreign aid and investment to strengthen the state. The government used those prohibitions as a means of securing financing to maintain the status quo, not to fundamentally transform those regions affected by or dependent on the opium trade.

Things changed during the 1960s and 1970s, however. As the global illicit drug trade expanded, concerns grew about the sources of supply. Mounting international pressure, spearheaded by the United States, led the Afghan state to create, and more important, enforce drug control laws. Chapters 3 and 5 demonstrate how the establishment of laws prohibiting opium production and smuggling were important aspects of the state becoming legible.[31] Moreover, the building of a drug control apparatus as a response to the growing global illicit drug trade, especially during the era of the US war on drugs, reinforced the state's need to project its power into the lives of Afghan citizens.[32] The Afghan state remained confined by its own political design, however. When the Afghan government did have to enforce prohibition and antismuggling laws to maintain access to American aid, the state's lack of integration into Afghan society and the increasing resistance to centralized governance prevented any meaningful or effective form of drug control.

Analysis of Afghan drug laws (chapters 1, 2, 3, 5), and the often impulsive implementation and enforcement of those laws, reveals complications of the lines between the legal and illegal that governments often present as black and white. By analyzing how and why drug laws were made, the line between smuggler and trader becomes increasingly blurred. What this reveals is not so much the rise of the smuggler and drug trafficker, but rather the rise of how the state defined these parameters to justify the control and expansion of its legal, and therefore, political boundaries. For Afghanistan, this is particularly important. The contemporary narrative that drugs reign and have reigned in the absence of law fails to consider how historically the drug trade has existed, not within the absence of law but in tandem with Afghan law that has tried to define a trade that long predated the existence of the state. In other words, these ideas are contested, often messy, and perpetually intertwined. This invokes the words of Christopher Tomlins, who states: "legalities generate illegalities, for the two are necessary conditions of each other's existence. Law, after all, makes outlaws, not law's absence. Their cheek-by-jowl intimacy, in fact, helps explain how easily, and frequently, legality and illegality trade places."[33]

Examining the history of drug policy in Afghanistan also reveals how Afghan citizens reacted to and influenced the state and its drug policy. In particular, the interactions between the state and Afghan society reveal the impact of *qawm* in perpetuating the inherent conflict between state and local governance, thus dictating the extent to which drug policy was implemented, complied with, or resisted. The government's lack of integration into society inevitably elevated the importance of *qawm* in determining outcomes. In fact, the aim of most who worked within the state was not to overcome the *qawm* through the power of the state but rather to insert *qawm* into the state. As Afghan historian Olivier Roy notes, "the state was no more than a stake in a larger game and the strategy of a *qawm* consisted in establishing an advantageous relationship with the institutions of the state."[34] Thus, false compliance, smuggling, aversion, and corruption—forms of peasant resistance described by James Scott[35]—should be viewed not only as forms of resistance but also as forms of support for local and individual interests. Ultimately, drug policy during the twentieth century was characterized by a sociopolitical culture that shaped why, how, and when the Afghan state decided to promote or prohibit opium and the extent to which individuals complied with, enforced, ignored, or resisted state control (see chapters 4, 5, 6).

Moreover, analyzing the cultural dimensions of drug policy brings to light deeper forces and non-national histories that are integral to the entire story of drugs but are often hidden in state-centric histories. The focus on social factors such as *qawm* reinforces the need to differentiate between the nation and the state as a set of ruling institutions in explaining the origins of the opium trade. The focus on non-national histories also reveals how Afghan leaders' attempts to stop smuggling along its borders were directly linked to broader ambitions to regulate the movement and mobility of people on Afhanistan's periphery.[36] Rural Afghans had been moving and trading across Afghanistan's porous boundaries since the country's inception, and opium, like other commodities, was considered a licit product (see chapters 1 and 2).[37] The establishment of an antinarcotics policy, however, allowed the Afghan government to portray Afghan traders as smugglers, posing a significant threat to Afghanistan and its neighbors and thus requiring an appropriate response from the state. In other words, "bandits helped make states and states made bandits."[38] The creation and implementation of drug control and antismuggling laws were vital components of the expansion of state power.

Drug policy, in this vein, is not only about the drugs themselves, but more important, about the regulation of people whose lives transcended the borders and laws that states imposed on them.[39]

Furthermore, the national history of Afghanistan has come to represent that of the Pashtun majority. Yet many tribal and ethnic minorities have their own national histories that have only been brought to light by anthropological research.[40] Moreover, the emergence of these subnational histories indicates the strength of these communities in the face of the state's overt ethnic and tribal biases.[41] Thus, Afghanistan represents the juridical state described by Myron Weiner: it is regarded as a national state in the international arena, yet its legitimacy is contested within its own space.[42] Ultimately, the many national, subnational, and tribal/ethnic strands that make up Afghanistan's history contextualize the political, social, and cultural underpinnings of the state building/drug trade dialectic.

The history of drug policy in Afghanistan during the twentieth century brings attention to broader issues of foreign influence in the development of the Afghan state, particularly the impact of the United States. However, this book does provide an overview of the complications of how drug control took shape prior to any interaction with the United States. As discussed in chapter 1, the development of harsh laws discouraging the use of drugs, while coinciding with the reduction of export taxes to increase drug smuggling, was all done without US interaction. Nevertheless, the United States did eventually play a significant role in building the Afghan state and shaping its drug policy. In this way, analyzing what role the United States played in Afghan drug policy reveals how changes to Afghan governance, especially the shifts in political dynasties, amplified the role of the United States, and drug control, as an important aspect of Afghan state formation. This invokes what Paul Gootenberg and Isaac Campos see as a critical need in the discourse on Latin American drug history, and drug history in general: the need to de-emphasize the US impact on drug control and identify how drug control was not just imposed by the United States but rather how US drug control was incorporated into preexisting forms.[43] As chapters 2–6 will show, examining foreign influence on domestic policies illuminates political culture in Afghanistan as well as the conflicts inherent within US foreign policy.[44] Although disputes between the state and rural Afghans existed well before the twentieth century, the Afghan state's increasing reliance on foreign money exacerbated the preexisting cultural disconnect between the state and people. Afghanistan's attempts to adhere to international drug regulations required the implementation of laws that reflected American values[45] more than Afghan ones. Opium thus emerges as a powerful symbol of the disconnect between state and society. For Afghan officials who believed American aid was the key to building a modern state, prohibition was synonymous with modernity. Yet for other Afghans, opium was a vital commodity that could help ordinary people thrive in the global market. It is certainly ironic that the state opted to prohibit the one commodity that had real potential to change the lives of thousands of Afghans.

Analyzing the impact of American-led drug prohibitions in Afghanistan reveals the extent to which the United States lacked a comprehensive understanding of the global drug trade. In Afghanistan, as in much of the world, American ambitions to extend drug control through prohibition inevitably helped to globalize local and regional drug markets. In particular, US drug policymakers failed to consider the deeper economic dynamics of the global drug trade. American supply side theory endeavored to use prohibitive and coercive methods, especially eradication, to curb drug markets in isolated nations, assuming that the respective drug systems were inelastic markets.[46] US antidrug crusaders failed to consider, however, that the variables of supply and demand were far more elastic than previously imagined and were by no means isolated by national boundaries or political systems. In particular, as chapters 4 and 5 show, the increases in opium smuggling into Pakistan and Iran during the 1950s, 1960s, and 1970s, despite prohibitions in both countries, indicates the limitations of American drug control policy. Not only did the regional prohibitions create new markets for Afghan opium to fill but the dramatic increase in demand in the United States and Europe helped to transform Afghan opium into a global commodity. As a result, the US ambition to control the supply of drugs worldwide by advocating or coercing nations to implement prohibitions proved to stimulate, not diminish, local, regional, and global drug economies. Thus, the Afghan government's eventual co-optation of American drug policy proved fundamental to the emergence of the contemporary Afghan drug trade.

As Paul Gootenberg notes, the study of a transnational commodity that respects no boundaries is ideally suited for more integrated global history.[47] The study of drugs in Afghanistan provides a unique lens through which to examine the various global forces at play in Afghanistan. As described in chapters 2, 3, 5, and 6, during the Cold War, Afghanistan's opium policy was affected as much by the broader geopolitical games being played by the United States, Soviets, Iranians, and Pakistanis as it was with the transnational nature of its drug industry. Afghanistan launched various opium policies because it saw that not only were its neighbors doing the same; they were also using opium policy as a conduit for greater American investment in the economy and military. Unlike Iran and Pakistan, however, Afghanistan was not an ideal site for American investment. Since Afghanistan was a neutral power with limited geostrategic benefits, the United States was reluctant to provide Afghanistan with the same funding it gave to Iran and Pakistan. In the Helmand Valley, however, the United States did invest hundreds of millions of dollars in creating a market-based agro-industrial sector for the Afghan economy. More important, the United States' attempt to develop a "little New York" in the western deserts of Afghanistan was also deeply embedded with the growth of the Afghan drug trade. As chapter 6 describes, as the demand for legal crops such as wheat and cotton subsided in the early 1970s, the demand for opium grew. Thus, farmers began to grow crops for the illicit drug market. As a result, the failure of the Helmand Valley Development Project was not a failure in building a market-based agricultural system but rather in building an agricultural sector that would be tied closely to the legal parameters of the Afghan state. As the state's legitimacy declined in the 1970s, so too did its claim to control the Helmand agricultural system. Opium emerged not simply because of the growth of the illicit market but also because of the failure of the state and its trade in licit agricultural goods.

In short, examining the history of opium in Afghanistan during the twentieth century further integrates the history of Afghanistan into the history of the global opium trade, drug policy, and the Cold War. The common tropes used to characterize the Afghan opium industry today, statelessness, lawlessness, and war are rooted in misinterpretations of the history of opium in Afghanistan, if not the history of Afghanistan itself. Examining drugs in Afghanistan during the twentieth century reveals that opium played an important role in shaping the Afghan state and its relations with Afghan society. More important, drug control, particularly the prohibitions of opium, contributed to the gulf between state and society, which laid the foundation for Afghanistan to become the stateless, lawless, war-ravaged place where opium thrives to this day.

Chapter 1

Colonial and Global Engagements

Afghan Opium on the Periphery of the Global Drug Market

> The problem of controlling production, whether of the raw material or of manufactured drugs, is full of difficulties. . . . It is undeniably true that given the same, or increasing demand, and an uncontrolled source of supply, any curtailment of authorized production and distribution will be answered instantly and *ipso facto* by increase of smuggling, along the line of least resistance.
>
> —J. P. Gavit, *Opium,* 76–77

In 1924, a British officer stationed in the northwest frontier of British India reported that the British trade in opium and cannabis, which was a significant portion of domestic tax revenue, was increasingly threatened by the smuggling of Afghan opium and *charse* into British territory.[1] Although smuggling was nothing new, especially among Afghans, this situation seemed different. The smuggling of Afghan drugs coincided with a significant decrease in the export of opium to China, long a bulwark of revenue for the British Empire. Opium was now being discouraged by British policymakers as the international community became more aware of the impact of opium use in Asia and the Americas. The decrease in exports, in turn, had a profound impact on British governance in India, as it forced many local and provincial governments in British India to rely on the domestic trade as a major source of tax revenue. The British were in a tight spot; on the one hand, they needed opium revenue to finance their empire, but on the other, the bad odor of the drug trade was restricting their ability to engage with the international community. But as the Gavit quote above depicts,

British attempts to reduce exports and control domestic production and use would have profound consequences beyond the boundaries of the empire. In other words, supply would always meet demand, and if the demand could not be met through legal means, people would get their supply through illicit channels.

It was during the end of the nineteenth and beginning of the twentieth centuries, when the global drug trade was flourishing and international drug control was in its infancy, that Afghan opium and other drugs began to enter into the global market. Throughout this period, the global drug trade was essential to both the growth of global capitalism and European colonialism. Asia, more than all other regions of the world, was vital to the production and consumption of drugs, particularly because it helped facilitate the growth and expansion of British colonialism. Despite opium's significance to the imperial system, the commodification of drugs for the benefit of European powers was not without its detractors. The creation of the international drug control system, particularly the role of emerging American imperial power, was a response to the European-dominated drug trade. Unlike the European powers who embraced opium, the United States had profoundly influenced the creation of the drug control system. The missionary fervor of the Americans helped push international drug control advocates closer to a total prohibition of the production and consumption of drugs.

By the late nineteenth and early twentieth centuries, the drug trade and the drug control system were beginning to take shape in Afghanistan. Under Abdur Rahman Khan (1880–1901), and later, Amanullah Khan (1919–29), Afghan opium and other drugs evolved from local or regional goods and started to enter the global market through British India. This forced Afghan authorities into diplomatic and trade engagements with colonial authorities in British India, ultimately exposing Afghans to the effects of international drug control. In particular, under both Abdur Rahman and Amanullah, opium and *charse* were exported to British India, but during the reign of Amanullah, a dual system was established whereby domestic drug use was largely condemned, with enforcement implemented through a series of draconian penalties (for opium users in particular). On the other hand, Amanullah, like Abdur Rahman before him, decreased taxes on the export of drugs in an effort to expand and grow the trade.

But the export of Afghan drugs coincided with major changes to the Indian production of opium. When India decreased its production of opium in an effort to conform to international drug control, domestic use remained high. Furthermore, the British maintained heavy taxes on imports from other countries. As a result of the high taxes and demand for opium, Afghan opium was smuggled into India in increasing numbers. The emergence of illicit Afghan opium eventually helped convince British Indian authorities to ban all opium imports, and as J. P. Gavit presciently described above, further increasing the smuggling of the drug. By the end of the reign of Amanullah, opium emerged as a significant component of Afghan trade (licit or illicit), as well as its foreign policy.

As Afghanistan was increasingly drawn into the colonial drug trade, it was, in turn, increasingly engaged with the global drug trade and the international drug control system. It is clear that Afghan drugs were entering both the Indian and Chinese markets. Afghanistan was only marginally influenced by the international drug control regime, however. Afghanistan was not party to any of the international conventions, and British India's movement toward greater drug control created vacancies in the regional market, which Afghan opium and *charse* began to fill. More important, this episode sheds light on how international drug control, essentially as an opposing force to the uninhibited free market exchange of drugs in the global market, often, and unintentionally, bolstered and expanded the global drug trade by introducing new producers and traders to the market. In the case of Afghanistan, the drug trade in India, as well as the impact of international drug control, helped build the networks and trade systems essential for the emergence of Afghan opium, licit and illicit, into India, and inevitably, the global drug market.

Pre–Twentieth-Century Opium in Asia

Afghanistan was very much a late bloomer in terms of its role in the regional and global drug trade. By the time Afghan opium and *charse* were making their way into British India and the global market in the late nineteenth century, drugs, opium especially, were already established as significant pieces of the global economy. Much of this was because various parts of Asia had long histories of drug cultivation, use, and commercialization. But the history of opium, of course, is long and tied to earlier civilizations in the West. Some of the earliest references to opium come from Sumerian clay tablets dating back to 3400 B.C. The Assyrians referred to opium as "the plant of life" and "medicine of the gods."[2] By the time of the Egyptians, Greeks, and Romans, opium was established as an important medicinal and spiritual product. But it was not until the eighth century, when Arab trade spread into Iran, India, and China, that opium took a firm hold in the Asian region. Arabs valued opium for its medicinal properties and exported much of that knowledge to Asia.[3] Opium, in turn, thrived in Asia; many of the social and environmental conditions throughout Asia were ideal for the use and production of opium. As David Courtwright suggests, "opium was uniquely suited to treat the ills of civilized peoples: anxiety, boredom, chronic fatigue and pain, insomnia, squalling babies in close quarters, and, not least, diarrheal diseases, ubiquitous and often deadly afflictions inherent to concentrated populations." The enduring prevalence of diarrhea and malarial diseases, especially acute in the warm and densely populated regions of Asia, made opium an essential medicine.[4]

During the sixteenth century, opium emerged as a commercial crop throughout much of India, Turkey, and Persia, with enough surplus being produced to meet the demand elsewhere. But even then, opium was isolated mostly to regional markets and was primarily an exotic good. It was in the eighteenth century with the British Empire that opium would be transformed into a global good. The British import of Asian goods, such as tea and porcelain, without any meaningful British exports, initially pushed the British Empire into a massive imbalance in trade revenue, often running at an average of a 5 percent loss per year. The British looked to opium as a key to rectifying its budgetary deficiencies, and began producing opium in India for export to China. As Carl Trocki has pointed out, "opium thus functioned, in the first instance as a source of virtually free capital which allowed the English to get their foot into the door of the Asian commercial system." Opium then followed the same path as other commodities before it, such as sugar, tobacco, and coffee. It required cheap labor for production and was organized on cheap monopolized or company-run land, control over collection and processing was centralized, and the consumer market was expanded, in this case into China.[5] By 1773, opium became an official monopoly operated by the East India Company (EIC) in Patna, and then spread to other regions, such as Uttar Pradesh and Benares. Although Warren Hastings, the governor of Bengal, understood opium to be a harmful drug, he believed the EIC monopoly "was quite defensible. It produced revenue where none had existed and a relative degree of order in an industry where confusion had prevailed."[6]

Although opium was already prevalent in Asia, use spread among migrant laborers, largely because of the brutal working conditions and prevalence of disease brought on by European colonialism and global commerce, and as a result, demand grew rapidly throughout Asia. China, in particular, grew very fond of the intoxicating effects of the drug, and by the 1800s, opium spread into the various middle and peasant classes of Chinese. Opium evolved into a unique culture of consumption, becoming an essential component of business life, general recreational time, the sex trade, and even eating out.[7] The demand for opium grew at an alarming rate. In 1775, British merchants exported roughly 75 tons of opium to China; by 1850, it was nearly 3,200 tons. And even though Qing officials banned opium multiple times, British smugglers continued to bring it into China. This conflict over the opium trade led to two opium wars, the first in 1839, the second in 1858, both won by the British. In both cases, British victories led to the massive expansion of the opium trade.[8] By the late nineteenth century, China itself was producing nearly 32 million pounds annually,[9] and by 1900 had roughly 13.5 million addicts smoking around 38,000 tons per year.[10]

Opium proved critical to the British Empire in Asia. When the British crown assumed full control of India in the early nineteenth century, opium revenue was next to land and salt as the largest increment to Indian treasury, more than one-seventh of the total income.[11] It often dictated the terms of economic and political decisions within the empire, exhibited by the monopolization of the opium trade and the defense of the trade in the two opium wars.[12] Carl Trocki sums it up best by stating:

> Opium had become like the other great commercial drug trades . . . It was now a market-driven system that was almost completely monopolized by a tiny privileged group. It also created, around itself, a system of trade, financing, banking, insurance, transportation, and distribution. Opium did for Asia what tobacco, sugar, alcohol, and tea had done for Europe. It created a mass market and a new drug culture.[13]

In essence, opium proved the critical commodity for solidifying Britain's place as the global imperial power, with Asia as its financial foundation.

What makes the study of opium so important is that over time, drug use proves itself to be remarkably universal. Although many of the political and economic intrigues of opium played out in Asia during the nineteenth century, as a global commodity its intoxicating power and recreational prowess eventually made its way west to Europe and the Americas. Opium use grew in popularity in Europe and the United States, as opium dens sprouted up across urban landscapes. But unlike Asia, the need for cheap, lifesaving drugs spawned a major evolution in forms of opium. Morphine, heroin, and cheap patent medicines emerged as panaceas to the ills of modern life. Patent medicines, especially, became mainstay commodities. They were cheap, easily accessible, and for some, lifesaving. But patent medicines were also unregulated, often coming with fantastic claims or carrying secret formulas, and more often than not, consumers were naive to the drug's detrimental qualities.[14] As to be expected when dealing with drugs with outstanding physical and psychological effects, the variations in opium forms were often for recreational rather than medicinal purposes.[15] As is the case with all drugs, they were abused, leading to addiction, and in some cases, death.

By the twentieth century, much of the world was well versed in the pleasures and pains of opium and other mind-altering substances. The drug trade itself had become an essential piece of the European imperial machine; it connected distant producers of drugs to an ever-increasing consumer demand; and drugs became more diverse, more potent, and more accessible than ever before. Many of these drugs were just as prevalent in the seedy opium dens of urban sprawls as they were in the posh private residences of the global elite. Opium, arguably more than any other drug, proved itself a phenomenal medicine, as well as an effective aphrodisiac. But the growth of opium did not come without its detractors. By the end of the nineteenth century, questions emerged about the drug trade and the growing evidence of addiction. Drug control, either through regulation or prohibition, became an essential piece of the opium narrative.

Although Afghanistan had very little role in the formation of the global drug trade and international drug control in the nineteenth century, it was, as were all other drug-producing nations, eventually drawn into the fold through its encounter with imperial consumer nations.

Colonialism and the Emergence of International Drug Control

After the British went to war over the right to bring opium to China in 1839, various reports from European missionaries and Chinese officials helped foster a growing resentment toward the drug trade.[16] It was not until 1874, however, with the formation of the Anglo-Oriental Society for the Suppression of the Opium Trade, that the movement toward the global prohibition of drugs began in earnest.[17] The Anti-Opium Society helped generate enormous scrutiny of the British role in perpetuating the opium trade in China, but in the end, they failed to generate the substantive political and economic change necessary to stop the British imperial machine.[18]

It was with the American colonization of the Philippines in 1898 that international narcotic control would assume an entirely new and powerful dimension, and one that would be more recognizable to us now. Unhappy with the role the European powers played in profiting from the opium vice, American missionaries, led by Bishop Charles H. Brent, sought to establish a new moral benchmark for imperial powers by creating a system of drug prohibition.[19] The American emphasis on prohibition was heavily influenced by Asian nations' previous attempts to completely prohibit the sale and use of drugs.[20] But unlike earlier attempts, the American push for drug control was imbued with a sense of religious fervor unlike any political movement against drugs beforehand. Moreover, American missionaries were not at odds with the political establishment. The American president, Theodore Roosevelt, was quite convinced by Brent's religious duty to save the world, and unlike previous presidents, was content in shedding the shackles of the anti-imperial Monroe Doctrine, allowing him to pursue ambitions of spreading America's moral empire across the world.[21] American missionaries presented to Roosevelt the idea that China and other regions of Asia were unprepared for the benefits of American commerce, largely due in part to the prevalence of the opium scourge. And as part of the much broader Open Door Policy, an attempt to secure for American goods access to the Chinese consumer market, the antiopium crusade became an essential component of broader American foreign policy objectives.[22] Arnold Taylor notes that the nexus of political action and religious missionary work against the drug trade was unique in many ways and should be "referred to as a missionary movement—or better still, as missionary diplomacy."[23] Certainly there is great irony in the role opium was playing in the confluence of empires during this period: on the one hand, it was an essential economic and political keystone, an utterly necessary piece of the British (and other European) empires; on the other hand, it was a political and religious keystone for the newfound American empire in Asia, and the attempt to justify its own expansion through moral and (relatively obscured) economic objectives. Nonetheless, the American antiopium crusade was the beginning of a political movement to rid the world of the scourge of drugs, a role that the United States has yet to relinquish today.

American efforts to jump-start an international drug control regime were due in large part to the fact that the United States was fast becoming one of the major drug consumers of the world. As Bewley-Taylor notes, "international activity, it was hoped, would help reduce the illegal flow of drugs into the United States and hence reduce drug use." As a result, for antidrug crusaders, a national prohibition failed to work because drugs were a global problem, to be solved only through the creation of an international system.[24]

In 1909, in Shanghai, and again in 1912 at the Hague, the United States and the world debated the challenges to drug control. The Shanghai Commission held both domestic and international significance. Prior to 1909, the United States had no federal drug laws, which was certainly a glaring, if not hypocritical, position for the Americans to take. Pressure around the Shanghai Commission helped the US legislators pass an act that prohibited opium for smoking to enter the United States. More important, the resolutions adopted by those attending the Shanghai Commission recognized the issues regarding opium use and addiction, and the broader objectives of, at best, prohibition, and at worst, "careful regulation." Furthermore, the Shanghai Commission brought the British and Americans to an ideological head. The British were unwilling to adopt the American stance on a total prohibition of nonmedical use, rather favoring some form of regulation.[25] It seemed that American ambitions to regulate other nations was seemingly too much for many nations to swallow. The British saw the activities of all sovereign nations as rightly their own and largely condemned the Americans' aims to interfere in others' business.

The Hague Conferences broadened the scope of drug control to encompass other drugs, including cannabis and cocaine, and tried to address issues of smuggling. More than anything, the conferences at the Hague started the process of licensing and record keeping, which would become a mainstay of international drug control.[26] Nations were also compelled by the conference resolutions to pass domestic laws that would more closely conform to the emergent forms of international drug control. As a result, the pressure from the Hague led to the United States passing the Harrison Narcotics Act in 1914.[27] For the United States, the new landscape of drug control reinforced the push for total prohibition abroad, while simultaneously justifying the expansion of the state through drug prohibition at home. In this sense, international and domestic drug laws were mutually constitutive, reaffirming the validity and need for expansion of each. With domestic drug laws now in place, American antidrug crusaders continued their push for the total prohibition of drugs across the globe.[28]

By 1925, when the League of Nations convened the Geneva Conference, the movement for drug control had gone global. Under the Geneva Narcotics Convention, drug control moved toward mandatory international regulations over the production and trade of drugs.[29] This new form of international diplomacy began the process of restricting the "rights of government to traffic in narcotics," based on the belief that the primary problem with drug abuse was the supply of drugs, not the demand.[30] This was not entirely a reflection of the American antinarcotics crusade, however, nor entirely an endorsement of the total prohibitionist stance. Because the convention was through the league, it took into consideration many of the differing viewpoints from other countries regarding drug use, often leading to vast divisions between American and other members.[31] Nonetheless, the focus on the supply of drugs was spurred largely by the United States. As David Bewley-Taylor notes, the United States' "single-minded pursuit of control at the source . . . overlooked the economic and cultural obstacles that producer states had to overcome to carry out any anti-drug convention effectively."[32] Thus, the Geneva convention marked an important step in the growth of international drug control by creating some form of consensus around the need to regulate the production and movement of drugs. At the same time, however, it also embodied the various obstacles preventing success in something as ambitious as global drug control; drug use did not go away and the production of illicit drugs continued.

Drugs in Afghanistan

Despite Afghanistan's central role in the drug industry today, throughout much of its history, it was merely a peripheral or small-scale actor in the broader drama playing out in India, China, Europe, and America. As the drug trade penetrated deeper into global markets, however, and various powers tried to control it to some degree, Afghan drugs slowly began to trickle into parts of Asia. In fact, exactly when opium made its way into Afghanistan is unknown. As in India, opium likely came through Iran as the Arab trade spread east, and knowledge of cultivation and use followed suit.[33] Certain regions of Afghanistan, particularly Badakhshan in the northeast, are often seen as "traditional" centers of opium production.[34] Even in the broader scope of time, however, opium is a relatively recent phenomenon.

Arguably the first historical record of opium and its relation to Afghanistan starts with Zahiruddin Muhammad Babur, who founded the Mughal dynasty in 1526. Babur's empire, which stretched from Afghanistan to the plain of the Ganges, strengthened the political and economic ties of Afghanistan to South Asia. During the Mughal period, one often defined by decadence, opium became a mainstay of recreational and medical life. Opium, particularly because of its popularity as a recreational drug, became an important source of revenue for the Mughals.[35] Although Babur was famous for his prodigious alcohol consumption, in his later years he used various hashish- and opium-laced concoctions.[36] *Majun*, a mixture of hashish or opium with various edibles, was the drug most commonly referenced by Babur and Mughal sources.[37] Babur's use of *ma'jun* makes it difficult to determine the extent of his opium use because opium, *charse*, and various other intoxicants were often used interchangeably and without specification.[38] Babur's son, Nasiruddin Muhammad Humayun, on the other hand, is most often associated with opium use. Although there are numerous references to his use of opium, and some claims that he was an addict, there is very little evidence to suggest that he was actually addicted to opium.[39] Nonetheless, opium use during Mughal rule was quite common, ordinary, and tolerated.[40] The revenue from poppy production, both for domestic use and for the growing export trade to Indonesia (through the Dutch) and later to China (through the British) undoubtedly contributed to the expansion of production and cultural acceptance of opium use.[41] Although it was quite clear that drug use during the period of the Mughals was common, what role Afghanistan played is rather limited. Abul Fazl, sixteenth-century emperor Akbar's vizier, claimed in *A'in-I Akbari* that poppies were one of three profitable spring crops, but that production remained centered around Lahore, Delhi, Alwa, and Malwa.[42] However, Abu Fazl also mentions that Akbar's governor in Kandahar, Shahbaj Khan, was a regular user of alcohol, wine, and cannabis.[43]

Despite opium's role in the Mughal dynasty, the wide-scale use and production of the drug in Afghanistan seem to be a recent phenomenon.

However, hashish, or charas (*charse*), appears to have a longer historical track than opium, and until recently, was more common in Afghan regions. Hashish has been a part of Afghan and central Asian countries for thousands of years, maybe predating Scythian hashish use. Although there is little textual recording of hashish cultivation and use, oral histories firmly plant hashish use into Afghan mythology. According to Afghan legend, Baba Ku, a central Asian herbal healer, came to Afghanistan to heal plague victims, and thus administered balls of hashish. Aside from spreading knowledge about the plant and its psychoactive and medicinal properties, he also taught Afghans how to smoke using a water pipe. To this day, *babas* (religious teachers) invoke Baba Ku when partaking in hashish.[44] It is interesting to note that the legend of Baba Ku also mirrors that of the thirteenth-century Persian Sufi, Sheik Haidar. Haidar was said to be from present-day Khorassan in northeast Iran (not too far from Baba Ku's claimed origin of Samarkand), and is credited in Persian lore as the man who discovered hashish. It is quite possible that since both were proclaimed to have discovered hashish and spent much of their life exalting its use, they are likely regional incantations of the same "hashish origin myth, Sheik Haidar from a Persian perspective and Baba Ku from a Central Asian perspective."[45]

British sources also provide short glimpses into drug use prior to the twentieth century. T. L. Pennel, a British medical missionary, observed that *faqirs*, Islamic ascetics, or Sufis, "like the Hindu Sadhus, they are much addicted to the use of intoxicants (though rarely alcohol), and charas and bhang (Indian hemp) are constantly smoked with tobacco in their *chilams*. When thus intoxicated they are known as *mast*, and are believed by the populace to be possessed by divinity, and to have miraculous powers."[46] British observer Horace Alexander was even more judgmental of those using *charse*, noting that he was not sure the *faqirs* could "distinguish religious exaltation from madness."[47] Nonetheless, aside from these references to *charse*, bhang, and *faqirs*, there is little evidence of broader systemic trading in Afghanistan. Given the growth of production in South Asia during the nineteenth century, one could surmise that Afghan entrepreneurs participated in the drug trade, given the commercial and social connections between Afghanistan and India and China. As of yet, however, there is scant historical record of the depth of Afghan involvement in the broader South Asian or global drug trade during this period. It was not until Amir Abdur Rahman

Khan began the process of building an Afghan state in 1880 that opium emerged as a commodity to be taxed and regulated.

Opium and the Iron Amir

In 1880, as Abdur Rahman Khan ascended to the throne following the Second Anglo-Afghan War, he faced enormous obstacles in creating a functional, modern, and most important, strong Afghan state. Afghanistan had lost the war to Britain; however, fear of Russian encroachment further south from central Asia allowed Afghanistan to maintain its independence, in essence acting as a buffer between the Russian and British empires. Domestically, Afghanistan remained decentralized and tribal in character, and lacked social, economic, and political modernization. Disruption of trade routes by marauding tribes devastated both urban and rural economies, and many tribal leaders remained powerful bulwarks against the central government's authority.[48]

Abdur Rahman Khan rose to power by justifying his rule as a form of divine right of kings and highlighting his role in fighting against foreign occupation during the war.[49] Fear of Russian and English encroachment figured prominently in the khan's early years. To him, much of the disunity of Afghan tribes was a result of the "Great Game" between the Russian and British empires. In this sense, he succeeded by invoking Afghan nationalism in defiance of the imperial threats to the north and south.[50] Furthermore, unification of Afghanistan was not merely confined to rhetorical claims of a religious and patriotic nature. He also embarked on a major military campaign with his newly minted army, subjugating tribes one by one; he married off his sons to strengthen tribal allegiances; he played off of tribal rivalries to gain support; and he appealed to religious sentiments, as was the case with the Shi'a Hazara rebellion in 1891, to unite other Sunni tribes.[51]

Much of Abdur Rahman's success lay in the various reforms passed to help in the unification and creation of a strong centralized Afghan state. He passed a series of legal and social reforms that gave him greater control over the country. The amir created three separate legal categories to deal with the country's issues: Islamic laws (sharia), civil laws, and tribal laws. And although most laws were dictated by religious officials and based on sharia law, the amir had the final say in determining verdicts. Harsh sentences were doled out to criminals, something British observers seemed to think the amir "relished."[52] He also created a large, centralized, modern national army.[53]

Abdur Rahman placed a heavy emphasis on improving Afghanistan's economic situation. And even though his rise to power was imbued with patriotic and xenophobic rhetoric, he was still reliant on foreign assistance. He received an annual subsidy from the British, to be used to pay for his army, to strengthen the buffer state against the Russians to the north.[54] Trade remained a difficult and painstaking process for those involved, both merchants and government officials. Prior to the khan, previous Afghan rulers had levied enormous duties on both imports and exports. To ease the flow of goods and improve the flow of capital into Afghanistan, the amir simplified customs duties, initially assigning a 2.5 percent ad valorum tax on all imports and exports.[55] It was during this period that opium and charas emerged as important export commodities for Abdur Rahman.

In terms of use, there is very little evidence to suggest that opium and charas were used or abused in Afghanistan during the reign of the khan. More than anything, opium and *charse* were primarily export items to be sent to India, Russia, and China.[56] India, in particular, remained the primary destination for Afghan opium. In 1903–4, in the newly annexed Northwest Frontier Province (NWFP), British officials observed that use of opium and bhang was relatively common, especially in light of Islamic prohibitions regarding alcohol. This was in spite of the fact that opium production had been virtually eliminated in the region prior to the creation of the provincial authority in 1901. Moreover, most of the British supply from Bengal was being consumed in the larger urban areas of the Punjab, so most of the local demand in the NWFP was met by outside sources. Afghan opium, as well as that sourced from Kashmir and Malwa, filled the demand. It is interesting to note that British officials believed that the demand for opium in the NWFP could easily be filled by opium in production in the Jalalabad valley in Afghanistan alone (what is now Nargarhar Province, one of the primary opium-producing regions).[57] Whether this was because the local demand for opium was so small or the production in Jalalabad valley was so large, sources do not say. But it certainly hints at the reality that Afghan opium production was increasingly entering the local, if not global, marketplace.

Although Afghan opium showed up in markets in British India, especially the NWFP, there were considerable issues with how opium fit into the broader trade between Afghanistan and British India. As Shah Mahmoud Hanifi details in his book, *Connecting Histories in Afghanistan*, Abdur Rahman monopolized the export trade in fruit and other commodities (including opium) as a primary form of financing the building of the state.[58] In an attempt to displace Indian traders while capitalizing on the large consumer base in India, the amir licensed brokers to funnel Afghan goods to Afghan-controlled merchants and brokers in British territory. Those who agreed to the arrangement (or were coerced) were pushed into specific trade routes, supply depots, and merchants all associated with the amir. And for those who evaded the monopoly, as many did, they faced financial ruin through confiscations or fines. There were certainly incentives to smuggle goods outside of the khan's export monopoly. The taxes levied against the Afghan traders was sometimes three times higher than those being levied by Indian colonial authorities. For Abdur Rahman, the consolidation of the lucrative export trade into a tightly bound monopolized system was seen by British colonial officials as "a new form of Durrani state tax that was being collected in India."[59] For the amir, on the other hand, it served to not only wrest away much needed capital from South Asian merchants but also to forge stronger commercial networks between Kabul and the commercial centers to the south.[60]

By the time of the death of Abdur Rahman Khan in 1901, Afghanistan had stabilized into a recognizable, albeit flawed, state. As Vartan Gregorian states, Abdur Rahman Khan was "largely successful. By 1901, when he died, Abdur Rahman had managed to unify Afghanistan politically and to establish the first thoroughly centralized regime in the county."[61] The amir's reforms were limited, however. Most of the benefits of his trade policies, including the export monopoly, were felt mainly in Kabul. Much of the rest of the Afghan economy remained subsistence based. More so, many of the amir's reforms did little to alter Afghan society, especially in rural areas. As a result, Afghanistan entered the twentieth century with a modern army and new critical commercial connections to the outside world, but they were limited by the reach of the state. As was the case then, as it is now, Kabul remained the focal point of change, for better or worse.

Opium was a part of the amir's bigger plan to increase exports and capture much-needed South Asian capital, and more important, raise revenues for the building of the state. But there remain questions about the impact of opium within Afghanistan. This, of course, is tied to trade issues. In a broad sense, Abdul Rahman pushed to decrease imports as an important means of curbing the flow of Afghan capital abroad. And in many cases, consumption of foreign products declined.[62] But how and in what ways do the issues over trade influence our understanding of drugs in Afghanistan, especially consumption? Does this then explain why the amir would discourage use? During the time of the khan, there is not enough historical evidence to answer any of those questions definitively. It is clear that opium and charas were becoming commodities for export and that the revenue was important for the growth of the amir's state, although the extent of this is still unclear. What is certain is that two decades after the death of Abdur Rahman Khan, the rise of Amanullah would put to rest many of these questions about domestic consumption of opium and its ties to trade.

Amanullah: Modernization, Opium, and the Beginning of Drug Control

Abdur Rahman Khan was succeeded by his designated heir, Habibullah. Habibullah took the throne without a war for succession and maintained the internal stability of the country. It was during this period that Afghanistan broke from the self-imposed isolation of Abdur Rahman and was genuinely influenced by the outside world. Many people who were exiled by the Iron Amir returned to Afghanistan and brought with them religious and secular ideas that were blossoming in other parts of the world.[63] Many of these individuals would profoundly shape the future trajectory of the Afghan state.[64] Furthermore, significant changes were occurring beyond the borders of Afghanistan. In 1914, the Great War broke out in Europe, ultimately enveloping the Muslim Ottoman Empire, and subsequently forcing Habibullah and other Afghans to think deeply about Afghanistan's place in the changing political arena. Especially for the Afghans inspired by European secularism and notions of modernity, the war was a stark reminder that Europe did not have the answers "to the needs of modern society."[65] On the other hand, for religious leaders or pan-Islamists, Habibullah's neutral position in the war and unwillingness to support the Ottoman caliphate was seen as a failure.[66] Furthermore, the militant nationalist uprising in India in 1919 was straining the British raj, and many Afghans recognized that British influence was waning in Afghanistan and the rest of South Asia. For them, now was the time to act and finally break the British hold on Afghanistan.[67] By 1919, tensions and discord against Habibullah (either for his war policy or unwillingness to take advantage of the unrest in the British raj) led to his assassination.

Following Habibullah's death, his brother Nasrullah would lay claim to the throne, but he would remain in power for a mere ten days. It was Habibullah's third son, Amanullah, who would challenge Nasrullah for succession and ultimately win the throne. Amanullah, unlike others in his family, was closely connected to the main sources of political power in Afghanistan. Upon his father's death, he served as vice-regent of Kabul, allowing him to take control of the army and national armory. He was also popular among the nationalist modernists. Nasrullah, on the other hand, lacked a support base in Kabul (although he did have greater support among border tribes and the ulema).[68] Once Amanullah took power, he instigated the Third Anglo-Afghan war, a brilliant political move that united tribal groups, religious factions, and modernists under a nationalist banner. The war forced the British to sign the Treaty of Rawalpindi in 1919, enshrining Afghanistan as a fully independent and sovereign state.[69] To the north, Amanullah also brokered a treaty with newly formed Bolshevik Russia, the Russo-Afghan Friendship Treaty of 1919. This treaty not only guaranteed Afghan independence, but also brought much needed Russian technical and economic assistance.[70] Amanullah's sense of nationalism, one infused with a deep sense of self-determination and independence from Western powers, mirrored many of the other movements of the non-Western world following the World War I.[71] More important, by securing friendly relations with Afghanistan's two most important neighbors, Amanullah was able to focus on domestic policy.

Amanullah Khan embarked on a series of aggressive social and economic programs aimed at bringing Afghanistan to the forefront of the twentieth century. The task was certainly monumental. Amanullah took over a country plagued by poverty, a weak health-care system, limited access to education, and an administrative system plagued by inefficiencies and corruption.[72] To provide a road map for Afghanistan's future, Amanullah passed the Fundamental Law in 1923. The first of its kind in Afghan history, it served as the foundational legislation defining the role of the king and the administration, and the rights of Afghan citizens.[73] Many of the regulations that stemmed from this and subsequent laws provided Amanullah with the necessary template for his ambitious reforms. For example, new tax laws were introduced, slavery was abolished, and the education system was expanded to include women. He also pushed for more stringent social reforms, such as those that sought to restrict child marriage and polygamy, and tribal customs regarding women.[74] To Amanullah, Afghanistan was in desperate need of modernization, and that modernization came primarily through "educational, social, and cultural change."[75]

Opium Consumption and Law under Amanullah

Among his many reforms was a series of administrative and legal reforms aimed at centralizing and institutionalizing "the administration of justice."[76] The Criminal law, originally passed in 1923, and based on Hanifi law (one of the four schools of thought on religious jurisprudence), was seen as an important tool for the Amanullah administration to not only strip the *qazis* (Islamic judges) of autonomy but also to tackle corruption.[77] Largely because the laws were widespread and sweeping, the criminal code was not popular among the mullahs and *qazis*, especially, because it gave the state the authority to administer punishments, a right traditionally reserved for the *qazis*. In many ways, this law embodied the aggression of Amanullah's reforms, as well as the justification for the dissent and rebellion that would come later. Not even Abdur Rahman Khan dared strip the ulema of their century-old authority to mediate conflicts and administer justice.[78] More important, the new criminal code represented "a major attempt to increase the power of the secular authority at the expense of the religious establishment," and to bring "tribal justice (Pashtunwali), too, under the control of the monarchy."[79]

The Criminal code went through a series of revisions after 1923, ultimately leading to the Penal Code of 1924–25. The final version of criminal law had hundreds of provisions and bylaws, all of which reinforced the monarchy as the central arbiter of justice. The code outlined three categories from which to disperse justice: serious crimes, such as adultery and alcohol consumption; major crimes, such as murder and intentional bodily harm; and lesser crimes. The code specified punishments (*hadd*, or *jazaw*) for serious crimes, which were already mandated by Islamic law, as well as those punishments for major crimes (*qesas*) and lesser crimes, for which *qazis* would apply "public and exemplary punishments (*ta'zirs*)" at their own discretion. It also provided a series of laws on civil and property rights, such as outlawing forced labor and animal cruelty.[80] Despite the legal system's aims to encourage modern reforms and push for more humane laws in some cases, the penal code remained remarkably strict, particularly regarding things such as the use of opium, bhang, and alcohol.

It was through the Penal Code of 1924–25 that opium, and other drugs such as *charse* and bhang, were more clearly placed under government regulation. In Article 125,[81] both the production and use of alcohol and drugs were forbidden by law. It was clear from previous regimes that the use of drugs or alcohol, or both, remained a problem. Nasrullah Staanekzai notes that prior to the passing of the penal code, the Amanullah government, despite trying to prevent use, allowed adult addicts (*mehtaad*) to continue to use it.[82] However, the 1924–25 penal code exacted rather harsh penalties for the use of drugs and alcohol. Smokers of hash, users of bhang, and opium eaters under the age of twenty-five would receive anywhere from twenty-five to thirty-nine lashings. Older addicts would be given fifty to seventy-five lashings; the harsher sentence apparently was seen as a deterrent to further use.[83] The punishments (*jazaw*) of the penal code embody many of the broader legal issues between the Amanullah regime and traditional forms of Afghan jurisprudence administered by *qazis* and mullahs. In most Islamic countries, intoxicants are defined as *al-khamr*, and stem from the root word, *khamara*, meaning to cover. In this sense, some strict adherents of sharia law saw drugs as products that cover or veil the mind, causing one to lose control, and ultimately, are forbidden (haram) under sharia law.[84] More important, by predetermining punishments, Amanullah was stripping mullahs of their traditional right to place judgment on an individual user. Thus, it is not the punishments that were really severe that caused concern, but rather the willingness of Amanullah to take ownership of the punishment for such acts.

There are other indications that Amanullah was using the newfound power of the state to address the issue of consumption. Along with the draconian penalties, he also passed a steep tax on consumption as a means of deterring use and addiction. As the table below indicates, the Amanullah government levied heavy tax penalties on the use of drugs, especially opium.

Tobacco	15% (30% in Kabul)
Snuff	20% (50% in Kabul)
Charse and bhang	50%
Opium	100%[85]

The new penal code represented an important step in Amanullah's attempt to increase the power of the state by giving it the moral authority to regulate individuals' behavior, a right traditionally held by the religious establishment.[86] But with regard to drug policy, it is unclear whether domestic drug policy was enacted to deal with a real problem of addiction (i.e., was drug addiction much of a problem, and if so, how much of a problem was it?), or as an indicator of Afghanistan's ascension to the global pantheon of antidrug moralizing, by which drug addiction was seen as the antithesis of modernity. Similarly, during this period in the United States and Europe, much of the emerging discourse of the early 1920s centered on drug addiction as an inherently Eastern vice, one that kept the various Asian peoples downtrodden and easily controlled. Many of the early antidrug crusaders believed that opium use was a primitive act, and therefore, stood in the way of progress. For example, Leslie Keeley, one of the most well known purveyors of addiction cures during the late nineteenth century, often linked drug addiction in the United States to the "well-known" fact that opium was the drug of choice for Arabs and Easterners. He claimed that "he who, in this mighty continent of the West, delivers himself over to a life of Opium torpor, falls from his high estate and passes into a world which, by contrast, is even more dreary and monotonous than that of the Arab tribes. . . . He passes from the living progressive world into a desert whose extent is limitless."[87] In other words, to be an addict was to be anti-Western and antimodern.[88] Whether that was the case in Afghanistan is unclear. It may very well have been that this law was intended as nothing more than justification for the expansion of state power, and given the attention paid to the export of the drug and the lack of evidence regarding the extent of use and addiction, that seems to be the case.

Opium Exports and British Entanglements

Although the domestic drug policy was rather strict, approaches to the role of drugs in trade and foreign policy was an entirely different story. By the time Amanullah came to power, opium emerged as an important part of Afghan trade. British authorities estimated that Afghanistan was producing 25,900 pounds in 1922.[89] Production was believed to be concentrated primarily in the north, particularly in Herat and Badakhshan.[90] Much of Amanullah's trade policies centered on standardizing and institutionalizing an inconsistent customs system. One of the more important trade reforms was the standardization of export and interregional trade using a base 5 or 7 1/2 percent ad valorum tax.[91] For example, *charse* and bhang were exempted from the scrutiny of Article 125 in the penal code if the drugs were intended for trade abroad.[92] In the Kabul, Kandahar, and Afghan Turkestan areas, traders were required to pay a 10 percent ad valorum tax on opium for export. Furthermore, the new tariff granted the government the authority to enforce the law in both urban and rural areas.[93] In terms of scope, a law taxing and regulating consumption of opium, *charse*, and bhang was unheard of, and in all likelihood, symbolic more than anything. But this disparity between import and export taxes raises some important questions about the role of drugs and drug control under the Amanullah regime. Clearly, the Amanullah government recognized that the drug trade, while not to be tolerated within the borders of Afghanistan, was still lucrative enough to export abroad. Moreover, given the very real budget concerns facing the Amanullah regime, this certainly explains this contradiction.

By 1924, the British were becoming weary of the increasing presence of Afghan opium and *charse* coming over the northwest frontier. Despite the fact that Amanullah and the British had seemed to reconcile their differences by 1924,[94] the British were entering a new phase in their opium trade. The increasing pressure from the international community to stop the export of opium to China and the concerns about drug addiction worldwide were pushing the British toward the international drug control regime and the eventual cessation of the licit drug economy. As a result, the interactions with Afghanistan over the opium trade were muddled by regional issues over taxation, loss of revenue and smuggling, and broader concerns about the implications of such a trade in the changing international drug control environment.

For the British, the growing threat of Afghan opium came at a time when international pressure to decrease their long-standing drug trade was growing to a fever pitch. At the Shanghai conference in 1909, organized by the ardent American antiopium crusader Bishop Charles Henry Brent, the British came under enormous fire for their role in the massive drug epidemic in China. Although the conference was nonbinding, it was the first of many global conferences that pushed drug producers and consumers to work toward greater control over the leakages and excesses of the global drug trade. Among the most important stipulations was the need for greater control over opium and morphine not intended for medical use. For the British, in particular, much if not all of their opium exports to China were used for nonmedical purposes, which largely explained why the British were reluctant to jump into the new global drug control paradigm with the same zeal as the Chinese and Americans.[95] More important, Indian farmers and merchants, provincial governments, and the Indian government wanted the opium trade to "continue indefinitely," as they had become utterly dependent on the tax revenue to fund important local and regional governmental functions.[96]

Not long after the Shanghai Opium Conference in 1909, the British government passed the Morley-Minto reforms as a means of addressing the increasing international pressure to crack down on the drug trade and the emerging fears of declining opium revenue. The reforms gave Indian members of the government greater say in the financial issues facing India, particularly as it related to opium and taxation. Internationally, animosity was growing toward the British drug trade to China, symbolized by the Shanghai conference. But ending the drug trade was not an easy endeavor for the British, as its cessation would immediately affect the financial situation in South Asia, especially at the provincial level. By giving greater political agency to local Indian authorities, the Morley-Minto reforms overrode international diplomatic efforts to curb Indian exports to China. As a result, Indian members were given the authority to maintain the opium trade to provide much needed funding for local programs. The Morley-Minto reforms opened the door for a series of tax reforms aimed at elevating the role of drugs as a form of revenue for British authorities, but Britain could no longer rely on export to China as a major form of revenue. Thus, they abandoned their policy of "export maximization and minimum consumption which had prevailed since 1813," and production for export was dramatically reduced. The Patna factory, which had long symbolized British economic power in India and the important trade connection to China, was closed. Other regions where area was devoted to opium production were reduced as well. For example, in Bihar, production fell from 304,000 hectares in 1906–7 to 68,000 in 1913–14.[97]

To offset the loss of export revenue, the British pursued an increase in domestic consumption, despite this conflicting with the goals of the Shanghai conference. The British then passed the Montford reforms to further distance the central government from pressures to achieve greater drug control. The Montford reforms of 1919 gave provincial governments authority to control the excise revenue from drugs. Thus, pressures to restrict opium consumption lay not with the central government but rather with provincial authorities. The central government, on the other hand, retained control of cultivation, exports, customs, and finances.[98] This conflict of authority allowed the British government to justify the growth in domestic consumption on the grounds that it was up to provincial authorities to restrict use and sale. Moreover, provincial authorities were not likely to take any action to curb domestic consumption. Revenue sources for provincial authorities were already limited, and drug revenue had become an integral piece of the budget for education, welfare, health services, and public works. As M. Emdad-ul Haq has pointed out, "neither the people nor their elected representatives in the provincial legislatures had any choice, but to continue to promote the sale and consumption of drugs."[99]

By 1924, the political and economic climate changed so much so that the British question about whether to prohibit Afghan opium was no longer a matter of if, but when. After boycotting previous Geneva summits, the British were compelled to participate in the 1924–25 Opium summits. Pressure from the United States had largely coalesced around the need for governments to control the supply of drugs. Finally succumbing to the enormous international pressure, the British agreed to suppress the smoking of opium by 1935.[100] The following year, the Indian government began the process of eliminating the export trade altogether. This increased scrutiny over the role of opium exports and excise revenue not only transformed India's position within the global market, and the emerging international drug control regime, but drew opium-producing neighbors, such as Afghanistan, who were fast becoming the major sources for Indian consumption, into the fray as well.

Although most of the international attention focused on India's export of opium in 1924, domestic consumption remained relatively unaffected. Provincial authorities still relied on the taxation of drugs as a major form of revenue. Local opium production was on the decline, however. Furthermore, the taxation on opium was proving to make licit imports so expensive that most opium traders were simply smuggling to evade the exorbitant costs of the regulatory system.[101] Analyzing prices of licit and illicit opium shows why many Afghan opium traders would evade British taxation. According to British authorities in the Northwest Frontier Province, the base price of opium on the border was around 55 rupees per seer, but with the export duty of 56 rupee per seer, and a vending duty of 40 rupees per seer in the bazaar, the average retail price for a seer of legal Afghan opium was 151 rupees. British opium, on the other hand, averaged around 111 rupees per seer. The impact of the regulatory system did little more than instigate the growth of the illicit trade, however, as most Afghan opium traders simply stopped trading opium on the legal market altogether. For example, the average price of smuggled Afghan opium in Northwest Frontier bazaars was around 65 rupees per seer, making all other competitors, especially licit opium, virtually impotent to compete. As British officials noted, "excise opium has little or no chance." Furthermore, not only were sales of British excise opium dropping but the demand for illicit Afghan opium was growing. To raise the fear of Afghan smugglers running amok in British India, rumors persisted that illicit Afghan opium was making its way deep into the Punjab.[102]

Naturally, British officials were concerned about the prospects of Afghan opium flooding the Indian market, as they tried to balance local demands for opium with the growing international drug control regime. Local authorities demonstrated very little concern for global drug control efforts, instead fearing the loss of excise tax revenue. As the chief commissioner of the Northwest Frontier noted, "the smuggling trade is now so rife that Government's Excise revenue is seriously affected, and urgent drastic action is called for."[103] The excise reports from Northwest Frontier Province clearly indicate that smuggling was affecting British opportunities to tax Afghan imports of opium. As figure 1.1 shows, within a span of nine years, excise revenue from Afghan opium decreased nearly twenty times, from 8,999 Rs in 1914–15 down to 460 in 1922–23.[104]

British officials were clueless as to what caused the growth in smuggling. Some British officials grew more suspicious about this being an organic reaction to an overtaxed commodity, while others worried if this was by design, a quasi-official state policy, similar to Abdur Rahman's trade monopoly. To the further dismay of the British, Herr Ebner of the German and Oriental Trade House in Kabul, sent an inquiry to British customs agents on behalf of the German government to request passage for Afghan opium through India to Germany.[105] Now it seemed that not only were Afghans smuggling opium into India; they were also expanding the licit market as well (and in competition with the British, no less). It was obvious for many British officials involved in the trade issues with the Afghans that knowledge of the capacity of Afghanistan to produce and trade opium was still a major unknown. C. Latimer, then deputy secretary of the government of India, remarked that British officials should try to determine to what extent the Afghan government was involved in the trade, whether

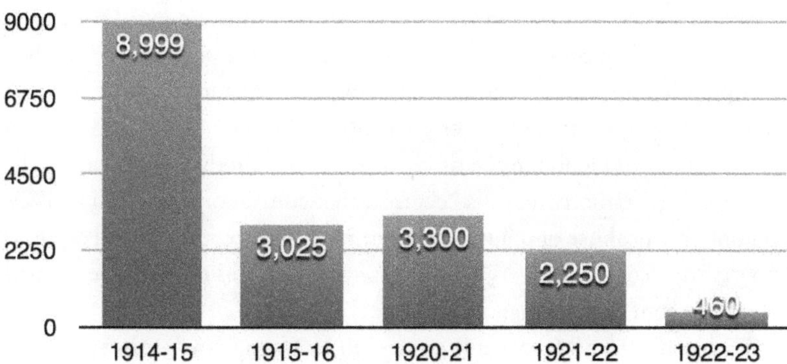

Figure 1.1. Annual excise revenue of opium from Afghan importers

opium was still produced by a government monopoly, or if smuggling was nothing more than entrepreneurial Afghan traders doing their best to avoid taxation. Latimer noted that if the Afghan government was supporting the smuggling of opium into India, their official exports could not exceed that amount from which they were expected to pay taxes.[106]

Ultimately, the most logical solution for British officials was to ban Afghan opium altogether. However, this was easier said than done. A potential prohibition of opium carried with it an enormous amount of diplomatic baggage, especially because it could threaten the tenuous peace between Afghanistan and India. Article VII of the Anglo-Afghan Treaty (the Treaty of Rawalpindi) mandated that no Afghan article could be prohibited from India "except as included in a general prohibition of the import of that article from all countries outside India." In other words, India would have to prohibit opium completely, from all sources, to justify a ban of Afghan opium.[107] In September 1924, the chargé d'affaires in Kabul, R. R. Maconachie, reported to authorities in India about his inquiries to the Amanullah government about the growing threat of illicit Afghan opium in India. Not surprisingly, the Afghan Foreign Office had very little verifiable information about the extent of production and trade in Badakhshan, Herat, and Jalalabad, the three major opium-producing regions in the country. It did confirm, however, that the government no longer operated a monopoly of opium and anyone was free to trade in opium. Furthermore, the Foreign Office also made a series of unofficial and paradoxical claims to Maconachie about the extent of drug production and trade in Afghanistan. For instance, Afghan authorities claimed that the government reduced production by 10 percent in 1922.[108] How they could do this, or even know that it was occurring, when not operating a monopoly is undoubtedly contradictory to their previous claim that the government no longer controlled the trade, or knew little of the extent of production in the three major opium-producing regions of the country. Furthermore, they also claimed that cultivation decreased in 1924, and only medical use of opium was permitted in the country. And as far as exports were concerned, very little was sent to India, as most opium exports were sent from Badakhshan into China.[109]

The report from Maconachie seemed to reaffirm many of the suspicions lingering among provincial and central government authorities in India that Afghanistan was clearly encouraging the trade of opium into India by reducing levies on exports, while cracking down on domestic consumption. Maconachie summed it up by stating, "It appears that the duty has been recently lowered, possibly with intention, in combination with the prohibition of eating and smoking . . . of simultaneously encouraging export and discouraging local consumption." He added further, "it seems doubtful whether the Afghan government have made or would make any sincere effort to restrict the production or consumption of opium." For the British, Afghanistan was playing a duplicitous game. It would try to hold the British to the stipulations of the treaty, but willingly or unwillingly, fail to do so on its own. It then comes as no surprise that Maconachie advocated for the prohibition of Afghan imports into India.[110]

On November 24, 1924, in a modification of section 19 of the Sea Customs Act of 1878, the government of India announced the prohibition of "the bringing of opium by land into British India from any country situated on the land frontier of India."[111] Evidence suggests that the threat of Afghan opium and obvious duplicity of the Afghan government with regard to the extent of control or knowledge of smuggling influenced the passing of the prohibition of all foreign opium. It is not entirely clear, however, whether the passage of this law was due to international pressures to end the opium trade altogether or frustration about the obvious growth of Afghan opium smugglers. The passage of this law can likely be explained by a combination of international pressures to end the opium trade and frustration with the growth of smuggling. Nonetheless, smuggling was rampant across the country after the official end of the drug trade. In 1928–29, Indian opium was still being smuggled into China as well as South Africa and Australia.[112] Furthermore, the British were already making motions toward acquiescing to international drug control efforts and ending the entire opium trade for good. By the end of the Geneva Opium summit in 1925, the British promised to end the drug trade, and most important, the prohibition of all opium in British-controlled India was inevitable. The next year, the British government announced an annual decrease in opium production of 10 percent, in effect ending the production of opium by 1935, and more important, putting the British in line with the Geneva convention for greater drug control.[113]

Conclusion

As was the case with much of rest of the world, Afghanistan was eventually drawn into the global drug trade. Although both opium and *charse* existed in Afghanistan prior to the twentieth century, the extent of production and use was limited at best. However, Afghanistan was not isolated from the broader machinations of the global market for drugs. As the demand for opium in India and China grew, it eventually forged important connections among the disparate regions of Afghanistan. But the connections forged were not entirely organic makings of the market; on the contrary, both Abdur Rahman and Amanullah embraced opium and *charse* as exportable commodities. Moreover, they seemed willing to lower tax burdens on the export trade to improve the drug trade. In this sense, drugs became part of the broader goal of using the export of goods to improve the financial situation of Afghan traders by bringing much needed capital out of the subcontinent, and a critical tool for bolstering the growth of the nascent Afghan state.[114]

Afghanistan's ascension into the global drug market brought with it political baggage that forced Afghanistan, and particularly Afghanistan's neighbors, to adjust their policies regarding the trade in drugs. As Afghanistan increased its trade with India, the British were gradually moving from a regulated market system to complete prohibition. This transformation played an important role in forcing the Afghan government to balance local demands for financial capital against diplomatic pressure for tighter regulation of the drug trade. In this sense, we must reconsider the Iron Amir and

Amanullah's drug policy. As the British viewed it, the prohibition or tight regulation of domestic use in Afghanistan, coupled with the official or unofficial support of the drug trade in contravention of British regulatory systems, was a seemingly duplicitous political and economic game. But we should know better: that one man's smuggler is another man's trader. Given the pressures on both Abdur Rahman and Amanullah to transform their Afghanistan by building stronger state systems, while simultaneously maintaining the balance between urban and rural political, cultural, and economic systems of power, the tacit support of the drug trade in spite of British efforts to tax and regulate seems less deceitful and more pragmatic. Certainly the need for money trumped diplomatic concerns with the British, especially given their history of frosty relations.

The issues with smuggling, however, posed challenges to the Afghan government as well. Based on the colonial records, one could assume that Afghan drug traders were paying taxes in Afghanistan only to be subverting laws once they crossed into British India. Yet even then, there is very little evidence to suggest that Amanullah was even able to tax the drugs as they passed Afghan customs and went south. Smuggling within Afghanistan was also an issue under Abdur Rahman, although in his case, the prevalence of smuggling was influenced by the amir's monopoly on exports,[115] something that did not exist extensively under Amanullah. Amanullah's restructuring of trade and taxation, however, and the creation of joint-stock companies (*shirkats*) were helpful in expanding trade with Russia and Persia.[116] In a similar vein, Abdul Ghani noted that the dual tax system (low taxes on exports and high taxes on imports) was intended to keep the "social tastes of people within the bounds of simplicity," while also developing "the economic resources of the country by inducing home manufacture."[117] In this case, the implementation of the tax makes sense. But what we do not know is how much the state benefited from this arrangement; in other words, how much revenue did the state actually make from this new tax system? And how much was smuggled? These questions were as impossible to answer then as they are today. More important, they reflect, in their most basic sense, the challenges of studying a commodity in a time and place whereby not only are records hard to come by but the changing environment of the trade in relation to its illegality reinforces the lack of textual record.

Regardless, the drug policies of Abdur Rahman and Amanullah may not have even mattered much in relation to the growth of the drug trade. As

Thomas Gallant argues, bandits and smugglers, were in many cases, both integral to the growth of markets and states. Via smuggling or looting, bandits often brought much-needed monetization to the places that were often beyond the capacity of the state.[118] Moreover, they also connected farmers to global markets in ways that states often could not.[119] As a result, we must come to view this period of the drug trade as one in which the market and the state both influenced the trade, but often in countervailing ways. On the one hand, the growth of the global drug market clearly provided impetus for Afghan drug producers and traders to participate in the trade. The movement toward drug prohibition at the international level clearly forced the British to reconsider its dependency on the opium trade, despite the fact that much of its local and provincial political systems remained dependent on opium for revenue. On the other hand, state policies, on both regional and international levels, also influenced the drug trade. The gradual decline of the legal opium trade in India provided an avenue for the Afghan drug trade (both licit and illicit) to fill the void. As a result, we can conclude that the two primary exogenous factors that worked to catalyze the Afghan drug trade were (1) the global drug trade and (2) international drug control. The second factor remains an important part of this book. The attempt by international drug control advocates to restrict the production and sale of opium, a product that had proven itself a lucrative source of capital for colonial powers, peripheral states, and even nonstate actors, inevitably instigated the growth and expansion of the global drug trade by strengthening the linkages between global and regional drug trades. This was in spite of the fact that the surging drug trade remained in contrast to the moral and political prerogatives of the nascent international drug control system seeking to control, if not destroy, it.

Although Amanullah would be ousted from power in 1929, the impact of his attempt at drug control and the response from the Afghan drug trade would reverberate in the years to come. Future leaders would come to recognize that the ideals of the international drug control regime, primarily in the form of the prohibition of drugs, would not easily conform to the local realities of political, cultural, and economic life in Afghanistan. Nonetheless, the drug trade would provide new opportunities for both the growth of markets and the growth of the Afghan state, and as we saw here, sometimes in contravention of each other.

Chapter 2

The Politics of Prohibition

How Diplomacy with the United States Shifted the Drug Control Paradigm in Afghanistan

In June of 1929, customs authorities in Paris attempted to deliver a package to the residence of the Afghan minister to France, Ala Ghulam Nabi. Ghulam Nabi was a notable figure since his arrival in France; he had served as the Afghan envoy to Russia, where he worked to get the Soviets to come to the aid of the now deposed Amanullah Khan.[1] But the delivery of the package had aroused the suspicions of French authorities who had spent weeks trying to get Ghulam Nabi to file the necessary customs paperwork for the package's delivery. Repeatedly, however, he circumvented official procedures. After three weeks, in a seemingly benign gesture of diplomatic goodwill, French customs officials decided to deliver the package. During the delivery, however, a box was dropped, and several bags containing a white powder fell to the ground. Given Ghulam Nabi's dubious behavior, French customs officials decided to test the contents of the bags.[2] Tests revealed that the bag contained heroin, refined somewhere east of France (likely in Germany), from opium of South Asian origin. Later, when authorities examined all of the contents of the boxes, they discovered the large cache of heroin (250 kilograms) and cocaine, believed to total an approximate street value of 1 million francs. Ghulam Nabi was subsequently arrested for smuggling 250 kilograms of heroin and a minor quantity of cocaine into Paris.[3]

After the incident, French and US officials contemplated the meaning of Ghulam Nabi's arrest: Was he just an ordinary criminal? Or was there a connection to something more nefarious? The size of the haul hinted at the most obvious concern that Ghulam Nabi was a big player in the illicit global narcotics trade. While somewhat true, this perspective disregarded the deeper connections to the political and social events in Afghanistan during 1929. His arrest was significant because, in the most basic sense, it revealed that Afghan opium was reaching well beyond Asian markets. But Ghulam Nabi's arrest also demonstrated that opium was now playing a greater role in the political, social, and economic events in Afghanistan following the end of the Amanullah Khan regime. In fact, from 1929 up to the Afghan prohibition of opium in 1945, both the export of raw opium and the import of Western-manufactured narcotics played increasingly significant roles in the development of the Afghan state. During this period, the export of raw opium to generate revenue for the state and the import of Western pharmaceutical narcotics to support the development of a struggling health-care system greatly influenced domestic and foreign policies implemented by the newly established government of Nadir Shah.

Throughout the 1930s and early 1940s, the global opium trade and international drug policy were increasingly entangled in the formation of the state under Nadir Shah and the new Musahiban dynasty.[4] The attempts of the Afghan government to attain pharmaceutical opiates to build and expand its moribund health-care system pushed Afghanistan into broader diplomatic engagements with the international community, especially the United States. In particular, Nadir Shah's vision for creating a modern Afghanistan revolved around the establishment of an advanced health-care system. This included building hospitals and clinics, as well as gaining access to modern pharmaceutical drugs. Access to pharmaceutical opiates, in particular, was important for Nadir Shah's new state, as dysentery, malaria, and cholera remained significant obstacles to the well-being of many Afghans. More important, the demand for pharmaceutical drugs forced the Afghan government to engage with the outside world in a way that no other Afghan government or leader had done before, forcing it to participate in the League of Nations and other early formulations of international drug control.

Meanwhile, the Afghan government was also exporting opium to various countries around the world, and opium exports emerged as a small but lucrative source of revenue for the Afghan government. On an annual basis, more and more Afghan opium entered the global market, making its way to Russia, Britain, France, Japan, and Germany. But with the onset of World War II, and the subsequent disruption of the conventional channels of the global drug market, Afghanistan would drift into its first formal engagement with the United States. Moreover, the relationship with the United States would come to define Afghanistan's drug policy. Throughout the war, the United States became one of the major buyers of Afghan opium, thus helping to nurture an otherwise nonexistent diplomatic relationship. Although the United States had concerns about the Afghan government's lack of control over the production and distribution of opium, the need for new sources of opium and hopes of creating a new ally in central Asia overrode any such fears. More important, drug diplomacy developed into an integral piece of America's central Asian war strategy, as the drug trade helped lure Afghanistan away from German and Japanese influence.

As the war drew to a close, American ambitions for international drug control reemerged as part of the US foreign policy paradigm. The changing dynamics of international relations, whereby the United States arose as a major potential force on which the Afghan government grew dependent, forced Prime Minister Hashim Khan to reassess the government's approach to drug control, health care, and the building of the modern Afghan state. More important, it forced Afghanistan to choose what role opium would play in its future. In one way, ending the lucrative and dependable opium export trade with the United States threatened to further destabilize the struggling Afghan economy and the government's tenuous control over the Afghan people. But expanding the legal opium trade also raised important questions about the production and trade of opium, and the capacity and willingness of the government to control it. In other words, was the export of opium so valuable it was worth risking alienating a new and potentially lucrative diplomatic relationship with the United States? Ultimately, Afghan leaders decided that maintaining access to modern pharmaceutical drugs and expanding its diplomatic relationship with the United States were essential to the design and future expansion of the Afghan government, and as a result, implemented a ban on the cultivation and trade of opium in 1944–45.

A ban on opium is no easy task for a state to enact and enforce; it requires enormous political will and substantial resources, and even then, it is almost always unsuccessful.[5] Then why would Afghanistan do it? This episode reveals how and in what ways the drug trade and drug policy were mutually constitutive forces in the formation of the Afghan state. On the one hand, maintaining access to foreign money was an important aspect in the design of the Afghan state under Nadir Shah and subsequent Musahiban leadership. It allowed the government to use foreign money to expand without relying entirely on domestic taxation. As a result, the government was more than willing to comply with American and international demands for drug control as long as it offered more lucrative opportunities elsewhere. On the other hand, the Afghans exhibited incredible cunning in manipulating American ambitions for drug control. By appealing to American fears of an ever-expanding illicit drug industry, the Afghans touched a nerve from which to exploit. The exploitation of American fears as an important tool in foreign relations would become an enduring aspect of Afghanistan's relationship with the United States, especially as the US presence grew in Afghanistan in response to the Cold War. As a result, this period of dialogue over drug control contributed to defining the core characteristics of the Afghan government under Musahiban leadership: that by acquiescing to international norms, such as drug control, and manipulating the global ambitions of the United States, it gave them access to money and resources that allowed them to perpetuate and maintain their predominant position in the Afghan political hierarchy without risking insurrection against the state. Ghulam Nabi was merely a microcosm of this period, for the global drug trade and international drug control policy became tools in the internal, and external, political narrative of Afghanistan.

1929 and the Fall of Amanullah: Setting the Stage for the Musahiban

Under the rule of both Abdur Rahman Khan and Amanullah Khan, the government of Afghanistan in Kabul was embroiled in a bitter struggle for control against the traditional tribal and religious authorities of rural Afghanistan. To varying degrees, these leaders tried to reform a rural society that for centuries had resisted forms of centralized governance. In a deeper vein, however, resistance to state control has not always been a product of innate rejections of institutionalized governance. On the contrary, the state itself was often limited by an acute lack of resources, accessibility, revenue, and man power, if not a general disinterest toward engagement with rural Afghanistan. Amanullah Khan had tried to change that; he was, in many ways, the first Afghan ruler to make an earnest effort to transform and modernize the vast expanses of Afghanistan. With neighboring countries, such as Turkey and Iran, revolutionizing previously feudal kingdoms into modern republics, Amanullah hoped to transform Afghanistan into a beacon for modern Islamic nations in Central and South Asia. However, his ambitions were met with the stark reality that change in a place like Afghanistan would require great skill, resources, and time, none of which he possessed.

By the late months of 1928, Amanullah was losing his hard-fought battle to change Afghanistan. The reforms that he had passed throughout his decade-long reign proved to be increasingly controversial, ultimately leading to open resistance against his attempts to modernize the country.[6] Much of the resistance stemmed from his reforms to education and health-care sectors, which required heavy taxation of both rural and urban Afghan, as well as some social reforms, such as those that gave rights to women or required Afghans to wear Western clothing.[7] More than anything, his policies were ambitious and idealistic, and when combined with the lack of personnel, resources, and poor planning, were doomed to fail.[8] Ultimately, Amanullah's attempt to transform Afghanistan into a modern, quasi-secular Islamic state in the matter of a decade, one to rival Turkey and Iran, created widespread animosity toward the Afghan government, leading it to crumble on its own very shaky foundation. By January 1929, Amanullah was forced into exile, and a bitter conflict ensued over the future of the mountain kingdom.[9]

From January to October 1929, Habibullah Kalakani, otherwise known as "the Bandit Amir," ruled Afghanistan. A Tajik, he rose to power amid a flurry of anti-Amanullah sentiment among the rural and tribal elements of Afghan society, and promises to restore Afghanistan to its traditional foundations of tribal and sharia law. While Kalakani laid claim to Afghanistan, the nation itself eroded into political anarchy and economic ruin.[10] Even though he claimed ownership of the Afghan throne, Afghanistan remained chaotic throughout the country, due in large part to the lack of consensus among the various tribal groups legitimizing his rule. As a result, many

European powers portended his demise. In exile, Amanullah remained active trying to reestablish his rule. Many Durrani Pashtuns in Qandahar, who originally opposed him, began to change their tune, because Kalakani's chaotic rule, and probably more important, his Tajik heritage, proved difficult for most Pashtun tribes to stomach. Amanullah promised to revoke many of Kalakani's reforms and to work extensively with the tribal and religious authorities, attempting to regain favor from the tribes that opposed him only months earlier.[11]

One of the major agents leading the fight for the rebirth of Amanullah's rule was none other than Ala Ghulam Nabi. Having served extensively as the Afghan ambassador to Moscow (as well as France), Ghulam Nabi became a key player in gaining Soviet favor to help fight for the return of Amanullah. Throughout the struggles of 1929, Ghulam Nabi led a small army across the Afghan-Soviet border to muster support for Amanullah and in hopes of creating a pro-Amanullah base of operations in the north. He would inevitably fail and be forced into exile; his quasi-military career was apparently short lived.[12]

Ghulam Nabi is relevant, not necessarily for his military escapades, but rather for how this connects to the Afghan drug trade. Certainly, his arrest in Paris was alarming because of the sheer quantity of heroin seized. But what does his arrest suggest to us about opium as an agent of political and economic change, if at all, in relation to Afghan history? I think it is safe to assume that Ghulam Nabi was not using for personal reasons, for such a quantity would, as Thomas De Quincey writes, "do what is particularly disagreeable to any man of regular habits, viz. die."[13] But more important, there is greater symbolism in the connections to the political events occurring in Afghanistan. In this sense, opium, as a lucrative illicit commodity, presented an opportunity for Ghulam Nabi to raise money for Amanullah Khan's attempt to recapture his throne. Norman Armour, the chargé d'affaires ad interim for the State Department in Paris, was in some ways right about a connection to Russia. He stated in July 1929:

> The *MATIN*[14] sees in this incident evidence of a world-wide scheme by the Soviets to poison the public with drugs, from a "center of intoxication" located in British India, and working through foreigners of position and influence such as Ghulam Nabi who, it is stated, is in the employ of Moscow, acting as a "blind" for an organized band of drug vendors.[15]

He did note that "the Afghan legation was admittedly hard pressed for funds after the fall of King Amanullah; the Minister was always in possession of large sums of money and is known to have spent 150,000 francs in one evening at Montmartre," but "this money comes from Moscow."[16] Armour concluded that Ghulam Nabi's economic motivations were mainly a product of the limited funds brought on by the downfall of Amanullah's regime.

But Armour was also shortsighted; after an extensive investigation by the United States Division of Foreign Control (part of the Treasury Department), it was revealed that Ghulam Nabi had worked with French national Joseph Raskine to obtain the heroin. Raskine was well known among French authorities for his long and lucrative engagement in illicit narcotics traffic. Raskine traveled extensively throughout areas of Asia that produced large quantities of outlawed narcotics, such as Turkey, China, and India. Raskine apparently received $10,000 from Ghulam Nabi, whereupon Raskine purchased the refined opium product from a manufacturer in Alsace. But in ascertaining Ghulam Nabi's motives, US and French officials were "convinced that the deal in question was financed with Soviet money through Ghulam Nabi, and the evidence goes to show that the drugs were to be sent to Bombay, where, the theory is, they were to form another insidious arm of the Soviet campaign to undermine British authority in India."[17]

The interpretation of Ghulam Nabi's arrest as a part of larger global conspiracy derived from a consensus in both Russian and American circles that the fall of Amanullah was largely a product of the "Great Game" between the Soviet Union and Britain. Soviet officials, and portions of the French and German press, viewed Amanullah's downfall as a product of British intervention. This was given greater salience when officials took into account the history of contention between the Afghan state and the British, as well as the close affinity of Amanullah toward Russia.[18] The various views put out by Western sources as to why Amanullah fell focused almost exclusively on the larger global powers. Most failed to credit the political events of Afghanistan as impetus enough.

The British, on the other hand, were more reluctant to fall for communist conspiracy theories. They were not quite convinced that this money was in some way connected to the events in Afghanistan. Apparently, Ghulam Nabi claimed that the revenue from the drug sale was for the benefit of the king, something that Amanullah most clearly declined.[19] However, the British were unnerved by a series of illicit drug-related actions involving Afghans. In

October 1929, British officials were notified that Afghans at the consulate in Delhi were connected to a scheme whereby they were trying to import cocaine from Britain to Afghanistan, to then be smuggled into India.[20] Why Afghans would do this, they did not explain. But it does suggest that given the political conflict in Afghanistan, there was a need for money and resources. But for what purpose? Were they raising funds for Amanullah's war against the Musahiban? Or were they out for personal profit? French authorities hinted that the money was being used to undermine British influence in Asia, much of the same argument presented in the media.[21]

To go back to the bigger question here, again, why would Ghulam Nabi smuggle drugs, and in what way was it connected to the conflict facing Amanullah in Afghanistan? The lack of sources certainly prevents us from fully understanding the motivations and connections to the Afghan conflict. Furthermore, Ghulam Nabi failed to sell the heroin, and failed to help Amanullah reclaim the throne. The evidence we do have, however, still indicates that there was a connection to the upheaval in Afghanistan. Given that this event occurred during the period in which Amanullah was deposed from rule, and that most foreign agents held a broad consensus that Ghulam Nabi was trying to raise money to undermine British influence, which was seen as somehow involved in the overthrow of Amanullah, it is clear that a connection existed, no matter how nebulous.

In a deeper vein, the episode of Ghulam Nabi demonstrates how, as Thomas Gallant states, "bandits helped make states, and states make bandits."[22] Opium money could fuel rebellions, insurgencies, or even the retaking of a state. In this manner, the banditry of Ghulam Nabi could have proved fruitful for the reascension of Amanullah to the throne. But Ala Ghulam Nabi failed, and Amanullah never recaptured the throne; nonetheless, the production and trade of opium continued. Thus, the episode of Ghulam Nabi is a good starting point for examining the future role opium would play in shaping the political, social, and economic development of the Afghan government and the country.

The Musahiban Dynasty and Medicinal Opiates

By October 1929, Afghanistan would be transformed by a new dynasty, the Musahiban. The Musahiban were descended from the line of Muhammadzais,

Peshawar sardars not directly part of the dynastic line of Dost Muhammad who ruled Afghanistan for the better part of a century. Nadir Shah, the new Musahiban leader, established the dynasty fully cognizant of the need to differentiate himself from Amanullah. Amanullah and Nadir Shah had both appealed to modernizing factions of the Afghan urban elite, but Nadir Shah recognized that most of the rural tribal groups of Afghanistan were directly opposed to state-run modernization reforms. So rather than change Afghanistan overnight, as Amanullah tried, Nadir launched a policy of gradual social change combined with economic development.[23]

In the past, most rebellions in rural Afghanistan were launched under the banner of Islam, usually in reaction to aggressive state policies. For the Musahibans to survive in Afghanistan, stability must be paramount. To ensure stability, the Musahiban government had to be delicate in dealing with the religious and tribal elements of Afghan society. One of Nadir's first moves was to rescind the secular laws of Amanullah and to reinstitute sharia law.[24] His constitution, passed in 1931, was infused with Islamic sentiments. Although Nadir did manage to pass some moderate reforms, such as those for women and in education, the constitution made important compromises to the tribal and religious authorities. *Loya jirgas*[25] were to be a regular exercise in the political mediation between the state and the tribes. This allowed tribal authorities to regulate the political and social policies of Nadir. The constitution also differentiated between civil and religious courts, giving the ulema broader powers over legal matters in the country. To appease both tribal and religious fears, the rights of foreigners were restricted and women's quest to vote was denied.[26]

Another important facet of Nadir's government was a focus on expanding access to public health. Afghanistan had one of the poorest health-care systems in the world. To deal with the abundant health-care concerns, the Public Health Department was upgraded to a ministry, and further attempts were made to reorganize the current health-care system. For example, a Faculty of Medicine was established at Kabul University to expand health-care education. And by 1938, the Bacteriological and Hygiene Institute was founded.[27] Although the health-care system remained a work in progress for many decades thereafter, its development indicated the growing importance of health care as a fundamental aspect in the development of the Afghan state.

Gaining access to pharmaceutical opiates was viewed as one of the major components of improving health care. Opiates, such as morphine and heroin (depending on the country manufacturing it), were revolutionizing modern medicine. In the United States and Europe, opium was marketed as a panacea. Doctors, pharmacists, and even entrepreneurs prescribed opium and morphine for a variety of chronic illnesses, such as asthma, bronchitis, diarrhea, dysentery, malaria, and arthritis.[28] Heroin transformed medicine by allowing doctors to experiment with longer and more intrusive operations. By the twentieth century, opiates were the primary analgesic for modern medicinal practices, and for Afghanistan, gaining access to pharmaceutical narcotics was essential to building its health-care system. Nonmedical use of opiates continued to be viewed as a social problem. Just as Amanullah targeted drugs as a threat to Afghan society by increasing punitive measures for smokers of marijuana, hashish, and opium a decade before,[29] Nadir endeavored to maintain a similar stance.

Nadir Shah was assassinated in 1933, however. In an ironic turn of events, it was believed that his killer, Abdul Khaliq, exacted *badal* (a core tenet of Pashtunwali, meaning revenge) against Nadir Shah in retribution for the execution of Ghulam Nabi in 1932. Unlike previous eras when sibling rivalry would have led to a war for the throne, the Musahiban family sought to preserve family stability. Mohammad Zahir Shah was proclaimed king, but being only eighteen, he acceded legitimate rule to his paternal uncles.[30] Muhammad Hashim Khan assumed the role of prime minister and took complete control of domestic and foreign policies.

The relatively peaceful rise of Hashim Khan as prime minister led to a renewed wave of interest in Afghan nationalism and modernization. For some Afghans, modernity meant the building of education, media, and industry, all of which were to emerge as significant forces during these years. The national bank, the Bank-i-Milli, reorganized and rebranded under Nadir, helped fund significant development projects throughout the country, particularly roads. Moreover, Hashim Khan desired to modernize the industrial and agricultural sectors of the economy to lessen dependence on foreign aid. The Bank-i-Milli used both state and private funds to invest in fifty trading and industrial holding companies to expand import-export trades.[31]

Hashim Khan was in a dangerous predicament; despite the emphasis on imports and exports, much of the economy remained small. Hashim Khan wanted to expand the state by developing the moribund economy but was reluctant to incite resistance to state expansion through taxation. Hashim

Khan decided to reduce the dependency on taxation as a means of limiting opposition to state encroachment.[32] As a result, foreign aid became a fundamental component of state formation. But to secure access to foreign aid and investment, Hashim had to break down the barriers of isolation that had long characterized Afghanistan's role in the international community. In 1934, Afghanistan joined the League of Nations.[33] Joining the League of Nations proved fruitful for the Musahiban government: it facilitated greater trade with the Soviet Union and led to Afghanistan's inclusion in the Saadabad Pact (1937), formalizing relations with neighboring Islamic nations to the West: Iran, Iraq, and Turkey.[34]

Afghanistan's inclusion in the international system ignited a wave of import and export trade. Exports, in particular, were fundamental to the growth of the Afghan economy because they provided a market for the two largest agricultural products in the country: karakul[35] and fruit.[36] Karakul, in particular, was the primary export making up 40 to 50 percent of all Afghan exports in the years from 1936 to 1946. In that decade, exports grew from 1.5 million skins to 3.3 million.[37] Grains, cotton, wool, and opium made up the rest of Afghanistan's exports. As table 2.1 shows, both imports and exports increased between 1937 and 1944, indicative of the growing importance of imports and exports to the Afghan economy.

Furthermore, exports were essential to the Afghan economy because they provided the only source for the accumulation of capital, thus allowing for the expansion of key industries. Trade increased so much that the bank increased its capital a hundredfold between 1932 and 1938.[38] Exports also served as the only form of foreign exchange.[39] It was apparent throughout the 1930s and leading up to World War II that the growth of the Afghan economy depended almost exclusively on foreign trade. This reliance on foreign trade meant that Hashim Khan had to maintain foreign relations that preserved the importance of foreign investment in Afghanistan's economy.[40]

As a result of Afghanistan's new role in the international community, Hashim could forge new relationships for investment and aid that previously did not exist. One of Hashim Khan's main goals was to improve relations with the United States. The United States was seen as a major opportunity, because it had the potential to provide significant infusions of private American investment and technical expertise.[41] Although both sides issued diplomatic pleasantries, including the recognition of Zahir Shah's govern-

Table 2.1 Afghan Trade, 1936–1944 (in millions of afghanis)

Year	Afghan imports	Afghan exports
1937–38	324	258
1938–39	332	411
1939–40	394	492
1940–41	512	444
1941–42	308	461
1942–43	340	578
1943–44	627	734

Source: Franck, "Problems of Economic Development in Afghanistan," 299.

ment and the appointment of a formal diplomatic mission, neither side was willing to acquiesce wholeheartedly to the other's demands.[42] The United States was slow to approach Afghanistan partly because the they were not granted primary diplomatic treatment.[43] Afghanistan, on the other hand, aimed to maintain its policy of neutrality, *bi-tarafi*, on all foreign policy matters. Furthermore, by the mid-1930s, Germany had become the major source of aid. Thus, giving the United States primary status in Afghanistan was deemed unnecessary.

Much like Nadir Shah, Hashim hoped to expand foreign relations to transform the health-care system, and in the 1930s those health-care issues were daunting. The young but expanding health-care system struggled to keep up with the growing list of epidemics ravaging the country, as the demand for hospitals, doctors, and resources greatly exceeded supply. In 1935, for example, the small number of hospitals in Kabul treated 93,168 patients, and hospitals in the provinces, 105,907.[44] In 1938, a cholera epidemic devastated the tribal regions along the Pakistan border. The intensity of the cholera epidemic was due in large part to the insufficient supply of medicines, especially pharmaceutical opiates, as well as the ignorance and skepticism of the local populations toward Western medications and vaccinations. Afghan officials were particularly concerned about the possible impact on the population of Kabul, given the devastating effects of previous cholera epidemics.[45]

It was clear by the late 1930s that to increase the well-being of the Afghan population through improved health care (and in some ways to bolster the legitimacy of the state), Afghanistan needed modern medicines. But to get legal access to them, Hashim Khan would have to participate in the international regulatory system of narcotics, the obligations of which would most certainly require the state to take a more direct, if not invasive, role in regulating drug production and trade. But would the Afghan government follow through? In other words, the decision to obtain pharmaceutical drugs from abroad would at some point demand that the Musahiban leadership implement policies that would disrupt and conflict with the social, political, and economic norms of many of Afghanistan's inhabitants, otherwise upsetting the delicate design of the Musahiban state. For Hashim Khan, the pros outweighed the cons; Afghanistan needed this. Furthermore, becoming a member of the narcotic regulatory system meant that Afghanistan, in some way, shared similar social values as the West and was accorded legitimacy in the international regulatory regime. This would be convenient when courting more foreign investment, which was becoming an important component in the design of the Musahiban state.

In previous years, the purchase of medicinal opiates went off without a hitch. But as the international regulatory system that emerged from the Hague Convention of 1912 took hold, Afghanistan's ability to obtain opiates decreased. The basic issue was that by the mid-1930s, Afghanistan had yet to recognize the core tenets of the convention, and as a result, all nations that were party to the convention (mainly Western nations) could not legally trade with a nonsignatory nation. When Afghanistan joined the League of Nations, the hope was that trade restrictions would be lifted. Moreover, there was a general hope that Afghanistan would be free to purchase Western pharmaceutical opiates. Because Afghanistan had yet to sign the official Protocol of Powers ratifying its acceptance of the 1912 Hague Convention, however, all attempts to gain licit sources of opium were put on hold while the Musahiban government tried to navigate the inefficient bureaucracy of the League of Nations.

One such case in 1934 highlights the newfound difficulties facing the Hashim government. In November 1934, Afghan officials submitted a purchase order to the Martin H. Smith Pharmaceutical Company of New York City. The Bureau of Narcotics (then a function of the US Treasury Department) denied the company's request to export ten, sixteen-ounce bottles of Glykeron (pharmaceutical heroin) to Afghanistan. In a letter to Harry Anslinger, commissioner of the Federal Bureau of Narcotics,

Martin H. Smith's manager, M. Reich, challenged the decision. Reich had received a letter from the Health Department of Afghanistan stating that Afghanistan had in fact signed the International Dangerous Drug Act[46] and was still in the process of familiarizing itself with the specific regulations and processes.[47] The International Dangerous Drug Act mandated that a certificate system be put in place whereby no government could export dangerous drugs to an importing country without the necessary certificates to prove that such drugs were needed by the importing nation.[48]

While the Afghan government may have signed the International Dangerous Drug Act in 1934 when it was admitted to the League of Nations, it had not ratified the 1912 Hague Convention. Assistant Secretary L. W. Robert noted that Afghanistan needed to ratify the 1912 Hague Convention to be considered for certified trade in pharmaceutical narcotics. But Afghanistan was not a member of the league when the Hague convened, something Afghan officials were keen to point out.[49] Nevertheless, Afghanistan would need to adhere fully to the international system to gain full access to the trade for pharmaceutical narcotics, leading Afghanistan to sign the 1931 Convention for Limiting the Manufacture and Regulating the Distribution of Narcotic Drugs in March of 1937. The convention required that all signatory nations submit estimates regarding the amount of licit narcotics each nation intended to consume for that year and nations were to cease import or manufacture, or both, when they surpassed annual estimates.[50] For the first time in its history, Afghanistan was a part of the international drug regulatory system and it submitted formal amendments to the League of Nations to alter the annual statement for the world requirements of dangerous drugs.[51] This was seemingly an important step for Afghanistan. It appeared that Hashim's government could trade for pharmaceutical opiates legally and give the state new access to medicines and sciences that could help in building a nonexistent health-care system.

But there was still a lingering issue; because they had not ratified the 1912 Hague Convention, Afghanistan never fulfilled the necessary requirements to be fully approved for licit trade in opiates, despite signing the 1931 convention. Furthermore, it failed to submit statistics and estimations as required by the 1931 agreement; it also failed to work with the Preparatory Committee on new regulations. Much of Afghanistan's difficulty in adhering to statistics and estimates had little to do with its import of pharmaceutical narcotics; rather, it stemmed from its emerging role as a significant exporter of raw opium.

Opium Exports, World War II, and the Beginning of a "Legal" Opium Industry

The lack of full or official participation in both the Hague Convention of 1912 and the Geneva Opium Convention of 1925 was putting both signatory and nonsignatory nations in odd situations, yet it did not prevent states from trading opium. In the early 1930s, prior to ratifying any of the international drug control conventions, Afghanistan exported increasingly large quantities of opium, especially to Japan and Russia. This created quite a diplomatic quandary, however, as opium exported to Japan had to first pass through British India. The issue of the transit of Afghan opium forced the British to weigh local political concerns, particularly the hope for good diplomatic relations with Afghanistan, against those of the international drug control system, which required participating nations to prohibit all trade with countries not adhering to the convention.

Questions arose as to why Japan, which already had a well-established and flourishing monopoly of opium, needed any Afghan opium at all, and more important, what impact this would have on the future of Afghan opium production. The British estimated annual production in Afghanistan to be around 80,000 pounds, with roughly 53,670 pounds being sent to Russia. These estimates also did not factor in the illicit trade going to India, nor that from Badakhshan to China and Russia.[52] Repeatedly, Afghanistan mentioned that Soviet authorities would happily grant Afghan opium transit through Russia. Moreover, if this arrangement led to a larger trade deal, it could help facilitate an expansion of the exports up to nearly 100,000 pounds per year.[53] Despite a much-belabored discussion, it was agreed that on "political grounds" the transit of Afghan opium to Japan via India would be approved. Expectedly, the political concerns centered largely on fears that the denial of the Afghan request would push Afghanistan toward the Russians.[54] In this way, the British approval of the transit of Afghan opium highlights the limitations of international drug control when drug controls came into conflict with local and regional political concerns.

For Afghanistan, however, the issue with the British highlighted the pressure to acquiesce to the international drug control system. In an attempt to standardize and regulate the process of production and trade, the government created the Shirkat-i-Taryak (Afghan Opium Company), a monopoly controlled by the Bank-i-Millie. It first began exporting raw opium in 1935, sending 1,500 kilograms to Germany. To obtain raw opium, government agents, or *alaqadars*, purchased crops from farmers who were registered and licensed by the government. Independent farmers who desired to plant poppies were required to submit applications through their local supervisor (*alaqadar*) to the National Department of Agriculture. The *alaqadars* were ultimately responsible for regulating who planted poppies for the sale of opium to the Government Opium Company.[55] By 1936, the Afghan Opium Company was exporting to Germany, the United Kingdom, Japan, and Russia to be used in the manufacturing of pharmaceutical narcotics.

Other than the basic structure of the opium industry, little is known about the specifics of the process. Not until World War II, when the major players in the international opium trade, particularly the United States, began to deal with Afghanistan, did more information emerge about the industry and its production, use, and regulation of the drug. Nonetheless, as shown in Table 2.2, early statistics indicate that from 1937 on, opium was had become a significant source of revenue for Afghanistan.[56]

Initially, the market was rather broad. The USSR and Afghanistan agreed in June 1936 to a trade treaty covering the exchange of goods valued at $10.5 million over the course of three years. Part of the deal was that the USSR received 90 tons of opium from Afghanistan.[57] It is not clear how the Afghan state differentiated between opium and pharmaceutical narcotics. Even though the medicinal qualities of raw opium were always known, a modern health-care system required the standardization of medicine, so raw opium was of no use. Moreover, Afghanistan did not have the infrastructure or international approval to manufacture pharmaceutical opiates. As a result, Afghanistan was drawn into a strange predicament for a nation that produced opium: raw opium was exported to foreign nations, whereby it would be manufactured into modern pharmaceuticals, and then imported back into Afghanistan. This arrangement was attributable mostly to the United States, because it had the largest stake in upholding strict international narcotic

Table 2.2 Afghan opium exports, 1937–41

Opium exports	Pounds exported
March 1937–February 1938	54,614
March 1938–February 1939	74,060
March 1939–February 1940	53,438
March 1941–February 1942	50,246

regulations. For example, the United States began importing opium from Afghanistan with the understanding that Afghanistan would fully comply with league regulations. In 1938, US pharmaceutical companies imported some four tons of raw Afghan opium into the United States. And yet, by 1939 Afghanistan's full compliance with the 1931 convention was still very much in question.

Other nations watched to see how the United States would react given its avid stance against noncompliance. Certainly cognizant of American hypocrisy, Clem Sharman of the Canadian government (an avid antidrug crusader in his own right), was curious about how the United States could justify trading opium with Afghanistan given its noncompliance. Noting that Afghanistan was supplying the raw opium that was eventually being reimported to Afghanistan as pharmaceutical opiates, he envisaged "an even more intriguing situation wherein she would be the non-signatory country which will be supplying the non-signatory consumer."[58] This letter foreshadowed what became the major problem with Afghan opium. Pharmaceutical companies had first jumped at the opportunity to import Afghan opium the minute it ratified the 1931 convention. Afghanistan never fully complied with its provisions, however, and as a result, the formal inclusion of Afghanistan as a party to the convention and legally allowed to trade opium was still contingent on it fulfilling the obligations of party nations. Afghanistan would not attempt to fulfill such expectations until the latter stages of World War II.

As the US chief of the Federal Bureau of Narcotics, Harry Anslinger, responded to Clem Sharman: "I learned of the importation of Afghan opium some time after the permit had been issued. At that time our permits did not specify the source, but they do now. I lowered the boom on the manufacturers and told them that there should be no further importations of this opium. *They informed me that it is of high content and very cheap.*"[59] Anslinger's reply highlights the major issue regarding Afghanistan and the trade of opium. It was clear that Afghanistan, despite its formal acceptance of the 1931 convention, was not capable of fulfilling its obligations. Yet US pharmaceutical companies were either unaware or willfully ignorant of this fact as they pursued the cheap opium. Ultimately, the US Federal Bureau of Narcotics prevented the sale of pharmaceutical opiates to Afghanistan in 1939.

The issues surrounding Afghanistan's ability to adhere to international drug control regulations certainly limited the expansion of the trade in the 1930s, but the onset of the World War II would change the way that both the United States and Afghanistan approached the global drug trade and international drug regulations. When World War II started, many of the established global systems of trade broke down. The economic and political development of nations such as Afghanistan, which were reliant on foreign aid, slowed to a halt. With Germany preoccupied by war, Afghanistan had little access to foreign aid. Understanding that the global order was shifting rapidly, Hashim reiterated the neutral stance of the state rather than reaffirming its support for Germany.[60] Although neutrality had the potential to open new doors for engagement, Afghanistan's economy suffered tremendously from the loss of its German donor. Most reform and development programs were interrupted or abandoned. Foreign trade, a major source of revenue for Afghanistan, was hardest hit. In particular, the karakul trade, one of the most important commodities for the Afghans, virtually disappeared. The growing economic hardship forced Hashim Khan to forge close relations with the other nations, especially the United States.[61]

Although most sectors of the Afghan economy struggled during the war, the export of raw opium did not. Afghanistan emerged as a consistent source of raw opium during this period. Because the war closed many customary sources of opium, competition for Afghan opium increased significantly. The Afghan government was fully aware of the potential for opium as a major source of revenue. *Iqtesad*, a trade journal published by the Afghanistan Chamber of Commerce, stated: "Opium is one of the important natural products of the country and as it is greatly in demand, more especially in wartime, in many countries steps have been taken to develop its production. It is hoped that, during the current year, good results shall be achieved."[62]

And the early 1940s were good for Afghan opium. In Badakhshan, opium purchased by the Opium Exporting Company increased from 7,772.6 kilograms in 1942 to 13,001.4 kilograms in 1943.[63] The government considered Badakhshan opium to be the best opium because of its high morphine content. The opium was of such high quality that Thailand sent a commercial mission to Afghanistan in 1940–41 to inquire about significant purchases of Afghan opium.[64] In 1943, Russia also purchased an unspecified quantity of opium from opium export companies in both Herat and Badakhshan.[65]

Land devoted to opium production also indicated the importance of opium as a commodity. Although the government claimed to dedicate 20,000 acres to opium, it is unclear how much of the land the state actually utilized or how much of the opium was supplied by independent farmers. Nonetheless, the increasing use of land for crops demonstrates the point. In 1940–41, 3,650 acres were utilized. In 1941–42, only 1,500 acres were used, but in 1942–43, production increased dramatically on state-controlled opium farms, as 6,870 acres were used, producing 8,930 pounds. These numbers, however, provide only a limited scope of total opium production. Exports, on the other hand, provide a better glimpse of the increases in opium production. The export of opium from the Government Opium Company rose sharply in 1942–43 from two years earlier. In 1940–41 and 1941–42, Afghanistan exported 6,700 pounds and 3,300 pounds, respectively. Both years' exports were sent to Thailand and Singapore. But in 1942–43, Afghanistan exported 19,740 kilograms, mostly to the United States.[66] Unlike the 1930s, when the Bank-i-Milli exported government-licensed opium only, the demand for opium led nonlicensed farmers to grow larger amounts of opium. As a result, much of the opium exported was grown independent of government regulation. The 19,740 kilograms exported to the United States would translate to nearly 43,000 pounds of opium, 34,000 pounds more than the government estimated was produced on government-run farms for that year.[67] Clearly, the majority of opium produced in Afghanistan was outside the scope of governmental control.

Numerous regionally based companies also emerged to capitalize on the trade. During the early 1940s, opium companies around the country were busy purchasing large quantities of opium for export. In an effort to open up business to private industry, the government allowed these businesses to compete with the Government Opium Company and each other. Two of the major companies, the Shirkat-e-Saderat-e-Taryak (the Opium Exporting Company) of Herat and the Shirkat-e-Sahami-e-Taryak (the Opium Joint-Stock Company), became major players in the opium trade. In 1944, for example, the Opium Exporting Company purchased 10 tons of opium during the first harvest and an additional 3,533 kilograms of Badakhshan opium at the end of the year.[68]

It is important to note what these numbers mean. They should not be read as comprehensive evidence but rather as indicators of opium's economic importance. The general increase in production and trade stems from the changes to the structures of the opium trade. Whereas during the 1930s Bank Millie ran the Opium Company as a monopoly, private companies now purchased opium from independent farmers. Why this shift occurred is unclear, but it is likely that the process was much more efficient, if not less controversial, when operated by nongovernment entities.

Trading with the Americans

The trade in raw opium between the United States and Afghanistan began in earnest in 1941. In December, the Afghan American Trading Company responded to a request by the US government for Turkish opium. The national bank of Afghanistan, the Bank Millie, cabled the Afghan American Trading Company in New York claiming it could "deliver forty cases Badakhshan opium, each 140 lbs net, first of February. Ninety cases fifteenth April provided license obtainable granted. Sixteen percent morphine 2170 dollars per case for Karachi Payment India Rupees."[69] The Afghan government saw an opportunity to fill a void in the global market since production of opium in places such as Turkey and Iran was disrupted considerably by war. Moreover, Western nations needing raw opium to manufacture pharmaceutical narcotics were cut off from their usual sources, in some cases compelling those nations to produce their own opium.[70] Despite the political holdups via international regulations, the United States saw Afghanistan opium as a prime opportunity. US Treasury Department officials were willing to agree to terms for price per pound depending on the percentage of morphine content. The first forty cases were of better quality, at 16 percent morphine. The second shipment of ninety cases was lower in morphine, at

13.5 percent. The United States would pay $15.50 per pound for 16 percent morphine content or $13.10 per pound for 13.5 percent morphine content.[71]

Harry Anslinger, who previously criticized American pharmaceutical companies for exporting pharmaceutical opiates to Afghanistan before it had fully ratified the 1912 convention, apparently was less concerned with international regulations when Afghanistan was willing to supply the United States with high-quality opium. Rather than deny the entry of raw Afghan opium because Afghanistan was not party to international conventions, he instead immediately referred the matter to J. J. Kerrigan of Merck Pharmaceuticals.[72] However, pharmaceutical companies apparently shied away from Afghan opium because of what they saw as excessively high prices.

The US government, on the other hand, was willing to purchase the opium directly, even if private pharmaceutical companies saw little potential for profit, largely because this was seen as an opportunity to generate Allied support in Central Asia.[73] In a confidential telegram in 1942, the American commissioner in India noted that the United States needed to consider the "possibility of supplying the United States with Afghan raw opium as the Far East markets for this product are now cut off."[74] The US stance was clearly changing as its role in the war changed. As a noncombatant, the United States had little need for opium, but with the bombing of Pearl Harbor and the German declaration of war, the United States was embroiled in conflict on both oceans. What was once a casual arrangement built on economic principles and loose political objectives was now, because of the war, one of great necessity.

Within a few days of the telegram, the US State Department issued a request for the commissioner to talk with the Afghan government about the availability of Afghan opium. He stated, "the Indian Government is reluctant to approach the Government of Afghanistan because this would tend to aggravate still further the price situation, which is already enormously inflated,"[75] referring to the previous offer from the Afghan American Trading Company. The United States hoped that the Indian government would have some leverage in possibly lowering the price, but the commissioner made it clear that the initiative might have the opposite outcome.[76]

The price of opium was the major sticking point, especially because US officials thought it could still obtain cheaper opium from other sources in the international market. If the US government were to buy Afghan opium, it would do so either out of charity for the Afghan state or its own self-interest.[77] But this benevolence would have consequences elsewhere, as noted by Herbert Gaston, assistant secretary of treasury to the Division of Far Eastern Affairs, "It would become necessary to increase the price of morphine and codeine manufactured from this opium, and . . . the increase would have to be borne by the sick and injured."[78] Furthermore, the United States had yet to increase its own prices for pharmaceutical narcotics during the war and would not change this policy for Afghanistan. Given the high prices of Afghan opium, and the potential impact with other buyers, the United States opted out of the sale.[79]

The high price of the Afghan opium suggests two things: on the one hand, it is possible that the Afghans were cognizant of the strain on the global market, and that the high price for opium was what they thought they could charge given the high demand and limited supply. On the other hand, the price of opium may have been dictated by more immediate needs. In 1942, the foreign investment that the state relied on, particularly from Germany, was quickly evaporating. In this way, it is possible that their motives were not mutually exclusive, but instead mutually reinforcing, because Afghanistan was losing revenue every day the war dragged on, and at some point, it needed to find ways to generate revenue.

It is not surprising that the export of Afghan opium for US production of pharmaceutical opiates did not generate the sort of uproar that the Afghan attempt to purchase US pharmaceuticals for import had. The United States consistently used its position as leader of international narcotic regulation as validation to impose its moral and ethical will on other nations. Why would Afghan need for pharmaceuticals be improper and illegal if it had yet to ratify the 1912 Hague Convention, whereas the United States purchasing raw opium from that same nation would be not? This dilemma was certainly contradictory, if not hypocritical. For any student of US drug policy in the twentieth century, this contradiction is not surprising; in many ways, it defines US policy.

As attempts to sell raw opium failed earlier in 1942, the Afghan government adjusted its pricing to accommodate the market. In September 1942, Muhammad Omar, consul of Afghanistan in New York and president of the Afghan American Trading Company, contacted Harry Anslinger about the sale of thirty tons of Afghan opium. Unlike the earlier attempt to sell opium, the Afghan government "would agree to sell it at a reasonable price, as the main idea is to establish friendly commercial relations with the United States."[80] Friendly commercial relations with the United States were becoming increasingly important to Afghanistan since the loss of major assistance from states such as Germany.[81] The lowering of the price and the Afghans' overt political objectives made this a deal of great importance, with Anslinger giving it his personal approval.[82]

Within three days, the Defense Supplies Corporation (DSC) made the move to purchase Afghan opium if private pharmaceutical companies did not. The DSC offered to pay the same amount for the Afghan opium as it did for Turkish opium, $18.70 per kilogram. The DSC was authorized by the Board of Economic Warfare to purchase 400 tons of opium, 333 tons of which were already contracted out to manufacturers for production.[83] The Afghan supply would not necessarily fulfill demand, being only 30 tons. It served to fulfill an immediate need, however, and perhaps more important, had the potential to expand in the future given the uncertainty of the global supply.

Both Anslinger and John Goodloe preferred that private corporations purchase the opium. Both men seemed to be sending mixed signals to potential buyers, however. They did not want anyone to make a finalized purchase, only to inquire about the potential for purchase.[84] The reason for this is not entirely clear. It is safe to assume, however, that the Bureau of Narcotics feared a free-for-all and wanted to keep the first official purchase of Afghan opium within the confines of their regulatory apparatus. The process of finding a suitor who would adhere to the demands of the Bureau of Narcotics took time. Muhammad Omar wrote a letter to Anslinger asking him why the deal was taking so long to happen.[85] Anslinger was reluctant because private companies were overstocked with opium and were in fact losing money. To purchase more opium would simply overburden their already strained finances. As a result, Anslinger urged the DSC to purchase the opium.[86]

The US government finally purchased the opium on October 5, 1942. The DSC agreed to pay $18.75 per kilogram for thirty tons of 13.5 percent morphine content opium, to be picked up in Karachi. The DSC wanted to contract the shipping process to Merck and Co., which had experience in dealing with this process in South Asia and Turkey.[87] But as the Afghan American Trading Company sent the agreement to Kabul, the response from the Afghan government marked a considerable change in the original agreement. On October 20, 1942, in a letter from Mohammad Omar to Harry Anslinger, the Bank Millie stated:

> Can deliver within one and a half months 8 tons of Badakhshan opium 16 percent morphine 3 tons Heart 10.5 percent. Can deliver another 11 tons within 4 months same quality and proportion total 22 tons. Prices 20 dollars per kilo basis 13.5 morphine difference in morphine percentage will be counted for. You arrange Indian transit permit and shipping space.[88]

The response from the Bank Millie contradicted much of what Mohammad Omar had told Anslinger. The opium was clearly not standardized, nor was it ready. More so, Afghanistan wanted the United States to pay for transport from Kabul to Karachi. Anslinger noted that paying for transportation costs would raise the price considerably and that this would most certainly be a deal breaker.[89] Rather quickly, Omar contacted Afghanistan and clarified the deal. The United States would only be responsible for transportation from Karachi to the United States, nothing else.[90]

The costs of transportation were reflected in the final price, as the Afghan government was still charged $20 per kilogram, an increase from the $18.75 initially agreed upon.[91] Despite the price increase and the issues with the transparency of the transaction, the United States agreed to the purchase.[92] Although American pharmaceutical companies were enticed by the Afghan opium crop again in 1944, the issues with the previous sale left a sour taste; they were particularly dismayed by the apparent inefficiency and unprofessionalism of Afghan opium traders. US State Department officials notified American pharmaceutical companies that nearly twenty-five tons of Afghan opium was harvested, of which thirteen to twenty-three tons of opium were available for export to the United States.[93] But apprehensions about dealing with the Afghans remained. Reporting to the US government, J. J. Kerrigan of Merck & Co., advised other pharmaceutical companies to approach business transactions with the Afghans with caution. When Merck representatives went to Karachi to inspect the product and approve of the delivery, "it was found that the weight of each case differed from the other. Moreover, the net weight of opium in each case exceeded 160 lbs."[94] The inconsistencies in both deliberations and delivery reinforced the notion that Afghanistan's opium industry was inefficient, unprofessional, and maybe worst of all, unregulated.

For American pharmaceutical companies, strict regulations and highly organized procedures were to be expected. Kerrigan, who was hesitant to purchase more Afghan opium for Merck, was willing, however, to notify Mallinckrodt Chemical Works and New York Quinine & Chemical Works of the available opium for purchase, especially if they were willing to manage the risks.[95] But the problems with Afghanistan were not so much the lack of efficiency or standardization in dealing with individual businesses. Rather, the inconsistencies that plagued their multiple deals with US pharmaceutical companies were indicative of potential issues with the entire Afghan opium export system. Was there more underneath the cover of this legal trade? And was the strain of the war leading the United States into a relationship with a nation that was not able to, and likely could not, fulfill the expectations of a legal producer and exporter of opium?

Although American companies and government officials complained about the lack of standardization and professionalism, the United States recognized the devastating impact of the war on the Afghan economy. And given the Afghans' previous affinity for the Germans and the present neutral stance in the war, the US State Department saw the purchasing of Afghan opium as an effective way of encouraging sympathy for the Allied cause. On the other hand, State Department officials also questioned how much of the industry the Afghans truly controlled.[96] What concerned US officials was that the exports of opium in 1942–43 exceeded the production value that Afghanistan stated for acreage used. From the US point of view, independent farmers were too large a source of Afghan opium.[97] For many of the US delegates in Kabul, the reality of the industry contradicted the majority of the claims made by the Afghan government. To offset growing concerns about the Afghan government's claims about its opium industry and to satisfy drug regulators' need for proof of control, State Department officials launched an investigation into the Afghan opium industry.

The investigations revealed that the strict regulation of production and trade claimed by the Afghan government was actually a farce. US officials believed that acreage and production control was far more lax than indicated, and that most of the time *alaqadars* took small bribes. But what concerned

US officials more than government corruption was that the majority of opium was produced outside of government control. The eventual acreage dedicated to opium production and export of raw opium often far exceeded government numbers, a clear indication that illicit production existed, and on a much larger scale than previously imagined. Moreover, the Afghan government repeatedly commented that opium use and addiction was nonexistent in Afghanistan. Yet one Badakhshan official believed that one in five people in Badakhshan were addicts and that large black markets for raw opium existed in the country's larger towns and cities. US officials also learned from talking to Afghan officials that the black market price for raw opium in Kabul was between $4.50 and $6.10 per pound, compared with the invoice price of licensed opium, which was around $3.00 per pound.[98]

Throughout the first half of the twentieth century, the United States established itself as the strongest advocate for the regulation of narcotics. With respect to Afghanistan, the United States feared the emerging illicit market for opium. But how to deal with it was another matter altogether. Direct intervention by US officials was not considered an option, given the still young diplomatic relationship between the two countries. But the United States did believe the Afghan government genuinely wanted to stop the illicit traffic in opium, indicated by the increased punitive measures for the illegal use or trade, or both, in opium. It is unclear whether the Afghan government wanted to control the illicit industry, so as to make it legal, or whether it shared in American aspirations to eventually stomp out the illicit opium industry because of moral and ethical considerations. It is likely, given the general ambivalence toward opium production and use, that Afghanistan desired greater control for economic gain. The difficulty for the Afghan government, however, was how the government would control a trade that existed generally in the places where the state's power was often at its weakest, mostly in the outlying provinces. Both US and Afghan officials understood that trying to control opium production in the outermost provinces would likely lead to dissent and rebellion against the state. More important, it was increasingly evident that the growth of opium as a global commodity could not be controlled by the Afghan state. For US officials, it seemed that the best tactic was to bolster the strength of the Afghan state so that it could either provide alternative employment or be strong enough to control the industry.[99] For that to happen, a major change would have to occur.

The Import of Pharmaceutical Narcotics during World War II

The effects of World War II on the production and export of raw opium were eventually felt in the production and trade of pharmaceutical opiates worldwide. Before the war, the supply of raw opium for American and British pharmaceutical opiates came primarily from Germany. German manufacturers imported opium from Turkey, Iran, and India. France imported nearly sixty tons annually from Iran and Turkey to French Indochina. However, the war completely restructured the global trade in licit and illicit opiates.[100] Many nations had to adapt to the changing global supply. The United States in particular adapted by manufacturing its own pharmaceutical opiates.[101]

For nonindustrialized nations with small health-care systems, getting access to pharmaceutical narcotics during the war proved increasingly difficult, straining already debilitated health-care systems. In the 1930s, Afghanistan struggled mightily to establish a functioning health-care system, which the war put under increasing pressure. The presence of diseases such as cholera, typhoid, and dysentery grew as decreasing supplies and increasing costs restricted access to vital medicines. In 1938, 400,000 people were inoculated against typhoid and an additional 164,000 against smallpox.[102] The need increased for pharmaceutical narcotics to deal with the growing list of epidemics ravaging the country.

By 1941, the pressures of World War II led Afghanistan to approach the United States to purchase large quantities of pharmaceutical narcotics. Although the United States recognized the dire situation in Afghanistan, it took the Afghan desperation as an attempt to bolster its drug control measures in the region. Afghanistan needed to ratify the 1912 Hague Convention and become a full party to the convention; otherwise, the Americans would refuse the deal. Afghan officials had already begun taking the necessary steps. The Afghan ambassador to the United States responded to the US decline for narcotics by reaffirming the Afghan ratification of the 1931 Narcotic Limitation Convention.[103] This was not, however, primarily a crude display of American power and manipulation. Rather, the lack of diplomatic interaction and want of basic knowledge clouded the validity of the Afghan request. If Afghanistan needed American narcotics as it suggested, it would have to jump through the various bureaucratic and political hoops to do so.

By the next year, it seemed as though Afghan officials were taking the steps necessary to get access to American drugs. The Afghan minister of foreign affairs, on behalf of the Ministry of Public Health, sent a letter to the US State Department in Tehran requesting assistance in the urgent acquisition of American-made pharmaceutical narcotics. It stated:

> The Ministry of Public Health has not been successful in obtaining narcotic drugs from the United States of America for three years as the Bureau of Narcotics of the United States does not permit the supplying of narcotic drugs to Afghanistan. It states that Afghanistan did not participate in the International Opium Conference held at the Hague in 1912, although the Afghan government has signed and ratified the International Convention for Limiting the Manufacture and Regulating the Distribution of Narcotic Drugs . . . which is supplementary to the Hague Convention of 1912. The Legation will note . . . that Afghanistan has legally adhered to the 1931 convention and that our adherence has been accepted. . . .
>
> Since the signing and ratification of the 1931 convention by Afghanistan, the Ministry of Public Health has imported its requirements without difficulty from other countries such as England, Germany, and France. Now owing to the conditions prevailing in the world it cannot purchase from other sources. Therefore it desires to purchase its required drugs in America. Great efforts have in this respect been made by the Afghan Embassy in Tehran in collaboration with the American Legation. Mr. Mohammad Omar Khan, Afghan trade Representative at New York, has also done his best, but without results.
>
> As the Ministry of Public Health is in great need of a certain quantity of narcotic drugs, and in view of the above statements, the Ministry of Foreign Affairs would appreciate whatever cooperation the Legation of the United States of America can render to the Ministry of Public Health, and requests that a telegram be sent to its government asking that the necessary facilities be given to the Afghan Trade Representative at New York to acquire and ship the above drugs.[104]

Similar to the situation in the mid-1930s, Afghanistan sought American pharmaceuticals. In the 1930s, however, with the relative ease of obtaining narcotics from other nations, American drugs were not a high priority. Furthermore, political relations between the two states were far colder at the time. But by the 1940s, with the war closing supply channels, Afghanistan appeared more desperate than ever. This need for pharmaceuticals appeared genuine, particularly because of the overwhelmingly poor health-care situation and the almost constant battle with disease. Yet despite the desperate calls for assistance and growing empathy for the Afghan situation within the State Department, the Federal Bureau of Narcotics continued to drag its feet.

The bureaucratic wrangling over Afghan drugs was indicative of a bigger struggle between the State Department and the Bureau of Narcotics over the future of American drug control. As John Collins notes, when the Judd Resolution was passed in 1944, it ceded much of the power of drug diplomacy to the State Department, which provided a more balanced and focused approach to international drug control.[105] The State Department began applying pressure on the Bureau of Narcotics to answer to the letter. The State Department sought a response from Anslinger either to approve or deny the Afghan request.[106] Although the Bureau of Narcotics responded that it was willing to ratify a trade agreement, it was not going to do so without getting the Afghans to ratify the 1912 Hague Convention. Narcotics officials responded:

> The Treasury Department is fully prepared to issue export authorizations for the shipment of a limited quantity of narcotic drugs to Afghanistan, within the limits of its estimates to the Supervisory Body, with the understanding, however, that Afghanistan will ratify the Hague Opium Convention of 1912.[107]

Urging Afghanistan to ratify the Hague convention also reinforced American efforts to bolster international drug control regulations. As deliberations continued, the United States used the opportunity to argue that the Afghan problem was not a bilateral issue but a multilateral one. For the United States to approve of a sale of pharmaceutical narcotics to Afghanistan, Afghanistan would have to ratify the Hague convention. But the United States had no authority to approve of such a request; rather, it was the Netherlands that had to approve of Afghanistan's formal adherence to the 1912 convention. Ultimately, it was "the opinion of the Department that any communication by the Afghan Government for that purpose should be addressed to the Netherlands Government."[108] Although this was a seemingly positive step for Afghanistan, the issue of Afghan legitimacy as a licit consumer of opium was now subject to the formal processes of the League of Nations and The Hague. Time, which was clearly an issue for Afghanistan, would no longer be relevant; Afghanistan would simply have to wait.

As formal political dealings awaited Hague approval, the US Legation in Kabul began to arrange the more pertinent matters of actually obtaining the specific quantities of narcotics desired by the Afghan government. This was another seemingly positive step for the Afghan government, as specific quantities and required numbers would further satisfy Hague officials that Afghanistan was a responsible consumer of narcotics, and more important, that its needs were sincere. The Ministry of Health sent the list to the US Legation specifying the drugs and quantities desired.[109] The State Department expedited arrangements for this purchase assuming that at some point in the near future Afghanistan would be granted permission to purchase narcotics and would receive the drugs it so desperately needed.[110]

As the list of pharmaceutical requirements made its way to the Federal Bureau of Narcotics, questions arose over quantities of various medicines. The bureau believed that the amounts Afghanistan requested for codeine and ethylmorphine hydrochloride exceeded the estimates of the Narcotics Supervisory Body.[111] Moreover, the Netherlands government received no notification from the Afghan government about whether it was willing to adhere to the 1912 Hague Convention.[112]

Afghanistan was at a crossroads. The future of Afghan opium exports and the more desperate need to acquire American pharmaceuticals were becoming entrapped in a larger political discourse of international opium regulation. It was quite apparent that there were growing concerns about the exports of Afghan opium and the potential for growth in the illicit trade. Moreover, the overall situation in the country was deteriorating. Health care, in particular, was becoming a major issue. With US and League of Nations officials increasing the scrutiny of Afghanistan's export of opium and imports of pharmaceuticals becoming more and more difficult to obtain, soon Musahiban leadership would have to decide between nurturing the export industry or securing the import of pharmaceutical narcotics. There were risks and rewards for either decision: First, Afghanistan could break from international regulations and continue to produce and export opium. In doing so, it could support the development of its own production of manufactured pharmaceutical opiates. However, this would ultimately incur the condemnation of the international community and likely alienate a potentially massive source of aid and investment. Or Afghanistan could adhere to the desires of the international community for opium regulation. In doing so, it would eliminate the lucrative export of opium but gain access to pharmaceutical narcotics and likely the favor of the international community. This, of course, would be a major factor in obtaining foreign aid and investment. Underlying both options was the risk that the Musahiban leadership could push the delicate balance between the people and state to the brink. A decision would be made with this in mind.

The Prohibition of 1945

By mid-1944, Afghanistan was becoming entangled with the ambitions of the United States and the League of Nations to establish greater antinarcotics controls over global opium production and trade.[113] The opium trade established between the United States and Afghanistan had benefited from the instability in the global market as a consequence of the war. As the war drew to a close, however, it became apparent that the Afghan state could not meet the requirements of the Hague convention because it could not regulate the production and trade of opium. Not only was regulation weak; it was practically nonexistent. Moreover, illicit production and trade was more widespread than previously thought. For the United States to secure the international drug control system from the growing threat of the illicit global narcotics trade, Afghanistan would need to suppress the production and trade of opium. Furthermore, the United States, as the leader of the international antinarcotics regulatory system, would have to provide the aid and motivation to push Afghanistan to prohibit opium.

Yet Afghanistan's decision to prohibit opium in 1945 was not an act of goodwill or mutual disdain for opium use. Rather, it was an act of calculated diplomacy, for the Afghans placed their new opium policy within the larger context of nurturing a new United States–Afghan diplomatic relationship, one that could potentially reap large economic rewards. In this way, the strategy employed by the Afghans centered on using American antinarcotics ambitions to secure substantial aid and investment in the Afghan state and economy. The United States, on the other hand, realized that to achieve its antinarcotics agenda in Afghanistan, it would have to help in bolstering the Afghan state and economy.

Moves to join the League of Nations and the international drug control system had begun before the war ended. In October of 1943, after various attempts to obtain American pharmaceuticals and consistent complaints about Afghanistan's unsystematized export system, Afghanistan finally made the move to adhere to the 1912 Hague Convention.[114] In a letter to the Hague, the Afghan government wrote:

> Whereas Afghanistan did not ratify the Hague Opium Convention of 1912 it is now desired that this convention should be ratified in order that certain essential drugs may be purchased from other countries subscribed to this convention and we, the undersigned, hereby signify our intention to adhere to all those terms of the convention which shall concern our country, which is confirmed by our signature herewith.[115]

Thus, on May 5, 1944, Afghanistan finally made the move to comply with the Hague conventions.[116] Adhering to the 1912 Hague Convention was a necessary start for Afghanistan, but in its acceptance to the Hague, the expectations of what the Afghan government was required to do to changed.

By becoming signatory to the 1912 Hague Convention, governments were to enact laws against the illicit use and trade in opium, while maintaining full and strict control over the legal industry. At this point, Afghanistan lacked any effective antiopium laws and regulation, which ultimately meant that Afghanistan failed to meet the requirements of the 1912 convention. And concerns about the Afghan opium industry were warranted; the State Department had repeatedly called to question the claims to control by the Afghan government. They saw a limited and weak state unable to control much of the trade in opium, with the illicit trade and use of opium alive and well. In other words, Afghanistan needed to create legislative distinctions between the legal and illegal trade in opium, and more important, begin earnest enforcement of antiopium laws.

In a letter to Cornelius Van H. Engert, American minister in Kabul, Secretary of State Adolf A. Berle laid out the tactics of the US delegation to try to convince Afghanistan that it needed to create laws regarding the cultivation and trade of opium. The letter from Berle was essentially a detailed list of orders for US delegates to push the American antiopium agenda onto Afghanistan. First, it seemed vital to Berle that the United States specify that the trade with Afghanistan for opium, which existed for the better part of two years, was a product of the war and American benevolence, not basic market dynamics.

> You are requested, at an opportune time, in any manner you choose, to explain to the Afghan Foreign Office that the United States has found it expedient, owing to the exigencies of the war and in order to improve Afghanistan's economic situation, temporarily suspend its practice of not purchasing opium from countries which have not enacted laws or regulations governing the control of trade in opium, including a system of import permits and export authorizations at least equivalent to that described in the Geneva Drug Convention of 1925, and that unless such a system is established and enforced in Afghanistan, the United States authorities may be obliged, after the war, to refrain from approving applications for the importation into the United States of Afghan opium.

More important, Berle wanted Engert to set the foundation for the future regarding Afghan opium. The war made this trade possible, but to continue in the future, Afghanistan would have to make significant moves toward bolstering the regulation of the opium industry. Berle continued:

> You are also requested to state that the Government believes that Afghanistan would be likely to avoid obstacles to post-war trade in narcotics with the United States and other countries if its Government would take legislative and other measures, if it has not already done so, to fulfill the provisions of article 15 of the Narcotics Limitation Convention of 1931, to which Afghanistan is a party. . . . You may wish to reiterate that the laws of the United States permit, among other requirements, the exportation of narcotic drugs only to a country which has ratified the International Opium Convention of 1912 and has instituted and maintains, in conformity with that convention, a system, which the Commissioner of Narcotics deems adequate, of permits or licenses for the control of imports of such narcotic drugs.

Playing the diplomatic game, Berle was also keen to reiterate a friendly stance.

> The statements suggested above should be made in the most friendly spirit, giving assurances that the manufacturers of opium alkaloids in the United

> States are desirous of being able to continue making imports of Afghan opium, and in return, of selling morphine, codeine, and other narcotic drugs to Afghanistan.

Berle's suggestions certainly reveal the underlying motivations within US policy. Adhering to international drug laws was certainly a desire of Berle, but not for reasons concerned with illicit drug trade and use per se. Rather, the Afghan trade in opium was valuable. It was more important for Afghanistan to adhere to the Hague conventions to continue the trade of opium with the United States than it was to control illicit opium trade and use.

After Berle outlined the issues with the present and future trade of opium with Afghanistan, he began to frame the important task of getting Afghanistan to launch a prohibition of opium.

> You may draw the attention of the Afghan authorities particularly to the statement of the British Government that "the success of the enforcement of prohibition will depend on the steps taken to limit and control the production of opium in other countries." At the same time, you are authorized to state that the United States Government is deeply interested in and is prepared to cooperate with all nations in efforts to solve the problem of the limitation and control of the cultivation of the opium poppy and to suppress the illicit traffic in opium.

The problem of the illicit trade and use of opium was an international one. It required global cooperation.

> As it now appears that there will be no legitimate market in the Far East for smoking opium after the war, those countries which have in the past produced and exported opium for use in the manufacture of smoking opium will be obliged to curtail production and to seek a share of the world market for opium for medical and scientific requirements. *It is probable that the contemplated poppy limitation convention will limit to a minimum the number of countries which may produce and export opium and will regulate production and exports strictly. In as much as Afghanistan produces opium of high morphine content, it would be unfortunate if Afghanistan could not qualify to become an exporter and to share in the world's legitimate trade in opium. In order that Afghanistan may be on an equal footing with other opium producers, it is imperative that*

> *the Government of Afghanistan prepare without delay to establish control over the area to be devoted to poppy cultivation in Afghanistan and over the collection and distribution of all opium harvested* (my emphasis).[117]

Berle's "suggestions" for Engert were essentially a list of tools to either convince or manipulate the Afghans to finally adhere to the 1912 Hague conventions. This would entail, for the first time in the history of Afghanistan, a concerted attempt by the state to control all facets of the production, trade, and use of opium. As a result, Afghanistan would have to come to terms with identifying what was legal and illegal, in a country where both production and use were regarded with general ambivalence, and the government clearly lacked control in certain areas. But the implications of expanding state control went beyond the issue of appeasing the obligations of international drug control. The Afghan government would have to exert greater control over peoples' lives; this was a political dilemma that the Hashim Khan government wished to avoid.

The cursory steps taken by the Afghans to adhere to the 1912 Hague Convention were taken as a green light to continue to expand both exports and imports of opium. Afghanistan pressed harder to get access to all of the medicines that it requested from the United States. Muhammad Omar, president of the Afghan American Trading Company, tried desperately to convince US officials that the quantities of narcotics desired by Afghanistan was unique, in that their annual requirements were "stretched over a period of years."[118] Anslinger's response was typical in reiterating that Afghan estimates exceeded the Hague's estimates for that country.[119]

Afghanistan also tried to expand exports with the United States, which had been fruitful the previous year. Muhammad Omar contacted Anslinger about the prospects of the United States buying six tons of raw Afghan opium (for thirty dollars per kilogram).[120] The almost unanimous response from potential buyers was that the price was too high. But the high price was indicative of how desperate Afghanistan was for money, especially with foreign aid money drying up. Unlike the exports of 19,740 kilograms to the United States in 1942–43, the amount of opium exported to the United States in 1943–44 dropped significantly to 871 kilograms, an astounding 4 percent of the previous year's export. Officially, Afghan officials chalked up the decrease in exports to external factors associated with the war.[121] But buyers were also turned off by the fluctuations in price and inconsistencies in both production and delivery. Ultimately, Afghanistan was desperate for money; this desperation reinforced Musahiban leaders' desire to find new ways to generate revenue for the struggling state.

As exports declined and access to imports slowed, the United States increased pressure on the Afghans to write into law the boundaries of licit and illicit production and trade of opium. Part of the postwar antinarcotic strategy spearheaded by the United States and enshrined in the Judd Resolution was an attempt to secure the periphery of the global drug market, particularly the traditional suppliers of opium, coca, and marijuana.[122] Countries such as Afghanistan were targeted as areas of particular concern, and US officials were tasked with motivating governments to establish basic controls over opium. America was especially motivated by the prospects of the global narcotics system postwar. The Narcotics Supervisory Board at the Hague estimated the required global opium usage for scientific and medical purposes after the war to be somewhere around 400,000 kilograms per year. However, real output would be closer to 2.4 million kilograms/year. This meant, of course, that governments worldwide would have to prohibit illicit cultivation and trade in opium to prevent the 1.8 million kilograms of surplus opium from hitting the illicit market.[123]

Given the circumstances, Afghanistan had little options left other than to launch a prohibition of opium. First and foremost, Afghanistan was still in dire need of pharmaceutical narcotics. Second, the export of opium, though lucrative, was limited. Third, the dialogue about drugs between the United States and Afghanistan was drawing the Americans closer to Afghanistan diplomatically. The more the United States understood the issues concerning the political, social, and economic development in Afghanistan, the more likely the United States was to get involved. In this way, aid and investment emerged as primary tactics to combat the growth of the illicit opium industry in Afghanistan. More important, Hashim Khan had larger concerns than the growth of the illicit opium economy. The war had not only devastated the economy but had dramatically impaired any state development. Afghanistan needed revenue to survive, let alone grow, and the United States was willing to provide it. A prohibition of opium, though devastating to the relatively small export industry, could now serve as the nexus of the new United States–Afghan relationship.

The Afghan government sent a letter to the US delegation responding to its previous discussion about the need to uphold the 1912 Hague Convention by prohibiting opium:

> Although opium is considered one of the export products which enjoy a ready and profitable market abroad at present, its cultivation in view of the non-existence of the necessary controlling organizations, has evil effects, both morally and materially, upon the public health. For this reason the Council of Ministers has passed a resolution that the cultivation of opium be prohibited as from the beginning of 1324 (March 21, 1945). The Ministry of National Economy should notify, by means of signed orders of the Prime Minister and the publication of notices in the press, all provinces and districts of the prohibition of opium cultivation.[124]

The semantics of the letter from the Council of Ministers reflected both the reservations and aspirations of the Afghans. The end of the export trade was clearly an inconvenience economically, made all the more inopportune given their economic struggles. With the lack of "controlling organizations," however, and more important, the moral and material consequences of addiction, the government was willing to take necessary steps to prohibit opium. This letter suggested two things that could be used in the Afghans' favor in the future. First, the lack of controlling organizations could be remedied with necessary support, something the United States stressed to the Afghans on numerous occasions. Second, the acknowledgment of the moral and material consequences of opium addiction served to bridge the cultural gap. This essentially notified the West that the Afghans shared similar cultural concerns regarding opium. All of these points would make Afghan attempts to court American and Western aid that much easier.

The government posted the formal declaration of the opium prohibition on November 6, 1944, in *Islah*. The government also ordered that all people possessing opium were to deliver it to government authorized dealers by September 23, 1945.[125] American responses to the Afghan prohibition were overwhelmingly positive. Walter Judd, representative from Minnesota and figurehead of the Judd Resolution, remarked:

> The other day the Government of Afghanistan announced that after March 21, 1945, all cultivation of the opium poppy in Afghanistan is to be forbidden.

> This action is wholly to be commended, particularly since the loss of revenue resulting from the ban on opium-poppy cultivation will be felt by a nation whose resources of income are not very great. But the progressive leaders of the middle eastern kingdom acted as they did because they are fully aware that the only effective way of eliminating the opium evil is to strike at its root.[126]

While Judd saw Afghanistan's prohibition as a boon for the United States and the world, and some Afghans would later question the decision, many Afghans saw this as the only option. Most Afghan officials knew that revenue from the opium industry would not surpass the potential gains from foreign investment in industry, transportation, health care, and education. For example, Minister of Afghanistan Abdul Hosayn Aziz believed that Afghanistan was willing to prohibit all cultivation (versus limit, as proscribed by the 1931 Limitation Act) because opium was not a significant export commodity, and it seemed wiser to stop the trade altogether given the potential benefits of doing so. Aziz also noted that opium was forbidden by Islamic law.[127] All in all, the prohibition of 1945 was seen as a positive and effective policy, especially as the Government Opium Company and various subsidiaries adapted to the prohibition and began to export other commodities.[128]

Yet news of the prohibition did not lead to an immediate disruption of the production and export of opium. Some opium companies, unaware of the specifics of the prohibition, were still active in purchasing opium up to March 20, 1945.[129] Indeed, various opium companies, with the help of the Bank-i-Milllie, still actively purchased opium that remained from previous stocks and was left over from independent farmers, to export to foreign nations. The Opium Company of Herat purchased 32,358 kilograms, the Opium Company of Badakhshan purchased 8,773 kilograms, and the Amanat Company (Herat) purchased 10,700 kilograms.[130] Since the opium was officially cultivated before the prohibition, it was therefore legitimate and legal, and open for sale on the market. The US delegation in Kabul made a special point to "help" the Afghans sell the remaining opium.[131]

Conclusion

By April of 1945, with the Afghan government formally announcing the prohibition of opium, all government-sanctioned production and trade seemed to cease. For both the United States and Afghanistan, the prohibition was an important step in their future relations. The delineation of legal boundaries and the appearance of drug control gave Afghanistan a new foreign donor, the United States, from which to get aid and build their nation. The United States, on the other hand, saw Afghanistan's apparent acquiescence to international drug control as an important step in their ambitious drive to create a strong international drug regulatory system. From initial accounts, the prohibition of 1945 had eliminated all clandestine cultivation and trade of opium.

Things were not quite as they seemed, however; rumors persisted that opium was still being produced and traded. By 1947, the State Department in Washington had no other choice but to inquire about the effectiveness of the prohibition. The US Legation in Kabul relayed that according to reliable Afghan sources, the prohibition eliminated all clandestine opium cultivation.[132] Yet the US Treasury Department reached a far different conclusion about the success of the prohibition. Furthermore, by late September 1945, and despite some claims that the exports were merely leftovers from prior to the ban, the British minister in Kabul notified Bureau of Narcotics officials in Washington, DC, that Afghanistan had not enforced the prohibition of opium, and was indeed continuing to produce opium for export.[133] In sum, the persistent rumors dogging the total prohibition of opium, which was widely hailed as a success early in 1945, appeared to be an aberration. If there was any success in the prohibition, it was that the opium ban marked the end of most of the government-run opium industry, particularly those companies most visible to other nations. But for those nongovernment companies, or those outside the scope of the state, or those merely willing to ignore the state, opium continued to be an economic force, with or without government sanction.

Throughout Afghanistan, for both government and citizenry, there was a general ambivalence toward the production and trade of opium; this was certainly reflected by the government not taking significant steps to enforce the ban. Most glaring, the prohibition was published only in *Islah*; virtually no attempt was made by the state to enact any legal measures. Furthermore, the state was well aware of its own limitations; it did not have any real capacity to control the legal, let alone illicit, opium industry. In this way, the formal declaration of a prohibition was more a political device to appease the United States than a genuine attempt to stop opium. Thus, at best the 1945 prohibition can be seen as an attempt to start restricting opium, and at worst, as a masquerade to get American money.

This episode unveils two important factors about the mutually constitutive relationship between opium and state building in Afghanistan during the early Musahiban dynasty, a relationship maintained by the function of opium as an economic and political tool. It reveals how Afghanistan used global ambitions for drug control to their advantage It functioned directly as an economic tool, as raw opium was exported to the United States. But indirectly, opium emerged as an important political device, used to bring the United States and its vast money and resources, into the Afghan political sphere. By replacing Germany with the United States, the Musahiban opened a new avenue from which to extract resources from abroad. More important, it allowed the state to use this money to expand without relying entirely on domestic taxation. As a result, the prohibition of opium (or at least the formal appearance of a prohibition) proved essential to the Musahiban and their ambition to base the growth of their state on foreign rather than domestic revenue.

Second, this episode highlighted the limitations of American drug policy and the cunning of Afghan foreign policy that proved instrumental in laying the foundation of Afghan political culture under Musahiban leadership. While American pressures certainly factored into the Afghan governments eventual opium ban, this perspective obscures more important Afghan developments. The United States managed to get Afghanistan involved in the international drug regulatory system but only because the Afghans saw benefits to such inclusion. Moreover, the United States had limited access to Afghanistan and knew very little about Afghan history, society, and culture, let alone the opium industry, and therefore was limited in its ability to understand and ultimately manipulate the Afghans. The State Department investigation is a good case in point. It took nearly two years for Americans to realize that although Afghans had signed the Hague convention and appeared to regulate its drug industry, the Afghan government remained limited in its ability to regulate the trade. This fact alone reinforces the idea that it was the Afghans, not the United States, who exhibited tremendous cunning in manipulating changes in the global political environment to their advantage.

Ultimately, by opening up to the outside world and embracing international drug control as an important aspect of their state, Musahiban leadership gained access to money and resources that allowed them to preserve and build their government. However, the result of this political design ultimately negated any real or meaningful political dialogue between the Afghan government and the Afghan people about drug control, which had profound effects on the future of the Afghan state, future resistance from rural Afghan peoples, and the eventual expansion of the opium trade.

Chapter 3

The Consequences of Coercion in Badakhshan

The 1958 Prohibition of Opium and the Issue of Culture in Drug Control Policy

Opium cultivation has become like a spring for the people. If my opium is not eradicated, I will be able to settle my debts. If it is, I will have to sell animals in order to repay the debts.

—Farmer from Khash, Badakhshan Province, 2012

In 2013, opium was a pervasive component of the political and economic environment of Badakhshan. The revenue from opium provided farmers with the capital to repay debts; it improved individual farmers' economic, if not social and political, conditions. As opium production expanded, however, so too did the impact of the Afghan government's counternarcotics programs. In 2011–12, the government eradicated four times the amount of land devoted to opium production than the previous year. Although the eradication of large swaths of opium poppies would seem to be good for Afghanistan, over time, the consequences of the deployment of coercive counternarcotics policies are revealed. Most significant, and as the quotation above depicts, the Afghan government failed to provide farmers with the economic opportunities to shift from the opium trade (which at this point was firmly illicit); quantities or access to alternative crops were often inadequate, reinforcing farmers reliance on the poppy cultivation. As one farmer told Fishstein: "It is possible that the situation will get even worse, if the government doesn't find work for the people. If the situation doesn't improve, maybe I'll grow 100 percent of my land to opium."[1] So why then would the Afghan government eradicate opium if they had no alternative to offer farmers in Badakhshan? In the most basic sense, the pressure on the Afghan government to eradicate crops is deeply entrenched in the perceived political success of the current Afghan government, or as David Mansfield says, "eradication is to be celebrated and seen as evidence of a capacity and a will to 'act like a state.'"[2] Essentially, the perception of success is tied directly to the international donors who continue to compel Afghanistan toward a drug-free future.

While the idea of a poppy-free Badakhshan certainly makes great political fodder, it rarely makes for good policy. As Mansfield notes, as the political cadres in Kabul and Washington, DC, celebrate eradications, "the rural population often sees quite the opposite."[3] In other words, without viable economic alternatives, the eradication of opium often forces farmers deeper into economic debt and desperation; celebrate they do not. More important, eradications (especially those that seem to reflect political posturing more so than genuine sustainable attempts at change) create deep cleavages between the local population and the state; the cleavages factor directly into the ability of the government to build and establish political legitimacy in rural provinces.[4]

What is most disheartening about this episode is that it has happened before. In fact, the eradications from 2011–12 seem to share many similarities with events that occurred more than a half century earlier. In 1958, the Afghan government, under the leadership of Mohammad Daud Khan, launched an eradication of opium in Badakhshan. And like 2012, the failure of the state to provide viable economic alternatives, which were compounded by deeper ethnic and tribal relationships, not only reinforced the importance of opium production in Badakhshan but also undermined the legitimacy of the state.

Despite the fact that the 1945 prohibition failed to halt the production and trade of opium, the vestiges of its failure reignited the dialogue over drug control throughout the 1950s. As a result, the desires of US and UN antinarcotic officials to curb the illicit production and trade of opium through the 1953 Opium Protocol, and Afghanistan's pursuit to establish a legal opium export industry, had a profound impact on the implementation and enforcement of the opium prohibition in 1958.[5] Unlike earlier efforts, this prohibition marked an entirely new direction for the Musahiban government: for the first time, Afghan leaders were willing to enforce the prohibition and eradicate opium. The willingness to eradicate opium was a significant step for the Afghan government, and it raises important questions as to why they chose to do so, especially in light of the delicate balance between the Afghan state and the people of rural Afghanistan. The answer lies in the external pressures applied by the international drug control regime, the United States in particular, and the needs of the Afghan government to placate foreign donors. After World War II, prohibiting opium became an integral component of the Afghan government's strategy to get greater access to American aid and investment that was increasingly vital to the state. By targeting Badakhshan, the opium ban allowed the state to use coercive force in a region populated largely by ethnic minorities, thus negating the risk of inciting rebellion from the contentious Pashtuns in the south. More important, despite the short-term success of the ban, the reemergence of opium production in 1959 suggests how deeper social, political, and cultural issues between the Musahiban government and the people of Badakhshan were fundamental to the effectiveness of drug control, and the future opium trade in Badakhshan.

The process leading to the Afghan government's decision to implement a prohibition and eradicate opium in the Badakhshan province, as well as the impact of that policy on the people of Badakhshan and the future of opium production and trade, are essential to understanding the evolution of drug control in Afghanistan. Following the systemic failures of the 1945 prohibition, mainly the lack of a legal and structural framework for drug control, the Afghan government had demonstrated to much of the international community that it was unable, if not unwilling, to effectively stop the production and trade of opium. This inaction on the part of the government proved instrumental in shaping the Afghan government's attempt to restart the legal production of opium for international trade in the 1950s. The production and trade of Afghan opium was increasingly problematic and worrisome for the international community and Afghanistan's neighbors, and as a result, forced the Afghan leadership to take measures that largely broke from its more conventional modes of governance. Ultimately, for Afghanistan to gain international approval for the legal trade, especially under the 1953 Opium Protocol, it would have to implement and enforce legal measures. It seemed that by the time Mohammad Daud Khan took power in 1953, Musahiban leaders were finally preparing to do just this.

Although Afghan ambitions for a legal opium trade received tacit support from American officials, especially because American pharmaceutical companies desired its potent raw opium, the increasing threat of illegal Afghan opium in neighboring Iran forced American and international officials to refocus attention on the extent of opium production, trade, and use in Afghanistan. The growing demand for Afghan opium in Iran deterred Daud's attempts to gain acceptance in the protocol. Eventually, the fact that illicit production and trade of opium was far more widespread than the Afghan government was willing to acknowledge forced Daud to launch new policy measures. By late 1957, Daud had one of two choices: he could either continue trading opium in the international market, but in contravention of international law, thus further isolating the country, or he could implement a new prohibition, effectively stop the opium trade, and use the new drug policy as a means of gaining access to US and UN funds for the development of his state.

By November 1957, Daud announced a nationwide prohibition of opium. Unlike previous bans, Daud would actually enforce the opium prohibition, but with one very important stipulation: the ban would only go into effect in the province of Badakhshan. Why would Daud chose Badakhshan when opium was also being grown and traded in Nangarhar and Herat? Badakhshan, in the northeast, was historically a major source of opium in the country. By targeting Badakhshan, Daud made a symbolic statement to the international community, since most countries recognized Badakhshan opium to be some of the best in the world, something valued highly by foreign pharmaceutical companies, and vital to the local economy. Although the symbolism of banning opium in Badakhshan was important, it was, more significantly, a calculated policy maneuver. The opium ban allowed Daud to garner international praise and financial support, while enforcing the eradication in an area inhabited by ethnic minorities, thus ensuring that the Afghan government would not generate resistance from rural Pashtun tribes historically opposed to these types of state interventions.

Although the opium ban was hailed in international circles as a shining example of international drug control, in 1959, opium production was again present in Badakhshan. Opium's reemergence in Badakhshan reveals how deeper socio-political relations in the region were fundamental to either the ban's success or the enduring production and trade of opium. More important, the eradication of opium in Badakhshan revealed a paradox between the government's justification for intervention and the underlying causes of opium's enduring production and trade. On the one hand, by making opium illegal, the Afghan government established legal as well as economic and cultural parameters about the improper uses of opium. The production and trade of opium defied what Willem Van Scehndel and Itty Abraham call the "norms and rules of formal political authority."[6] But whose norms, and whose authority? It was one thing for the Afghan government to establish and enforce such norms in Kabul, but another altogether to do so in Badakhshan. In Badakshan, opium was a vital, if not normal, aspect of cultural, economic, and political life; opium's role is pivotal in this sense. The eradication of opium not only disrupted the economic livelihoods of people in Badakhshan, but cut against cultural norms and political relationships. In this way, the opium ban exacerbated deeply rooted sentiments that government policy was overtly pro-Pashtun, reinforcing the growing cultural chasm between the Musahiban government and the people of Badakhshan, and ultimately fragmenting an already fractured state–society relationship.

Paradoxically, the prohibition reinforced the economic, as well cultural and political, role of opium. As long as Daud's government failed to build effective and responsive political and economic institutions, in particular those forms of aid and development that were tied to international and western machinations for drug control, and also perpetuated the governments' overt racial bias, opium would remain a vital part of the social, economic, and political fabric of Badakhshan. The more Daud and other Musahiban leaders pushed for drug control while neglecting other aspects of state building that were indirectly tied to the drug trade, the more drug policy enflamed preexisting political tensions, fragmenting the country, and, ironically, creating a political and economic environment that was ideal for the expansion of the drug trade.

Rethinking Drug Production in the Age of Daud

Shah Mahmud, brother to Hashim Khan, replaced Hashim as prime minister in 1946. Much like his predecessor, Mahmud was encouraged by a growing educated elite to continue the push for social, political, and economic reforms. As a result, the years following the war and the 1945 prohibition saw substantial increases in foreign aid and investment. The United States, in particular, eventually became one of the major investors in the future of Afghanistan.[7] Musahiban leaders understood that US financial aid and investment would provide more than economic benefits: it would also generate political confidence in the Afghan government. Initially, however, the United States shied from forthright involvement in Afghan politics. Although aid and investment in Afghanistan was seen as an opportunity, resources from Afghanistan were not vital to American interests.[8] Moreover, Afghan neutrality perpetuated American reluctance. With regimes in both Pakistan and Iran strongly supporting American foreign policies, and Afghanistan offering little economic or political return, Afghanistan was a secondary option.[9]

Nonetheless, the United States still saw value in expanding the relationship with Afghanistan. Afghanistan was a buffer state to the Soviet Union and could be a key arena in a future conflict with the Soviet Union. In late 1945, the United States agreed to help with developing rural Afghanistan launching the Helmand Valley Project. The project, contracted out to the Morrison-Knudsen Company, began with an estimated cost of $63.7 million. The Morrison-Knudsen Company was hired to build dams, roads, and canals in the Helmand Valley to improve agricultural output and connect the region considered the breadbasket of Afghanistan with the rest of country.[10] The project was ambitious and beset with problems from the onset. After a few years, various inconsistencies and poor planning led to a major explosion in costs.[11] The loss of the foreign exchange surplus forced the state to cut costs where possible and to search for new sources of revenue. As a result, policies that restricted revenue growth, such as prohibiting opium, were placed on the chopping block.

By 1950, rumors circulated that Afghan leaders desired to reestablish the cultivation of opium for export. Abdul Wahab Haider, Afghanistan's head of the Commercial Section of the Ministry of National Economy, believed that the 1945 prohibition of opium was a serious mistake given the potential for raw Afghan opium in the pharmaceutical market. The Afghan government believed that exporting opium was fast becoming a necessity, given the country's greatly reduced foreign currency holdings.[12] Wahab's explanation was likely related to general issues regarding the Helmand Valley Project but nonetheless proves an important point. Afghanistan needed more development. It needed major investments in the bureaucracy, the military, and economic infrastructure, and could not enforce policies, such as the prohibition, without outside aid. Moreover, the enforcement of regulations was impossible since most opium was grown by individuals and smuggled along Afghanistan's vast borders, which could not be effectively patrolled.[13] Afghanistan had previously shown the ability to play on American paranoia, so the rumor very well could have been an attempt to stoke fear, but it is also likely that Wahab understood that American desires for a strong antiopium regime in Afghanistan could be used to benefit the Afghan government.

Despite US narcotics officials' concern about the threat of illicit opium cultivation and smuggling, the export of raw Afghan opium to manufacture in the United States continued, especially because Afghan opium was proving to be an ideal source for high-morphine content opium. In various discussions between Wahab and State Department officials, Wahab was keen to reinforce the fact that Afghan opium, especially from Badakhshan, was some of the best in the world. For a poor country such as Afghanistan, opium could provide a stable source of revenue for the growing state. Wahab estimated that if Afghanistan could again export opium, it would produce upward of one hundred tons of opium, adding $1.5 million to Afghanistan's foreign exchange reserves.[14] In repeated meetings with US officials, Wahab was keen to emphasize the point that the high-morphine opium from Badakhshan was valuable to both American pharmaceutical companies and the Afghan government.

The problem for both parties was that Afghanistan's legal status remained in flux. Although American pharmaceutical companies continued to pursue the opportunity to buy Afghan opium, they did so reluctantly. The variable for American companies was whether they carried licenses allowing them to import large quantities of Afghan opium.[15] US antinarcotics officials were disinclined to grant either American companies or the Afghans the right to openly commence trading. They feared that granting Afghans rights to trade opium again would undermine the most recent American effort to strengthen international regulation of opium supplies.

In 1953, the United States and France had coordinated the Opium Protocol to reorganize and reestablish international efforts to control the production and trade of opium. The treaty aimed to get producer states to regulate production strictly through rigorous adherence to the monitoring of quantities of opium planted, harvested, consumed domestically, exported, and stockpiled. It also gave the provisional body the power to make inquiries about discrepancies, conduct inspections, and impose trade embargoes. Only seven countries were granted rights to produce licitly under the protocol.[16] In exchange for being signatories to these strict regulations, nations were granted monopolies on all licit sales.[17] In other words, if the United States were to trade with Afghanistan, it would ultimately undermine the treaty the Americans worked so hard to create. By 1954, Harry Anslinger was urging the US Embassy in Kabul to vigorously discourage the Afghans from restarting export trade.[18]

Yet the conflict over Afghan export of opium was not limited to purely narcotic matters. Rather, the Cold War transformed the opium question from an ethical and moral crusade by the West into a political conflict between the United States and the Soviet Union. During the Avuncular period (1933 to 1953), so called because both Hashim Khan and Shah Mahmud pushed for relatively liberal reforms in social and political institutions, both leaders looked to the West for political and economic guidance, with little effect. By 1953, public pressure mounted against the liberal Parliament, and Daud Khan launched a bloodless coup in September and announced himself as prime minister. Daud promised to modernize the country but refused to continue the aggressive policies of the liberal Parliament.

One of the principal aims of Daud's rule was to reestablish Afghanistan's neutrality.[19] In an effort to rebalance Afghanistan's foreign policy, Daoud forged closer ties with the Soviet Union. Part of his lean toward Moscow was the belief within Daud's government that the United States placed Afghanistan low on the geopolitical totem pole. In particular, Afghanistan was upset that the United States denied requests for military aid, yet continued to arm Pakistan to protect South Asia from Russian expansion, even though Afghanistan bordered the Soviet Union.[20] To make matters worse, Afghanistan was denied US aid under the Mutual Security Program, while Iran and Pakistan received increased funding.[21] Conversely, US foreign policy under Eisenhower and the Dulles brothers viewed neutrality as an indication of leftist inclinations. With the United States focusing on larger nations, the Soviets positioned themselves to take advantage of Afghanistan's need for aid. By the mid-1950s, there were substantial increases in Soviet military sales to Afghanistan.[22] They even managed to barter for substantial quantities of Afghan opium.[23]

Afghanistan continued to push to the international community its case for inclusion in the 1953 Opium Protocol. In 1955, Afghanistan presented its case to the United Nations. A. Hamid Aziz, permanent representative of Afghanistan to the UN, argued that Afghanistan was not included in the 1953 protocol because it was unable to attend the conference due to extenuating domestic circumstances.[24] As a result, the government of Afghanistan was taking the necessary steps to amend the 1953 protocol so as to include Afghanistan in the licit import and export of opium. By demanding the urgent amendment of the protocol, Afghanistan was hoping to reflect the seriousness and urgency of the request, if not the desperation. Aziz stated, "My Government considers it to be a matter of the most vital importance to her economy that the said protocol should be amended with the least possible delay."[25] Afghan requests seemed logical; Egypt became the first significant Middle Eastern nation to support Afghanistan's inclusion in the 1953 protocol, arguing that since Afghanistan was poor and remote, the export of opium could be a valuable crop to increase its desperate need for hard currency.[26]

The arguments presented by Afghanistan were reasonable enough that the United States supported Afghanistan, albeit reluctantly. Harry Anslinger, the icon of American antidrug control, noted that Afghanistan would have undoubtedly been included in the 1953 protocol had it been represented at the conference. Moreover, Afghanistan's urgency was reinforced by the expectations of twenty tons of opium being produced in 1955. Anslinger thought "they are entitled to this production; their opium is of the highest quality, and, as far as I know, has not been found in the illicit narcotics traffic."[27] Anslinger's statement reveals the two primary concerns for US officials. First, the quality of Afghan opium was valuable to American pharmaceutical companies. Afghanistan's inclusion in the protocol would be of great benefit to the US pharmaceutical industry. Second, Afghan opium had yet to become a significant component in the illicit narcotics trade. The United States could not allow Afghanistan to resume licit production if illicit production and trade of opium was widespread.[28] If the United States wanted Afghanistan to control opium, decisions needed to be made, and soon.

Iran and the Regional Implications of Afghan Opium

Afghanistan's push for a legal opium industry, which had been laid forth before the international community and was seen by many as reasonable, was not without its detractors. Iran, Afghanistan's neighbor to the west, struggled to deal with a very large and active opium-consuming population.[29] Some observers believed that in 1955 Iran had a staggering 2.8 million opium addicts. Opium use was so widespread that there were 1,200 opium dens in Tehran alone.[30] The black market for opium was estimated to earn nearly $61 million dollars in 1955, three times the amount of revenue generated by Iran's legal industry. That year, the shah and Parliament imposed a ban on poppy cultivation and outlawed the sale and possession of opium. Unlike previous measures to curb opium trade and use by the state, the shah's prohibition was unyielding in its implementation. All opium, including opium used for medicine and export was banned.[31]

The shah's ban on opium had profound implications for the region. Even though the prohibition was successful in eliminating opium production and closing down large numbers of opium dens in Iran,[32] demand for opium remained high. Iranian officials feared that Afghan and Turkish opium would quickly meet the massive demand. Iranian fears had a considerable impact on Afghanistan's push for legitimization of the opium trade. Had opium concerns been isolated to Afghanistan, considerations for inclusion in the protocol likely would have been different. But Afghanistan's opium trade was not isolated, and was beginning to threaten neighboring countries, especially those with deeply entrenched American interests. Iranian officials and State Department officials in Tehran believed granting Afghanistan rights to expand such an industry would only make matters worse in Iran. As a result, Iran was staunchly opposed to Afghanistan's push for a legal opium industry given the potential for Afghan opium to fill the massive void in supply as a result of the shah's ban.[33]

During the Eleventh Session of the United Nations Economic and Social Council's Commission on Narcotic Drugs in 1956, both Afghan and Iranian delegations were granted the opportunity to advocate their stance. Iran pressured the United States to advocate on its behalf given the strength of the relationship between the two nations. The Iranian Mission to the UN regarded the Afghan request for inclusion in the protocol as a dangerous proposition, given the already substantial quantities of opium flooding the global market. The Iranian Mission stated:

> Recalling the fact that at present those countries which produce opium are producing more opium than the world requires for medical and scientific use, and noting that Iran, notwithstanding her loss of national income, has banned the cultivation of the opium poppy by law, and emphasizing the fact that the annual world production of opium by the five countries remaining as opium-

> producers is 500 tons—almost 50 tons more than is required by the world consumption of opium, the Government of Iran reaffirms that the recognition of another country as an opium-producer for export would not only add to the unnecessary production of opium, but it would also intensify illicit traffic in the world market, and in this special case, it would totally cripple effective enforcement of the law banning the cultivation of the opium poppy in Iran and make futile any efforts toward the treatment of opium addicts.[34]

The State Department Legation in Tehran strongly supported many of the Iranian government's concerns. They feared that legalizing the export of opium from Afghanistan would undermine Iran's attempts to curb production and use of opium. This was already underscored by the fact that Afghan opium smugglers were increasing along the borders. Given the large numbers of opium addicts in Iran, along with Iran's geostrategic significance, the State Department urged the UN to side with Iran.[35] While the commission recognized the dilemma facing Afghanistan, it opted to postpone any decision until its twelfth session, when they determined that Afghanistan could put the entire 1953 Opium Protocol in place as well as finally adhere to the 1925 Protocol.[36]

The next session of the commission convened in July 1956. Various delegations discussed Afghanistan's desire to be included in the 1953 Protocol. India, Pakistan, Iran, and Turkey all displayed varying degrees of reluctance toward the Afghan request, mostly because they were either major producers, major consumers, or both. Some members of the Social Committee supported Afghanistan's request because they believed that the regional prohibitions in Iran and Pakistan, regularly cited as the most obvious reasons why Afghanistan should not be allowed to export opium legally, gave Afghanistan an opportunity to fill voids in the licit market. Furthermore, one Afghan delegate cited the fact that Afghanistan prohibited opium eleven years before Iran and never had an addiction epidemic.[37]

However, UN and US officials began to question the sincerity of Afghan motivations. Not only was Afghanistan actively trying to restart the export of opium (preemptive to official inclusion in the 1953 Opium Protocol), but it was also raising alarms with its import requests as well. A major issue for the UN was the inordinately high quantities of pharmaceutical narcotics requested by the Afghan government. Dr. Abdul Zahir, minister of Public Health, wrote the UN to explain Afghanistan's large request for pharmaceutical narcotics.

> The spread of modern medicine and its whole-hearted acceptance by the remote villagers throughout our country has been remarkably rapid during the past few years, due mostly to availability of more medical and paramedical personnel, increased national and governmental financial help and the technical assistance of the World Health Organization. Private and group medical practice, clinics, pharmacies have increased. The government budget for the Ministry of Health alone has grown in many fields during recent years. There was an increase of 17 percent in 1953 over the previous year and an increase of 100 percent in 1954 over the year 1953. Next year there will again be an increase of 75 percent over last year's budget. This increase in the government budget is a good index of the general trend of the growth of modern medicine in this country.

Although keen to emphasize the increasing role of modern medicine in Afghanistan, Dr. Zahir did not agree with the Afghan government's request for pharmaceutical narcotics. He stated, "This increase in availability of medical facilities, although very appreciable, however, does not explain, in my opinion, the requests made during the past three or four years for a relatively large increase in the quota of the Narcotic Drugs for Afghanistan." He explained that the government requested such high numbers "in anticipation of the expected future expanded medical programs." However, making such a remark could be seen as proof of Afghanistan's inability to effectively and responsibly control the import of pharmaceutical narcotics. However, Dr. Zahir cited the issue as the source of motivation for the government to act. As further proof of Zahir's claims, the government created the Central Office for Narcotic Drugs within the Ministry of Public Health to regulate the import of pharmaceutical narcotics.[38] Although the creation of the Central Office for Narcotic Drugs was initially considered a boon for Afghan import of narcotics, the Central Office had yet to prove that it controlled opium production and use.

The first real step toward real drug control occurred with the launching of the Opium Act of 1956 (Aswalname Tariawk 1335). Unlike the 1945 prohibition, the Opium Act outlined definitive rights of the government, farmers, and traders regarding the opium trade. The first article declared that the government had the right to control the cultivation of farmers (*zaareh*) and export (*saader*) of opium.[39] The law also addressed the historical role of the government in the opium trade and how this role was to be restructured along the present political and economic conditions. Article 2 acknowledged that in many places in the country, opium cultivation (*kesht kardan*) was previously licensed by the state. In these regions, cultivation would still only be permitted with a government-issued license, and farmers would have to engage directly with government representatives to have their product exchanged for cash. Furthermore, farmers would undergo compulsory audits by the government to keep their license to grow.[40] The subsequent articles outlined the steps farmers had to take to acquire or renew their licenses, particularly the planning around meetings with government auditors and negotiations for exchange (Articles 3–5). Mirroring the laws of Abdur Rahman and Amanullah, use of opium (*estemaal tariawk*), as well as the buying of opium, was prohibited (*mamno*) under Article 7. But users would also have access to treatment for opium use through the Ministry of Health (Article 8). In this way, the act was a big step toward realizing how drug control was to manifest under Daud; it provided guidelines for legal production and penalties for illegal production and trade.

But possibly the most interesting aspect of the 1956 act was that it created a cultural bridge in the government's approach to opium that further aligned Afghan drug policy with that of the international and American drug control community. Article 10 states: "The Ministry of Health, Royal Afghan government, will launch a vigorous program against the eating, smoking, and the other use of opium and bring to the notice of the public the evil effects on health and anti-social repercussions of this drug."[41] Adopting the more dramatic rhetoric characterizing drugs as evil and morally reprehensible (quite akin to the American stance), the opium act suggested that the state had taken sides in approaching opium cultivation, trade, and use as both a legal and moral dilemma, a decision that was sure to play well with the Americans. This cultural shift carried both positive and negative connotations, however, either of which could hamper or aid state development. In a positive sense (for the Musahiban), a clear cultural shift would ideally lead to increased technical and financial assistance from the United States and the UN, much like the 1945 prohibition. On the contrary, how could the state, one so limited in its reach, possibly control a commodity so widespread, and in some regions, so culturally accepted, as opium? Moreover, how could the state balance the control of opium with broader concerns about economic development and diplomacy without inciting resistance to its policies?

For some Afghan officials, the moral qualms about drug production and use were irrelevant compared to the needs of the state. Abdul Malik, the finance minister, sent a letter to the UN and made it quite clear that the law had a specific purpose: to justify the international court's decision to grant Afghanistan the right to produce and trade opium legally. He stated:

> The Government of Afghanistan strictly controls the production and sale of opium in accordance with all International conventions and regulations already in existence. We hope, as the Economic and Social Council have expressed sympathy for the right to production and export of Afghanistan opium, the Narcotics Commission in its coming sessions will consider this in order to include the name of Afghanistan in the Single Convention and also among the exporters of countries mentioned in Article VI of [the] 1953 Opium Protocol.[42]

Moreover, the law was partially influenced by Iran's prohibition of opium in 1955. Iran had secured substantial technical assistance and financial development aid from the United States to implement the ban. Afghanistan hoped to do the same.[43] But Afghanistan had done this all before in 1945, so why was the 1956 Opium Act any different?

The Opium Act of 1956 was divergent from the 1945 ban in a variety of ways. First, it created a true legal framework for delineating the government's control of opium. The 1945 prohibition appeared as a government announcement in *Islah* but never actually became law. Second, the act marked a substantial change in the state's role as arbitrator of economic development. In 1945, the state had been hampered by the war, and a lack of foreign donors. The government was limited in its ability to effectively monopolize the opium industry, largely because of the state's structure under Hashim Khan. Third, by this time the government was taking steps to institutionalize opium control. The 1945 ban was reflected in the almost complete lack of institutional transformation. By 1956, as the law indicated, the state would now be in control of all aspects of the opium trade, and it would build the apparatus to do so.

The United States saw the Opium Act of 1956 as a positive step toward becoming a legal opium producer, but Afghanistan still needed to follow the American strategy and patiently wait for the international system to ratify Afghan involvement (which the United States admitted could take some time) within the ongoing debates over the Opium Protocol. If it could maintain this course, Afghanistan would eventually become the eighth licit producer of opium in the world.[44] But Afghanistan could not wait. In 1956, the New York Quinine & Chemical Works company received an unlawfully imported sample of Afghan opium from the Ministry of Finance of the Royal Government of Afghanistan.[45] This event was not unique; in fact, foreign officials were notifying American authorities that Afghanistan was actively seeking buyers for their opium. French officials from the Ministry of Social Affairs reported to Harry Anslinger that the government of Afghanistan was actively and regularly shopping its opium to prospective clients in France. The Chief of the Central Pharmacy Service in France noted, "It seems to me that the Afghan government is prejudging rather rapidly about the decisions that could be made concerning the eventual modifications of the opium protocol of 1953."[46]

By pushing for opium exports, Afghan officials indicated broader Afghan sentiment that there was little reason for reluctance on the part of the United States and the UN to approve opium production. A legal opium industry could become a core export for a state in dire need of one, and through increased trade with the United States, the state would become a powerful ally in a vital region of the world. Dr. Massouli, an economist and the Afghan delegate to the UN, exemplified the Afghan view that its request was reasonable given the potential economic and political benefits. Massouli believed the aim of the Afghan government was to export seventy-five tons a year. Such exports would greatly enhance Afghan's foreign exchange and its internal economy. Seventy-five tons a year would hypothetically add $1.5 million to Afghanistan's foreign exchange reserves. Given the outflow in foreign exchange that started at the end of World War II, this was advantageous. The opium export would also provide a stable source of revenue for poor regions of Afghanistan, Badakhshan in particular. Dr. Massouli noted that if Afghanistan began to manufacture morphine, it would reinforce the desire to expand opium production.[47]

Yet the unwillingness of the Afghans to follow protocol guidelines rubbed many US narcotics officials the wrong way. Harry Anslinger, who previously advocated on behalf of Afghanistan, tired of Afghanistan's persistence. He sympathized with its desire to begin production of opium but wanted to wait for the proper legislation. In a letter to his colleague Gilbert E. Yates, he wrote:

> I am reaching the point of exhaustion on the Afghanistan question. They are milling around New York trying to get Assembly action and we are sticking

> to the line that their request has been noted and will be considered by the Narcotic Commission.
>
> I have talked with the State Department and they have no suggestion in relation to the proposal. I just read the PCOB [Permanent Central Opium Board] report on Afghanistan's statement. They expect to produce 100 tons. Also the idea of going into the manufacturing business is all wrong. Possibly at the next meeting we can drive them away from both production and manufacture by a little adroit public opinion with the Iranians leading off.[48]

Anslinger's changing tune reflected a broader change in most of the US government. It was becoming increasingly obvious that although Afghanistan could benefit from a licit opium export trade, it would simply be unable to do so under UN protocols. The issue lay not in the benefits of a government-run opium industry, but rather in an opium industry the government could not control.

The official stance remained unchanged, as the United States still declared its public support for Afghanistan, but behind the scenes the United States was putting itself in a position either to get the Afghan government to act or to withdraw support based on the Afghans' inability or unwillingness to meet the specific guidelines put forth by the protocol. The primary issue American officials raised with the Afghans was the persistent issues with the smuggling of illicit Afghan drugs into Iran, and the perceived total lack of enforcement by the Afghan government. If Afghanistan could not control the opium industry now, what would change in the future? Second, Afghan responses to UN requests for information regarding production, trade, and enforcement were lacking. As a result, both issues reinforced and exacerbated concerns the United States, the UN, and neighboring nations had about Afghanistan's ability to control the opium trade.[49]

On the other hand, the Afghans saw the lack of support as an indication of Afghanistan's inferior status within the American diplomatic hierarchy. More specifically, Daud and Afghan officials interpreted the shift as an indication of the United States' priorities to support regimes in Iran and Pakistan. The Afghan Mission to the UN stated:

> In the last session of the Narcotics Commission, which, after long delay and much study showed great possibility of settling this question once and for all, the United States Mission, unlike its previous stand and support for the just

> claim of Afghanistan which was recognized by the majority of members of the United Nations, because of the opposition of one member, (Iran) took a stand which delayed the final settlement of the question for another year. The Mission of Afghanistan is surprised that the United States Mission has taken such a step, in a case which they themselves on principle and technical grounds have supported from the beginning.[50]

In response, the US Mission denied such accusations, sticking to the formal diplomatic stance. It responded:

> The Permanent Mission of Afghanistan to the United Nations may be assured that the position of the United States with respect to the request of Afghanistan has not changed and will not change unless there is incontrovertible evidence which indicates that Afghanistan opium is entering illicit traffic or there is some other compelling reason for the United States to reconsider its position.[51]

It seems that the United States was positioning itself for the inevitability that Afghan opium would emerge as a large component of the global illicit market. As the *New York Times* reported on May 18, 1957, during the May meeting of the Economic and Social Council, the Narcotics Commission voted to defer, yet again, Afghanistan's request. Then, in October 1957, the State Department sent out a memo that would be the death knell for Afghanistan's hopes of being a licit opium producer. According to the memo, embassy officials in Tehran met with the Swiss minister to Afghanistan, Anton Roy Ganz, who reported that Iranians were traveling en masse to the bazaar in Herat and trading gold rials for opium to smuggle into Iran. According to Ganz's source, opium was traded openly. In fact, opium was so widespread that even Afghan government officials, including the vice president of one of Afghanistan's largest government-owned companies, owned extensive opium plantations.[52] Whether or not the allegations were true is another story. But the allegations were effective in stoking American fears that illicit Afghan drugs were flourishing amidst the diplomatic wrangling over the Opium protocol.

This was a critical point. Daud's bid for inclusion in the protocol hinged on Afghan opium remaining out of the illicit market. When news hit, however, it appeared to the international community that the Afghan state could not enforce its own law; to keep the bid alive, Daud needed to launch and actually enforce a prohibition of opium. But to enforce a prohibition without threatening the delicate balance between the state and rural Afghan society was another matter altogether. Daud needed to find a place where (1) there was significant symbolism to garner attention from the Americans, and (2) the government could enforce a ban without inciting widespread resistance to the state.

Targeting Badakhshan: The 1958 Opium Prohibition

As US and UN officials discussed the regional and global implications of ratifying Afghanistan's membership in the 1953 Protocol, in November 1957 Daud surprisingly announced a ban on the cultivation and trade of opium. The prohibition was launched largely in response to growing skepticism regarding the government's ability to control and regulate the production and trade of opium. But for the Musahiban leadership, the 1958 prohibition was a calculated policy risk. Enforcing an opium ban in conjunction with broader policy objectives allowed the government to exert greater control over territories inhabited by tribal minorities. But Daud's government needed to prove to the antiopium establishment that it had the power and will to uphold the requirements of the 1953 Protocol. In this way, the 1958 prohibition was far different from previous efforts. Unlike the 1945 prohibition, or even the 1956 Opium Act, the 1958 prohibition was exacting and precise. Daud's government chose to target the one province where opium was historically cultivated and traded extensively, Badakhshan. This ban was intended to send a loud message to the rest of the world, particularly, the United States and Iran, that Afghanistan could in fact control, and even suppress, its opium industry.

In choosing Badakhshan, the Afghan government targeted the one area that opium played its most significant role. It was common knowledge at this point that opium was a staple crop in Badakhshan. Previous decades of trade had raised awareness to the superior quality of Badakhshan opium. Symbolism aside, this prohibition was a serious challenge for the state, not only because of the limitations of state power, but particularly because of the unique challenges the province provided.

Badakhshan was one of the most remote provinces in Afghanistan. High altitudes and steep river gorges isolated it from the rest of the country.

Communications with other provinces were relatively undeveloped, and one road connected Faizabad, the center of Badakhshan, with other provinces. Most of the population lived in small, remote villages and imported and exported goods by pack animal.[53] Historically, opium from Badakhshan was traded to areas in western China. But when the border closed in 1949, traders shifted into the region, placing greater emphasis on market goods. This had a major impact on farmers. The increasing demand for market goods led many farmers to devote more land to grow opium as a cash crop.[54] Most other provinces in Afghanistan had relatively diverse economies, but Badakhshan depended on thousands of small farms that cultivated and harvested opium. The opium harvest was especially important for the roughly 15,000 migrant workers who came down from the hills to harvest poppies in April and May each year. Unlike wheat and barley farms, the opium harvest required a great deal of labor. And for most migrant workers, the poppy harvest was the only way to earn cash, which was vital for the purchase of supplies to survive the long cold winters. Although the Afghan government knew that opium was an important crop in Badakhshan, it was intent on making a bold statement to the international community. Thus, it targeted the one province where the new ban would have its most significant, and visible impact.

The opium ban went into effect on March 21, 1958, stopping all opium cultivation by the nearly 3,000 small opium farmers in the districts around Faizabad, Jurm, and Kishim. All farmers who were licensed by the state were forced to transition to wheat and barley, and unlicensed farmers were being forced to transition as well.[55] According to US and UN officials, the opium ban was relatively well received by local farmers and government officials. Two village conferences were held between Afghan government officials and local village and tribal leaders, and according to US representatives at the meeting, most farmers accepted the opium ban and agreed to work with Afghan officials to stop opium cultivation.[56]

The significance of the opium ban garnered global media attention, most of which was positive. The *London Times* summarized the plight of the people of Badakhshan but was quick to frame the importance of the antiopium law, especially given the recent trend by Asian producer states to prohibit opium production. It stated: "The Afghan Government has boldly decided to ban the cultivation and export of opium. It will not be an easy decision to implement in such a country, where it is not the population's addiction to the drug that it is the problem so much as the livelihood of those who grow poppy in places where few other crops are possible. But the intention must be welcomed and aided."[57]

The opium ban was remarkably effective. The government eradicated opium throughout the province, ceasing production in all major opium growing regions of Badakhshan. According to US officials, farmers took the prohibition in stride as they shifted to new crops. Reading between the lines, however, it is hard to believe that farmers were so easily convinced by the government to accommodate the eradication, especially given the fact that the government was more representative of distant Pashtun and Kabul interests. Rather, it is more likely that American and Afghan officials understood the delicacy of this action and were less inclined to highlight the potential controversies of forcibly eradicating a crop so vital to the region. Furthermore, the effectiveness of the eradication had severe consequences for much of the region. The 15,000 migrant workers and their families who depended on the opium harvest, estimated between 75,000 and 100,000 people in all (10 percent of the total population in Badakhshan), suffered tremendously from the prohibition. The plight of the migrant worker typified the critical state of the Badakhshan economy. In the matter of a few months, tens of thousands of people in Badakhshan were unemployed. To make matters worse, there was absolutely nothing to replace the employment offered by the opium harvest. During the warm summer months, it was only a matter of work, but by fall, the lack of jobs was fast becoming a matter of life and death.

Afghan and US officials recognized the urgency of the situation shortly after the implementation of the ban; tens of thousands of Afghans were without work, could no longer provide for themselves or their families, and faced the possibility of famine during the winter. In Afghanistan, as elsewhere, banning opium was often contingent on broader forms of economic development and more localized forms of crop substitution. Ideally, as Graham Farrell notes, drug control efforts could succeed if the state could improve "road and communications infrastructure," which "could facilitate law enforcement and eradication." In addition, however, economic alternatives would create "competitive economic opportunities that restrain others from taking up illicit cultivation or induce migration of labor and farmers away from areas of illicit cultivation."[58] In the case of Badakhshan, the UN Technical Assistance Mission and various Afghan government departments contributed materials and advisers to boost agricultural output. The public works department of Afghanistan recommended improving the road into Badakhshan, completing the irrigation canal in Faizabad, and improving the airstrip. Although the recommendations seemed a reasonable way to address the issues of opium cultivation, there were more obvious impediments: the Afghan government had no funds to act on these recommendations. For both the Afghan government and the UN, the recommendations of each would take time and failed to deal with the immediate issues facing many in the province.[59]

In April, Afghan officials approached the UN in hopes of getting aid for the farmers and workers in Badakhshan. While the UN agreed that aid was needed to help the people of Badakhshan, negotiating who would coordinate aid and how it would be dispersed took time. Abdul H. Tabibi, Afghan delegate to the UN, tried to appeal to Harry Anslinger to advocate for some expediency.[60] Anslinger responded: "Will you kindly send me a proposal covering the assistance that you desire in the area. This should be very specific in relation to the amount needed for an agricultural or other project you have in view and should be in complete detail in relation to funds required for this purpose."[61] Anslinger was dragging his feet. Why is not entirely clear, but it took three months for Anslinger to respond to Tabibi's initial request. It is unlikely that Anslinger wanted to make the thousands of inhabitants of Badakhshan suffer, but given his obvious vexation over the Afghans before the prohibition, willfully delaying action seemed highly predictable.

As various departments haggled over the details and official protocols, the issue of Badakhshan soon gained substantial international attention. The *New York Times* looked at the serious danger facing the thousands of farmers and migrant workers now without their primary source of income. In Badakhshan, "there 100,000 persons, prohibited by law from growing the opium that has sustained them and their ancestors for centuries, are threatened with destitution unless the loss of revenue from the highly remunerative opium crop can be at least partially offset."[62] Although not critical of US antinarcotics policies, the article was quick to advocate assistance to Badakhshan. The potential for the Badakhshan prohibition becoming a humanitarian disaster was tangible. And for the United States, blood would be on its hands.

It was not until October, a few weeks before the harsh Afghan winter, that the State Department began to push for a more urgent response to potential and expected requests for Afghan aid. US officials knew that the political backlash from the opium prohibition leading to a famine was quickly becoming a reality. The United States did not want the people of Badakhshan to starve for a policy that largely reflected American wishes. State Department officials suggested that Afghanistan file for a P.L. 480 designation, otherwise known as the Agricultural Trade Development and Assistance Act of 1954. P.L. 480 would approve urgent US aid to Badakhshan. One of the major stipulations was that Afghanistan had to make a formal request, and for this to happen a prominent US official knowledgeable about the issues in Afghanistan would have to advocate on its behalf. The State Department immediately turned to Anslinger, feeling that he was "deeply interested in Afghanistan retaining the ban on opium production. . . . you might be prepared to support the recommendation that Afghanistan be furnished appropriate assistance."[63]

Afghanistan had requested aid through the UN but did not specifically seek aid from the United States. The State and Agriculture Departments were prepared to distribute aid to Afghanistan at a moment's notice but awaited on official request from the Afghan government. On the contrary, US Embassy officials in Kabul noted that the Afghan government was fully prepared to distribute its own aid regardless of the availability of US aid.[64] But no one was sure what the Afghans were thinking. Between the various departments, urgency was palpable. To avoid a political disaster, however, someone needed to spearhead the cause, and in this case, most fingers pointed at Anslinger and the Bureau of Narcotics.

As a part of the US Treasury Department, the Federal Bureau of Narcotics faced increasing scrutiny. Assistant Secretary of the Treasury A. Gilmore Flues figured prominently in the urgent push for Afghan aid. Flues sent letters to the heads of the Departments of State and Agriculture as well as the International Cooperation Administration (ICA) to garner support for Afghan aid. He wrote to the Department of Agriculture, which was responsible for P.L. 480:

> This Government, it seems to me, has some moral obligation to help in the situation since over the past several years, through our Bureau of Narcotics and our representatives at the international conferences on illicit narcotics problems, we have urged Afghanistan to suppress the growth of the opium poppy and to prevent its opium production from falling into the hands of the traffickers of illicit narcotics. This is a case where the Afghan Government has succeeded just too well.[65]

Flues noted that even if the Afghan government could provide aid on its own, it would still lose any surplus resources of grain, thus further straining its already depleted stocks. Flues undoubtedly felt responsible in some degree for the desperate state of Afghanistan. Not long after his letters, Harry Anslinger followed suit, mostly reiterating the sentiments of Flues.[66]

By mid-November, all of the various departments were prepared to act on behalf of Afghanistan. But Afghanistan had yet to make a formal request to the US government for aid.[67] The Afghan government's mixed messages to the United States, such as those from Tabibi, and its seeming lack of urgency toward the Badakhshan issue were largely due to Afghan plans to depend on P.L. 480. The Afghan government planned to use its existing wheat stocks to alleviate the most immediate issues, hoping that P.L. 480 would be used to refill its depleted reserves.[68] This was the plan all along, but the failure of US and Afghan officials to meet over the issue prevented a more coordinated effort. The United States, on the other hand, was more concerned with the global implications if it sent aid without a formal Afghan request. Most US officials feared that sending a large contingency of US officials to the province, which borders the Soviet Union, would raise big concerns for both Russians and Afghans. And if the United States did not adequately respond to Afghan requests, it would push Afghanistan further into the Soviet sphere.

As 1958 came to an end and winter approached, the US and Afghan governments seemed comforted in the steps taken to stop both opium production and avert an international relations tragedy. Food aid was provided to those in need, and for counternarcotics officials, opium was no longer the primary crop in Badakhshan. They also laid plans to provide a long-term solution to the Badakhshan problem. With the help of the UN, the Afghan government enacted a five-year plan to provide the population of Badakhshan with alternative livelihoods. The government would provide food, clothing, shelter, health care, and residential facilities for inhabitants of former opium-growing regions.[69] The government also took on the task of enforcing the broader aims of stopping the traffic of opium. Immediate concern was placed on the cannabis trade, which most UN officials assumed would grow in size in the absence of opium.

But as the years followed and the development that had been promised to the region failed to come, opium cultivation reemerged throughout the region. British observers noted that opium was the only cash crop in the region and that many of the small plots of cultivable land were devoted exclusively to opium.[70] The reemergence of opium in Badakhshan forces us to ask why the prohibition failed, and how opium cultivation responded, if at all, to the impact of Afghan governmental policies in the region.

Conclusion: The Meanings of the Opium Ban

The ban on the production and trade of opium in Badakhshan was unlike any other social policy enacted by Musahiban leadership to date. The use of force to stop a culturally accepted commodity with significant value to the local population was enacted not out of goodwill or a sense of benevolent humanitarianism, but rather with the aim of allowing the state to project power in a way that would garner increased foreign assistance without instigating the vital Pashtun tribal base. Historically, drug laws have been about social and political problems concerning states' desires to control certain groups of people, not necessarily the drugs themselves.[71] However, analyzing the 1958 prohibition of opium in Badakhshan sheds light on how the production and trade of opium responded to the political and social interactions between the Afghan government and the people of Badakhshan, and such interactions reinforced the mutually constitutive relationship between opium and state building.

Part of the reason opium production restarted after the ban in 1958 stems from how the Afghan government, as well as the United States and the UN, misunderstood the role of opium in Badakhshan. For people in Badakhshan, opium had a variety of uses. Opium was a vital source of nutrition, as many farmers used poppy seeds to make breads and oils. It was also used to make soap. More important, opium was an essential medicine. For a region so isolated from the rest of the country, health care was a serious problem. Opium provided people with a way to treat the persistent cases of cholera and dysentery. Therefore, much of the understanding of why opium was so widespread in the region rested on culturally misinformed tropes regarding the use of opium.

Such misinterpretations as to why opium was widespread in Badakhshan reinforce how cultural misperceptions of opium use influenced American, and eventually Afghan, drug control policies. American perspectives have been shaped by a history of seeing opium as nothing more than a social vice.

When American missionaries colonized the Philippines in 1898 and assessed the extent and impact of opium use, they failed to see that many Chinese and Filipinos were trying to use opium revenue to build schools, hospitals, and infrastructure that local and colonial governments failed to build. Rather, the Americans viewed opium only through a dialectical lens, that is, a matter of good versus evil, and organized governments to introduce international legislation against opium, despite its seemingly benevolent uses for people in the Philippines.[72]

The UN and the United States could not see opium as anything other than an addictive drug, concluding that the wide-scale cultivation, trade, and use of opium in Badakhshan was due primarily to "social addiction."[73] They described social addiction as a "mass phenomena, where the taking of the drug is socially acceptable in the community, and is to a large extent due to stresses caused by factors such as exhaustion, hunger, and poverty."[74] They failed to interpret opium use as anything more than a social vice, justified by deplorable social and economic conditions. In this sense, given the American one-dimensional view of opium, it is easy to see why the Americans considered the extensive production of opium to be an indicator of widespread addiction and a threat to neighboring regions.

Such cultural misinterpretations of opium use between Western and Persian societies were not, however, unique to history. In Safavid, Iran, the medicinal, spiritual, and recreational uses of opium were often indistinguishable, making it difficult for European observers to determine the existence, let alone the extent, of addiction.[75] Although many members of the Afghan government understood that opium was used for a variety of purposes beyond getting high, they certainly perpetuated, if not reinforced, American misperceptions of opium addiction to serve immediate political purposes. By elevating the fear of addiction in Badakhsan as well as its potential to spread throughout the region, Daud played to the emotional heartstrings of the Americans. This gave Daud the justification to exert pressure in a region that had a small Pashtun population and therefore posed very little threat to Kabul.

The larger question is what impact this prohibition had on the future of the opium trade and state–society relations with the Afghan government in Badakhsan. The Afghan government implemented and enforced a drug policy that conflicted with local norms of opium production, use, and trade; in this way, the drug ban reinforced the profound disconnect between the people of Badakhshan and the Afghan government. By defining the opium trade as illegal, the Mushiban government was projecting its authority and further shaping the contours of what was legal or illegal, right or wrong. But as Itty Abraham and Willem van Schendel state, drug laws are

> relational, culturally inflected, and act asymmetrically along the contours of power and social mores. Legal restrictions often come up against socially sanctioned practices, and while this may have the effect of driving these practices into the sphere of criminality, it does not eliminate them, nor does it necessarily force them into hiding.[76]

The imposition of halting a culturally accepted practice and trade without enacting other social and economic policies that would have mitigated its loss not only served to elevate the role of opium in supplementing resources in a way that the government could not but also exacerbated preexisting cultural and political schisms. In other words, although the state defined opium as illegal and stopped its production (temporarily), the opium trade would continue in contravention to the distant and foreign government.

The broader cultural and political issues inherent in the Afghan government's relations with the people of Badakhshan also reinforced the cultural issues surrounding the opium trade. This stemmed from the structural and cultural contours of Musahiban state relations in Badakhshan. Structurally, the government was not integrated into Badakhshan. Thomas Barfield noted that in Qataghan, just west of Badakhshan, Afghan "officials were part of the national system which was laid on top of the area it administered but which was not organically linked to it. Afghan officials looked upon residents as ruler to subject, not as public official to citizen."[77] One British observer described the government in Badakhshan simply as an "instrument of oppression from which there is no redress."[78] Furthermore, the rampant corruption and oppression that often characterized the local government was mainly a product of the cultural gaps underscoring state relations. Tajiks, as well as Uzbeks and Kirghiz, populated Badakhshan. Although Tajiks were a majority in the north, state officials were overwhelmingly Pashtun and often overt in their favoritism toward policies that reinforced Pashtun hegemony. The role of tribal influence in the state was so profound that in northern Afghanistan the word *Afghan* was synonymous with *Pashtun*.[79] Thus, for the Musahiban government it was much easier to justify a prohibition of opium in Badakhshan given the lack of ethnic concern.

The ban on opium in Badakhshan also reveals a paradox in the mutually constitutive relationship between opium and state building. Enforcing a ban in Badakhshan was an important, if not convenient move, on the part of Daud and the Afghan government. Its implementation was closely tied to the role of foreign aid in the design of the Musahiban state. But the use of coercive force (reinforcing the cultural and political disconnect of the state) to enforce state law and the lack of infrastructural development reinforced many of the reasons local residents of Badakhshan grew, traded, and used opium in the first place; without meaningful and lasting alternatives, opium would remain the primary good in the region.

The success of the opium prohibition and its enduring production and trade were also connected to how the Musahiban government was designed, where it got its money, and how it intended to wield its power and influence. When Daud came to power in 1953, the state was increasingly financed by foreign revenue and developed into a rentier state.[80] The problem with this was that development was contingent on the amount of aid received by a foreign donor. The ability to develop Afghanistan was only as good as the state's ability to maintain support for its aid programs.[81] The design of development programs was also greatly influenced by foreign powers. Many state planners, under the guidance of both Soviet and American officials, did not recognize the importance of agriculture as the foundation of the national economy and instead put overwhelming emphasis on manufacturing and industry.[82] Thus, rural Afghanistan was increasingly marginalized by the designs of its own state.

The Musahiban government was increasingly reliant on foreign aid, and retaining aid consistently remained a significant challenge. As Richard Newell states, "Donors are convinced that Afghanistan is important enough—largely because of its strategic location—to try to influence, but is not valuable enough to risk domination."[83] In other words, nations would donate money and resources to influence the country and to draw it into their sphere of influence, but were not willing to make Afghanistan an exclusive part of their bloc. In this way, the opium ban was an important step in the American vision for global drug control. But its lasting success required substantial improvements to the country, and to Badakhshan more specifically. The Musahiban government could not get access to the amounts of money it desired from the United States to develop Badakhshan. Daud's reigniting of the Pashtunistan issue was leading to major diplomatic breakdowns with Pakistan and the United States, and was reinforced by his growing relationship with the Soviet Union. Furthermore, even if Daud could get American money, it is likely it would have gone to the Helmand Valley, where the United States had already begun a massive agro-industrial project in the Pashtun-dominated area and not to Badakhshan.

And herein lies the paradox. The more Daud implemented culturally misinformed and divisive policies, such as the opium ban in Badakhshan, the more local residents either became disaffected by or ignored state policy altogether. The only viable solution was to provide the economic and political infrastructural improvements to alleviate the needs of those who took part in the opium trade and to improve political relationships between the state and local inhabitants. More than a decade later, British officials observed that Badakhshan remained predominantly impoverished and unintegrated into the broader Afghan economy.[84] The promise of economic development and political integration clearly never happened. Thus, the more Daud pushed for drug prohibition, using force to eliminate a culturally accepted and economically vital commodity, while neglecting the broader economic and political improvements needed in Badakhshan, the more he delegitimized the state's role, ultimately creating the economic, political, and cultural environment for the people of Badakhshan to continue to grow and trade opium in the future.

The case of Badakhshan also has some important parallels to the contemporary situation in Afghanistan. In 2000–2001, the Taliban launched an effective nationwide prohibition of opium, reducing land devoted to opium poppies from 82,000 to 8,000 hectares.[85] The ban was much heralded by the international community, and provided the Taliban with "the moral high ground" regarding a universally humanitarian issue.[86] The Taliban ban, much like the 1958 ban in Badakhshan, demonstrates the ways the respective governing bodies utilized the eradication of opium to legitimize themselves to the international community, as well as how such actions affected poppy farmers. The most prominent narrative about the Taliban ban has centered on the idea that it was a result of the elevated prices due to the oversaturation of the market; this seems an oversimplification of the situation. Rather, as David Mansfield shows, the Taliban prohibition was most likely a result of an attempt to redirect discussions with the international community, which prior to the ban, focused primarily on the Taliban's relationship to Osama bin Laden and its deplorable human rights record.[87] Similarly, the 1958 ban (possibly the 1956 Opium Act, too) reflected the Daud government's placating the international community in hopes of reorienting American–Afghan relations, which prior to the ban, had proven increasingly fractious and burdensome. In this sense, both the Daud ban in Badakhshan and the nationwide Taliban ban, were deeply intertwined with the hopes and aspirations of the international community for global drug control.

The ties to the international community also highlight the role of aid and development packages that have become part and parcel of the international drug control regime. Much like Daud in 1958, who promised aid (which was slow to come and contingent on the international response) and development (which never came), the Taliban were ill prepared for the consequences of their ban. In fact, Taliban representatives expected European nations to provide development assistance, and similar to 1958, feared that without it, a potentially large humanitarian disaster loomed. Their fears seemed justified; the prohibition greatly impacted rural communities, disrupting their access to food and forcing many to sell their important assets (such as livestock and land). Furthermore, the broader impact of the Taliban ban mimicked the consequences of the 1958 ban, in that many of the itinerant laborers dependent on the harvest lost their jobs, without any viable alternative form of income.[88]

The connection between the bans in 1958 and 2001 exposes many of the harsh realities of the impact of the ambitions of international drug control: as they manifest into coercive forms, such as eradications, they create incredible strain on the local population. Eradications often force farmers to adapt in ways that minimize the impact of the ban, either by relocating or planting more crops.[89] For governments (if we care to refer to the Taliban as one, as unorthodox as they were), they were most certainly aware of the possible outcomes that would arise from disrupting the opium trade. In the case of Daud, the prohibition in Badakhshan was calculated in that it would not only garner (or force) an international response but the local impact would have a minimal effect on the government or the broader Afghan populace; in this sense, the ends far outweighed the means. The Taliban also recognized that eradication of opium would not only give them much desired international respect (and development aid to support the policy), but the political consequences of the ban were relatively small. As Mansfield notes, the Taliban realized "that the international political support gained by prohibiting opium outweighed the unpopularity the ban would engender."[90] The prohibition of 1958, as well as the 2001 Taliban ban, are indicative of the ways international drug control can be subsumed into local contexts, sometimes with potentially disastrous political and humanitarian consequences.

But these gambles are also essential to understanding how international pressures can factor into the fractures and fissures during the formation of states. In particular, for the UN and the United States, the advocacy of drug-free policies is part of the predominant view of what Antonio Guistozzi refers to as "virtuous state-building"; according to this viewpoint, coercive forms of governance, such as eradications, are often antithetical to Western ideals of governance.[91] As this historical study shows, however, coercive policies often factor directly into the process of state formation. Thus, the similarities between these bans (1958, 2001, and 2013) reinforces the idea that international ambitions for drug control often manifest at the local level largely in coercive forms. If that is the case, then international pressures driving drug control are linked, in some cases directly, to the deeper and more localized negotiations of governance. As a result, prohibition as coercion is an essential component of the ties between illicit drugs and governance. As the ban in 1958 shows, the role of the state in influencing the drug trade through coercive prohibition can prove to catalyze both discord toward the state, and in turn, the necessity for the continuation of the drug trade in contravention to state law.

The ties between the state, prohibition, and the opium industry also shed light on the need to redraw the picture of opium in Afghanistan; the drug trade that defines Afghanistan today emerged not simply as a by-product of the statelessness and lawlessness of the last four decades but also as a result of the historical consequences of drug control as part of state formation. Furthermore, the historical antecedents of the Afghan drug trade must make us rethink how the formation of the state was, and still is, deeply intertwined with the opium trade. In other words, we must look at how opium was and is tied to deeper political and social issues in Afghanistan that seem to permeate state–society relations. As David Mansfield suggests, "It is impossible to isolate illicit drugs from the wider issue of governance in Afghanistan; the two are intrinsically linked."[92] In 1958, as in 2001 and 2012, prohibitions and eradications carried political, cultural, and economic weight that often did more to undermine the broader goals of Afghan governance than they did to help the state. History, like the annual harvest of opium, seems doomed to repeat itself.

By the 1960s, people in Badakhshan, as well as in many other parts of rural Afghanistan, were increasingly prepared to defend their local communities in the face of a government whose rule proved increasingly contentious. Opium, on the other hand, continued to grow and expand. New questions arose as to whether or not the government could, or even desired, to stop it.

Chapter 4

East Meets West

Hippies, Hash, and the Globalization of the Afghan Drug Trade

If you are carrying drugs from Afghanistan, drop them in the basket.

—David Zurich, *Errant Journeys: Adventure Travel in a Modern Age*

For centuries, travelers, traders, and armies have passed through Afghanistan in awe of its mighty mountains, deep valleys, and vast deserts. The imposing physical features serve as one of the cornerstones of Afghanistan's intrigue. Much like the travelers of centuries past, during the 1960s and 1970s, the allure of Afghanistan brought thousands of American and European travelers to explore its borders. Some of them were there on journeys of self-discovery; others in rejection of society and culture that was increasingly foreign to them. As Erik Cohen remarked, the foreign traveler "reject[s] his home society and culture and seeks in the strangeness of the world of others, at the very least, experience of real, authentic life . . . an alternative to that modern world which he has rejected."[1] Whatever their needs may have been, Afghanistan, as did other parts of Asia, offered a palliative to their needs.

Whether travelers were searching for spiritual enrichment or to escape Western culture, their journeys also had an important impact in the history of drugs; such trips led thousands of Westerners to one of the prime hashish-producing regions of the world. Similar to the mystics who praised the plant for its spiritual powers,[2] these Westerners were drawn to the spiritual and cultural world of hashish in which they hoped to immerse themselves. Tourists were enticed further by a political and legal environment that regarded hash production and use as a nonissue. However, not all travelers sought refuge in Afghanistan's perceived cultural and social isolation. Rather, the more people descended on Afghanistan, the more they became aware of its superior-quality hashish, the popularity of which helped link the consumer markets in the West to Afghanistan. Eventually, the networks they created would serve as a critical link between the growing demand for drugs in the West and the supply of hash and opium in Afghanistan.

And yet, travelers were coming to an Afghanistan that was undergoing a period of relative political turmoil, marked by a series of protest movements and scathing free press publications. The movements highlighted what was becoming increasingly obvious to many Afghans: that the government was either incapable or unwilling to make the changes needed for Afghanistan to prosper. In other words, the legitimacy of the Afghan government was waning. Furthermore, this coincided with events to the West. Changes to Iranian drug policy were reshaping the domestic drug market, creating a large demand for illicit opium produced in Afghanistan. By the 1960s, various global forces seemed to converge in Afghanistan, and the mystical Afghanistan, famous for its isolation, became increasingly entangled with the political, social, and economic changes influencing the rest of the world.

The waves of tourism in the 1960s and 1970s came on the heels of a series of important shifts in politics and drug policy. Following the 1958 prohibition, both Afghanistan and the United States heralded the law as a successful example of US–Afghan cooperation in antinarcotic matters. However, neither side seemed to recognize the fundamental flaws in endeavoring to eliminate opium in Badakhshan, or in Afghanistan, for that matter. The potential success of the prohibition was predicated on the state successfully transforming the social, economic, and political environment in the province, as well as the country. But during the 1960s, the hopes of building a modern Islamic state were lost amidst the fray of an increasingly chaotic political environment, both in Afghanistan and globally.

The political dynamics in Afghanistan and the geopolitics of the Cold War reflected and underscored the limitations of the Afghan government and, more important, signaled the beginning of Afghan hashish and opium's entry into the global illicit narcotics market. During this period, the economic and political role of drugs in Afghanistan was influenced heavily by local, regional, and global movements, initiating its emergent role in the global market for narcotics. Locally, Afghan politics became increasingly chaotic. Zahir Shah launched a series of reforms in hopes of democratizing certain elements of Afghanistan's social and political arena. Known as the Decade of Democracy (1963–73), the policy shift was intended to bridge the gap between the disillusioned populace and the state. However, these reforms magnified the disconnect between the Afghan government and its people. Policies aimed at modernizing Afghanistan became increasingly contentious, especially as the economy stagnated and the government became progressively dysfunctional. Various political factions emerged, emboldened by the state's continual mishandling of its domestic and foreign affairs. The Decade of Democracy exposed critical fissures between the Afghan government and society, fractures that would prove critical in the following years.

Regionally, the growing political turmoil in Afghanistan coincided with the rising demand for Afghan opium in Iran, which had a profound impact on the growth of the Afghan drug trade. The attempts to curb illicit use and smuggling in Iran prompted the shah's government to reintroduce state-regulated opium production and distribution in 1969, alongside draconian penalties against drug smugglers. Despite this policy change, Afghan opium became the primary source for illicit opium use in Iran by the end of the 1960s. Although Afghans had a long history of smuggling contraband into Iran, something was different this time around: Iran was not only emerging as a major market for Afghan drugs but was also becoming a significant transit point for drugs heading to emergent markets in Europe and America. Hashish, a widespread and common drug in Afghanistan, was being smuggled through Iran to markets in the West. Iran emerged as a key link in a burgeoning commodity chain that connected Afghanistan to new markets, transformed the regional trade, and ultimately contributed to expanding the reach of the Afghan drug trade.[3]

The entry of Afghan drugs into the global illicit drug trade was largely a consequence of the influence of Western European and American tourists traveling to Afghanistan. What began as drug tourists traveling to Southwest Asia to experiment with drugs evolved into something entirely different; Afghanistan was increasingly inundated with entrepreneurial drug traffickers. The new traffickers established important physical links between opium (and hash) producers in Southwest Asia and the ever-increasing consumer markets in the West. Although the quantities of drugs shipped from the region to the West were nominal during the 1960s compared with today, the cumulative effect of Western drug traffickers, and the Afghan smugglers in Iran, established critical links from Afghanistan to the global market, setting the foundation for the expansion of the Afghan drug trade in the following years.

Analyzing Afghanistan in the 1960s illustrates how global, regional, and even domestic forces coalesced to transform Afghan drugs into global commodities. This period was instrumental to the future of the Afghan drug trade for two major reasons. First, drug tourists increased awareness about Afghanistan's drug trade and in the process forged vital links between Afghan opium (and hash) producers and markets abroad. The early formulation of this chain between Afghanistan and markets to the West (Iran and Europe/America) linked geographically segregated regions of supply and demand, transforming production and consumption in the process.[4] Second, this chain also carried social, political, and cultural meanings.[5] As Western tourists arrived in greater numbers, Afghans became increasingly aware of the lucrative potential of the drug trade. Although opium and hashish were illegal, they emerged during this period as viable commodities to be traded on the global market. The ascent of opium and hashish came as the rest of the Afghan economy struggled and social and political conflict continued. Ultimately, the growing drug trade in Afghanistan and its increasing connections to markets abroad indicate how the drug trade both responded to and influenced the political and social environment, reinforcing the mutually constitutive relationship between state formation (characterized by the increasingly dysfunctional policies of the government) and illicit drugs.

Democracy Now!

By 1963, Daud's authoritarianism and his hard-line Pashtunistan policy had seemingly trumped the various successes he accumulated modernizing the political and economic infrastructure of the country, and many Afghans were united in their opposition to his rule.[6] To ease tensions, King Zahir Shah forced Daud to resign and appointed Dr. Muhammad Yusuf as prime minister. Yusuf's plan to change the country centered on constitutional reforms and a more representative government.[7] Zahir Shah hoped that opening democratic channels, such as reforming the electoral process and promoting free speech, would unify the country and ultimately lead to modernity.[8] However, the Dimukrasi-yi Naw (Democracy Now) movement emboldened large numbers of students to challenge the politics of the Musahiban regime. The ideal of gradual modernization and development, a concept that had guided Afghan leaders since the reign of Amanullah, came under intense scrutiny from the increasingly popular and vocal left-leaning political parties, as well as from conservative tribal leaders.

The shining achievement of Yusuf's reforms was the 1964 constitution. On October 1, 1964, after long and contentious deliberations, both the Parliament and the Loya Jirgah accepted the new constitution, and Zahir Shah signed it into law.[9] Soon after ratification, its many flaws became evident. Some fundamental problems centered not on long-standing frictions between the state and tribal authorities but rather structural flaws, which created the potential for future political conflicts.[10] More important, the new constitution changed the structural components of the government. Former US diplomat and Afghan historian Leon Poullada points out that the new constitution isolated the legislative and executive branches, allowing the Parliament to impede any executive action, essentially immobilizing the political process.[11]

The increased political dialogue resulting from the Democracy Now movement generated very little attention outside Kabul, however. Most rural Afghans were illiterate and "knew little and cared even less about the new constitution and New Democracy."[12] Most preferred to avoid government interaction at all costs. Some, however, were keen to use the democratization of politics to advocate limiting government intervention in rural areas, such as taxes. In Kabul, on the other hand, the growing intelligentsia was enveloped by democratization. Most visible were leftist intellectuals, many of whom wanted greater participation in creating and implementing policy.[13] Although political parties were outlawed by the constitution, it could not prevent their formation. Most of these parties used the new political system to put supporters into key positions of power and to further their particular agendas.[14]

By 1965, the new democracy in Afghanistan exposed the hard realities facing the government: modernization was ill conceived and ineffective; the economy was failing; the state was corrupt; the gap between rural poor and urban communities was increasing; and beneath the veneer of hope behind the democratization movement, deep-rooted political tensions started to boil over. Leftist groups and leaders, especially Babrak Karmal, openly began to express not just frustration but also anger and rage toward the government. These conditions gave many critics of the government from around the country plenty of ammunition. As a result, various newspapers used new political freedoms to decry the government policies.

One newspaper, *Afghan Millat*, became a leading critic. The newspaper was largely pro-Afghan and pro-Pashtunistan, and often denounced the role of foreign powers, particularly the British, the United States, and Iran, in Afghanistan. The newspaper especially emphasized corruption.[15] In its March 28, 1967, issue it stated: "In present modern countries persons must acquire high ranking jobs on the basis of education and capability and not on the basis of family connections, riches, giving bribes and parties."[16] Various cartoons criticized the government for everything from corruption in the economy (figure 4.1) to increasing poverty among the rural and poor (figure 4.2).

At one point, *Millat* even suggested that "a dictatorship with a stomach full of naan is better than a naanless and unfair democracy as this."[17] *Millat*, like many other periodicals of this period, became increasingly critical of the government and its policies. The young intellectuals who wrote for such periodicals found their influence was confined mostly to the literate urban populations, not necessarily the country as a whole. Their views were important, nonetheless, as their cartoons and commentaries reflected the growing political and social unrest that came to embody the era of democracy.

Criticism of the government was not confined to assaults from the press but was increasingly voiced by youth and student groups in Kabul. The various attempts by Babrak Karmal and other leftist leaders to intrude on formal parliamentary processes were becoming increasingly violent by the fall of 1965. The Siyyum-i Aqrab tragedy of October 25 became a galvanizing point for various political groups opposing the government. Students marched on Parliament, clashing with police along the way. When students approached the house of Prime Minister Muhammad Yusuf, Afghan troops fired on the crowd of nearly two thousand students, killing three and wounding many more.[18] The tragedy led King Zahir Shah to force Yusuf to resign as prime minister.

For many, the Siyyum-I Aqrab incident and Yusuf's resignation marked the end of an optimistic era. Although the new constitution and increasing

Figure 4.1. **"The way of our democracy, ear-twisting telephone calls to secure jobs for one's children." (*Afghan Millat*, March 28, 1967)**

freedom of expression were welcome signs, the outpouring of grievances toward the government signified its waning legitimacy. In rural Afghanistan, tribal authorities increasingly believed that the government's modernization program was no longer targeting rural Afghanistan, only the cities. To the chieftains, the balance of power was shifting heavily in favor of Kabul.[19] On the other hand, for many in urban Afghanistan, the reforms

Figure 4.2. Caption reads "Hunger is frightening people, instead of bread, fathers are carrying their daughters home from the bakeries like this." (*Afghan Millat*, April 4, 1967)

and policies of the government were simply too slow. With poverty, corruption, and violence mounting by the day, modernization, like democracy, had to happen now.[20]

The successive governments of Mohammad Maiwandal (October 1963–November 1967), Nur Ahmad Itimadi (November 1967–July 1971), and Abdul Zahir (July 71–September 1972) each faced waves of student unrest. Both Maiwandal and Itimadi tried hard to maintain stable political environments, but the violent interactions between the state and its people led to a rapidly deteriorating relationship.[21] A major cause of tension between state and students was the increasingly socialist leanings of student groups. Although not theoretical purists like some communists who only advocated class struggle in complex industrial societies, students were responding to social and political inequities that they saw as consequences of religious fanaticism or Western economic exploitation.[22]

The political factors were exacerbated by the government's response to a series of crises. Abdul Zahir, appointed prime minister in July 1971, faced a dire situation that further intensified criticism and anger toward the government. In 1971, a severe drought was followed by widespread flooding, culminating in a devastating famine. Rural areas were hardest hit. News reports cited examples of farmers selling their livestock, and even their children, to survive.[23] The government's slow response in distributing aid and widespread corruption involving the selling of food aid created immense anger at government officials.[24] Most Afghans faced desperate situations. Newspapers reported that student groups in Kabul openly attacked government authorities while in rural Afghanistan, while thieves and bandits had killed dozens of foreigners.[25] By 1972, some parts of Afghanistan were ablaze in political, economic, and social strife. The democratization of Afghan politics had rendered the already weak Afghan government dysfunctional. Moreover, the corruption and oppression that characterized the Musahiban state remained. But now Afghan citizens began to recognize the relationship between the government and their own marginalized positions. By the end of the Decade of Democracy, a cohesive and unified Afghanistan was nothing more than a dream.

The political chaos of the 1960s grew out of frustration over the government's inability to chart a viable path forward for the country, as well as its inability to deal with the problems facing Afghans. But drugs and drug policy would factor into this political dynamic. The Afghan government was playing a duplicitous game in which it could benefit from tourism and the illicit drug trade while also remaining engaged with the United States. For the United States, not only was Afghanistan a low diplomatic priority but illicit drugs from Afghanistan was not yet a major threat to national and international security. That would begin to change, however. The increasingly chaotic political environment in Afghanistan was indicative of a state that was quite limited in its capacity to control its population. In other words, for antidrug crusaders, it was an ideal environment for illicit drugs to thrive. But Afghan drugs' ascendancy in the global market resulted from not just these internal factors but also from the increasing impact of regional (illegal smuggling in Iran) and global factors (foreign demand and international drug policy).

Rekindling an Old Flame: Iran and the Afghan Opium Industry

After the coup of 1953, the shah of Iran, Muhammad Reza Shah Pahlavi, sought to bolster the military, the gendarmerie, and the state bureaucracy as a means of consolidating state control.[26] The shah had a long history of working with the United States on various regional and global issues, and grew to depend on American aid and investment to expand state power.[27] His willingness to cooperate on various issues such as narcotics control was a natural outgrowth of this relationship. Iran had a deep and complicated history of opium production and consumption. In 1955, the Iranian government estimated there were close to 2.8 million opium addicts in the country, consuming nearly two tons of opium a day.[28] Even though opium was a fundamental component of life in Iran,[29] the shah imposed an absolute ban on production, consumption, and trade of opium in 1955.[30] Certain aspects of the ban were sensitive to the plight of both farmers and users of opium. Addicts were granted six months to overcome their addictions.[31] Farmers were given long-term assistance for alternative crops.[32] Although the law made all opium illegal, it was biased toward addicts who had been supplied with government opium.

Dealing with illicit and unregulated opium was a different matter altogether. In 1959, the government passed a second statute to increase punitive measures against the continued cultivation and use of opium.[33] Specifically, the new law incorporated elements intended to deal exclusively with illicit drug smuggling. Article 8 of the law stated, "[If] the person in whose possession narcotics are detected is not the owner, but is merely a carrier for some other person, the former shall be regarded as the accessory and the latter as the principal." Both the 1955 and 1959 laws were intended to reduce the supply of and demand for opium.[34]

Cultivation and certain types of consumption decreased or were put under greater control by the government. Larger and larger swaths of opium-producing land were eradicated each year, and most opium dens were abolished. According to McLaughlin and Quinn, "If the government's policies in banning opium cultivation and in closing opium dens can be characterized as successful, its policy-objective of containing smuggling ended in failure."[35] What the government accomplished was the suppression of previously government-sanctioned production and traffic. What the ban had not done was decrease the demand of an estimated 2.5 million addicts. This created a prime opportunity for growers and traders. Not only was there massive demand for Afghan opium but its illegality made it far more lucrative than ever before.[36]

As McLaughlin and Quinn note, the 1955 and 1959 laws had misidentified the nature of the opium industry in Iran. The Iranian government "had conceived of the opium problem as a self-contained medical-social problem. The opium consumed in Iran was mainly grown in Iran and distributed by Iranians," and "the strategy might have worked had Iran been an island," but "Iran did not exist in isolation, and programs directed at what superficially appeared to be a purely domestic concern carried international consequences."[37] By 1960, the international dynamic of Iran's drug problem prompted its government to approach the United States for greater financial and technical support for its border patrols and gendarmerie, as well as diplomatic support to conjure greater regional cooperation from governments tied to Iran's opium industry, mainly Turkey and Afghanistan.[38]

US assistance to Iran for military and policing matters began as early as 1942 when the famed US general Norman Schwarzkopf was sent to Iran to help bolster the Imperial Iranian Gendarmerie (IIG). Schwarzkopf implemented a new program, the United States Military Mission to the Imperial Iranian Gendarmerie, also known as GENMISH, whereby US military advisors trained the IIG in advanced military and police techniques.[39] Through the 1940s and a large part of the 1950s, GENMISH worked on training and literacy. In 1959, however, after repeated failures by customs guards and army patrols to impede smugglers, the IIG and GENMISH were sent to the borders to act as the primary antismuggling units. GENMISH incorporated various American antinarcotics agents in its training of IIG personnel to increase the efficacy of antismuggling operations. Simultaneously, the United States granted Iran significant increases in military aid, providing new planes, helicopters, and motorcycles to the IIG.[40] The shah was concerned with the rise in smuggling, and the appearance of heroin on the streets of Tehran renewed joint efforts by both Iran and the United States to stop all illicit traffic in opium as soon as possible. To counteract the growing wave of opium into Iran, the IIG and GENMISH established antismuggling squads—armed with Alsatian dogs from West Germany—in major districts along the borders of Turkey, Pakistan, and Afghanistan.[41]

The fears of Iranian and American antinarcotics officials were warranted given the increased smuggling activity.[42] In 1961, for example, two Germans were arrested in Karachi, Pakistan, with two pounds of heroin. The details of the arrest corroborated concerns of US antinarcotic officials that drugs were flowing from Afghanistan to Iran; the heroin was reportedly cultivated in Afghanistan and processed somewhere along the Afghan–Pakistan border, with the intent to smuggle and distribute in Iran.[43] By 1964, Afghan opium had begun to fill the hole left by the Shah's prohibition, as nearly five tons of Afghan opium were seized every year.[44] Aside from Afghanistan, efforts to create greater collaboration among the countries tied to the opium trade seemed to be working. Both Turkey and Pakistan were willing to work with the IIG along their boundaries to fight smugglers, but the US Bureau of Narcotics reported, "the Afghans ignore any overtures of mutual cooperation on anything including narcotic smuggling."[45] Yet cooperation never materialized as narcotics officials envisioned. The relative indifference of Afghan government officials suggests that they simply did not care to stop smugglers, particularly those who benefited (either directly or indirectly) from the trade, or that they did not have the capabilities to effectively enforce counternarcotics measures, particularly in the border regions of the country. Most likely, the Afghan government could not or did not enforce the boundaries because it had far greater priorities, such as curbing the political and economic tensions of the 1960s. The Afghan government was struggling to maintain control in Kabul, and its influence on the Afghan population waned as distance from Kabul increased. Patrolling the western border was a task the Afghan government was unprepared to perform.

Moreover, the impetus to enforce narcotics laws in Iran, Pakistan, and Turkey stemmed largely from American political and economic assistance. Afghanistan was an afterthought in the broader machinations of the Cold War. Both Pakistan and Iran, backed by the United States, were motivated to stop narcotics because of US financial and political backing. I contend, however, that Iran's and Pakistan's eagerness to enforce antismuggling laws on their mutual boundary had as much to do with efforts to exert greater control in areas dominated by ethnic minorities as it did with narcotics and Cold War politics.[46]

Desperate Measures

By 1969, the ban on opium was becoming increasingly difficult to enforce. In an effort to regain control of the industry in Iran, the shah embarked on a multifaceted approach to deal with the opium problem by regulating domestic opium production for a program for a small number of registered addicts; increasing rehabilitation; and instituting new, draconian measures for convicted smugglers.[47] Both the Government of Iran and the United States deemed such steps necessary given the high demand for opium and the increasing role of illicit opium in meeting such demand.

In 1970, GENMISH, responding to a request from the French government, conducted a study of narcotics smuggling along the Afghan–Iranian border. The study, "Narcotics Traffic Originating in Afghanistan," seemed to confirm antinarcotics officials' fears from the previous decade that Afghan opium was becoming a larger component of the illicit narcotics trade. More important, the report was fundamental in shedding new insight into the process, tactics, and motivations behind Afghan smugglers' growing presence in Iran. Historically, the supply of illicit opium in Iran came from Turkey. Following the new 1969 opium law, however, which made drug smuggling a capital offense, Turkish smugglers were rapidly abandoning operations. BNDD officials in Meshed, in Khorassan Province bordering Afghanistan, noted that "prior to 1970, there were approximately equal amounts of raw opium illegally imported from Afghanistan and Turkey (45 percent each)," and "during 1970, the situation changed radically, 90% of seizures of smuggled raw opium were made on the Afghanistan border, 3% on the Turkish border, 4% on the Pak border, and 3% within Iran."[48] Furthermore, Turkish smugglers were described as being the consummate "business[men] whose prime interest was . . . making . . . the most amount of money with the least amount of risk."[49]

The changing dynamics of illicit drug smuggling presented new challenges to the IIG and GENMISH. Afghan smugglers, in contrast to Turks, came from a much different background. Most Afghan smugglers were from nomadic or seminomadic tribes of western Afghanistan and Pakistan. The majority of them were illiterate, poor, heavily armed, and seemingly predisposed to violence. Yet this only partially explains their increased involvement in smuggling. Although poverty might seem the most obvious justification for Afghan willingness to smuggle opium into Iran, many Afghans captured by the IIG offered a much different explanation. Several captives pointed to coercion, stating that members of their families were held hostage by the person who sent them into Iran, in the event that the smuggler did not return the money, failed to deliver the goods, or was caught.[50]

Afghan smugglers overcame daunting odds to bring opium into Iran. Individual smugglers were paid a flat fee of one thousand Iranian rials (thirteen dollars) to carry a knapsack containing roughly twenty to thirty kilograms of raw opium across hundreds of miles of harsh and mountainous desert terrain. Because the threat of violence and capture increased with the 1969 antismuggling law, most Afghan smugglers traveled in larger and larger groups. If a family member was held hostage, smugglers would take every precaution to ensure that they would not be caught or surrender out of fear that their families would be sacrificed. For US and Iranian officials, the challenges presented by the increasingly militarized smugglers were a consequence of this coercive element. The image of a desperately violent smuggler would certainly be helpful for antidrug officials trying to garner greater institutional support for counternarcotic efforts. But it was also impossible to determine the validity of the smugglers' claims, as a captured smuggler would be likely to give a story to present himself as less nefarious and more a victim. Rather, the reasons for increased smuggling were more complex if not nebulous. For example, corruption was also a very large factor in drug smuggling. Some smugglers were doing the bidding of their tribal chieftains, many of whom held key positions in the Afghan government.[51] IIG officials complained that many Afghan smugglers were aided by Afghan border guards and were often paid by corrupt government or tribal officials to aid smugglers across the border.[52]

Prices of both hash and opium rose significantly during this period, which indicated the growing importance of illicit drugs as a major commodity in both Iran and Afghanistan. The price increase in raw opium as it penetrated further into Iran provided the lure that enticed many Afghans into smuggling. In 1969, a kilogram of raw opium garnered $43.28 in Taybat along the Afghan–Iranian border. That same kilogram could fetch as much as

$196.72 in Tehran.[53] Areas along Iran's eastern border were inundated with opium. In particular, the city of Meshad in Khorassan was emerging as a major transit zone for Afghan smugglers coming into Iran. Of the 13,447 kilograms of opium seized in 1971, 9,116 kilograms were seized in Khorassan, all of it believed to be of Afghan origin.[54] And in March 1973, the IIG seized 12.7 tons of opium in Khorassan, the largest haul in Iran's history and one of the largest in the world. The numbers of executions reflected the growing opium trade as well.[55] By February 1972, 134 smugglers had been executed under the 1969 antismuggling law, the majority of them Afghans.[56]

As a response to the escalating smuggling along the Afghan–Iranian border, the shah increased funding, technology, and training for the IIG. The IIG received upward of 5,000 motorcycles to improve mobility, particularly along the Afghan border, as well as night-vision goggles, light aircraft, 8 Huey helicopters, and antinarcotics and antismuggling training from both US and UN narcotics advisers.[57] Yet despite the increase in funding and attention, smuggling continued. The political, economic, and social climate in Afghanistan undoubtedly played a major factor in the increase in smuggling, but the IIG also faced a variety of hurdles impeding its border patrol and antinarcotic capabilities. The 885-kilometer border with Afghanistan, made up mostly of mountainous desert, was patrolled by IIG posts of six to eight men, located anywhere from 8 to 40 kilometers apart. The additional training and technology made little difference as the IIG faced large groups of well-armed and notoriously fierce Afghan smugglers, who faced certain death if they failed to succeed, either in Iran or Afghanistan.[58]

Moreover, repeated complaints by GENMISH officers revealed deep fissures within the IIG apparatus that significantly inhibited the effectiveness of the IIG in curbing Afghan smuggling. In an exit interview, one GENMISH officer noted that most gendarmes were totally unmotivated to act. Low morale pervaded most of the lower-level officers. Even though IIG officers got free education for their families, paid no income tax, and received two weeks' paid vacation, many were remarkably underpaid, with most civilians making three to five times as much as IIG personnel.[59] Given the violent nature of antinarcotic enforcement along the Afghan border, it is no surprise that many lower-level IIG officers were ill inclined to observe GENMISH standards.[60]

A lack of coordination among relevant agencies also impeded efforts to stop the illicit trade from Afghanistan. In particular, the National Police and

IIG rarely coordinated with each other, partly because of rampant corruption at all levels of the Pahlavi government. In 1975, the Drug Enforcement Administration complained to the IIG and National Police (NP) that only minor smugglers were incarcerated and not one major trafficker was arrested because of corruption. Lack of coordination became a major issue between US and IIG officials as well. One DEA officer spoke of a "one-way street," where DEA intelligence was often taken by NP and IIG to stop internal trafficking, but nothing was given in return that would help stop international trafficking. This was due in part to the growing anti-US sentiment among IIG personnel by the mid-1970s. To make matters worse, the rewards systems often created competition and discouraged cooperation among the various agencies. And individual rewards were often small. For poorly paid IIG personnel, corruption proved far more lucrative than the government reward system.

The economic and political issues that plagued Afghanistan throughout the 1960s and 1970s coincided with a period of remarkable interaction between Iranian drug users and Afghan smugglers. The impact of this interaction had a profound influence in shaping the role Afghanistan would play in the global drug trade. By 1972, Afghanistan had replaced Turkey as the primary supplier of opium for the illicit market in Iran. American intelligence officials estimated that Afghanistan was supplying anywhere from 100 to 170 tons of opium to Iran a year.[61] Moreover, the political chaos and instability in Afghanistan, combined with the increasing demand in Iran, created a perfect opportunity for Afghan farmers and smugglers. Yet there remained a disconnect between Iran, the United States, and the illicit drug trade in Afghanistan. The increased smuggling of Afghan opium into Iran failed to produce a concerted response from the United States, primarily because Afghan opium remained isolated in Iran and posed little threat to the US market. The United States, on the other hand, remained concerned about a more direct threat, one that linked the production of hashish in Afghanistan with the burgeoning markets in the United States and Europe.

Bringing the West to Afghanistan and Bringing Afghanistan to the West

When the international community passed the 1961 Single Convention, the broadest and most progressive international narcotics regulation ever, it nullified the failings of previous treaties and placed all narcotics matters under one uniform international treaty.[62] The convention put great responsibility on the governments of producer nations to increase reporting requirements for domestic needs and production. However, this new emphasis also granted producer nations greater power in mediating global narcotics disputes, much to the Americans' dismay. Alternative approaches finally gained traction and producer states ended up retaining autonomy in dealing with supplies. Although considered a success by most in the international community, the 1961 convention still focused on supply as the primary problem. Yet by the end of the decade, political and social chaos created new social regimes that unleashed a misunderstood element of the global narcotics trade: demand.[63] By the late 1960s, the global market for narcotics was emerging from adolescence to maturity.

All over the world, but especially in Western Europe and the United States, the demand for drugs seemed to reach unprecedented proportions. Heroin addiction exploded in urban areas, American soldiers in Vietnam became opium addicts, and white, middle-class youths embraced the use of psychedelic and psychotropic substances.[64] Individuals such as Timothy Leary, Ken Kesey, and Allen Ginsberg were seen by some as vanguards in a movement to challenge the social norms that regarded the recreational use of narcotics as both amoral and criminal.[65] Although these figures saw themselves as leaders of a spiritual, political, and countercultural movement, the basic reality was that by the late 1960s, drug use had carried itself into the mainstream. As a result, the increased demand for drugs was expanding the illicit global narcotics trade and opening up many parts of the world that had previously played minor roles.

During the 1960s, numerous educated, affluent youth left the confines of their homes to explore the world. Many of them traveled to Turkey, Iran, and Afghanistan to smoke hash and opium, where it was readily available and cheap.[66] Soon some of these travelers discovered that major profits could be made from shipping large quantities of opium or hash (mostly hash at first) back to the West. In particular, the lax customs and border controls in Afghanistan made smuggling easy. With the consumption of heroin and other narcotics in the United States increasing during the late 1960s and early 1970s, these travelers set up networks to link up opium and hash in Afghanistan with the markets in the West, laying the foundation for the future expansion of Afghanistan's opium industry.

During the 1960s, "Afghanistan lived up to the wildest fantasies of the hippies." For these travelers, Afghanistan was different from other stops along the infamous "Hippie Trail"; hashish was "to Afghanistan what wine was to France."[67] In Kabul, Chicken Street, in the Shahre-Naw district, was famous for cheap and accessible hashish. The Noor and Mustafa Hotels were popular hangouts for drug-seeking travelers. Moreover, the political climate was ideal for Kabul's role as a drug-using safe haven. Officially, opium and hashish were illegal,[68] but drug laws were rarely enforced, partially because the government did not perceive drug use to be a significant social problem.[69] Aside from its widespread availability in the markets of Kabul, there were also special teahouses (*saqikhana*) dedicated to hashish use.[70] In fact, hash was proving to be such big business that in 1969 and 1970 Zahir Shah gave an official edict to farmers encouraging them to use fertilizers to improve hashish production. As a result, cannabis plantations flourished around Herat, Kandahar, and Mazar-e-Sharif, and cannabis plants lined many of the major roads between Kabul and neighboring cities.[71] For rural Afghans, the growing demand for hash was a lucrative business. The "hash craze" helped many farmers gain access to agro-industrial equipment, especially tractors, that in previously years were unattainable.[72]

The popularity of hash among Western tourists was not confined to just Kabul. All over the country, bazaars marketed hashish to Western tourists and Afghans alike. Moreover, the way it was marketed clearly demonstrated that Afghan vendors were aware that much of the hash was to be smuggled out of Afghanistan. Peter Levi, in his travels to Afghanistan in the late 1960s, noted that in Kandahar "it was a big industry and even small children tried to sell us hash in its various forms. . . . Every kind of smuggling device was for sale, strings of hash beads, hash belts, hash-heeled shoes and for all I know hash codpieces."[73] But the popularity of hash among Afghans further complicates our understanding of how much Western tourism influenced the growth of domestic production. Wazir Mohammad, an Afghan who lived near the Afghan-Pakistan border, told Levi that hashish was the opium of the people, and ideal for inducing sleep.[74]

Although some Afghans saw hashish as a relatively harmless pastime, others saw it as a dangerous and abusive drug. Asad Hassan Gobar, professor of neuropsychiatry at Kabul University, reaffirmed the notion that hashish use was prominent among Afghans, especially rural and lower classes, mainly because it was cheap and easily accessible. However, he also claimed hashish was one of the more widely abused drugs in Afghanistan, and a prominent source of psychotic breakdowns among Afghans. He noted that 751 patients were admitted to Sanayee Hospital in Kabul for psychotic episodes during the decade (1960–69). The number of patients admitted for drug use was 13 percent of all psychiatric patients that decade.[75] Gobar noted that hashish was generally frowned upon by Afghans, perceived to be a likely cause of insanity.[76] Gobar's view certainly contradicts many of the depictions of Afghan users and sellers that hashish was common and relatively harmless. This disconnect may be a product of Gobar's role as a doctor, or possibly class, given that hashish was most common among layman workers and farmers.

For Western tourists, however, the potential medical side effects were irrelevant; Afghan hashish was perceived to be some of, if not, the best hash in the world. There were believed to be twenty-five variations of Afghan hashish, and some of them with extraordinarily high THC content.[77] The variations in hash, as well as the variations in methods used to create it,[78] were certainly indications of an emerging vibrant market. In some ways, the expansion of hash use in Afghanistan mirrored much of what was happening in China with the growth of opium smoking during the early 1800s. In Qing China, opium use spread rapidly, "downward and outward" toward lower classes and beyond its original contexts, ultimately to a wider array of classes, including workers, government officials, and literati.[79] Similarly, the variations in types of hash, as well as the ways to make them, symbolize the "liquidation" of hashish to a broad spectrum of Afghans and Western tourists.[80] Moreover, both opium and hash were also cheap; opium could be purchased in Kabul for forty-five dollars per kilogram; high-quality hash would go for nearly twenty dollars per kilogram. Thus, the lack of enforcement of laws regarding hash use, combined with the quality of Afghan hash, contributed to an environment conducive to its growth and expansion. In 1971 alone, fifty-nine thousand tourists flocked to Kabul, many to partake in its vibrant drug industry.[81]

The trend of Western tourists going to Afghanistan, mainly to do drugs, was also garnering the attention of both Afghan and Western media. Afghan newspapers were more often critical of the impact of foreign tourists and the growing use of drugs. The newspaper *Afghan Millat*, which often criticized the government for its failed policies and inability to curb its dependence on foreign money, also criticized the presence of Western tourists and the many Afghans, including government officials, who catered to their needs.

Figure 4.3. "Fishing for tourists for the International Hotel." (*Afghan Millat*, February 20, 1967)

Many articles and cartoons, such as that presented in figure 4.3, criticized Afghans for apparent dependence on foreigners.

The *Afghan Millat* cartoon signifies a broader sentiment that progress in Afghanistan depended largely on foreigners, both governments and people. Other publications, such as *Karavan*, noted that throughout the late 1960s and early 1970s Western drug tourists, "hippies," were a constant presence, if not a nuisance in Kabul. Many Afghans often mocked the public drug use of Western tourists, and as the *Karavan* cartoon shown in figure 4.4 suggests, the expectation that it was their right (*huquq*) to do so.

Figure 4.4. "Drawn-out hashish protest: Give us our right." (*Karavan*, January 31, 1970)

Karavan also highlighted the discrepancies between drug use and the role of the state. The perceived indifference of authorities toward hash use, while a primary draw for Western tourists, was yet again another flaw in the state.

The cartoon shown in figure 4.5 best embodies the period and the entanglements of Western hippies and Afghan authorities. Aside from the hippies, clear reverence for the magic (memories) in the bottle, the policeman kissing the *chars* (hash) exemplifies the clear willingness to cater to the Western hippie and to the drug trade. There are limitations to the impact of such cartoons, however, particularly given the low literacy rate and, hence, relatively small numbers of readers. Nonetheless, they are still indicative of the sentiments of many Afghans during this period: that tourism and drug use were perceived to be integral parts of Afghanistan's future, and that was not exactly deemed a good thing.

American newspapers, on the other hand, publicized the growing trend of tourism and drug tourists in Afghanistan. Arnold Zeitlein reported in the *Eugene Register-Guard* on June 8, 1970, that universities, such as Bowling Green University, offered classes encouraging students to travel to Afghanistan (not necessarily to take drugs). The presence of Western tourists, many with the sole purpose of using drugs, generated a great deal of negative press. For example, James Markham wrote a story in the *New York Times* on

Figure 4.5. "Hippie: 'This is a memory I am going to take with myself!' Police: 'That is not a memory, it is *charse* (hash).'" (*Afghan Millat*, no date)

November 17, 1972, about Melanie R (her real name was hidden for the story), a nineteen-year-old college student, who left school to travel to Asia, only to die of an overdose after smoking twenty-six hits of opium. The same day, the *New York Times* ran another article about Melanie and the bigger picture of drug use in Afghanistan. The article was a damning indictment of the drug haven that was Afghanistan; both the Afghan who was suspected of supplying the drugs and the Afghan authorities who were supposed to enforce antidrug laws "appeared reluctant, embarrassed and incompetent." The police, in particular, came across as corrupt and sinister. In this case, the police were hesitant to arrest the suspected dealer because it "might cause difficulties with people, likely to be powerful, who had clearly afforded him protection to run his narcotics haven and engage in wholesaling on the side"; meanwhile, "the seized opium and hashish would, true to Afghan form, reappear on the market before long."[82] In the two articles, some persistent themes reemerge; that Afghanistan is an easy place to get high-quality drugs, and that authorities are generally reluctant to do anything about it. For young Westerners with a keen eye for travel and psychedelic experiences, the sensational *Times* articles probably did more harm than good; it presented Afghanistan as an ideal place to see Asia and get high, with little to no penalties for such behavior (except for possibly dying).

Although some Afghans derided the hippies or saw them as symptoms of an outwardly focused government, the drug-seeking travelers of the 1960s were in other ways innocuous. According to Mir Rod, a professor at the Academy of Sciences in Kabul, *naswar*, a potent form of tobacco snuff, was far more problematic than hash use. And Russian political agents, not hippies, were the biggest source of concern for Afghan authorities, particularly because the lack of alcohol apparently drove Russians to consume larger than normal quantities of *hash* and *naswar*.[83] While most incidents between hippies and Afghans may have appeared comical to outside observers, for foreign diplomats, they were a nuisance. Most incidents resulted from basic cultural differences. In one instance, four hippies were beat up by local police for washing clothes in Lake Karga, which was forbidden under local law. Afghan police were often noted for their brutality and Western hippies for their complete lack of sensitivity toward local customs.[84]

For American officials in Kabul, these incidents were not comical. Rather, Western drug-using travelers were a growing sign of a problem that was spanning across the globe. In the United States, heroin use was expanding, along with a significant growth in the use of cannabis and psychedelics, such as LSD and psilocybin. Most opium consumed in the United States, especially heroin, was supplied by areas in Turkey or Southeast Asia. This, of course, coincided with the Vietnam War, where American GIs were a major factor in bringing Southeast Asian opium back to the United States.[85] However, American officials could not help but note that many of the same types of users in the United States were now littering the streets of Kabul. In 1971, US and Afghan officials met to discuss the issue of the hippie community in Kabul. US officials seemed primarily concerned that tourists in Kabul were helping expand Afghanistan's illicit narcotic industry and that the Afghan government was not enforcing its own laws. Given the dramatic rise of smuggling into Iran and the enduring strength of the Kabul narcotic industry, most American officials were justified in believing that something much bigger was happening.[86]

Indeed, there was truth to this; hashish was becoming the first Afghan product to link Afghanistan with illicit markets in the United States. On May 16, 1970, a raid on the Shak-Foladi Hotel in Kabul seemed to reaffirm many counternarcotics agents' growing fears about the changing role of Afghanistan in the global drug trade. Thirteen foreign nationals were arrested for possession of 100 grams of opium and 200 grams of hashish.[87] At the time, it was a significant bust, not because of the quantity of drugs seized but because foreign nationals were involved. Moreover, the possession of opium and hash pointed toward an ultimate destination in the West. More significant, the raid came to embody the role of drugs and tourism throughout the early 1970s, as reports of hash seizures involving foreign travelers continued to proliferate in Afghan newspapers. For instance, two Italian tourists were caught with three kilograms of hash hidden in wooden statues;[88] a German tourist was caught at the border near Herat with sixty kilograms of hash in the gas tank;[89] Americans and German tourists were discovered making liquid hash when the pressure cooker used to make the hash exploded.[90] The regular occurrence of hash smugglers was pointing to the changing role of Afghanistan in the global illicit market.

Furthermore, American authorities were increasingly alarmed by the presence of the notorious Brotherhood of Eternal Love in Afghanistan. Influenced by the infamous 1960s icon Dr. Timothy Leary, the Brotherhood was a major producer and distributor of LSD. Dubbed the "hippie mafia" by police, the Brotherhood wished to liberate the consciousness of the global population by spreading the use of LSD. To achieve such ambitious goals, they also trafficked in drugs, including large quantities of hashish from Afghanistan.[91] The quantities shipped by the Brotherhood between 1970 and 1973 were large enough that they forced Afghan farmers to alter their methods of production to meet demand. In particular, the Brotherhood advocated the manufacture of hash oil, which was not only easier to smuggle but also far more potent, and thus, more lucrative.[92] The presence of such a notorious gang ultimately prompted the Bureau of Narcotics and Dangerous Drugs to assign their first agent to Kabul in 1972. The presence of American agents in Afghanistan surely marked an important event in Afghan drug drama; Afghanistan was no longer an afterthought in the world of illicit drugs.

At this point, hashish politics were becoming entangled with opium politics. For Iran, the increasing scrutiny of the hash trade did little to help Iran deal with the issue of opium traffic. Afghan opium, although in high demand in Iran, did not make up a major percentage of opium used in the West. This, in fact, was a major issue with Iranian and American antinarcotics officials. Iranian efforts focused mostly on Afghan opium, whereas Americans were increasingly focused on the global hash trade. US narcotics agents tried to get Iranian officials to stop the hash trade, but since hash was not seen as a major Iranian issue, it was often not pursued with the same ferocity as opium. Unbeknownst to both Iranian and American officials, hashish traffickers were laying the foundation for networks that could potentially traffic more lucrative and dangerous commodities, i.e., opium/heroin. A DEA intelligence brief summed up this transformation:

> While of somewhat secondary significance relative to opium, hashish has been important in our enforcement efforts because of the smuggling systems that have spawned. The drug seeking hippie who came to Afghanistan a few years ago and spent his last few travelers check to take home a kilo or so of Afghan hashish has been replaced by the well heeled young entrepreneur from the US.[93]

By 1972, American antinarcotics agents noticed that a new, professional type of smuggler was replacing the drug tourists who traveled to Kabul in late 1960s. Kabul was becoming a popular spot for known drug smugglers, many with extensive criminal records in the United States. For Afghans, these entrepreneurs were a welcome respite from dealings with low-level hippies. More important, these well-financed individuals had a major role transforming Afghanistan's place in the global narcotics market. Seizures included liquid hash, morphine, and heroin, and the sting operations discovered large hash distilleries and morphine conversion laboratories. What this signified was that Afghans and foreign traffickers were aware of the need to reduce the product to its most profitable and concealable form to "offset the increased detection efforts by international law enforcement elements."[94] Afghanistan was slowly emerging as a player in the global market for illicit narcotics. To defeat the growing professional drug trade, both the United States and Afghans would have to increase antismuggling efforts (see chapter 5). But as the map below indicates (figure 4.6), Afghan and American counternarcotics officials were facing expanding and more dynamic trafficking networks that would challenge their ability to secure the porous boundaries of the country.

Conclusion: The Ascending Drug Economy

Compared to the size of the drug trade in later years and decades, the period of the 1960s is quite nominal in the broader scope of drug history in Afghanistan. However, analyzing the role of hashish in the history of drugs in Afghanistan provides key insights into the changes that confirmed Afghan opium's ascendancy into the global market. Historically, the networks forged by pirates, bandits, and smugglers have played important roles in facilitating the spread of capitalism around the world.[95] In Afghanistan, drug tourists provided one of the earliest global links to the markets in Europe and the United States. Although they started out quite small in number, Western travelers in Afghanistan increased awareness among Afghan producers and distributors of opium and hash that a larger market existed beyond Tehran. Conversely, travelers returning to the United States and Europe brought with them the knowledge of an area of the world ideally suited for exploitation by the illicit market: a weak state, weak controls, abundant supply, and an increasingly eager population. Thus, the professionalization of the hash trade in 1972 signified the fundamental shift for Afghanistan's future role in the

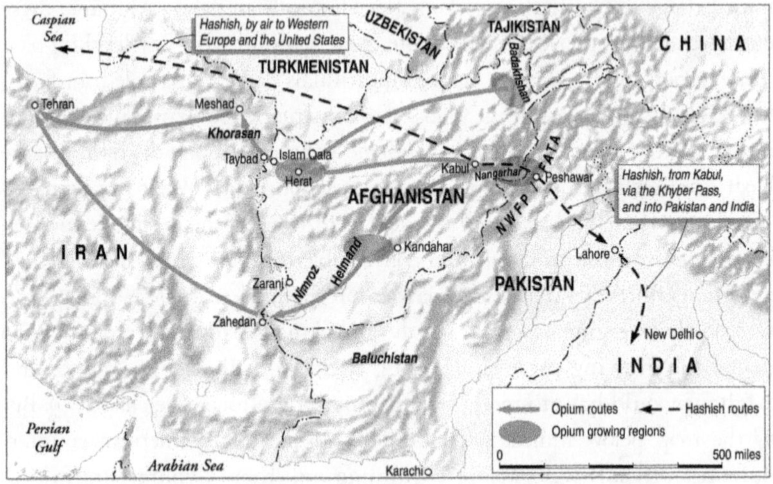

Figure 4.6. Map of drug trafficking routes, late 1960s to early 1970s. (Map by Philip Schwartzberg, Meridian Mapping, Minneapolis)

global narcotics trade. Although hash, and to some extent opium, were small compared to the profits generated by morphine and heroin, by the end of the 1960s, these factors were coalescing to create the perfect storm.

A bigger question emerges about the relationship between the political issues and the growing illicit drug trade. I argue that the illicit drug trade expanded during this period while the Afghan government was proving increasingly unable to improve the political and economic situation in the country, especially its ability to alleviate growing unemployment or implement effective policy responses to the issues raised by the Democracy Now movement. Drugs, in this sense, provided sources of economic revenue where the state was increasingly impotent. The cultural indifference regarding the trade of opium and hash only reinforced the economic needs. Furthermore, the importance of illicit drugs as a source of economic revenue was heightened by the expanding regional and global consumption of Afghan opium and hash. For some Afghans, the growing number of tourists traveling to Afghanistan to either use or buy its drugs were clear indications of the potential for economic growth, regardless of whether the government said it was right or wrong. This expansion in the Afghan drug trade coincided with the increased resistance to and frustration with the Afghan government during the 1960s, providing further evidence of the mutually constitutive relationship between state formation and the drug trade.

But the drug trade grew, not just from internal factors but also from the increasing impact of regional (illicit smuggling in Iran) and global factors (foreign demand and international drug policy). In Iran, the prohibition of opium amidst increasing demand opened new doors for smugglers and traders to traffic Afghan opium during the 1960s. In Europe and the United States, increasing consumption of opium, and especially hash, transformed the way Westerners used, and eventually transported, Afghan drugs. Initially, Western tourists traveled to Afghanistan to consume opium and hash. However, entrepreneurial traffickers smuggling opium and hash back to the West soon replaced those tourists. In both instances, the proliferating drug trade led to interlocking networks of both production and consumption, which transcended national and regional boundaries.[96] In this sense, the establishment of commodity chains to Iran and the West during the 1960s represent the early globalization of the Afghan drug trade.

This period also raises important questions about the relationship between illicit drugs and Afghan politics. Indeed, opium and hashish played a bigger role in the political conflicts of 1960s Afghanistan. As the cartoons from *Afghan Millat* and *Karavan* suggest, Afghans were increasingly aware of the presence and character of Western tourists. In many ways, the presence of tourists, most of whom were there to use drugs, represented the contradictions and dysfunctions increasingly characteristic of the Musahiban dynasty. To gauge the influence of opium on the political conflict of the time, we must turn to the political and social meanings often accompanying the illicit drug trade. Historically, the illicit drug trade has provided marginalized groups the economic revenue needed to confront or rectify political and social disparities resulting from dysfunctional or racially biased state policies. Many of the nations that were major producers of illicit drugs suffered from similar social, political, and cultural cleavages that heightened the role of drugs as an economic agent of power.[97] In Afghanistan, resistance to the government stemmed from ethnically charged social policies and the controversial modernizing policies of the Afghan state. In particular, the vision of creating a modern government, especially a drug-free one, depended increasingly on foreign aid from the United States. As a result, the Afghan government adopted both political and cultural stances that contradicted popular norms of use and trade or effectively broke down sociocultural systems that were vital to Afghan life (i.e., the 1958 Opium Prohibition). This reinforced political tensions stemming from the disconnect of the government (resulting from the tremendous influence of foreign governments and people) as a primary explanation for its dysfunction. Although the Afghan government had yet to make more concerted efforts to enforce drug control laws, the relatively lax enforcement of drug laws as they related to Western drug users reinforced sentiments that the Musahiban were not only catering to foreign powers but were largely driven by them.[98] Thus, the growing trade did, in some way, influence the political conflict of the 1960s.

By the beginning of the 1970s, Afghan drugs were becoming a larger part of the global illicit drug market. For many Afghans, the illicit drug trade was ideal for the period because, in one way, it allowed people to exist, if not thrive, outside the formal channels of governance; in others, the indifference by the state validated or justified the drug trade. As a result, the Afghan state was not only incapable of, or unwilling to, stop the illicit drug trade, but through its broader political failures, it also reinforced the growth and vitality of the illicit drug trade. Moreover, this interplay between local, regional, and global forces points to the complexity in the historical development of the Afghan drug trade. Some of the forces at play were circumstantial; others were mutually reinforcing and constituting, but nevertheless complex and nebulous. Nevertheless, Afghanistan, once a minor player in the global drug trade, was, as a result of the illicit hashish trade, emerging as a new source for the global drug market.

This period also marked the end of an era in Afghanistan. The relatively lax pursuit and enforcement of counternarcotics policy, evident in previous times such as 1945 and the period prior to 1958, could no longer be sustained. The political impetus to stop the production of drugs was fast becoming an integral component of American foreign policy. Ultimately, to remain engaged with the United States meant picking a side in the war on drugs.

Chapter 5

The Afghan Connection

Smuggling, Heroin, and Nixon's War on Drugs in Afghanistan

America's public enemy number one in the United States is drug abuse. In order to fight and defeat this enemy, it is necessary to wage a new, all out offensive.

—Richard M. Nixon

To wage an effective war against heroin addiction, we must have international cooperation. In order to secure such cooperation, I am initiating a worldwide escalation in our existing programs for the control of narcotics traffic.

—Richard M. Nixon

By the late 1960s, drug use in the United States escalated to seemingly epic proportions. Use of marijuana, heroin, and other hallucinogenic drugs became a mainstay of a youth culture that rejected the social and political constructs of the previous generation. When President Richard Nixon signed the Controlled Substances Act in 1970 and formalized the War on Drugs, he struck at the heart of the "silent majority's" fear that rampant and often romanticized drug use was a prime indicator of America's rapid social and moral decline. Throughout the 1960s, millions of baby boomers came of age in an era when youth culture romanticized drug use and made them increasingly susceptible to the visibly destructive use of drugs. Heroin addiction, in particular, became the primary gauge of social decay. Although heroin addiction was nothing new to the United States, the increased use among white suburbanites and soldiers in the Vietnam War transformed controlling drug addiction into prime public policy. Heroin became such an issue that by 1971, Americans listed heroin addiction behind Vietnam and the economy as one of the nation's most pressing problems.[1] Nixon cited drug policy as a fundamental barometer of the political, social, and cultural morass of the 1960s. As historian Daniel Weimer notes: "Nixon deliberately linked drugs with the challenges to the Cold War consensus, patriotism, patriarchy, and race relations. The anti-war movement, counterculture, feminism, Black Power, and the other ethnic and identity power/pride movements indicated that cultural modernity in the United States had become unstable and too permissive."[2] As a result, the once small group of zealous antidrug crusaders had evolved into a primary player in American domestic and foreign policy, demanding the attention of all departments and branches of the US government.

Although thousands of miles away, Afghanistan would be drawn into the globalizing war on drugs. As detailed in the previous chapter, in the 1960s Afghanistan emerged as a haven for drug users, sojourners, and amateur drug traffickers. Despite its popularity as a paradise for unregulated drug use and trade, it still remained a relatively small part of the global market, mostly fulfilling the demand for opium in Iran and feeding hashish to the West. Nonetheless, the demand for Afghan hash and raw opium was indeed growing. Smuggling across the border with Iran increased yearly, and more and more entrepreneurs were traveling to Kabul to purchase large quantities of narcotics to ship back to Europe and the United States. By the mid-1970s, opium from Afghanistan was trickling its way into markets beyond Iran and Pakistan; Afghan opium was emerging as a global commodity. More important, in response to domestic and international pressures for increased drug control, the Afghan government escalated its enforcement of antismuggling measures and its 1958 prohibition of opium. This was a significant turning point for drugs in Afghanistan. No longer would the government have a laissez-faire attitude toward drug use and trade. It could not. The American aid and investment the Afghan government had become so dependent on now hinged on adopting the more aggressive, supply-side interventions that were defining the Nixon-era war on drugs. In other words, to keep American money flowing into Afghanistan, the government would have to embrace the war on drugs. This period is significant because it shows how American drug control ambitions were taking shape in Afghanistan, and the political and social impact of such programs within the country. As a result, we are left asking two questions, fundamental to this book, about the history of drugs in Afghanistan. First, why, despite efforts in Afghanistan and around the world to stop the production and trade of drugs, did

Afghanistan emerge in the global market for illicit drugs? And second, what did the Afghan government do to stop it?

Much of the explanation lies in the evolving relationship between the supply-side interventions employed during Nixon's War on Drugs and the global supply for the illicit drugs market. Although the United States had been waging a de facto war on drugs since the beginning of the century,[3] Nixon's war ratcheted up the pressure and scale of US commitment. With renewed vigor, the United States applied more diplomatic pressure to states to employ more coercive supply-side strategies. Governments of drug-producing states now had access to the resources to create or expand institutions that could disrupt or eliminate the production and trade of drugs, particularly opium and heroin. But the reality of the war on drugs was that it was far more about political optics and Cold War diplomacy than it was about disrupting or eliminating the global supply of opium. When Nixon announced his war, most of the European and American supply was believed to be met by Turkish opium shipped by Corsican and French trafficking cartels, up to 80 percent of the US supply.[4] However, the sources of opium proved to be far more complex and dispersed than originally thought. Opium production in Southeast Asia and Mexico were also tied into the global market and proved capable of filling gaps in supply. In other words, the United States had largely misunderstood the scope, range, and malleability of the illicit drugs market.

At the time, it seemed that in nations with relatively strong states, the enforcement of eradication and interdiction programs was successful, as the customary sources of supply and trafficking routes were extinguished.[5] Those successes proved limited, however, because the war on drugs caused an important evolution in the market, as supply shifted to other regions, including Southeast Asia and Mexico.[6] Throughout this period, the market continued to evolve and adapt to the mounting obstacles to the global trade introduced by the United States. Eventually, as traditional sources of supply were disrupted by supply-side interventions, producers and traffickers found new sources of supply that were better suited for the new high-stakes environment, ideally, areas with weak or limited states, a preexisting drug trade, and a willing population. Thus, it is no surprise, that at some point, the global illicit drug trade would further integrate Afghanistan into its expanding webs.

Although the consequences of Nixon's War on Drugs are important to understand why the supply of opium was displaced or disrupted, it is the significance of the new enforcement strategies, particularly how they factored into the historical process of state formation, that is more important here. Afghanistan was a relatively minor producer of opium when Nixon launched the war on drugs, but the growing presence of Afghan opium in the illicit markets of Iran and Pakistan gave new life to the coalescence of international antidrug policy in Afghanistan. In particular, American antinarcotics officials in Afghanistan had a profound impact in shaping the government's implementation of new antismuggling laws and the creation of antismuggling units (ASUs) within the police and gendarmerie. By analyzing the antismuggling laws of 1969 and 1972, we see how US antinarcotics officials attempted to coordinate with Afghans to try to fulfill Nixon's vision of eliminating the production and trade of illicit narcotics in Afghanistan. Thus, exploring antinarcotics policy and infrastructure in Afghanistan during this period helps explain why, despite increased efforts from both foreign nations and the Afghan state, illicit narcotic production continued to thrive.

Ultimately, the success of Nixon's global antinarcotics vision was contingent on the governments of producer states effectively transforming and implementing domestic narcotics policies and subsequent structural changes—a daunting task indeed. In Afghanistan, the creation and enforcement of new legislation and antinarcotics structures indicated a renewed effort on the part of the state to use foreign ambitions for narcotics control to expand and bolster the state through the police and gendarmerie. Drug control in this vein emerged as a "modality" of state formation, justifying both the creation of a new state apparatus and the legal parameters to support the use of more coercive strategies.[7] However, despite this renewed effort, the state continued to fail to stop the production and trade of illicit narcotics. Analyzing the struggles and limitations of the antismuggling laws and the ASUs to stop the production and trade of narcotics reveals the tremendous difficulties facing the Afghan state and its ability to impose and enforce antinarcotic laws, particularly in the periphery of the country. Such failure stemmed partly from the subjective implementation and enforcement of antinarcotic laws by individual Afghan narcotics officials who often placed local needs and relations above state policy. In other words, the success or failure of interdiction and eradication was ultimately a by-product of the political culture in Afghanistan, whereby tribal, ethnic, familial, and/or local relations, the *qawm*, often dictated the extent to which state policy was enforced. Furthermore, the Musahiban government used the enforcement of anti-smuggling laws as a way of expanding power into the periphery of the country, attempting to regulate the movements of people whose lives often crossed the boundaries imposed on them. Consequently, by embracing Nixon's War on Drugs, and expanding drug control to a national level, the Afghan government contributed to the deepening fragmentation of Afghanistan and increased delegitimization of the state, all but reinforcing, if not instigating, the expansion of narcotic production and trade in subsequent years.

The Global Drug Trade circa 1972: Bringing Down the House

When Nixon launched the war on drugs in 1971, heroin use had reached epidemic proportions in the United States. A survey in 1974 estimated that nearly one million men between the ages of twenty and thirty had tried heroin at least once, and that nearly a third of those were regular users at some point in their life.[8] Part of the explanation for the more aggressive political response was the changing dynamic of use and addiction of heroin in the United States at the time. The emergence of white suburbanites and Vietnam soldiers as users put heroin addiction into the public sphere unlike ever before. Moreover, the relationship between heroin addiction and the increasingly unpopular war in Vietnam heightened public awareness of the increased use of heroin. By 1971, it was believed that over half of all enlisted men had tried heroin, with smaller numbers having become dependent. George McGovern, the 1972 Democratic presidential nominee, charged that the CIA was addicting American soldiers in Vietnam and pushing heroin on the American civilian population as well.[9] Although many politicians threw out numbers, mostly falsified, the stark reality was that heroin addiction was a significant problem in the United States.

Nixon spent much of his presidency building on previous federal legislation and infrastructural transformations to deal with the issue of drugs, including passing the Comprehensive Drug Abuse Prevention and Control Act in 1969. Although the scheduling of various substances and the public stigmas that surrounded their real impact on use and addiction were still clouded in highly subjective interpretations, the rapid growth in consumption seemed to justify an urgent, well-coordinated, and well-funded federal response. Nixon employed a drug strategy that was multifaceted, focusing on both consumption and production. He launched a series of treatment strategies, particularly methadone maintenance, to deal with alleviating addiction and curbing the demand for narcotics. Remarkably innovative at the time, Nixon's emphasis on treatment altered the traditional antidrug paradigm and its overwhelming focus on supply and production. From 1971 to 1973, for example, the federal budget for dealing with prevention and treatment increased from $59 million to $462 million.[10]

Yet despite the increase attention to demand, Nixon's new approach also reinforced and expanded efforts to curb production and supply. Nixon stated:

> America has the largest number of addicts of any nation in the world. And yet, America does not grow opium, nor does it manufacture heroin. This deadly poison in the American lifestream is, in other words, a foreign import. No serious attack on our national drug problem can ignore the international implications of such an effort, nor can the domestic effort succeed without attacking the problem on an international plane. I intend to do that.[11]

The increased focus on the international sources of supply was in some ways a continuation of old fears, but the convergence of demand and supply as a single interconnected issue led to reformulation of methods and infrastructure to curb domestic consumption and foreign production. In particular, the evolution of the Bureau of Narcotics of Dangerous Drugs into the Drug Enforcement Administration (DEA) in 1973 created a new infrastructure to enhance enforcement programs (or bolster preexisting ones) domestically and abroad, and increased capabilities to exert greater diplomatic pressure in major producer countries.[12] By making drugs an issue that required greater institutional support, the United States was now able to project its antinarcotic ideology in a way that fundamentally transformed how the United States and foreign governments dealt with the production, trade, and use of drugs. More important, by the early 1970s all of the major producers of narcotics, Iran, Pakistan, Turkey, Mexico, and Southeast Asia, were soon tied to America's new global antinarcotics strategy.

Alongside the various domestic programs, such as increased police enforcement and the innovative methadone treatment programs, Nixon's Drug War emphasized greater enforcement efforts abroad. However, the

United States had learned from its previous attempts to create a consensus on how to deal with the global drug trade that it could not fund antinarcotic efforts unilaterally. Many states were reluctant to take American money directly, either because of domestic pressures to resist the United States or because of broader questions related to the Cold War.[13] To circumvent possible problems arising from direct US relations, the Americans proposed forming an anti–drug abuse fund run by the UN. Financed by various government contributions and independent of regular UN programs, the United Nations Fund for Drug Abuse Control (UNFDAC) was formed in 1971.[14] As the primary source of revenue for the fund, however, the United States quickly dominated defining the objectives of the fund. The fund was initially envisioned as an international resource for suppressing all facets of the global drug trade, meaning both supply and demand. But the United States pressured the fund to emphasize enforcement and alternative crop programs, otherwise neglecting programs designed to reduce demand. As a result, despite the veil of international consensus and cooperation in the UN, the UNFDAC became a secondary conduit for the United States to exert pressure in its quest to suppress the global drug trade.[15] With the American public motivated to curb narcotics use and trade, and with new tools with which to implement its antinarcotics vision, such as the UNFDAC, the United States went about waging war against the global illicit narcotics market.

Turkey and the French Connection

The first target of Nixon's new war was the infamous French Connection, a system of trade in which Turkey supplied the opium (and morphine base) for the heroin laboratories in Marseilles, France, to be exported to the massive, and constantly growing, market in the United States and Western Europe. Although Turkish opium supply was rather limited within the global market,[16] it was perceived by American officials to be the primary source of opium and heroin coming into the United States, and by the 1970s it was estimated to supply 80 percent of the US market, making it the second largest producer of opium in Asia.[17]

Because of Turkey's long history as a producer of opium, the Federal Bureau of Narcotics focused a great deal of attention on its role in the illicit drug market and the French Connection. Throughout the postwar period, the Federal Bureau of Narcotics maintained a regular station of drug agents to monitor, with hopes of disrupting the trade.[18] By the 1960s, however, as heroin flooded American streets, Turkey emerged as a major culprit. As the Americans saw it, French and Corsican mafia expanded the import of heroin into the United States by buying large quantities of illicit opium from Turkey, refining it into high-grade heroin in laboratories in Marseilles, and ultimately transporting it to affiliated groups in the United States for distribution. For Turkey, the increased pressure in the United States to curb drug addiction, crime, and other forms of vice led to the elevation of Turkey's status as a focal point of US antidrug policy.[19]

By the 1970s, the French Connection faced increasing pressure from various circles. The Guerini family, who dominated the production of heroin in Marseilles and served as the virtual face of the French Connection for two decades, struggled to maintain a monopoly as competition increased from new criminal organizations. The rapid growth in heroin use in France transformed the narcotics issue into a primary public agenda topic in the country, particularly because the Guerini family had ensured its political protection in France by instituting a self-regulated embargo on heroin trafficking into France. As competing cartels expanded distribution into France, however, political scrutiny increased as well. Eventually, the domestic and international pressures proved too much.[20] By 1969, coinciding with the US war on drugs, French and US antinarcotics operations worked to end the French Connection, and by 1973, after numerous police operations, the Marseilles heroin industry was virtually annihilated.[21]

Although the effort from French and US antinarcotics officials proved effective in ending the role of Marseilles as the primary site of heroin production, there was also a concerted effort to cut off the major source of supply. While the United States and French were launching raids in Marseilles, American diplomats exerted tremendous pressure on the Turkish government to eradicate opium. As early as 1969, American diplomats began to press Turkey regarding its role in the global opium trade. Americans advocated the total eradication of the opium crop, but Turkish officials objected, citing the economic and political consequences of eliminating an important and widespread crop such as opium.[22] Moreover, similar to Afghanistan, American officials recognized that the Turkish government was limited in its control of certain regions of the country, especially those that grew opium.[23] Eventually, in 1971, after considerable US pressure (including promises of $35 million in aid), Prime Minister Nihat Erim announced a total ban on opium cultivation, including licit opium production, starting in 1972.[24]

For the most part, the details of American support for the ban were kept secret. Fifteen million dollars was allocated to the Turkish government as compensation for the loss of its licit industry, and an additional $20 million for future development and alternative crop programs.[25] Although the $35 million promised to Turkey was seen as too low by most accounts, the future political implications of Turkey's role in the global drug trade, specifically regarding the French Connection, and the US role as one of the major sources of aid certainly compelled Turkey to act. This was even more paramount when Turkish senator Kudret Bayhan was arrested in France for trying to smuggle 321 pounds of morphine base.[26]

Turkey's opium ban went into effect in 1972. Initially, US officials were pleased by the results of the ban. Laws were rigorously enforced; initially, farmers who were allowed to grow often opted for compensation instead, and cooperation between the DEA and the Turkish police and gendarmerie were at an all-time high.[27] Nonetheless, fissures emerged in the program, as many farmers complained about lack of compensation, and reporters feared the devastating economic losses from ending the illicit trade. By 1974, the opium ban became a major issue in the presidential elections. Bulent Ecevit, the young leader of the Republican Peoples Party who came to power that year, immediately set about rescinding the opium ban. Ecevit consciously distanced himself from the previous regime and its opium ban because "the ban had been the act of a non-representative government; a freely chosen one had no choice but to follow the will of the people."[28] In 1974, despite bitter condemnation from the United States, Turkey reinstituted the legal production of opium in seven provinces. Although reinstating the quasi-legal production of opium ran counter to American–Turkish diplomatic relations, particularly in light of increasing congressional pressure to cut off all aid to countries supplying drugs for the illicit market, the United States had to relent. A few weeks after Ecevit reinstated production, Nixon would resign amidst the Watergate scandal and Turkey would go to war with Cyprus.[29] Drugs, in this case, would take a back seat to more pressing issues.

As part of a broader coordinated effort to stop the entire French Connection, the ban in Turkey, at least temporarily, was seen as a success. It was believed that one hundred tons of illicit Turkish opium and nearly twelve tons of high-grade heroin from Marseilles vanished from the US market. The doubling of street prices and the decline in purity indicated that the disruption of the French Connection had led to significant shortages of heroin.[30] Despite the perception of success, things were not quite as they seemed. The decline in opium production, believed to be the primary outcome of this supply-side intervention, may have predated American-led intervention.[31] Furthermore, the Turkish government's larger role in regulating the production and trade of opium for pharmaceutical purposes did not end Turkey's role in the illicit drug trade. Rather, the country shifted away from being a supplier and manufacturer of drugs, to a more prominent role in the distribution and transit of drugs, primarily from areas such as Afghanistan.[32] However, with demand for heroin still high, and new markets continually emerging, the global opium supply shifted. As the French Connection was seemingly extinguished, Southeast Asia, known as "the Golden Triangle," emerged as both a key source of supply for the US market and the next target of Nixon's drug war.

The Golden Triangle

Unlike other parts of Asia, opium's fundamental role in the political economy of Southeast Asia is a relatively recent phenomenon. Before the nineteenth century, most of the Southeast Asian economy was subsistence based. However, as relations between the Qing dynasty and the Chinese people and colonial powers eroded, particularly in the southern province of Yunnan, various groups in Southeast Asia began to cultivate and trade opium in response to the chaotic political and economic climate.[33] When the Qing Empire attempted to expand its dominion south into the long-standing autonomous ethnic regions of China in the late nineteenth century, many of the ethnic hill tribes escaped persecution by fleeing to the mountains of Southeast Asia. Many displaced ethnic hill tribes and Muslim traders brought the knowledge of opium cultivation and trade with them. This displacement resulted in a new network of opium trade that linked Yunnan to the ports of Southeast Asia.[34] For the better part of a century, up to World War II, opium was an important, albeit relatively small, component of the Southeast Asian political economy.

After the war, however, Southeast Asia experienced a virtual opium boom. Unlike Iran, Turkey, and even Afghanistan, the nationalist fighting that unfolded after World War II had a profound impact on the production and trade of opium in Southeast Asia. After the war, the cessation of opium imports from major producers Iran, India, and China,[35] along with fears of communist uprisings, led the Thai police, the Nationalist Chinese Army, the French military, and the American CIA to adopt "polices that allowed Southeast Asia's mass opium addiction to survive and even thrive."[36] As Alfred McCoy detailed in his seminal work *The Politics of Heroin*, both the French and the CIA fought a covert war against Communist insurgents throughout Southeast Asia. McCoy notes that unlike other covert operations around the world:

> French and American operatives integrated their covert warfare with the Golden Triangle opium trade. An effective covert warrior had to find a strong local leader willing to merge his people's resources with the agency's operations. In a region of weak microstates and fragmented tribes, such strongmen usually combined traditional authority with control over the local economy. In the Golden Triangle, the only commodity was opium, and the most powerful local leaders were the opium warlords.[37]

These warlords used CIA resources—arms, ammunitions, and transportation—to maintain and expand control over opium production. Moreover, "instead of opposing the expansion of their ally's autonomous economic base, most CIA operatives embraced it, knowing it increased their client's effectiveness and independence from Washington's directives."[38] By either aiding the expansion of the opium industry or simply ignoring it, CIA officials could effectively arm and supply large groups of anti-Communist forces while avoiding possible political ramifications back home in the United States. Initially, the large addict population in Southeast Asia consumed almost all of the opium. This was, of course, important for political reasons, as American antidrug officials would be less concerned with opium addiction in Southeast Asia as long as the threat to the United States was minimized. By the late 1950s, the Golden Triangle was producing nearly seven hundred tons of opium, roughly half of the global illicit supply.[39] As a result, opium had become a primary vehicle for the CIA's covert war in Southeast Asia.

Although the CIA was complicit in aiding the expansion of the opium industry in Southeast Asia, it did not deter Richard Nixon from expanding his war on drugs to Southeast Asia. The disruption of the supply of heroin resulting from operations in France and Turkey had seemingly produced results in curbing supply in the United States, but it failed to recognize the international and multidimensional aspect of the illicit trade. This was partly because US authorities had misidentified Turkey and the French Connection as the overwhelming source of heroin in the United States. What US authorities discovered in 1972 was that Southeast Asian opium was in fact a much larger piece of the global heroin market than previously perceived.[40]

In 1972, US authorities estimated that the Golden Triangle produced between 750 and 1,200 tons of opium a year, much of which was believed to be consumed locally.[41] It was generally believed that the Chiu Chau syndicate in Hong Kong monopolized the heroin trade, facilitated by key connections with the police and local politicians in Hong Kong, as well as a large network of affiliated groups throughout Southeast Asia. US officials grew increasingly concerned with the changes in the local opium industry in response to the events in Turkey and France, however, and the changing dynamics of the US market. The opium trade in Southeast Asia had received a major boost in 1965 when American soldiers arrived *en force* in Vietnam. Before the American invasion of Vietnam, most of the local opium crop was refined into heroin no. 3, a brown crude heroin, smoked mostly by the local population. But when American GIs arrived, soldiers used various narcotics and stimulants to deal with the trauma of war, particularly heroin no. 4, a white and purer form of heroin. The overwhelming popularity of heroin no. 4 led the Chinese heroin manufacturers to increase refineries capable of producing heroin no. 4 to feed the growing demand among US GIs.[42]

Hong Kong, much like Marseilles, was a key city in the globalization of the Southeast Asian opium industry. Hong Kong was literally built on the revenue of the opium trade in the nineteenth century by the British and other opium traders. Little had changed by 1970. As a free port, a major international banking center, and a key transportation hub, Hong Kong was ideal for trafficking narcotics.[43] Hong Kong provided both a staging ground and financial hub for the Chiu Chau to exploit the East Asian opium industry. But the Chiu Chau had yet to break into the US market. Not until 1969, with the US government facing increasing resistance to the war at home, did the US begin to decrease troop levels. The Chiu Chau syndicates were left with a large surplus of high-grade heroin and no customers. The Chiu Chao used this opportunity to break into the US market, however. In essence, the Chiu Chau attempted to follow the GIs home, using Chinese and American seaman to smuggle nearly a thousand pounds of heroin into New York City in 1971–72.[44] The shift of consumer markets from Southeast Asia to the United States caused grave concerns among US officials. Not only was heroin use high in the United States but Southeast Asia was producing unprecedented quantities of heroin.

When knowledge of the GI heroin epidemic went public in 1971, US officials placed greater weight on stopping the flourishing trade in Southeast Asia. Concerned with preventing heroin from jumping across the Pacific to the United States, the BNDD (later the DEA) placed increased emphasis on interdicting heroin flowing from major narcotics hubs, Bangkok and Hong Kong, to the United States. The number of special agents grew from two in 1972 to thirty-one by 1974, and the budget increased to $12 million.[45] Almost immediately, the DEA succeeded in capturing shipments to the United States. As a complement to the US interdiction program, the UNFDAC launched a series of crop substitution programs encouraging farmers to grow fruit, coffee, and beans.[46]

Although the Southeast Asian opium trade had all the makings of becoming the primary source of heroin for the US market, it never did so. In 1975, seizures of Southeast Asian heroin in the United States dropped from 35 percent to 9 percent.[47] US interdiction efforts had made it increasingly difficult for traffickers to ship to the United States and they instead opted for more easily accessible and less prohibitive markets in Europe and Australia.[48] Moreover, by the end of the war, heroin addiction was emerging as a major problem in Southeast Asia. The increasing demand for opium at home diverted much of the product that was potentially going to the United States.[49] Lastly, Chinese and American syndicates struggled to bridge the ethnic gap that dictated many of the terms of retail street distribution in the United States, as most American distributors still seemingly preferred their European counterparts,[50] while the Chinese preferred to deal with other Asians.[51]

Much like the French Connection, increased American efforts to curb opium production and heroin trafficking into the United States from Southeast Asia were seemingly effective. By 1973 and 1974, the two major areas of concern for the United States, Turkey and Southeast Asia, had been dramatically reduced as sources of opium to the US market. However, US antidrug officials were quickly learning that the global illicit narcotics trade was far more reactive and capable of swift adaptation than previously perceived. As soon as supply dwindled from one area, a new source emerged. By the mid-1970s, a new source, Mexico, emerged as the largest source of heroin for the US market.

Mexico

Much like the Golden Triangle and the French Connection, Mexico's emergence as a major producer of narcotics stemmed from the events following World War II. During the 1920s, Mexican immigrants were largely responsible for introducing marijuana to the United States. During the war, fearing that the United States would be cut off from the major sources of supply, the United States turned to Mexico as a major source of opium.[52] After the war, despite Mexico's help in providing a key source of opium, the United States returned to the more traditional sources for opium from Asia and the Middle East.[53] In spite of the cessation of the licit trade with the US government, many Mexicans continued to produce opium and marijuana, feeding the growing demand in the United States. It was during the 1950s and 1960s, when schisms appeared in the American social and political fabric, and recreational drug use became a more visible component of American life, that the Mexican drug industry blossomed.

When Nixon came to power, he repeatedly urged the Mexican government to eradicate opium and marijuana crops. In 1969, he launched Operation Intercept, which increased border patrols and customs searches in an effort to stop the flow of Mexican brown heroin and marijuana from crossing the southern border of the United States. Mexico responded by launching an antidrug campaign of its own, Operation Cooperation, whereby Mexican soldiers eradicated opium plants manually using machetes.[54] Needless to say, the respective programs failed to curtail production in Mexico and trafficking into the United States. By 1972, Mexican heroin supplied roughly 40 percent of the US market, and by 1975, after the two campaigns in Southeast Asia and Turkey, it gained nearly 90 percent of the US market.[55]

It was not until Operation Intercept in 1975, a comprehensive interdiction program focusing on the highlands of Mexico where most of the narcotics were produced, that both governments were able significantly to cut back on supply. Twenty-five thousand Mexican troops uprooted poppy plants and planes (supplied by the United States) sprayed fields with herbicides. By the following year, 22,887 poppy fields were destroyed, decreasing the flow of Mexican heroin from 6.5 tons to 3 tons and its share of the US market from 67 to 25 percent. The apparent success of Nixon's drug war in Mexico seemed to indicate that the aggressive militarization of antidrug policy was an effective and sustainable solution to the drug problem.

However, the disruptions of the supply of opium on the global illicit market following the interventions in Turkey, Mexico, and Southeast Asia forced opium producers and heroin traffickers to adapt to the new global realities. Nixon's supply-side interventions, which focused on the major suppliers to the US market, were creating an evolution in the supply of opium. Often dubbed "the balloon effect," it describes the process in which supply-side interventions in one drug-producing area displace production in another area.[56] While there is some merit to this analogy, it also limited. In some ways, the "balloon effect" analogy oversimplifies the impact and influence of supply-side interventions, particularly as the only cause of crop dispersion.[57] On the other hand, the impact of supply-side interventions cannot be minimized. As Graham Farrell notes, supply-side interventions have, more often than not, been unsuccessful. Crop eradications can lead to expanded production in areas outside the eradication zone, or in anticipation of eradications. And more important, disruptions in supply in one country can lead to production moving to neighboring regions more conducive for illicit crop production. Moreover, the impact of supply-side interventions are often much greater than simple crop displacement, as traffickers may find sources elsewhere or produce other illicit goods, find other markets, or engage in other illicit activities.[58] The changing dynamics of the global drug trade suggest that the cumulative effect of cutting and disrupting supply in specific source countries, combined with the application of considerable political pressure on certain trafficking networks into the United States, stimulated the global illicit narcotics environment in some meaningful way. It adapted and evolved. More like bacteria than a balloon, the weak players in the illicit trade were eliminated or they changed their roles, while the strong became further entrenched in areas or political systems that were better suited for its success.

More important, the effects were unexpected for US antidrug policymakers. The DEA and the Nixon administration soon realized that the production of opium was not isolated in disparate production zones in Asia but instead was located in an "elongated highland zone" that "responded to stimuli from the global drug market with a surprising speed and unanimity."[59] The illicit drug market was proving remarkably resilient, and drug traffickers, not confined by national boundaries or laws, sought new sources. And herein lies the major point. The disruptions, displacements, and fissures that occurred to the global drug trade during this period ultimately elevated the importance of Afghanistan. On the one hand, Afghanistan was an ideal place for the illicit drug market to thrive; it had a relatively unstable and limited government, a history of drug production, and a population that was either culturally indifferent to or economically in need of participating in the expanding and evolving illicit drug trade. But on the other hand, and largely because of these reasons, it was a country that needed to be pushed more firmly to participate in Nixon's War on Drugs. It was at this point in history that Afghanistan would be enveloped by both the expanding global drug trade and the global war being waged to stop it.

Afghanistan: Building the Mechanisms for Drug Control

> Ours is a poor country. It's impossible for us to control the crops with the few police we have at our disposal. Nor are we equipped to combat the traffic. We don't have the money to pay informants. When we seize other kinds of contraband we sell it in the bazaar and pay fifteen percent of the receipts to the person who tipped us off. Obviously we can't do that with opium and hashish. And so far as our frontier with Persia is concerned, all we have is a squad of ten unmounted gendarmes for every forty kilometers. They have neither jeeps, telephones nor radios.
>
> —Afghan police chief Colonel Katawazi[60]

As the United States pushed its antidrug agenda onto the rest of the world, it focused on the areas of supply that were most closely connected to use in the United States. For countries such as Iran, Pakistan, and Afghanistan, their long traditions of opium production were relegated to secondary status given their limited impact in the US market. However, this did not discourage the United States from continuing to advocate greater drug control measures in those nations. And in Southwest Asia, as in other drug-producing regions of the world, drug control continued to emphasize supply-side strategies. But, as Colonel Katawazi's statement indicates, the attempts to build a strong military, police, and gendarmerie to suppress drug cultivation and trafficking took on new meaning in Afghanistan. During the late 1960s and early 1970s, the Afghan government, under tremendous pressure from the United States and the UN, expanded its antinarcotics repertoire. With the introduction of new prohibition and antismuggling laws in 1969, as well as the expansion of the police and the gendarmerie tasked specifically with combating drug smuggling, the Afghan government implemented and expanded on the American militarized supply-side strategy.

As discussed in the previous chapter, drug cultivation and trafficking increased in Afghanistan throughout the late 1960s and early 1970s. The influx of American and European sojourners, hippies, and young entrepreneurs contributed to the early globalization of Afghanistan's opium industry. Moreover, the large demand for opium and other narcotics in Iran and the rest of Asia was growing at a rapid pace, overwhelming authorities' ability to effectively manage addicts and smugglers. As a result, the attention given to Afghanistan as a part of Nixon's drug war stemmed not from Afghanistan's own domestic problems with addiction (which were limited, save for the drug tourists and Badakhshan), but from the potential of Afghan drugs reaching surrounding nations. In other words, the threat of drug addiction in the United States placed global counternarcotics strategies more firmly into the national security infrastructure. Fearing that American power was rescinding throughout the world because of the war in Vietnam and tinged by the shifting sands of Cold War geopolitics, Nixon's grand strategy called for a more active American engagement with the global community.[61] Afghan cooperation with American ambitions was increasingly important given Pakistan and Iran's role as important allies in the Cold War in Asia. Both Iran and Pakistan, opium producers in their own right, historically had been in relatively fortuitous positions on the American geostrategic spectrum, granting them easier access to funds and technical assistance that were seen as fundamental to controlling drugs at the source. Afghanistan as a neutral country, was not. However, the fear of Afghan drugs as an American security issue would change the US–Afghan relationship, and the war on drugs became an important tool for Afghanistan to gain much-needed funds and technical assistance from the United States and the UN to expand its police and gendarmerie.

Pakistan became increasingly concerned about its role as a trafficking route for drug traffickers coming from Afghanistan. While laws regarding the illicit production, use, and trade of drugs remained stern for Pakistani citizens, many Westerners continued to cross the Khyber Pass into Pakistan.[62] Meanwhile, the government continued to pursue the licit production of opium in hopes of expanding its nascent pharmaceutical industry. Eventually, in 1973, after significant pressure from the United States, Pakistan ended its licit production of opium and took a significant step into the realm of complete source control. Despite the government's formal prohibition of opium, however, opium continued to proliferate throughout the country. For many government officials, the money to be made from either trafficking or production was too much; some abandoned their political posts, moved to the frontier provinces, and essentially formalized their role in the illicit narcotics trade.[63] Others perpetuated the crisis of corruption that permeated the Pakistani political system.[64] Ultimately, US assistance for increased enforcement and crop substitution programs only affected Pakistan's settled areas. The frontier, where the government had little control and where many of the Pashtun tribal groups freely traded all sorts of contraband,[65] remained untouched by Pakistan and US efforts. As a result, despite the fact that the Pakistan government eventually conformed to American supply-side strategy, opium production continued. It was not until 1979, when the Zia ul-Haq launched the Hudood Ordinance establishing shariah law in Pakistan that the government enforced a nationwide ban on opium.[66]

Iran, like Pakistan, suffered tremendously from the expanding opium industry in Afghanistan as hundreds of thousands of addicts increasingly looked east for their opium fix.[67] When the shah announced the reestablishment of opium cultivation in 1969, he intended to bring rampant opium addiction under control by providing licit sources of opium in conjunction with increased measures to combat widespread smuggling.[68] The United States played an important role in helping to try to stop rampant smuggling. It had established a significant advisory presence during the 1950s with the GENMISH program and merely used Nixon's policy as a means of enhancing the preexisting system. In 1971, the United States agreed to expand financial and technical assistance to Iran, including a special police training program that provided access to training in the United States, as well as increasing the capabilities of border patrols and customs through new equipment.[69] Iran was a firm member of the American anti-Soviet bloc, and the shah's policies regarding narcotics were ardently supported by the United States. The increased enforcement had a major effect on the border between Turkey and Iran, as both nations' commitment to stopping the trade virtually eliminated the illicit traffic of opium into Iran. As a result, the threat posed to Iran from the Southwest Asian narcotics industry no longer came from Turkey, and a newfound emphasis was placed on interdicting opium from Afghanistan.

Afghanistan: Smuggling during the Time of King Zahir Shah

Although opium cultivation remained an important part of the rural Afghan economy, the Afghan state, and even the international community, recognized its own limitations in establishing effective and sustainable solutions. Both the 1944 and 1957 prohibitions stood as prime examples of how the Afghan government had attempted but failed, or did not care, to stop the production of opium. Things were changing by the 1970s, however. In previous decades, Afghan opium remained a domestic and regional concern, and its potential to surge into the global illicit market remained relatively low. But by the late 1960s, the ever-growing presence of Afghan opium in Iran and the increasing number of Western sojourners and drug-trafficking entrepreneurs in Afghanistan were transforming Afghanistan's role in the global drug market. Smuggling, not just cultivation, became the new focus of drug policy in Afghanistan.

In 1969, under immense pressure from the United States and its neighbors, Iran, and Pakistan, the Afghan government passed an antismuggling law to bring the proliferating smuggling trade under control. After a meeting of the Supreme Judicial Court in Kabul, the court concluded:

> The increase in cultivation of poppies and the increased production, sale, purchase, import, transportation, export and stockpiling of narcotics in recent years, and realizing the importance of Afghanistan's membership in the international community and her role in effectively participating in world

> narcotics control, the Supreme Court, in pursuance of the above mentioned points, and following the governments expressed wish it shall promulgate laws for the unification of the judicial process and court action on narcotic crimes.

The court also established a special tribunal in Kabul Province for dealing with special narcotics matters.[70] The tribunal indicated that the government was taking steps to centralize police and judicial structures in an effort to better combat the burgeoning drug trade. The 1969 Anti-Smuggling Law defined smuggling as three types of criminal acts: first, the import or export of goods without going through the proper customs procedures or without paying necessary taxes; second, the production, import, export, sale, purchase, and transport of prohibited goods or goods from government monopoly; and third, altering the quality of goods to avoid paying higher duties or taxes, thus decreasing revenue for the state. The state defined prohibited goods as "those whose production, import, export, purchase, sale, storage, and transportation the Government has proclaimed to be prohibited." The law also established the necessary procedures for departments, for policemen, and reward systems, as well as broad punitive measures.[71]

While the law marked the most significant effort on the part of the government to establish legal boundaries for the illicit import and export of goods since the days of Amanullah, it failed in two major respects. First, the law never outlined the specific goods prohibited by the government. As a result, for policemen arresting alleged smugglers or judges prosecuting suspected smugglers there was no specific guideline to define what was a prohibited good. Thus, policemen and the courts were tasked with stopping a growing smuggling trade without knowing what goods were illegal or how to allocate punishment. Needless to say, the arbitrary foundations of antismuggling laws in Afghanistan certainly did not help in stopping the burgeoning drug trade. Moreover, the law prohibiting the cultivation and sale of opium remained unchanged from its inception in 1957, despite the remarkable changes to the Afghan opium market. Second, and more important, the centralization of police and gendarmerie carried political and social implications that threatened the delicate balance between the state and the people. Would the authority of the state have similar results in Badakhshan or Helmand given the cultural and political differences distinguishing those provinces form Kabul? Although centralizing the narcotics system was deemed necessary, the success of such a restructured system would depend heavily on lower-level police, gendarmerie, and courts in provinces far from Kabul acquiescing to the demands of the Kabul government. In other words, would lower-level state officials abandon their *qawm* for the sake of the state? As we have seen, the state's legitimacy was always in question, particularly the further one got from Kabul. As a result, the centralization of Afghanistan's narcotic war was ideal in theory but flawed in practice.

Although the passing of the law was an important step in the antinarcotics campaign, the rather slow implementation and enforcement of the law prompted the United States and Iran to press harder for a more concerted Afghan effort. In 1971, Prime Minister Abdul Zahir met with ministers of various related departments to create a separate narcotics commission tasked with expanding customs police and border patrols by improving funding and technical assistance while increasing the crackdown on the production of opium and hash.[72] It was becoming increasingly obvious that the size and depth of the narcotics industry in Afghanistan was so large and widespread that narcotics matters could not be handled under the traditional judicial constructs. By 1972, Zahir's successor, Musa Shafiq, consolidated narcotics matters under two ministries: the Ministry of Interior to deal with smuggling and the Ministry of Agriculture to deal with production. Moreover, the Ministry of Interior created new antismuggling units within local police precincts tasked specifically with cracking down on illicit smuggling.[73]

Although there was a genuine desire to stop the influx of narcotics from some within the Afghan government, the new antidrug measures provided an opportunity for the Afghan government to continue its push for greater American financial aid. In meetings between Shafiq and the US Embassy, the prime minister repeated his intentions to increase the crackdown on drugs but continually stressed the importance of increased US aid to help provide for improved enforcement and, more important, increased funding for rural development.[74] Not only did this conflict with the American emphasis on enforcement but it also countered the US investments of hundreds of millions of dollars in large-scale agricultural development programs. The result was that Shafiq was pushing for more money for programs the United States had already contributed to (agro-industrial development) or had rejected in the past (police and military aid). As a result, despite the threat of Afghanistan as a significant source of illicit narcotics and drugs and its importance in American foreign policy, the United States was unwilling to contribute the type of funds the Afghans desired and that both governments actually needed to stop the flow of drugs.

Regardless of the dialogue between the United States and the Afghan government, the increase in enforcement of smuggling laws by both Zahir and Shafiq led to a dramatic increase in arrests of smugglers. According to official Afghan statistics, the number of arrests of smugglers increased from 72 in 1971 (1350) to 221 in 1972 (1351), before skyrocketing to 584 in 1973 (1352).[75] Although the statistics show a major increase in the number of arrests of smugglers, it is impossible to estimate the quantity of drugs being smuggled out of Afghanistan. Certainly, during this period there was a major increase in the smuggling of drugs and other products, but there is little statistical proof to show how much the industry was growing. If anything, these statistics demonstrate explicitly that the state was in fact trying harder to crack down on smuggling, implying that smuggling was on the rise.

Afghan smuggling successes also brought back old friends: American pharmaceutical companies. Mallinckrodt, which had purchased opium from Afghanistan in the 1950s, reentered the fray to try to purchase seized opium from the Afghan government. They successfully outbid a French firm and purchased the twenty-seven tons of opium for around $600,000.[76] Although Mallincrokdt was happy to once again be buying top-quality Afghan opium, issues emerged about the potential for criminal activity corresponding to the purchase. Rumors persisted that Afghan officials responsible for housing and packaging the product were substituting high-quality opium with more inferior product.[77] Moreover, Mallinckrodt didn't even know if they would receive the amount they purchased, as some Afghans stated they would receive anywhere from fifteen to twenty-five tons. American officials were clearly concerned. Not only did the lack of a definitive number point to the lack of professionalism of the operation; it also hinted that Afghan counter-narcotics agents might have been conning the system. To make matters worse, there were also fears that much of the product could also be diverted to the illicit market, where it would be worth an estimated $7 million.[78] Eventually, American Embassy officials' concerns that Afghans would be seizing opium not to stop drugs but rather to "seize to sell" it to American companies were satiated by the successful Mallincrokdt bid and export.[79]

The state's effort to combat smuggling was well publicized by government-run or progovernment publications, often extolling the virtues of the government's courageous campaign. In August of 1971, *Anis*, the government-run

Figure 5.1. "The opium was carried in large plastic bags on the vehicle's bed." (*Anis*, August 1971)

newspaper, reported that Kabul police had successfully captured smugglers in Sarobi, just east of Kabul, trying to smuggle nearly two thousand kilos of opium to either Pakistan or Iran (figure 5.1). The seizure was massive for the time. The smuggler was said to believe that the shipment would have fetched nearly 8 million afghanis, or nearly US$100,000.[80]

Moreover, the article noted that the police had adopted "the correct measures" by increasing the total area monitored,[81] particularly two major roads leading into Kabul.[82] It is interesting to note that the seizure was indicative of the improvement in Kabul police tactics in fighting smuggling, a characteristic that the United States and the UN urgently prescribed as the solution to Afghanistan's opium problem. The *Anis* article was followed by many others, including several in the *Kabul Times*, that emphasized, if not glorified, the state's new ambitious plan for stopping smuggling.

Despite this success and many others highlighted in various publications, however, American officials remained skeptical of the Afghan effort. Officials in the US Embassy questioned the purpose of the newspaper coverage. The *Kabul Times*, an English-language publication, was one of the most prominent of the Afghan newspapers to highlight the government efforts in cracking down on smuggling. Many American officials in Kabul questioned the sincerity of the *Times* given that it was generally aimed at the foreign community in Kabul. Furthermore, distrust was fueled by rumors circulating in Kabul that many within the government, including the king himself, were somehow complicit in the trade. Thus, many Americans in Kabul saw the crackdown not so much as a genuine effort but rather as a publicity campaign.[83]

Police, Drugs, and Qawm

Aside from the rumors of collusion at the upper levels of the Afghan government, all indications pointed to the continued expansion and growth of drug smuggling and cultivation in Afghanistan. Reports from US narcotics officials in Iran noted that Afghan opium was coming through the region in such quantities that it was not only spreading into Iran but also making its way by sea to Dubai.[84] Furthermore, in 1972, the Iranian gendarmerie made the largest seizure in the history of drug interdiction, capturing 12.7 tons of opium from a truck en route to Iran from Afghanistan.[85] All indications were pointing to Afghanistan's emergence as a major player in the global illicit narcotics market. Nevertheless, explanations for why Afghan drugs continued to expand in the region remain relatively obscure. Globally, the market was changing, yet narcotics officials had little foresight into how the market was evolving. Locally, however, much of the explanation rested on the suspected collusion at the top levels of the Afghan government. Although this was probably true to an extent, this explanation obfuscated the deeper issues tied to the role of the state in Afghan society. As a result, the continued rise in opium smuggling was never truly impacted by Afghanistan's narcotic policy because of the limited capabilities of the police and gendarmerie. Furthermore, political and cultural factors facing individual police and gendarmes tasked with enforcing antismuggling and antinarcotic policies, particularly surrounding the issue of *qawm*, amplified this functional incapacity.

When Daud took power in 1953, he wanted to bolster the police and gendarmerie so as better to protect state interests from the threat of local tribal authorities. In 1958, a small contingent of West German police officers was sent to Afghanistan to train police in Kabul. Despite this training, the Afghan police seemed to be the weakest link in the enforcement chain. Much of this stemmed from the role of police in both the Afghan state and Afghan society. Unlike the military, the police were held in low regard in Afghanistan. The police were generally made up of the bottom 10 percent of army conscripts. Most patrolmen received an average monthly salary of eighty cents a month. The low status and low pay of policemen often made even the most basic issues troublesome. For example, policemen were not given guns, badges, or ID cards because they often sold these on the black market to compensate for their meager pay. Illiteracy was endemic, virtually negating any record-keeping system or systematic application of narcotic laws. Moreover, officers who showed too much zeal in combating narcotics were often placed on leave as they threatened the status quo. In one case, a senior Afghan police official who cooperated with the BNDD was eventually sent off to Europe to "study" because his superiors feared he was too close to foreign narcotics officials.[86]

Corruption seemed to be rampant within the police force. In fact, some of the German police advisers commented that the overall result of their effort in Afghanistan was "to create the most highly organized criminal element in Afghanistan." Furthermore, any real and substantive progress was confined exclusively to Kabul. In the provinces, "even the inept efforts practiced in Kabul are virtually nonexistent. Lack of authority, know-how, initiative and equipment reduces the police virtually to a token presence." Similar sentiments would be shared by American counternarcotics officials. In 1972, BNDD agent Terry Burke was sent to Kabul to lead antinarcotics initiatives in cooperation with the Afghan police. Burke and other US narcotics officials struggled to coordinate with Afghan police because many of the "educated officials are well aware of the short-comings of their police and are less than eager to place these shortcomings in full view by attempting to do that which they know they cannot."[87] Ultimately, the low regard for Afghan police in broader Afghan political and social spheres made it virtually impossible for American officials to co-opt them in effective narcotics controls.

Although the Afghan police clearly failed to match the American zeal for narcotic control, many of the problems were much deeper than mere "lack of initiative" or limited "know-how." American desires to crack down on the highest-level drug producers and drug traffickers threatened the very foundations of Afghan political culture. As one BNDD official put it, the "BNDD won't be satisfied with token arrests of a few hippies, but is going to be pushing to stop the major Afghan suppliers and traffickers. For family, tribal, and political reasons, this type of action will be avoided at all costs by the Afghan authorities."[88] In other words, Afghan police, from the bottom to the top of the political system, were more concerned about their *qawm* than they were about the desires of the state.

Although American and European officials viewed this as nothing more than corruption, corruption implied that state rule superseded the power of local communities. In Afghanistan, particularly in rural communities far from Kabul, the state was not an entity that penetrates society but rather rests on top of society; corruption took on a different meaning altogether. Rural peasants used the state to enhance or protect local interests while simultaneously preventing the state from integrating into local society. As Olivier Roy notes, corruption for peasants (including those in the police) "makes it possible to resist regimentation, and to avoid dealing with issues which he does not understand. Corruption makes the official powerless and ensures that bureaucratic machinery can only function in a vacuum."[89] Thus, when the Afghan state's narcotics policy threatened local political, social, and economic relations, policemen often ignored the state directive.

The gendarmerie, much like the police, was just as ineffective at stopping drugs. Although structured as a paramilitary force under the Ministry of Interior, the mission was to maintain internal security and to supplement regular police forces. Although a relatively large paramilitary force, most of the gendarmes were located in key provinces just outside of Kabul. There were only a few border posts on the Afghan–Pakistan and Afghan–Iranian borders. As a result, the gendarmerie suffered tremendously from a lack of mobility.[90] Unlike the police, who were stationed throughout the country but lacked initiative the farther one got from Kabul, the gendarmerie had the potential to act as a significant antinarcotics force but simply lacked the mobility to do so. In this sense, the construction of routes provided the government with the opportunity to project greater power in rural regions,[91] but were ultimately restricted by the political and cultural forces limiting Afghan political culture in general. This also explains why the majority of seizures from the police and gendarmerie were located in or near Kabul while drug smuggling continued unabated on Afghanistan's southern and western borders.

By 1972, it seemed that Afghanistan was at a critical impasse. The steps the Afghan government had taken on its own were proving to be woefully inadequate. In a speech by Y. P. Maroofi to the UN General Assembly, Maroofi stressed that international desires for greater enforcement of drug controls would require greater investment in the country's enforcement capabilities:

> Traffickers are increasingly employing sophisticated methods of smuggling their contraband, both in and out of the country, [and] sophisticated and advanced methods of detection were needed to effectively cope with the problem. However, in order to effectively screen traffickers we are trying to have more check points and border patrols on all areas of our borders and such a measure is costly and cannot be implemented with the limited resources at our disposal.[92]

As had been the case in the previous decades, narcotics control ultimately rested on the willingness of the international community to fund such programs. On the other hand, this required greater institutional transformations in Afghanistan to fulfill international expectations for drug control. The UN Food and Agricultural Organization report, released in 1972, advocated a sweeping reform to Afghanistan's antismuggling and antiopium laws to allow the government to easily identify prohibited goods in conjunction with the 1961 Single Convention.[93] The UN proposed a three-year program valued around $2.5 million,[94] with an additional $2 million per year following the initial term. Of the UNFDAC funds, $790,000 would be used for agricultural development, while $255,000 would be used for enforcement.[95] American officials created their own Narcotics Control Action Plan that placed an overwhelming emphasis on enforcement. The United States recommended to the UN a program worth $9.5 million over three years, with the United States paying for $3.5 million, and roughly $654,000 for enforcement every year. The United States believed that the UN had undervalued the role of the gendarmerie and customs police in enforcing narcotics laws, and as a result, required far greater funding for enforcement.[96] Although significant questions about how to implement successful drug control remained, both the United States and the UN realized that enforcement was fruitless without development of the country. Although steps would be taken to bolster enforcement, the changes to legislation and the training of police and gendarmerie would take time. On the other hand, given their preexisting presence in Helmand and other places throughout rural Afghanistan, development assistance could be implemented immediately.[97] As a result, the United States and the UN began to pump money into Afghanistan in an effort to stop the proliferation of drugs in the region.

But in the summer of 1971, Afghanistan was hit by one of the worst droughts in its history. Although pleas were made to the government to provide much needed food, it did not respond until 1972. Thus, when American and UN officials were beginning their antinarcotics mission, the crisis of the Afghan state was deepening. The drought and slow response from the state contributed to a famine that killed thousands and pushed hundreds of thousands more to the brink. While the slow response was maddening enough, reports emerged that much of the food sent to the provinces was being hoarded by local officials and sold to desperate peasants. Other reports noted that most of the food went to the major urban areas, Kabul and Kandahar, and not the regions most affected by drought and famine.[98] Furthermore, student uprisings continued. Much of the unrest centered on the increasing levels of unemployment and a frustration over the increasingly disconnected and ineffectual government. During the 1950s and 1960s, the government employed almost all college graduates, but by the 1970s it could barely pay the workers it already hired. Moreover, the meager wages of government employees fed into the culture of corruption and bribery.[99] Kabul University continued to be a source of intense and sometimes violent political action. On both sides of the political spectrum, radical leftists and extreme Islamists clashed over how to overthrow the political and social order.[100] In the provinces, the drought and suspected corruption of government officials (often favoring one group over another) led to repeated violent clashes between tribal and ethnic groups as well as against the government.[101] Things were so bad that Louis Dupree, then working in the US Embassy, predicted that a coup would inevitably occur within five years of the events of 1971.[102]

Drug Control under Daud

Dupree proved prescient, albeit a little hopeful. In 1973, recognizing that the Afghan government was quickly losing its grasp, Mohammad Daud Khan launched a bloodless coup. Daud broke the traditional political paradigm that the Musahiban dynasty had embraced for nearly forty-five years by allying himself with urban leftists rather than the ulema and tribal authorities. Although Daud had placed himself on the left side of the spectrum with the coup, he initially faced little resistance from the tribal and religious authorities that historically played such an important role in shaping the political culture of the Afghan state. Many within Afghanistan viewed his coup as little more than a family dispute, and in some ways, the royal dynasty (despite its new socialist tint) as infallible.[103]

Daud took power promising to rectify the many problems facing the state, particularly corruption. However, despite his new power base of young and zealous leftists, little seemed to change. In fact, the transfer of power and the surprising lack of resistance to it "demonstrated that Afghan national politics was still the domain of a small elite based in Kabul that had little connection with the rest of the country."[104] But beneath the veil of ineffectual and disconnected government, Daud continued to pursue power for himself. He purged Islamists and Marxists from the government and military, established a one-party system, and bolstered the secret police and military by placing officials loyal to him in key positions. Furthermore, he continued to pursue foreign development aid as a means of meeting the significant challenges facing the country. Daud bolstered relations with Iran, Saudi Arabia, and even Pakistan, and continued to play the Soviet Union and the United States against each other to extract more foreign money.[105]

Daud, ever the strongman, embraced narcotics control as yet another way to bolster foreign aid for development and to bolster the strength of the police and paramilitary units. Initially, however, Daud was quite cold toward American antinarcotic initiatives. US requests for increased enforcement prompted aggressive responses proposing the radical development of Afghanistan. Furthermore, Daud refused to allow the United States or any other NATO country to take a significant role in designing and implementing any of the enforcement or development proposals, essentially confining narcotics control strictly to the UN. Other foreign embassies thought the United States sensationalized the narcotics issue, while some US Embassy officials noted that there was a growing anti-American sentiment floating around Kabul.[106] It is unclear whether Daud genuinely resisted the United States, but it seems likely that he was playing a delicate political game. Daud's second turn in control of the government resulted from the support of the leftist contingent in Kabul. To acquiesce to the United States would certainly create internal conflicts for Daud. Also, Daud had approached the United States before for aid, particularly military aid, and after being refused, turned to the Soviets. I would argue that his resistance to American overtures stemmed from the new political makeup of his power base (leftists) and largest donor and advocate (USSR), combined with lingering resentment against the United States from his previous go around.

By the end of 1973, however, Daud realized that his ambitious plans for his country would not be possible without massive infusions of cash. His government warmed to the United States and reasserted its commitment to improving drug controls. In October, Daud told the US Embassy that he ordered government officials to cooperate fully with US narcotics experts and that the matter of narcotics was "as much or more in Afghan interests than in that of the US." As a result, Daud made significant moves to curb the production and smuggling of opium and hash. The head of the Ministry of Interior, Faiz Mohammad, was put in charge of a new antismuggling unit. Unlike previous such units, which were under the jurisdiction of local police, the new antismuggling units, or ASUs, were given national jurisdiction, charged exclusively with suppressing the drug trade. The ASU was made up of twelve "eager" men, trained by UNFDAC and DEA experts to collect information and intelligence and launch covert sting operations against higher-level traffickers. By all indications, the new ASUs signified a new milestone in the US–Afghan relationship. Some US officials remained skeptical of Daud's intentions, however. Ambassador Theodore Eliot himself worried that Daud was using this as merely another avenue to increase funding for his large-scale development programs.[107]

Recognizing the limitations of Afghanistan's legal structure, the DEA embarked on an effort to improve the operational capacity of the ASUs throughout the country. Apparently, the moral campaign against drugs did not seem to foment the same sense of urgency and zealotry among the ASUs as it did among American narcotics officials. One proposal to improve initiatives among Afghans was to use US money (through the UN) to restructure incentives for informants and lower-level police officers to improve narcotic intelligence and prevent corruption. Both US and UN officials agreed that increasing monetary incentives would provide real motivation for raising the number of arrests.[108] Although the Americans were essentially dangling money in the face of the Afghans, the Afghans continued to resist, particularly at the highest levels. It seemed to US officials that Afghans were increasingly wary of US approaches because they knew it entailed greater

US involvement in internal Afghan affairs. And although the Afghan government continued to pursue antinarcotics controls, it continued to resist committing fully to American guidance on the matter.[109]

By 1975, the joint venture between the DEA/UNFDAC and the Afghan ASU was seemingly producing results, indicated by several large sting operations, one leading to the seizure of one ton of opium.[110] Moreover, the financial incentive program was helping contribute to the recent successes of the ASU, leading to improved morale and initiative.[111] Despite the success of the ASU, the question emerging was how much the enforcement campaign was merely nibbling at the edges of a much larger pie. The increasing prevalence of heroin in drug seizures was indicating that Afghanistan was in fact producing opiates that were moving beyond its regional market in Iran, as Iran was not a major consumer of heroin.[112] Furthermore, most of the enforcement successes occurred close to Kabul, where state control was strong. What worried both Afghan and US officials was not only that trafficking was spreading throughout the country, and virtually unabated in border regions, but also that opium cultivation was spreading. In 1973, the Helmand Valley, the site of the largest agro-industrial project in the country (and funded by the United States), was beginning to produce opium at larger and larger levels. As a result, by the mid-1970s, Afghanistan was emerging as a major supplier of opium for the global drug market. To make matters worse, the political conditions in Afghanistan were reaching a critical mass. For the United States, the hope of stopping narcotics in Afghanistan rested on a state that was quickly losing control over its people.

Conclusion

When Nixon began the crackdown on the consumption and production of drugs, he had hoped to eliminate the role of drugs in fomenting and perpetuating the social and political decay of the United States. Initially, the increased enforcement against the production and trafficking of drugs seemed to be working. By the mid-1970s, interdiction and eradication campaigns virtually eliminated the French Connection, reduced the role of Southeast Asian heroin in the US market, and decimated the Mexican heroin trade. All signs pointed toward a successful future for the war on drugs. However, underneath the veil of triumph loomed a stark reality that had yet to be understood.

Implementing the United States' new militarized supply-side strategy abroad led to a remarkable evolution in the production of drugs, ultimately diversifying the global market by introducing new actors that were better suited for the changing dynamic of the illicit drug trade. The impact of Nixon's War on Drugs cannot be understated.

Analyzing the impact of Nixon's drug war in Afghanistan reveals how American drug control ambitions were subsumed within the deeper political and social struggles of Afghanistan. In a broad policy sense, acquiescence to the American drug war simply meant more money for the government to improve the state's strength and reach. In many ways, this period in Afghan history reinforces the ways war, including a "war on drugs," can aid in the formation and growth of the state.[113] Under Zahir Shah, the state attempted to stop drugs by initiating significant reforms and institutional changes to achieve such goals. But the passing of the 1969 Anti-Smuggling Law, the creation of antismuggling units within the police, and the actual enforcement of the law indicated that the state was embracing more coercive and state-driven forms of drug control. Daud took it even further, embracing Nixon's enforcement-focused "War on Drugs" as a means of strengthening and consolidating his own power over the police and gendarmerie. The creation of the ASUs with national jurisdiction was a major step in transforming the role of the state in regulating its people. However, some important questions emerge about how American ambitions to suppress the global drug supply influenced, and were influenced by, the political dynamics at a more localized level: For what purpose did the Afghan state launch its own war on drugs? And what impact did this have on the relationship between the Afghan government and the Afghan people? In this case, Afghanistan's antinarcotics policy was a continuation of the long-standing American–Afghan narcotics relationship whereby American ambitions for drug control were used by Afghans as a means of enhancing other more pressing social, economic, and political needs or desires, or both.

However, the issues on the ground reinforced the broader political matters facing the Afghan state. The failure of drug control at the lowest level reveals the impact of *qawm* in the state drug control apparatus. This was most obvious at the lowest levels of the Afghan drug control apparatus, particularly the police. The success and failure of drug control ultimately rested on an individual's role within the state in relation to the local community. Thus, the power of the *qawm* was easily apparent in the decisions of both lower-

and upper-level police to pursue or ignore narcotics control initiatives. As Roy notes, for all Afghans working within the state, "the aim is to insert the *qawm* into the state institutions at a level which befits their own importance. The operation is intended not only to produce material benefits, but especially to ensure that the local power game carries on as it has always done."[114] Thus, the majority of policemen, especially those that Americans labeled corrupt, were in fact playing the Afghan political game. Narcotics control was inevitably subject to the whims of a police officer, border patrolman, or gendarmes who had to weigh the impact of a decision on his personal standing within his family, tribe, or community versus the state's demands. Given their low pay and low priority, it is easy to see why most Afghan officials either turned a blind to or lent a helping hand in narcotics dealings.

The enforcement of antismuggling laws also highlights deeper issues concerning people on the frontier and the attempts by the Afghan (and neighboring governments) to restrict mobility. Historically, regional nation-states and foreign powers interpreted the patterns of mobility as a "dangerous source of instability."[115] Many of the communities that traversed these borderlands were defined and shaped by this fluidity, however. In fact, the history of state encapsulation served as a significant source of identity for these peoples.[116] Although the history of cross-border trading would suggest that little had changed over time aside from the regional and global context of what was being traded, the transformation of the trader into a smuggler was ideally suited for the expansion of state power in the periphery of the country. Thus, the drug smuggler became an important piece of the state's narrative for the expansion of power into the periphery and the regulation of mobility.[117]

Ultimately, the biggest impact of Nixon's War on Drugs on Afghanistan was in influencing a massive transformation of the global narcotics trade and Afghanistan's role within it. Although Afghanistan was slowly emerging in the global market by the late 1960s, it could not compete within a market oversaturated with Turkish, Southeast Asian, and Mexican supply. Furthermore, the end of the second heroin epidemic in the early 1970s continued to restrict the consumer base.[118] However, the pressures applied to suppliers in Turkey, Southeast Asia, and Mexico created a demand for a new source of supply, which Afghanistan was ideally suited to fill. It is clear that American officials underestimated the ability of groups involved in the global illicit drug trade to evolve under these given circumstances. Metaphorically, Nixon's War on Drugs was much like the beginning of a game of whack-a-mole, wherein each successive whack produced or revealed another source of supply (a mole), often quicker and better suited to the conditions of the global illicit market and the war waged to fight it. Of course, in whack-a-mole, one uses a club to bash the head of the mole; in this sense, the club ideally resembled a robust and pliable state, and also one closely linked to American diplomatic engagements, neither of which characterize Afghanistan and its relationship to the United States. To take the metaphor further, once the Afghan mole popped its head, the Americans were trying to suppress it, not with a club, but with a small stick. As recent events indicate, the United States is still whacking away, and clearly to no avail.

The extent to which Nixon's drug war influenced changes in Afghanistan's politics is harder to discern. In Turkey, the eradication of the opium crop became a major political issue and helped usher in a new political regime emphasizing the "rights of the people" to grow opium.[119] However, narcotics issues were merely indications of much larger political and social dilemmas facing the Afghan state. Did the increased enforcement of narcotics control contribute to the growth of the drug trade in Afghanistan? To a degree, yes—by elevating the risk of production and trading, thereby increasing the value of the illicit crop. However, this is no different from anywhere else where drugs are illegal and those laws are enforced. The question is not so much about drugs as it is about politics and the extent to which more aggressive narcotics control strategies contribute to the declining legitimacy of the state. There is no concrete answer to this question. The implementation of narcotics policy was not sincere by any means, and the use of foreign money for development was not intended to build a cohesive national entity. On the contrary, the state's ambitions to build up infrastructure seem to be self-serving. As Roy notes, "the state itself seems to have no other goal than that of perpetuating itself."[120] Thus, it is hard to view Afghan narcotics policy as being genuinely about protecting its citizens or building a prosperous nation; rather, the policy seemed oriented around using the global concern over narcotics control to enhance and secure the state's standing to benefit the lives of a small, elite group of Afghans.

This state design, which had existed for the better part of five decades, was crumbling by the mid-1970s. State control was weakening, particularly in places well outside the state's stronghold for power, Kabul. In some places, such as the Helmand Valley, the state's waning legitimacy was transforming people's role in the global arena more directly. In particular, changes to the global market for illicit drugs were leading many farmers, landowners, and traders to convert to opium production and transportation on a large scale. As a result, the increasing demand for Afghan opium on the global market and the declining strength of the state, particularly in relation to its ability to enforce smuggling laws or increase agro-industrial development, converged to transform the Helmand Valley. And unlike the rest of the country, the Helmand's role as the breadbasket of Afghanistan, as well as the major site of American led agro-industrial development, coalesced in the mid-1970s to lay the foundation for what would inevitably become the largest producer of opium in the world and a shining example of the failures of nation building, narcotics control, and American diplomacy with Afghanistan.

Chapter 6

All Goods Are Dangerous Goods

Development, the Global Market, and Opium in the Helmand Valley, Afghanistan

If Helmand were a country, it would once again be the world's biggest producer of illicit drugs.

Following the attacks on the United States on September 11, 2001, and the United States' subsequent invasion of Afghanistan, opium has become synonymous with the conflict in Afghanistan. Helmand Province, in particular, has come to symbolize the role of opium as both a cause and consequence of the failures of the Afghan state. Helmand Province is by far the largest producer of opium in the world. In 2007, a year during which it was estimated that Afghanistan produced a record high of roughly 8,200 metric tons of opium,[1] Helmand Province itself produced an estimated 5,397 metric tons, nearly 66 percent of the total national crop, making it the largest source of opium in the world.[2] Underlying the contemporary situation in Helmand is that from 1946 to the Soviet invasion in 1979, the Helmand Valley was a cornerstone of US–Afghan engagement, particularly through the large-scale agro-industrial project, known as the Helmand Valley Development Project (HVDP). By building dams and irrigation canals to improve agricultural output, the United States hoped to bolster the market-based agricultural economy. Economic development of the agricultural sector was a key component of US diplomatic engagement with Afghanistan throughout the Cold War.

But the corresponding relationship between the Helmand Valley's history as a site of US–Afghan economic development and its latter role as a massive producer of illicit opium begs the question, how and in what ways they are related? The hazy historical picture of Helmand stems partially from the broader historiographical issues that motivate this study: mainly that the Helmand Valley, like the rest of the country, emerged as the major producer of narcotics primarily because of the Afghan-Soviet War of 1979–1989.[3] Although the war was an important catalyst in expanding the opium trade, it only explains *why it expanded*, not *why and how opium began* in the Helmand Valley. Given the role opium plays in Helmand today, there are many unanswered questions. Why, despite the hundreds of millions of dollars spent in the region, did farmers and traders turn to opium? Was it purely because of economic necessity? Or did social, cultural, and political factors influence the changing economic dynamics of the region?

The exploration of Helmand's history sheds light not only on the relationship between the project and the illicit drug trade but also on broader questions regarding the relationship between licit and illicit economies. As Itty Abraham and Willem van Schendel note, the distinctions between illegal and legal markets are far more complicated when they play out on the ground. Often, the state's claims to regulate certain goods as legitimate or legal, do not correspond with how certain people view such goods and the corresponding trade. In other words, what the state defines as "illegal" may very well be viewed as "quite acceptable, 'licit,' in the eyes of the participants in these transactions and flows."[4] The history of Helmand and the intersection of the US-led economic development program with the emergence of the illicit drug trade shed light on this complicated historical process. Questions emerge as to how and in what ways farmers and traders in Helmand responded to the changing conditions of the global market. And how did the illicit drug trade fit into or respond to those conditions? The analysis here reveals that the increasing entanglement of the rural development project and the illicit drug trade forced both the Afghan and US governments to respond in different ways, straining an increasingly difficult diplomatic relationship.

For Afghanistan, the evolution of the Helmand Valley from state development project to burgeoning producer of illicit opium reveals how rural development, as well as drug control, both became vital components of the state's attempt to become legible in the rural Afghan landscape.[5] The analysis of the Helmand furthers our understanding of how economic development was increasingly tied to security concerns about the production of illicit opium. In particular, this chapter explores how international donors, such as the United States, and donor recipients, in this case Afghanistan, balanced the objectives of economic development with drug control, the Cold War, and political legitimacy. This, of course, raises questions about how drug control and economic development can often serve similar purposes in justifying the expansion of state power into areas that have historically been resistant or posed challenges to state intercession.[6]

The emergence of illicit opium in the Helmand also sheds light on how American ambitions for global drug control influenced Afghanistan, ultimately becoming an integral piece of the Helmand narrative. As a development project driven by American modernization theory,[7] building roads, dams, irrigation, and canals was an integral element of the government's visibility in the Helmand Valley. But as the development project showed signs of failure and illicit drug cultivation grew, drug policy, particularly the eradications of opium cultivation and prohibitions on opium trading reflected the state's new attempts to penetrate and regulate the lives of rural Afghans. Both were heavily influenced by American ambitions to bolster capitalism, while simultaneously, if not paradoxically, trying to stop the cultivation and trade of opium. As this chapter will reveal, by the early 1970s the Helmand development project had actually led to increased yields and revenues for some Helmand farmers. Yet the illicit market for opium also emerged. Why?

Part of the answer stems from the economic primacy of opium over other agricultural goods. By the early 1970s, despite widespread political discontent, the introduction of high-yield wheat and cash crops resulted in a strengthening market-based agricultural economy. In other words, the Helmand did feel the effects of economic development. The creation of roads, dams, and highways, as well as more advanced farming techniques, integrated the Helmand economy with surrounding provinces and countries. The relative success of the Helmand agricultural economy did not result in a boost for the government's claim to legitimacy, however. Instead, economic development and agricultural output seemed to improve as the state's legitimacy waned. It is this paradox that highlights the emergence of opium as a historical phenomenon.

This is the part of the story I wish to emphasize. Although the development project showed promising returns during the early 1970s, Helmand was not isolated from the broader political and economic environment in Afghanistan. In one way, the state's failure to legitimize its rule throughout the country, evidenced by the increasing political chaos of the 1970s, especially the coup in 1973, influenced farmers and traders in Helmand. Conversely, the HVDP also served to delegitimize the state, especially in Helmand. The project itself was littered with issues of corruption, inefficiency, and ethnic and political strife, and was emblematic of the broader issues surrounding the Afghan government. More important, these issues served to delegitimize the state within Helmand. The destabilizing political and economic forces of the early 1970s in Afghanistan, and Helmand, coincided with profound changes in the illicit global drug trade; as Helmand faltered, the webs of the global narcotics economy finally reached Afghanistan in force. In this way, the history of the Helmand Valley development project becomes subsumed within the broader history of the global drug trade. Capitalism succeeded in Helmand, just not in the way the United States or the Afghans expected.

The history of illicit opium in Helmand also deepens our understanding of how the diplomatic relations between the United States and Afghanistan evolved from a focus on economic development to one of counternarcotics. The discovery of opium in the Helmand Valley, especially within the USAID (US Agency for International Development) project area, strained US–Afghan relations, and forced the Afghan government to adopt more stringent American-style counternarcotics policies. For the Afghan government, the discovery of opium in the Helmand Valley had the potential to undermine its relationship with the United States and threaten the project itself. The success of the Helmand Valley project, which Afghan officials viewed as an "unfinished symphony,"[8] depended entirely on the United States continuing to finance the project. As a result, Prime Minister Daud launched an eradication and prohibition campaign to stop the opium trade and maintain a steady flow of US aid. The prohibition was seemingly successful, as most farmers stopped producing opium. The United States, content with Daud's persistent antiopium policy, decided to continue to finance the project. Illicit opium production resumed in 1975, however, and by the end of the decade, the Helmand Valley had become one of the largest producers of opium in the country.

The obvious question emerges: Why, despite the ban on opium by the Daud government, did the opium trade continue to flourish in Helmand? The answer lies partially in a more nuanced understanding of how prohibitions function within the deeper political and economic relations between the state and its peoples. In this case, the temporary success of prohibition stemmed primarily from farmers' understanding of global markets, especially their recognition of how eradication of the crop could provide beneficial pricing in the following years. Opium emerged in the valley because local farmers, traders, and khans could no longer trust the Afghan (and by extension, the US) government to guide, effectively and efficiently, the economic transformation of the valley. In response, individual and group actors embraced opium, which by the mid-1970s was proving increasingly lucrative, despite the coercive prohibition policies of the Afghan government. In other words, as the market evolved to make opium more viable, a ban on opium only served to delegitimize the state.

The opium ban reinforced the political, economic, and social disconnect between the Afghan state and rural society. The new Republic of Afghanistan established by Daud after the coup in 1973 was increasingly leftist in makeup, and no longer representative of rural Afghanistan. Thus, when the webs of the global drug market reached the Helmand Valley and the state attempted to prohibit production and trade, it was stymied because it could not eradicate opium while also offering viable alternative sources of income without further risking its legitimacy. More important, the decision to continue to cultivate and trade opium contrary to state policy reinforced the power of the *qawm* and the priorities of local communities, tribes, and groups vis-à-vis the increasingly disconnected state. In this way, the emergence of opium in the Helmand Valley should be perceived not simply as a failure of the development project and prohibition policies of the Afghan government, but also as an indicator of the emerging role of opium in preserving the strength of individual and local communities, in this case the *qawm*, as the primary social and political unit in rural Afghanistan.

Ultimately, this complex interplay between global and regional economies, and international, national, and local political forces, provides unique insight into the emergence of the Helmand Valley as a global epicenter of illicit opium production and trade. In sum, illicit opium's emergence in the valley comes from market forces, diplomatic entanglements, and dysfunctional state–society relations. But there is also great irony in the story of the Helmand

Valley. At one moment in time, it represented the hopes of two nations. But in the end, it served only to symbolize the failure of the Afghan state, the failures of American diplomacy, and the power of the global illicit drugs market.

A Brief History of the Helmand Valley

When the noted Afghan American author Tamim Ansary was a young boy he and his family moved from Kabul to Lashkar Gah in Helmand Province in southwest Afghanistan. Lashkar Gah was unlike any other town or village in the country. Although hundreds of miles from urban Kabul and thousands of miles from the United States, it was a veritable oasis of modernity in an area otherwise seemingly untouched by the hands of change. Established by the Helmand Valley Authority (HVA), Lashkar Gah housed the American workers and their families dispatched to Helmand to build dams, canals, and schools. But as Ansary puts it, "the HVA's mission was not just to build dams but to impose Western progress on the Afghan people."[9] As one might guess, building modernity in the Helmand Valley was not without problems. More important, the myriad of problems that plagued the Helmand Valley development project reflected the deeper economic, social, and political schisms at the heart of constructing the modern Afghan state.

Helmand Province is the largest in Afghanistan, making up roughly 10 percent of its territory. The province contains rocky foothills in the north and gradually descends into clay and sand desert in the south. The capital, Lashkar Gah, and Girishk are the two largest cities/towns, although most of the estimated four hundred thousand inhabitants of the province live in rural areas.[10] Not far from the modern tenements of Lashkar Gah lies the ancient fortress of Qala Bist, where the Helmand and Arghandab Rivers meet. The Helmand River is the largest in Afghanistan and the most important geographic feature in the valley. It flows roughly six hundred miles from its source in the Hindu Kush, near Kabul, southwest into the Sistan Basin near the border with Iran. For centuries, inhabitants of southwest Afghanistan and southeastern Iran built canals, villages, and towns in an effort to harness the power of the river to make the desert bloom. In more recent times, the Afghan government, with foreign assistance, tried to exploit the power of the Helmand. In 1910, Habibullah built the first functional canal, and before World War II both the Germans and the Japanese lent technical assistance.[11] Not until after World War II, when the United States emerged as a key player in the development of Afghanistan, did the Helmand Valley begin the transformation to its more recognizable contemporary form.

The role of the United States in developing the Afghan state was fundamental to the design of the Musahiban dynasty. When Nadir Shah established the dynasty in 1929, he created a system in which state revenue was increasingly supplied by indirect taxation of foreign trade and customs.[12] The government's aim was to decrease its dependence on land taxes from the rural population, allowing it to continue its policy of gradual modernization while minimizing the risk of rural revolt.[13] As a result, foreign trade became fundamental to state expansion. Although the United States had diplomatic relations with Afghanistan before World War II, particularly involving the trade of opium, significant and formal engagement did not begin until the conclusion of the war. The war had eliminated the significant donors, Britain, Germany, and Japan, from Afghanistan, crippling the economy, and forcing Prime Ministers Hashim Khan and Shah Mahmud to reassess Afghanistan's engagement with the world. As a result, the United States emerged as the clear choice to fill the financial void.[14] In 1945, the Afghan government began negotiations with the Morrison-Knudsen Company, based in San Francisco and famous for building the Boulder (later Hoover) Dam and the Golden Gate Bridge. Unlike other projects throughout the country, the Afghans intended to use American money and knowledge to construct an important symbol of Afghanistan's future: a dam.

Throughout the world, dams in the mid-twentieth century were important symbols of progress, power, and modernity. In the United States, the Hoover Dam was a daunting representation of federal power carved into the American landscape. In India, Jawarhul Nehru envisioned dams as the temples of modern India. More important, dams were symbols of the power and reach of the modern state. As historian Nick Cullather states, "a dam project allows, even requires, a state to appropriate and redistribute land, plan factories and economies, tell people what to make and what to grow." For Afghanistan, reconstructing the Helmand Valley by building dams allowed it to not only project its emerging power in the rural countryside,[15] but further solidify its nascent diplomatic relationship with the United States.

Although building a dam in the Helmand Valley symbolized the state's power, it took on the characteristics of the political culture of the Musahiban state. Since its inception, the Musahiban dynasty designed and implemented policies recognizing that most rural tribal groups in Afghanistan, particularly the large Pashtun tribal majority, were directly opposed to economic and social modernization. As a result, a cultural policy was established to ensure Pashtun support of the new government. The Afghan government's social and economic policies combined gradual modernization with overt favoritism toward Pashtuns. The idea was simple: by assuring the allegiance of the largest and most important tribal group, the state would have unrivalled control of the country.[16] This cultural policy inevitably reinforced economic policy.[17] Although the Helmand Valley project was an enormous undertaking, certain to transform the region radically, the southern Pashtuns in the government wanted investment in the area.[18] Thus, justification for choosing the Helmand Valley stemmed from the government's hope that successfully modernizing Helmand would result in stronger state control in the region, and greater access to and control of the country's most important, albeit most threatening, demographic.[19] In other words, the project could ensure Pashtun primacy while simultaneously establishing greater state control in the region.[20]

For the United States, building dams was an important part of foreign policy during the Cold War. In an attempt to reshape the United States' role in the postcolonial world, it sought to ground itself in a new dialectic of developed/underdeveloped, rather than perpetuating the historically loaded colonizer/colonized. In particular, Western technological advancements became the focal point of the new development paradigm, and as a result, the United States began its new engagement with the world by building roads, dams, schools, airports, etc. American scholars and policymakers believed that technology would lead not only to the establishment of capitalist markets abroad but also to changes in behavior and thought, inevitably Westernizing foreign cultures.[21] This cultural transformation would not only strengthen the position of the United States abroad but would help counteract Soviet expansion. Advocates of modernization theory perceived American modernity to be the only tool for confronting Soviet influence abroad.[22] Thus, building modern capitalist economies was both financially and politically important. This took on an entirely new meaning in Afghanistan; the presence of both the the United States and the USSR in an environment of "competitive co-existence" was seen by both as a way to keep Afghanistan free and independent, as well as to deter each other from further expansion into Central Asia.[23]

Although this form of American-led modernization began to take root throughout the world at the onset of the Cold War, it often failed to generate the political impact Americans had hoped. Many world leaders of recently decolonized nations viewed modernization and economic development as the primary means of alleviating the significant inequities remaining from the colonial era. However, they did not see using American money and resources as a sign of political acquiescence in the Cold War. In India, for instance, Nehru was keen to use American money to finance the country's rapid industrialization, but he steadfastly maintained his neutrality in the Cold War.[24] Afghanistan followed a similar path. Despite Musahiban leaders' willingness to use American money to transform Helmand, they never relinquished their neutrality.

The Afghan government first approached Morrison-Knudsen in 1945, and after a series of preliminary surveys, signed a $17 million contract a year later.[25] Over the next few years, Morrison-Knudsen Afghanistan, Inc. (MKA) began building two dams, a highway, a power facility, and an extensive canal system, and trained technicians, to a cost of $63.7 million.[26] The project was beset with problems from the beginning, due in part to preexisting conditions. For example, much of the economy centered on the peasant and pastoral economy, and although it provided 90 percent of the labor in Helmand, crop yields rarely exceeded subsistence levels.[27] Furthermore, the massive scope of the project quickly exposed the difficult realities facing both the MKA and the Afghan government, such as the small dam at the mouth of the Boghra Canal that raised water levels too high, inevitably producing increased salt levels in the reservoir.[28] The early onset problems, such as those arising from the Boghra Dam, proved stressful for the Afghan government and the MKA. To save foreign exchange, the Afghans took over some of the more critical aspects of the project (e.g., constructing feeders and ditches to drain canals) and convinced MKA not to conduct vital surveys of soil and groundwater in the area. Both later proved to be critical errors.[29]

By 1949, costs skyrocketed. For MKA, the price of shipping to a landlocked country halfway around the world, through hostile Pakistan, proved costly. Afghanistan, on the other hand, saw its foreign exchange surplus dwindle because of the project. In 1949, after asking for a $55 million loan, Afghanistan received a $21 million loan from the Export-Import Bank. Despite the increase in funding, both MKA and the Afghans were forced to cut various minor projects to complete the more significant features of the project. Eventually, construction delays and rising costs led the Afghan government to hand over its own engineering projects to MKA. More important, the need for unification resulted in the creation of the Helmand Valley Authority (HVA),[30] now responsible for implementing the entire project.[31]

Reorganizing the project under HAVA led to completing the 200-foot-high Arghandab and the 320-foot-high Kajakai Dams. Although the completion of these large dams signified progress, much remained to be done. An extensive system of drains and canals had to be created, and maintenance had to be performed. Furthermore, acquiring land and the subsequent displacement of people failed to result in more land being farmed. Squabbles over land ownership were never resolved, and most of the land remained in the hands of farmers already affiliated with HAVA, not new ones as had been hoped.[32]

By 1953, HAVA had morphed into a project of unprecedented proportions. It was responsible not only for development but also for building schools, housing, hospitals, and infrastructure. The seemingly endless array of problems created numerous critics. Both the UN and the Afghan minister of national economy, Abdul Majod Zabuli, criticized the project for not being economically viable, focusing too much on large-scale investments with slow returns, and lacking culturally nuanced ancillary development.[33] Either to save face or to take greater control of implementing the project, in 1953 the Technical Cooperation Administration (TCA) of the US government took responsibility for completing the project. As a result, the failure or success of the Helmand Valley project rested "fairly or unfairly" on the joint venture of the Afghan and American governments.[34]

When Mohammad Daud Khan took power in 1953, he wanted to accelerate the development of Afghanistan. Facing a reluctant United States, Daud turned to the Soviets as the primary source of aid. The Soviets first gave a $3.5 million loan in 1953, but after a visit to Kabul by Nikita Khrushchev, opened a $100 million line of credit.[35] Daud claimed that the turn to the Soviets was an effort to restore Afghan neutrality, or *bi-tarafi*. However, he was certainly influenced by the conflict surrounding the Helmand project and broader disdain for US support of Pakistan.[36] Daud's frustration over the Helmand project was warranted. Rumors persisted of corruption and mismanagement within HAVA and bribes to MKA officials as well.[37] The United States, on the other hand, recognized the importance of Helmand to maintain good relations with Afghanistan, as well as to prevent a Soviet diplomatic victory.[38] Daud, of all the players involved, seemed victorious; he could continue with the project, maintain a balance between the Cold War powers, but also use both to reinforce Pashtun hegemony.[39]

Although the HAVA had an indirect impact on the politics in Afghanistan, more important was that it directly affected the lives of Afghans in the region. The reclamation and redistribution of land fundamentally altered the tribal and ethnic divisions that had defined much of the country. Daud resettled small groups of ethnic minorities in the valley, especially in Shamalan, so that the towns of Nad-i-Ali and Marja were essentially made up of the resettled nomadic Ghilzai Pashtuns. The impact of land reform was widespread. Between 1953 and 1973, nearly five thousand families immigrated to the province.[40] But land reform also cut across ethnic and tribal lines. As Louis Dupree put it, "old villagers," farmers who had lived for centuries along the river, now had to contend with "new villagers," resettled nomads.[41] Anyone who wanted to farm the land had to apply to the HAVA (including those that had lived there for generations), and after security screenings, they were housed in constructed communities, given a pair of oxen, two thousand Afghanis, and a year's supply of seed.[42]

For the Ghilzai, who for centuries had migrated between Afghanistan and Pakistan, the Helmand project resettlement program was particularly infuriating. The Ghilzai were not only wealthier and freer than the farmers but they were now being forced to cohabitate with minorities, most of whom they viewed with particular scorn.[43] For the state, however, the risk was worth the reward. Resettlement allowed the state to bring nomads under some semblance of control. This was important politically, because nomads, especially Ghilzai, were prone to resisting state programs. Moreover, gaining favor among the Pashtuns allowed the state to "crush the uprisings of the non-Pashtun people" and further its underlying aim of perpetuating Pashtun hegemony.[44] Nonetheless, for all Afghans displaced by the project, the experience of resettlement was disturbing at best. By the 1960s, many of the original participants had either moved outside the project area or to other parts of the country altogether.[45]

The project also proved to be a considerable source of conflict between the Afghan and American governments. In 1959, the Afghan government terminated its contract with MKA. Throughout the early 1960s, the Helmand Valley continued to fail to meet expectations, particularly because of problems with water logging and salinization.[46] With American credibility at stake, both the Kennedy and Johnson administrations renewed their commitments to the project, increasing the annual pledge from $16 million to $40 million. Through increased money and reorganization under USAID, along with new techniques accompanying the "green revolution," HAVA seemed to stabilize.[47] As Giustozzi and Kalinovsky note, "the political significance of it was too great for the Afghan modernizers and for the US cold warriors" to abandon Helmand.[48]

Many USAID officials remained skeptical of the program's future. Water runoff and drainage remained a constant problem within the project area. More important, embassy officials worried that the scope of the project was simply too large. Finishing the project too quickly would certainly lead to the failure of the program in the long term and could ultimately damage US–Afghan relations. On the other hand, the Afghan government faced increasing internal pressure to finish development programs as soon as possible.[49] Taking the time to ensure that the various development programs would be sustainable in the long term was not politically expedient for the Afghan government, particularly in the mid-1960s, when frustration with the government's ineffective development programs became a growing source of conflict.[50] In short, some US officials believed the project itself was doomed to fail.

In 1965, both the United States and the Afghans perceived the project to be at a critical juncture. In a meeting with Prime Minister Yusuf, Ambassador John Steeves set forth a new project proposal. Yusuf was disappointed and frustrated by the proposal, remarking that the scheme was "more of the same thing." He emphasized that his government was fully prepared to "pour in all the men and monies necessary to accomplish the job."[51] Feeling pressure from the Afghans to make the project fully operational in the quickest time possible while also ensuring that the project would be effective in the long run, USAID concluded that the best course of action was to remove the farmers, level the land, and redistribute land in larger plots. When HVA tried to implement the new policy, however, USAID tractors were confronted by farmers with rifles. Throughout the last half of the 1960s, USAID officials spent most of their time navigating the increasing resistance to HAVA from the farmers.[52] By the end of the 1960s, the Helmand Valley project had yet to meet its lofty expectations.

Resistance to HAVA projects was suggestive of the broader political conflict over the role of the state in the development of Afghanistan. By the early 1970s, the democracy movement continued to generate protests against the corruption, mismanagement, and overt chauvinism within the government. These problems were amplified by the drought in 1971 and 1972, and the famine that followed. The Helmand Valley project struggled as the drought destroyed most crops because the Helmand River and Arghandab Reservoir virtually evaporated.[53] Meanwhile, détente led both the United States and the Soviets to decrease aid to Afghanistan in 1970. When Daud launched his coup in 1973, the future of the Helmand Valley project and of Afghanistan remained very much in doubt.

The Global Market and the Helmand Valley: HAVA in the Early 1970s

Part of the impetus for Daud to launch a coup in July 1973 (beyond a pure power grab) was his desire to accelerate the modernization of Afghanistan. In 1959, when Daud was prime minister, he remarked that "Afghanistan is a backward country" and that he would do everything in his power to modernize the country.[54] But by 1973, much had changed. Resistance to the government was growing because of the rampant corruption and mismanagement within the state bureaucracy. To achieve his goal of modernizing Afghanistan, Daud had to break from the established foundations of Musahiban power. Rather than seek the customary support of the ulema and rural tribes, Daud allied himself with the urban leftists who had played such an important role in vocalizing popular discontent against the corruption and incompetence of the government.[55] More important, Daud identified corruption as a major impediment to modernization. In his first address to the nation, he stated that the government and "system became so corrupt that no hope for its reform existed. Consequently all patriots decided to put an end to this rotten system."[56]

As much as Daud portrayed himself as somehow different from the monarchy and King Zahir Shah, however, many of the core characteristics of the Mushiban state remained. In particular, the government continued to rely on foreign aid as a foundation of state revenue. The oil boom in 1973 increased Daud's access to foreign money, evidenced by the new relationship with the shah of Iran that in principle would have provided Afghanistan with

$2 billion for development.[57] On the outside, Afghanistan's economic situation under Daud seemed to improve dramatically.[58] However, the reliance on foreign aid and grants to grow the Afghan economy and strengthen the state negated any motivation Daud's government had to be responsive and accountable to the Afghan people.[59] As a result, Daud's state grew, but his ties to the people did not. More important, the combination of economic growth and sociopolitical fragmentation led to a vivid transformation in the Helmand Valley.

The Helmand Valley project remained an important component of Daud's engagement with the United States. As noted earlier, Helmand was an "unfinished symphony."[60] However, initial discussions between the United States and Afghanistan centered on dealing with the rampant corruption and mismanagement that had come to characterize the project. The United States, fearing the project was lost and concerned with Daud's new alliance with leftists, contemplated ending its involvement altogether. During Ambassador Theodore Eliot's meeting with the new Helmand governor and president of the HAVA, Fazil Rabi Pazhwak, both sides seemed to see Daud's coup as an opportunity to rectify the failures of the project under the monarchy. However, underlying the diplomatic platitudes was a seething frustration over the handling of the project. Governor Pazhwak believed that the United States had been complicit in contributing to corruption and mismanagement of the project. In particular, Pazhwak noted that there was a discernable difference between the development of Lashkar Gah and the surrounding villages, something that local residents were keenly aware of as well.[61] Pazhwak's concern was well founded. Lashkar Gah stood as a shining example of the impact of the state development program in rural Afghanistan. For the Americans and Afghans who worked as engineers and administrators, life was similar to that of suburban America, with wide streets and modern housing. As historian Arnold Toynbee wrote, the Helmand Valley "ceased to be a part of traditional Afghanistan. It has become a piece of America inserted into the Afghan landscape."[62]

For the farmers and villagers outside of the project area, Lashkar Gah was not a beacon of modernity but rather a somber token of the disconnect between the state and people and of the corruption that underlay it. US officials noted that the general sentiment among farmers regarding the project was "depressing," despite the relatively good agricultural output.[63]

Much of this frustration stemmed from the obvious corruption. For political and practical reasons, both the United States and Afghans endeavored to fix the problem.[64] Daud removed scores of HAVA administrators and engineers, including the heads of six departments. Furthermore, rumors circulated that many of the department heads would be put on trial for criminal prosecution.[65] Although removing these administrators slowed the progress of the project, the changes were needed. By 1974, the United States, despite opposition from USAID,[66] agreed to continue funding the project.

Building a Market-Based Economy in the Helmand Valley

Although the political aspects of HAVA proved divisive among local Afghans, by the early 1970s the project was finally producing agricultural dividends. This success stemmed primarily from the introduction of high-yield varieties of wheat and cash crops. In the past, farmers in Helmand grew corn, wheat, and various fruits, mainly at the subsistence level. However, the introduction of varieties of high-yield wheat and cotton provided them with incentives to utilize American technology and resources to grow crops beyond the subsistence level, creating a market-based agricultural economy. From 1970 to 1975, land devoted to growing high-yield wheat increased from 6 percent of total cropland to nearly 44 percent. The increase planting of high-yield wheat, which required chemical fertilizer and irrigation (ideal for farmers in or near the project), decreased the total area farmers needed to devote to wheat to meet subsistence levels, allowing farmers to grow cash crops to increase personal income.[67]

Cotton emerged as one of the major cash crops.[68] First introduced by the British in the mid-1960s, cotton was initially an unpopular crop because cotton prices remained low and the government took a substantial share of the profits. But in the early 1970s, USAID worked with various Afghan tractor owners to "ridge and row-plant cotton and increase production."[69] After the coup in 1973, the government began to pay more for cotton and also offered a credit system for fertilizer.[70] Moreover, the global demand for cotton prompted the government to offer greater incentives for farmers who sold the cotton to government-run processing plants.[71] By 1975, nearly 29 percent of total cropland was devoted to cotton (up from 5 percent in 1970), much of it devoted to double cropping of cotton.[72]

When farmers expanded output of wheat and cash crops, substantial problems arose. Growing high-yield wheat and cotton created depleted soil fertility. The solution was to use more chemical fertilizer, which in turn increased farmer's costs.[73] Increased labor costs drove farmers to expand the cultivation of cash crops.[74] Although during the early 1970s incomes increased significantly throughout the project area, the increased costs of operating these farms often offset their greater revenues.

Aside from the economic problems, there were significant social and political ramifications from the project as well. New farmers suffered the most from the problems with the project; they overwhelmingly experienced the problems with soil quality, especially increased salinity, sodicity, and drainage problems.[75] Moreover, the government program of settling heterogeneous groups led to social and political disputes over the allocation of land and resources. In particular, the disparity between new and old farmers often fell along tribal and familial lines, as most of the new farmers were not Pashtuns. Most new farmers also had smaller plots of land and less access to loans and government resources. As a result, new farmers were not only economically marginalized by the environmental impact of new forms of agriculture but also politically marginalized by the overwhelming prominence of well-connected Pashtuns within HAVA and the project itself.[76]

The overarching effect of introducing varieties of high-yield wheat and the expansion of cash cropping was a profound shift in the agricultural practices of the valley. This shift was not just rooted in technological improvements or changes in cultivation methods, however. Rather, farmers became more astute at understanding the global market and adapting their land to grow crops to maximize their profits. A USAID survey conducted in 1973 asked farmers, "How do you think you as a farmer can do better and make more money from your farm?" Farmers answered that they could get a tractor or increase fertilizer, or both. This, of course, implied that they needed some connection to the government-run project. But more important, farmers also answered that they could "watch the market and plant the most profit making combination of crops." USAID officials noted that farmers had become more adept at understanding how various combinations of crops could result in increased profits.[77] The increase in double cropping during the early 1970s, from 9 percent in 1970 to 23 percent in 1975, substantiates the incredible impact of the market-based agricultural economy on the farmers of the Helmand Valley. This was important for Afghanistan as well,

Figure 6.1. A Helmand farmer scratching the heads of poppies during harvest. (Owens and Clifton, *Poppies in Afghanistan*, 1972)

as Helmand made up nearly 20 percent of the total agricultural land in the country.[78]

The farmers' answers lead to an important point about the future of opium in Helmand. For farmers to have access to tractors and fertilizer, they had to participate in HAVA, which many did not. Knowledge of the global market was not confined to the project area, however. As a result, the dissemination of knowledge by farmers regarding the global market, particularly the profit maximization of cash crops, had an unforeseen consequence. As the market for cotton and wheat grew, so too did the global demand for illicit opium. The knowledge gained by farmers and traders to double-crop wheat and cotton for the global market was also beneficial to other goods, including opium. As figures 6.1 and 6.2 indicate below, opium was emerging as a larger piece of the Helmand economy and was possibly aided by the development project itself.

Figure 6.2. A poppy field near the Qala Bist in Helmand. (Owens and Clifton, *Poppies in Afghanistan*, 1972)

Opium Blossoms

Before the 1970s, the majority of Afghan farmers grew opium for individual needs or as a minor source of income, but it was not a significant cash crop. By the early 1970s, however, opium transformed into an important cash crop for farmers and traders in Helmand, as well as in other parts of the country. Markets dedicated exclusively to opium emerged in Herat and Kandahar in 1970, although they remained small compared with the markets at the end of the decade.

For farmers involved in the Helmand project or those who were in close in proximity, planting poppies fit well into the double-cropping schemes that had become a foundation of the Helmand project. Farmers would plant poppy seeds in the fall and harvest in the spring, and then plant cotton or vegetables and harvest them in the fall. Wheat, which was the most prevalent crop, was planted in the fall and harvested in the summer. As a result, poppies were often grown with corn, not wheat, because wheat and poppies competed for seasons and water.[79]

Initially, poppy prices remained low, ranging anywhere from 1,400 to 3,600 afghanis per kilogram depending on the quality. Part of the explanation for the low prices was that Helmand opium was still relatively low in demand, indicative of its relatively limited connections to the global market. The primary market for Afghan opium was still Iran. But even by the 1970s, Helmand opium faced stiff competition in a limited market. The shah of Iran restarted domestic opium production in 1969, Turkey produced significant amounts until 1972, Pakistan was also a major producer, and other areas of the country, particularly Badakhshan, continued to produce opium. Furthermore, many poppy farmers sold their opium short, meaning they agreed to accept payments before harvest, selling for a much lower price.[80] Revenues for farmers were also hampered by the high costs of labor and bribes. In fact, bribes often constituted the largest cost for poppy farmers and seemed to be the main impediment to devoting more land to the poppy.[81] As a result, until 1972 the cost of growing poppies seemed too high to be a profitable business.

In 1973, however, something changed. Opium production in the Helmand Valley went from being a limited crop with high costs and relatively low returns to one of growing financial importance that threatened to undermine the Helmand Valley project itself. In May, Bernard Weinraub of the *New York Times* reported: "Afghan farmers are harvesting a bumper crop of opium poppies on newly irrigated land that has been developed with foreign aid. American officials are furious and embarrassed because the land was developed by the aid mission here to spur food production. Instead, farmers have grown opium because of the fast and easy profits."[82] Weinraub's article sent shock waves through the American diplomatic establishment. DEA, State Department, and USAID officials all feared that Weinraub had uncovered a political catastrophe; Americans becoming addicted to opium grown on fields that had been leveled, irrigated, and perfected using American technology, know-how, and money.

In July, the State Department cable entitled "Poppies in Helmand Valley" confirmed fears that poppy cultivation had indeed emerged in the Helmand Valley.[83] It is interestingly to note that the cable, as a half policy, half intelligence brief, aimed to refute his claims by revealing the extent of poppy cultivation in Helmand while simultaneously establishing the official US posture on the issue. US officials quickly contextualized the opium problem in

Helmand as a nationwide issue and not "a Helmand problem," and more important, did not want policymakers to see it as "a problem to be approached with a panic mentality."[84] State Department officials remarked, "the observation of extensive cultivation of illicit opium on project lands in the Helmand Valley is erroneous." They noted that when Weinraub went to the Helmand Valley to research his article, "opium poppies were in full bloom in one, repeat one, field," and he photographed that one field. More important, the farmer had been working with the USAID and Peace Corps and was likely to lose US financial assistance.[85]

Although the revelation that opium was being produced had major policy ramifications, within USAID conflicts arose over why and how the problem emerged. Some AID officials only understood the opium problem as a problem of poverty and basic economics. They believed that poor farmers were enticed by the lucrative crop and that the improvements in the project area would allow farmers to "resist the extraordinary economic incentives" to grow opium. However, others understood the cultural and political nuances that underscored opium production. They countered that the very notion of resistance was tied to American perceptions of opium as an evil, whereas one official noted, "farmers don't think like that, they don't 'resist' poppy growing because we think it is evil."[86] Moreover, the effect of USAID assistance went far beyond the project area. It was impossible for the "US to completely close off supply of new technology to offending farmers since they can learn from their neighbors."[87] Efforts to withhold technology or information would be counterintuitive, panicky even. Instead, USAID needed to influence Afghan policymakers and administrators to make decisions that would curtail poppy production.[88] In essence, US officials hoped that the Afghan government could exert greater political influence in the area. This was easier said than done.

So was Weinraub right? Or was he merely being sensationalist? The truth was that opium did exist in the Helmand project area, yet it remained a small percentage of the total area devoted to opium in the region. Officials noted that "its obvious manifestations" were outside the project area supported by USAID, around 10 to 15 percent of the total cultivation area, and that only 1 to 2 percent of land within the project area was devoted to growing poppies.[89] Poppy cultivation was most prevalent in the northern parts of the valley, from Girishk to the areas around the Kajakai Dam. Although not part of the US project, farmers undoubtedly benefited from being in close proximity to the project area.[90] If anything, Weinraub proved prophetic, as opium was not grown in substantial amounts in the project area in 1973.

Yet his article pointed to an important process occurring in the Helmand region: the growing prevalence of opium as a lucrative cash crop. For both the Helmand region and Afghanistan as a whole, 1973 was a benchmark year. In 1972, farmers in the Helmand Valley were planning on decreasing their poppy harvest because prices remained low. In 1973, however, something triggered a substantial increase in poppy cultivation. Officials estimated that cultivation had increased sevenfold. In May, US and Afghan officials conducted a flyover of the Helmand-Arghandab area and noticed that poppy cultivation was so extensive and widespread that it was easily visible from an altitude of eight hundred feet.[91] So what exactly triggered this increase?

Although local factors, such as improvements in agriculture, certainly led to the increase in poppy cultivation, there were also significant changes regionally and globally that contributed to the expansion of poppy cultivation. One of the most significant developments in Afghanistan was the building of a ring road, which for the first time in the nation's history connected previously isolated regions and transformed rural life by shrinking travel time and transport costs.[92] In the south of the country, the United States committed $130.4 million to transport infrastructure, highlighted by the highways connecting Kabul and Kandahar, as well as to Spin Baldak on the Pakistan border.[93] The building of roads in general had a significant influence on social and economic systems. Throughout the country, the proliferation of goods and services led formerly self-sufficient regions to grow gradually dependent on economic exchanges lying beyond their domain,[94] with impacts as well on the growth of a cash economy and on migrant labor.[95] The creation and expansion of highways and roads, while important for the growth of state power,[96] was more significant because it increased the mobility of people, and therefore trade. Given that smuggling and trade are often seen as one in the same, smuggling increased, too.

Globally, disruptions with other suppliers of opium created an evolution in the global market, which provided an opportunity for Afghan opium to step in. As discussed in the previous chapter, Nixon's supply-side interventions, which focused on the major suppliers to the US market, was creating a "balloon effect" to the supply of opium. Turkey, which was considered the major supplier to the US market, launched a ban on opium production under considerable pressure from the US government. Although production decreased after the ban and subsequent eradication, evidence suggests that considerable crop displacement occurred before the ban, indicating the limited impact of the ban.[97] Nonetheless, the reduction in supply from Turkey, possibly a by-product of traffickers' choice or a consequence of international pressure, coincided with the expansion of production elsewhere.

In reaction to the cessation of supply in Turkey, Southeast Asian suppliers increased supply to the US market. What was once an insignificant amount in the late 1960s, by 1973, Southeast Asian heroin was accounting for nearly 30 percent of all street-level heroin in the United States.[98] The DEA responded in due kind, and with the help of the Thai police ramped up efforts to stop production and trafficking. Again, the market adapted; production of opium increased in the Shan and Kachin regions of Myanmar, and much of the Southeast Asian opium supply was diverted into European and Australian markets.[99] Mexico, too, entered the fray shortly thereafter following the myriad of disruptions to the opium producers in Asia.[100] But the disruptions in supply were not isolated to the pressures of supply-side interventions, as environmental problems contributed to supply disruptions as well. The interdiction campaigns in Southeast Asia were compounded by the drought in Southeast Asia, and the drought and famine in Afghanistan in 1971–72 produced considerable economic strain on the entire rural population of Afghanistan. Ultimately, the exogenous and endogenous forces, whether it was the weather, or pressure from supply-side interventions, or traffickers choosing more advantageous markets, or improved infrastructure that increased mobility and trade between Afghanistan and the outside world, all contributed to a larger presence of opium in the valley in 1973.

Back in Helmand, Weinraub's article pointed to an ominous future for HAVA, although the extent of opium production within the project area remained limited in 1973. However, both US and Afghan officials believed that the potential to stop opium from taking over the Helmand Valley rested in the ability of the state and HAVA to transcend the economic, social, and political problems that plagued the project and the surrounding area. In other words, to stop opium from taking over, the United States and Afghanistan would have to succeed in developing the Helmand Valley.[101] Both US and Afghan officials failed to recognize how economic development of Helmand could invite adverse consequences; in this case, preparing farmers to grow for the global illicit drug market. Moreover, the broader political and economic system, whose success was necessary to keep farmers within the licit market, needed to improve. By the mid-1970s, however, the political and social fabric that (loosely) tied the nation together began to unravel. More important, so too did farmers' and villagers' faith in HAVA. As a result, opium production increased, not just because of economic necessity, but more important, because of the social and political conflicts that increasingly characterized relations between the Afghan government, the United States, and Afghan society.

Prohibiting Opium in the Helmand Valley

The political impact of Weinraub's article was far-reaching. Shortly after the publication of the article, the US Congress investigated the extent of poppy cultivation in the USAID areas of the Helmand Valley. In September 1973, Daud announced a nationwide prohibition on opium. The prohibition was enacted to increase enforcement of bans on the cultivation, use, and trade of opium. On closer inspection, however, Daud's prohibition reflected the deeper political problems plaguing the new republic. In line with his efforts to increase military and police power, Daud established new enforcement apparatuses, particularly the ASUs, which he granted national jurisdiction.[102] The ASUs, financed by the UN and the DEA, were far more aggressive than the previous regime in cracking down on smuggling networks. But Daud's augmented enforcement and eradication programs did not hide his desire for massive increases in US funding. The United States, on the other hand, remained wary of Daud's true intentions, steadfastly maintaining that increases in development aid had to be matched by increases in enforcement programs.[103] At this point, rural economic development and counternarcotics were becoming increasingly intertwined. The unwillingness of the United States to pour more money into the Helmand project forced Daud to ease up on enforcing bans on opium cultivation and production compared with his zealous implementation of antismuggling laws, and it signified the Afghan government's tenuous control in Helmand.

The September prohibition was part of a larger dialogue about the future of US–Afghan relations. US officials hoped that Daud would recognize the delicate political situation the Americans were in. If US policymakers had proof that American money was being used to grow "bigger, better, and more opium poppies," this would threaten not only the future of US support for the Helmand project but of other proposed joint US–Afghan development projects in Nangarhar and Badakhshan.[104] However, Daud and the Afghan government were still in no position to flex their muscles in rural Afghanistan. Fresh off of the coup in July, Daud was still consolidating power. Exerting power in Kabul was one thing, but in Helmand, the government, regardless of who was in power, remained a contested political entity.

Ismail Osman, a UN official and also nephew of Daud, met with Afghan government officials to gauge their willingness to enforce prohibition measures in the Helmand region. Osman found that Daud was reluctant to prohibit opium production, fearing that it would be unpopular. Daud planned to prohibit opium cultivation only in the small project area. Outside the project area, rather than targeting opium farmers, Daud planned to concentrate on "big traffickers who gain most of profits and who are currently target of new regimes' anti-corruption campaign." Daud wanted to "avoid [a] full scale anti-opium production ban in [the] Helmand area until regime has had time to consolidate its power in the area" and instead would focus on trafficking because that was "all the Government of Afghanistan could realistically do for the moment."[105]

The opium prohibition, as well as the United States' hope to stop Helmand from becoming a major source of the drug, depended on the future of Daud's government. But for Daud, the situation was far more complex; drug control was ultimately dependent on the willingness of local government officials and community leaders to comply with national drug control policy. For many local government officials enforcing a national ban on opium could hurt farmers economically, inevitably straining the already tenuous relations between the government and local peoples. In February 1974, Peter Constable and Charles James of the State Department met with Governor Pazhwak to stress the United States' grave concerns about the discovery of opium in the Helmand Valley. However, despite pressure from the United States to enforce the prohibition, Pazhwak could not simply eradicate the opium crop. Pazhwak responded that the opium problem was a simple issue of the "poor little farmer" and that the solution would be to find suitable alternatives and rectify the income gaps among farmers.[106] Pazhwak's clever response eluded to an important point; if the United States provided more money and resources, the problem would eventually go away.

But the issue was not simply a matter of poverty. Pazhwak's reluctance to prohibit opium spotlighted the fragile role of the Daud government in the Helmand Valley in 1974. Pazhwak had been an ardent critic of the project as a whole but remained steadfast in his efforts to increase US aid. His various meetings with US officials regarding opium suggested that he was rather indifferent to opium cultivation and trade, believing the opium trade "was a fact of life in the area."[107] No matter how much US officials pressured Pazhwak, his concern rested in maintaining good relations with the people of the region rather than appeasing the United States. On a deeper level, Pazhwak's constant concern about his political standing reflected the simmering conflict between national directives and parochial realities. Prohibiting opium made little political sense for Pazhwak as a provincial governor when tensions between the people and the state were already high. Moreover, farmers were finally benefiting from the project, either directly or indirectly. Thus, his general cultural and economic indifference toward the opium trade, combined with political pragmatism, certainly reinforced the notion that Pazhwak was less than enthusiastic about enforcing national antiopium laws in the Helmand Valley.

By early 1974, rumors circulated throughout Helmand that Daud would finally crack down on poppy farmers and enforce the ban on opium. In February, to gauge the extent of the narcotics trade and the impact of narcotics policy in the valley, Richard Scott and Frank Denton of USAID met with three wholesalers and middlemen operating in the raw hash and opium trade in Lashkar Gah. Scott and Denton's survey revealed that hash and opium prices had made substantial gains from the previous year, confirming fears that the global market was making inroads in Afghanistan. Between 1973 and 1974, profits from the sale of a seer[108] of hash increased 59 percent. As table 6.1 indicates, opium profits increased 68 percent (both percentages based on the lowest sale price).

Although prices fluctuated depending on the market, the increasing demand for opium was undoubtedly escalating prices, partly because the market for Afghan opium was no longer exclusive to Iran. Some traders noted that foreigners had entered the markets in Herat and were sometimes offering double the market price.[109]

In early 1974, fearing the cessation of US funding if opium production continued unabated, HAVA declared a prohibition in the project area and promised to turn any farmer growing poppies over to the police. USAID

Table 6.1 Hashish and opium prices (afghanis per seer)

	Hashish		Opium	
	Buy	Sell	Buy	Sell
1972–73	120–300	250–280	300–360	450–500
1973–74	180–250	300–400	400–450	600–650

Source: Vincent Brown, director, US AID Afghanistan, "Memorandum on Narcotics in the Helmand Valley," USAID, March 9, 1974, RG 84, Records Relating to Afghanistan; NACP.
Notes: Hashish prices were based on first quality. All prices varied within ranges listed.

officials seemed comforted by the notion that opium would be eradicated from the project area. However, State Department and DEA officials remained more concerned about opium outside of the project area. The project area was only a small fraction of the total farmland in the valley, and more important, the opium trade was growing throughout the valley and country. Ultimately, to stop farmers outside the project area from growing opium, Governor Pazhwak would need to enforce antiopium laws, something HAVA, provincial, and national officials were clearly reluctant to do.[110]

Still, the Afghan government imposed a prohibition outside the project area shortly after HAVA's ban. Unlike earlier prohibitions, particularly the 1958 ban in Badakhshan, the prohibition in Helmand received little fanfare. There is little evidence that an eradication program was actually enforced by the police or gendarmerie, but rather the opium ban was self-imposed by farmers, local khans, and landlords. In June, US officials reported, "poppies are not being grown on a commercial basis anywhere." According to the United States, subtle and informal pressures from Afghan authorities led farmers to stop growing. In any event, the apparent success of the prohibition was a clear political victory for the United States. Embassy officials cabled Washington to notify Congress about this important development.[111]

Although the United States perceived a significant victory in the war on drugs, evidence suggests that the ban succeeded for other reasons. For some farmers, the costs of opium still outweighed the benefits. However, by complying with the ban, and waiting a year to harvest opium, farmers could benefit from the expected hike in price due to the shortage of opium supply. When Scott and Denton conducted their survey in February 1974, the three narcotics traders noted that the shortages in supply caused by the prohibition would potentially increase prices nearly 200 to 300 afghanis per seer. Most farmers seemed aware of the impact of the prohibition on their profit margins. As a result, despite increases in customers buying opium, many farmers held onto the year's crop because they expected an even higher price in the future.[112]

Farmers exhibited tremendous agency in manipulating international and national drug control programs. However, fear of coercive action from Daud's government influenced farmers and traders to self-impose the opium ban. Government pressures under Daud, especially the introduction of ASUs, began to change the way the opium trade operated. The men interviewed noted that things had become more secretive but also more accurate. The threat of coercive action by the government raised the stakes for traders, and as a result, required them to be more precise in their business. Farmers were also holding onto their crop because if they did not have regular buyers, they feared that the government's use of local contacts and informants would eventually lead to their arrests.[113] More important, traders indicated that growing scrutiny from the central government was pressuring the local structure of production and trade. Conventionally, farmers who grew hash or opium sold it to a local khan or large landowner who, in turn, sold it to traffickers.[114] These networks mostly followed ethnic and tribal lines. However, the government's strength, particularly in rural Helmand, depended on coopting local khans and large landowners in supporting government projects and policies. Thus, farmers had to be careful in dealing with wealthy landowners who might be acting on the state's behalf. On the other hand, Daud's government was also walking a thin line. If the prohibition was not enacted properly and without due consideration of these powerful characters, the state risked further alienating them, and the rest of the local population.

The question arises as to what caused the adaptations in the illicit drug market. Was the prohibition a matter of effective state enforcement or market manipulation by farmers? The answer lies somewhere in between. The growth of double cropping certainly gave farmers a way to maximize their individual profits, given global market conditions. The increasing demand for opium, evidenced by foreigners showing up in Herat and Kandahar, strengthened awareness among local Afghan farmers and traders of the lucrative potential of the global narcotics market. They understood that demand showed no signs of subsiding. As a result, withholding supply rather than complying with the prohibition (despite the massive demand for their product) would improve future profits. Meanwhile, since opium was often double-cropped, farmers could survive the year by growing wheat and cotton. Complying with state policy allowed farmers, khans, and large landowners to avoid Daud's crackdown on corruption and crime while simultaneously improving their future prospects.[115] The Afghan government had a history of being indifferent when it came to enforcement, and undoubtedly used informal pressures to maintain political support from local khans and landowners while satiating the feverish demands of the Americans. In effect, the prohibition was essential to the future growth of the opium trade in the Helmand Valley.

Amid US elation over the apparent success of the prohibition, it seems odd that the Americans never questioned the role of corruption. Corruption plagued HAVA and local provincial authorities throughout its history, and State Department and DEA officials were convinced to some extent that Afghan authorities remained involved in the drug trade. Indeed, this casts a shadow of skepticism over the whole prohibition. Is it likely that local officials withheld product, enforcing the prohibition, to protect themselves from potential prosecution while profiting in the future? The answer is yes. The potential impact of prohibition on future prices further reinforced local officials' willingness to acquiesce in state directives. As an informal prohibition of sorts, whereby subtle pressures were applied, this scheme protected larger traffickers and khans (who played important and profitable roles in moving product) from prosecution by allowing them temporarily to halt the trade while projecting an image of compliance with the government. In the assessment of the ban, success was short lived. The ban was not a result of moral compliance or of effective state policy; it seems rather that political and economic opportunities were presented by the prohibition that proved advantageous to multiple parties.

This ban, like many others in the history of drug control, did not stand the test of time.[116] Despite the cessation of opium production in 1974, by 1975 and 1976 opium cultivation had once again sprouted up in the Helmand Valley. UN narcotics advisers noted that roughly 106 fields were identified near Lashkar Gah and surrounding areas (although not in the project area). US officials scrambled to offset the political damage, fearing that opium's reemergence in the valley and, worse yet, the project area would lead to the end of US presence altogether.[117] Daud issued stringent orders to his ministers and provincial governors to eradicate all opium. The United States even helped fund a propaganda campaign to try to convince farmers not to grow opium. Despite US pressure, however, Daud seemed politically impotent. Again, the effectiveness of Daud's orders depended on cooperation from the heads of ministries and provincial leaders.[118] Yet by 1976, many within the government were more concerned about their own survival than with implementing drug policy. Unemployment skyrocketed and peasants continued to be exploited by landowners. Furthermore, the country's trade deficit continued to rise.[119] Local khans and landowners, who had proved so instrumental to the prohibition in 1974, were no longer willing to acquiesce to government demands. By 1975, Daud's republic faced increasing resistance in the countryside from Islamic radicals, who in turn were met by even greater repression from Daud. In sum, by the mid-1970s, Daud's government did "not have the capacity to implement policies that challenged entrenched local interests."[120]

The Afghan government's ability, or willingness, to stop drug trafficking was on the decline as well. In fact, by 1976, the emphasis on counternarcotics efforts decreased rapidly, as border patrols and antidrug police were increasingly absent from the state payroll.[121] Meanwhile, as the state receded from many parts of rural Afghanistan, opium flourished. In 1978, the CIA estimated that Afghanistan and Pakistan together produced roughly 1,000 tons of opium, double the 500 tons UN officials had predicted.[122] Moreover, the opium trade was increasingly tied to the deepening political conflict in Afghanistan. As early as 1976, opium production was growing, and much of it was being used for the purchase of arms and munitions, as resistance to the Afghan government spread.[123] By 1977, the CIA estimated that the Helmand Valley produced nearly 51 tons of opium, a significant portion of the estimated total 200–250 tons produced throughout Afghanistan.[124] It was quite apparent that by the Sawr Revolution in 1978, opium had become an integral part of the Helmand Valley.

The Helmand Valley during and after the War

When the Soviets invaded Afghanistan in 1979, opium was becoming a primary source of revenue for farmers, khans, and resistance leaders. Although Afghanistan had a growing addict population, most of the opium produced in the country was heading west to Iran and then on to Europe. In the early stages of the Afghan-Soviet war, Pakistan experienced a boom in the production of opium, particularly in the frontier provinces. However, as the mujahideen took control of rural areas in Afghanistan, opium production shifted primarily to Afghanistan.[125] The results were astounding. In 1983, it was estimated that Afghanistan produced nearly six hundred tons of raw opium.[126] By the mid-1980s, most mujahideen commanders operated within a system in which opium was grown in Afghanistan, refined into heroin in Pakistan, and then sold domestically or shipped to neighboring markets or the west.[127] Some leaders even managed to establish heroin laboratories in Afghanistan. The *Washington Post* reported on May 13, 1990, that Gilbudin Hekmatyar, leader of the Hizb-i Islami and one of the major figures of the mujahideen, established six heroin refineries in the Helmand during the early stages of the war.

Part of the reason opium production increased so dramatically in Helmand and the rest of the country during the 1980s was that heroin consumption increased significantly around the world. The reemergence of heroin consumption in the United States in the late 1970s and early 1980s solidified Afghanistan's role as the major supplier for the US market. In particular, in the northeast United States heroin addiction and overdose were on the rise. American officials estimated that 54 percent of the US heroin supply came from Afghanistan in 1981.[128] Regionally, both Pakistan and Iran emerged as major consumers of heroin in the early 1980s.[129]

By the end of the war, as the mujahideen broke into rival ethnic and tribal wars, the fight for control over opium took form. Warlord Mullah Nasim Akhunzada took control of the Helmand Valley and used the opium profits to continue his fight versus his rival Hekmatyar and also to build schools and roads amid the political vacuum nationwide.[130] The role of opium warlord and local leader was reminiscent of Republican-era China when local warlords encouraged opium production so as to tax it and use its revenue to build local states.[131] Control of Helmand Valley was extremely profitable for Akhunzada, as it was producing nearly 250 tons a year, earning him the nickname "King of Heroin."[132] Following the end of the war, Akhunzada was so powerful that the United States offered him $2 million to stop cultivating opium. Although the sum was to be paid in the form UN development aid, Akhunzada agreed and reduced Helmand production considerably in 1990.[133] Although Akhunzada managed to stop growing poppies in 1990, Helmand remained an important region for opium producers and traders. It remains even more so today.

Ultimately, there is a sad irony to the story of the Helmand Valley. In 2002, the Helmand Valley produced nearly 56 percent of the country's opium. Nad-i-Ali, once an important settlement in the Helmand Valley development project, itself produced nearly 8 percent of the country's output in 2003.[134] Although thirty years of war and political instability led to the expansion of the opium industry in the Helmand, its origins remain closely intertwined with the building of the Helmand Valley, the Afghan state, and globalization of Afghan opium.

Conclusion

> The farmers have lost confidence and respect for the government and the donor community. They understand that the inconsistencies in word and action reflect uncertainty, indifference and disorganization. The opium buyers continue to offer credit and a good market. Violence increases and the farmers continue to cultivate ever increasing crops of opium poppy.[135]

As Richard Scott indicates above, many of the problems that plagued the Helmand Valley development project during the Musahiban era continue to this day. Many projects launched by the Afghan and donor governments are poorly managed and conceived, and there remains a vast gap between local concerns and input versus those of national and international governments. More important, farmers continue to grow opium as the Afghan government and its various international supporters remain disconnected from local realities that buttress the opium trade. For historians, as well as social scientists, there are important lessons to be learned from this episode in history.

The examination of opium production in the Helmand Valley sheds light on the important factors shaping why opium production began in the region. Economically, the introduction of cash crops created an awareness among local farmers and traders of how to maximize profits in the global market. This proved to be a vital component in the transformation of Helmand as the global narcotics market adapted to the restrictions in supply stemming from the US-led war on drugs. The prohibition on poppy growing in 1974 was also important to stimulating the local opium economy, as the decrease in supply amid growing regional and global demand helped increase prices for locally produced opium. Politically, the republic established under Daud proved an important factor in the deteriorating relations between the Daud government and local Helmand officials. Daud broke from the conventional Musahiban political model using leftists as his primary support base. The prohibition emerges in a different light as a result. Local officials did not acquiesce per se but rather co-opted the prohibition to eliminate potentially violent interactions with the Daud government while improving future economic prospects. As a result, the emergence of opium in the Helmand Valley was not a product of the Afghan-Soviet war but rather a by-product of the political, social, and economic engagements between local Afghans and the Afghan government, and changes to the global narcotics economy.

Except for the ring road, the Helmand Valley development project was unprecedented in size, scope, and impact. Not only did the Morrison-Knudsen Company build dams, canals, and roads but it also settled nomads and built schools and housing. It constructed a new way of life in Afghanistan. This transformation was branded indelibly with American identity and visions of modernity. On a deeper level, however, the Helmand development project was about the expansion of state power into rural Afghanistan.[136] In this way, development took on a new "meaning." Thus, resistance to development was really about resistance to the political attachments that came along with development. The prohibition took this even further. The threat of coercive force by Daud, seen by Americans as an important step for the aspiring modern nation, was a symbol of the increasingly invasive character of the Afghan government. Thus, in a country where the economic disparity and cultural differences between urban and rural societies was stark, the transposition of American modernity into rural Afghanistan, in the form of both development and prohibition, was even more radical. The impact was profound.

The social and cultural issues revolving around the planting of American modernity in the Helmand Valley were reinforced by structural deficiencies within the Musahiban state, especially the pervasive strength of the *qawm*. The Musahiban dynasty never established a consensus or uniformity around an imagined national identity as Afghan.[137] Rather, state officials "inserted the *qawm* into the state institutions." The net effect, of course, was that Afghans rarely developed a fealty toward the state. As Afghan historian

Olivier Roy states, "the state was no more than a stake in a larger game and the strategy of a *qawm* consisted in establishing an advantageous relationship with the institutions of the state."[138] Specifically, the development of the Helmand Valley was not an effort to unify and strengthen the national allegiances but rather to aid and perpetuate Pashtun hegemony.[139]

What impact did this have on opium in the Helmand Valley? During the early 1970s, when farmers' incomes had grown beyond subsistence levels, the state was not credited with the success of improved agricultural systems. This was mainly because the state was rarely integrated into rural society; rather, it merely encapsulated "local political structures in order to prevent them from causing trouble."[140] Furthermore, relations between the state and people were weakest at the provincial and subprovincial levels. As a result, when opium burst onto the scene in 1973 the state was incapable of introducing the sorts of measures that would effectively stop opium production.

In many ways, the emergence of opium highlights the problems surrounding the *qawm* and state governance. In particular, the state's attempt to prohibit opium happened at a time when the local farmers and traders were benefiting from the global opium trade. And even when the state managed to enforce a prohibition in 1974, the ban succeeded only because it served local interests to do so. Thus, the false compliance by farmers and traders in the Helmand represented a form of peasant resistance to the state.[141] More important, opium emerged because it benefited the *qawm*, which ultimately had the irreducible effect of delegitimizing the state in the region as it tried to uphold coercive prohibition policies. Furthermore, the hopes of developing legal crops as an alternative carried the historical weight of nearly twenty-five years of government corruption, mismanagement, and misguidance in HAVA. Thus, it is not surprising that given the history of the project and the potential of the opium trade, local farmers and traders continued to produce opium and ignore or manipulate the directives of the increasingly disconnected Afghan government.

The linkages between the Helmand Valley development project and its subsequent role as epicenter of the global narcotics trade also lead to questions about the legacy of the United States in the Helmand Valley. The legacy of the role of the United States in the Helmand Valley is one in which it succeeded in teaching farmers to grow crops for the global market. However, it happened at a time when local political and social schisms were increasing, the state was weakening, and the tentacles of the global illicit narcotics trade finally reached into the fields of Afghanistan. Consequently, Afghan farmers learned to master a system that happened to be in direct opposition to the ideologies of the American donors who helped them learn and achieve such mastery. More important, America was exporting competing visions of its own modernity, one rooted in building a free market, the other in prohibiting opium.[142] Ironically, the two American visions were not necessarily juxtaposed to each other but rather were increasingly interwoven. As a result, by co-opting the Afghan state in its own inconclusive and misguided ideology, the Americans contributed to the cultural and political malaise brewing in Afghanistan. In other words, by failing to achieve either of its objectives, the United States contributed to the failure of both. Now the opium poppies, which riddle the Helmand countryside, serve as reminders of a vision of modernity gone awry.

Epilogue

In 2008, an Afghan from the Nimroz Province, Hajji Juma Khan, was arrested for violating a recent established narco-terrorism law. American authorities described him as "perhaps the biggest and most dangerous drug lord in Afghanistan," who worked with the Taliban to funnel drugs and weapons to fuel the insurgency.[1] To casual observers, Juma Khan's case was an affirmation of the shady world the United States was engaged with since 2001, one where warlords and drug lords were indistinguishable from governors and parliamentarians. The great fear, of course, was that this would undermine the American state-building project. Yet people like Hajji Juma Khan were essential to the United States; Khan was more than an ordinary drug trafficker—he was an American informant for the CIA and DEA, who offered information for protection, as well as other perks, such as lavish shopping trips to New York. The question for many was why, then, was he arrested? Was he not an asset in the war on terror in Afghanistan? Conversely, how responsible was he for the heroin being smuggled and consumed in the United States? The answers to such questions are as vague as the policies that drive them.

If we push aside the charges laid against him, Hajji Juma Khan's arrest was indicative of the messy, often convoluted, ways the drug trade, the war on drugs, and other policy initiatives, in this case the war on terror, intersected in Afghanistan. The United States, in particular, has played a critical role in this entanglement. This relationship has been defined by constant change, and political inconsistencies, and yet, with the shifting sands of political players and their policy objectives, some of the same questions linger historically. What role has the Afghan state, or other governing groups, played in the drug trade and forms of drug control? What issues with governance, at local and national levels, influenced, or were influenced by, the drug trade? Furthermore, the contemporary problems with the drug trade share a great deal with those events of the past century. In this way, what does the case of Hajji Juma Khan tell us about issues of governance and the connections, or not, between governing bodies (the Taliban and the Afghan state) and the drug trade, and how that fits within the scope of the Afghan–American relationship? Although a great deal has changed in Afghanistan since 1978, opium remains an important link, revealing that the issues that plagued authorities in the prewar years still remain today: mainly limited state control, countervailing policy initiatives, limited economic and political opportunities, ethnocentric enforcement of drug control initiatives, and the growing global illicit drug trade. In this way, understanding how and why the drug trade emerged is more important than ever.

Since the Soviet invasion of Afghanistan in 1979, the production, trade, and use of opium exploded. As the war ravaged much of the Afghan countryside during the 1980s and state systems failed in rural parts of the country, opium emerged as an ideal crop for farmers, especially those facing inconsistent water access and drought, since opium required little. But opium had other advantages as well: it was easily transported through borderland regions lacking state surveillance; skills needed to grow and harvest the plant were easily learned; as a labor-intensive crop, it provided work for landless poor; and more than anything, it was a lucrative crop. Throughout the decade, as other social and economic systems broke down amidst the deepening conflict, opium production expanded into lowland valleys and closer to urban centers, beyond the upper valleys and borderland regions that were the historical locus of opium production. The opium trade further reinforced the shifting power dynamics brought on by the war and the mujahideen, the Afghan freedom fighters resisting the Soviet invasion. As opium was trafficked into neighboring countries and sold into the illicit market, the accumulation of capital reinforced the ability of fighters to purchase more weapons, as well as political influence, thus reinforcing the role of opium within the conflict economy.[2]

After the war, much of the Afghan economy remained in shambles. Opium thrived, not only because it was a lucrative crop, but now there was virtually no governmental oversight. Figures such as Nasim Akhundzada emerged as archetypal warlord-opium kingpins. In the fertile Helmand Valley, Akhundzada decreed that half of all agricultural production be devoted to opium. The desire to produce opium (upward of 250 tons) was compelled by the devolving political and economic situation in the country. Akhundzada was not merely trying to make a profit; he was also using the money to fund a bitter territorial struggle with the notorious mujahideen commander, Gilbuddin Hekmatyar.[3] During the Taliban years, opium production and trade expanded even further, with multiple areas, not historic producers of the plant, trying their hand at opium cultivation.[4] Although the Taliban were credited with a ban on opium production in 2000, one that virtually eliminated the production of opium, the ban seems to have been limited in other ways. Opium was still visible in urban markets, produced on the sides of major roads and highways, and checkpoints and trade barriers virtually vanished. Furthermore, heroin laboratories propped up throughout the country and in urban centers, sometimes in close proximity to Taliban authorities credited by the international community for curbing the production and trade of opium.[5]

Following the US invasion of Afghanistan and the ouster of the Taliban regime in 2001, many thought the formation of a new state system would eliminate the lawlessness that gave rise to the opium trade. The opposite occurred, however. If anything, the establishment of a new Afghan state under Hamid Karzai only further amplified the production and trade of opium. When the new government was established, it was largely dependent on power holders from the periphery of the country.[6] For many power brokers in Afghanistan, the drug economy became a primary vehicle for accumulating political power, and the influence of drug money could be felt from the lowest levels of the state to members of Parliament, even to Karzai's own brother.[7] As a result, cultivation exploded throughout the period of 2002–2004, showing up in all of the 34 provinces, and in 194 of the 364 districts in the country, a fourfold increase compared with during Taliban rule.[8] By 2005, it was estimated that Afghanistan was the supplier for nearly 87 percent of the world's illicit heroin.[9]

Paradoxically, the illicit drug trade in Afghanistan blossomed amidst an environment in which billions of American dollars and thousands of American troops descended on Afghanistan. In this way, the irony is too hard to ignore: that the most ardent antidrug nation on earth was responsible for the reconstruction of the state that supplied most of the world's illicit opium supply, and not only were they not stopping drug production, but it was in fact, thriving. As the drug trade continued to expand, the Taliban reemerged. For the Americans, there was a dramatic shift in thinking about the role of drugs in Afghanistan, and how to combat the drug trade. As a result, the war on drugs converged with the war on terror; drug policy became a security issue.[10] The idea that drugs comprised a unique security threat remains an enduring piece of the American effort in Afghanistan to this day. The Department of Defense states, "revenue from drug trafficking, taxation/extortion, illicit mining/agriculture, and foreign financial support continues to sustain the insurgency and Afghan criminal networks."[11] As a result of drug control being "securitized," the United States has provided most of the funding for counternarcotics programs; between 2002 and March 2018, it provided a total of $8.78 billion to combat drug production and trafficking throughout the country.[12]

While the massive amount of money devoted to the reduction of drug production and trade seems necessary given the enormity of the drug trade, counternarcotics policy plays out differently at the local level. For Afghan leaders, the dependence on American money, which requires them to uphold American policies, often contradicts their more immediate political and economic needs at the local level. On the one hand, waging the war on drugs may increase the legitimacy of Afghan leaders among international donors seeking to curb the supply of illicit drugs. On the other hand, many Afghan farmers see counternarcotics policies as driven by the West, and they became disillusioned with the Afghan power brokers responsible for initiating such policies; this is further complicated by the failure to compensate farmers with alternative livelihoods or legitimate opportunities elsewhere. In turn, the demand for significant reductions in drug production and trade, while looking good on paper and in front of congressional committees, "ultimately . . . run the danger of undermining the more fundamental goal of state-building."[13]

And yet, counternarcotics policy endures year after year, with the same set of ambitions and goals, and little, if not adverse, effect. Eradicating opium remains one of the cornerstones of US–Afghan efforts to stop the production of drugs in Afghanistan. The United States and Afghan authorities often cite recent examples of successful drug eradications, such as the 94 percent reduction of opium cultivation in Nangarhar in 2005, or in Balkh in 2006–7. In both cases, local strongmen were employed by the state to reduce drug production. To achieve such goals, however, the central government granted individual strongmen greater political autonomy. On paper, the significant reduction of opium looked good to international donors, but at the local level, the state was subsumed by the local figures, not the other way around. As a result, not only did the state lose the ability to shape and construct a more durable and lasting solution (as drug production reemerged in following years), but by opting for more short-term solutions, and relying on local power brokers to employ eradications, they sacrificed the chance to build arguably greater political legitimacy.[14]

Furthermore, eradications undermine the state at its most critical juncture. Those who suffer the most from eradications are often those most dependent on opium as a source of income: poor farmers. In many cases, eradications are counterproductive to the larger goal of building a stable Afghan state. David Mansfield argues that eradications fuel "instability precisely because it exposes the rural population to significant economic shocks; it destabilizes the political order due to the fluid and fragile nature of local leadership . . . and finally it damages the bond between state and periphery, fueling violence and rural rebellion." As Mansfield notes, the end result of eradications is that they "present an image of a state and a local leadership that does not care about the welfare of the population but prioritizes its own interest and those of foreign benefactors."[15] The issues Mansfield highlights are not exclusive to contemporary Afghanistan. We see a variety of historical parallels between eradications happening now and those that happened in Badakhshan in 1958, or in Helmand in 1974. In almost every case, the goal of eradicating opium seems predicated on assuaging international players; at stake is a great deal of money, and thus political influence. But the poor farmers and traders, those with the least, suffer the most. If we consider eradications within the broader historical lens that is included in this study, what we see is a cyclical nature of drug control in Afghanistan whereby the United States provides money and aid to eliminate drugs, drugs are eliminated short term, usually through eradications, but the policy itself was often divisive or incomplete, and the state failed to come through with alternative livelihoods. As a result, people regrow opium, and more important, become increasingly disillusioned by the state; the state loses political ground and to gain ground, it needs more foreign money; foreign donors search for policies that placate internal political ambitions and narratives (in this case, eradicating the scourge of drugs); and the cycle continues.

Interdiction is the other pillar of US counternarcotics strategy. Both the DEA and DOD (Department of Defense) actively train Afghan army and police to interdict drug smuggling. From 2008 to March 2018, Afghan and US units have interdicted over 463,000 kilograms of opium. Unfortunately, that is estimated to be roughly .05 percent of the opium produced in Afghanistan for only 2017.[16] Trafficking, too, is very difficult to combat, particularly in Afghanistan, as most of the value of drugs is in trafficking. As a result, the financial stakes are much higher when dealing with traffickers. To combat drug traffickers, US and Afghan antidrug units often employ local militias to aid in drug interdiction. More often than not, however, the same people being employed to stop drug trafficking come from the same pools as those involved in drug trafficking. Thus, the lines between the legal and illegal are blurred, fueling corruption, and ultimately, undermining state authority.[17] Again, we see historical parallels. Similar attempts were made in the 1970s with the establishment of the antismuggling units, and much like contemporary Afghanistan, the same problems persisted: the value of the drugs was much more than many of those working to fight drug trafficking, thus compelling many to become corrupt; at the local level, the state expected local authorities to enforce national antismuggling and antidrug laws, but many of those smuggling were drawn from the same communities, if not families, as those enforcing those laws; and lastly, even if there were successes, the amount of drugs seized was negligible compared with the amount being smuggled.

Ultimately, we must consider what the history of drugs in Afghanistan can teach us about the drug trade and drug policy in Afghanistan today. I have argued throughout this book that the focus on the formation of the Afghan state is critical to understanding the drug trade, not merely because the state has done the most to try to stop drugs (and mostly unsuccessfully for that matter), but conversely, it has also done a great deal to perpetuate the existence and expansion of the illicit drug trade. The issue stems largely from the perception of why and how drug use and trade emerge. The more recent period provides some clues. In the last decade, some have argued that Afghanistan's drug woes stem from a lack of state building; in other words, building greater state capacity will yield reductions in drug production.[18] This is, of course, consistent with what I showed here historically, that Afghan and American authorities saw drug control as a vehicle for state formation and as a way of expanding state power, which would, in turn, eliminate the illicit drug trade.

However, something is amiss with this perception, historically and contemporarily. The United States has pumped trillions of dollars into Afghanistan and the state has certainly expanded, but drugs remain more problematic and present than ever. Why? The existence of the state does not preclude the elimination of the drug trade. Thus, we must think how the state governs and how it legitimizes itself as critical to not only the formation and expansion of the state, but to the power and stability of its governing power at various levels and regions. In this way, the existence of the illicit drug trade is not merely a "threat" to or juxtaposed with the state (e.g., in the form of antistate actors such as the Taliban); rather, it is a symptom of the failures of the state and governance. We can see this in the very drug control apparatus. The need to proclaim the reduction of areas devoted to the cultivation of poppies or drug seizures as justifications for the success of drug control further obfuscate how the problem has been incorrectly diagnosed. As David Mansfield and Adam Pain note, the "elimination of opium poppy is being pursued at a dramatic rate, using opium area statistics more as an indicator of dealing with the causes of the disease rather than as a symptom of them."[19] In other words, what has developed, arguably over the last century, and has become most acute in Afghanistan in the last decade and a half, is the perception that drugs are the cause of instability, crime, and political chaos.

However, underscoring these conceptions is a lack of historical understanding about the mutually constitutive relationship between opium and state formation that has shaped the conditions that now characterize the opium trade in Afghanistan. Throughout the last century, drug control often amplified the issues of governance that gave rise to, or sustained, either nonstate actors or criminal organizations. Even more recent examples reinforce how groups such as the Taliban or the Islamic State increased their political legitimacy, not by fulfilling vague and often overly simplified goals of reducing drug-producing territory, or seizing certain amounts of smuggled goods, but rather, by simply improving governance.[20] Thus, analyzing the historical antecedents of the Afghan opium industry broadens and enriches our understanding of the contemporary drug trade in Afghanistan. In particular, analyzing this period reveals the between-state formation in Afghanistan and the growth of the Afghan opium industry; drug control was both a response to the drug trade and a stimulant for it. Moreover, the increasingly coercive nature of drug control, often contradicting social, cultural, and economic norms regarding opium production, use, and trade reinforced the growing illegitimacy of the Afghan government. As a result, drug control contributed to the political, social, and cultural problems that increasingly characterized the relationship between the Afghan government and its citizens. Therefore, the globalization of Afghanistan's opium industry was not simply a by-product of war and statelessness, but rather a consequence of the deeper political issues stemming from the formation of the Afghan state, of which drug control played an increasingly important role. As a result, we must look beyond the opium trade as the cause of Afghanistan's woes and instead recognize it as a symptom of the deeply entrenched political, social, and economic issues that continue to plague Afghanistan today. And to do that, we must better understand the history that has so fundamentally shaped, and continues to shape, the present.

Notes

Introduction

1. UNODC, *Afghanistan: Opium Survey 2011*, 15.

2. SIGAR, *Quarterly Report to the United States Congress*, 193.

3. UNODC, "Afghan Opium Crop Cultivation."

4. For more on the alleged connections between the Taliban and the opium trade, see Peters, *Seeds of Terror.*

5. For more on the relationship between counternarcotics and counterinsurgency, see Felbab-Brown, *Shooting Up.*

6. Mansfield, "Alternative Development in Afghanistan," 13.

7. Among the most important and clear analyses of the contemporary drug trade in Afghanistan is Mansfield's *A State Built on Sand.*

8. On labor, see Mansfield, "Access to Labour." On credit, see Mansfield, "The Role of Opium," and Pain, "Opium Poppy and Informal Credit." On root causes, see Mansfield, "Diversity and Dilemma." For analysis of the role of poverty in the opium trade, see UNODC, "Is Poverty Driving the Afghan Opium Boom?" As it relates to the War on Terror, see the growing number of UNODC reports that analyze the role of drugs and the threat of violence. See, for example, UNODC's *Afghanistan Opium Survey 2012.* For connections between opium eradication and political instability, see Rubin

and Sherman, *Counter-narcotics to Stabilize Afghanistan*, and Chouvy, "Drugs and the Financing of Terrorism." For criticisms of the drug war and the impact on the broader conflict in Afghanistan, see Carpenter, "How the Drug War in Afghanistan Undermines America's War on Terror," and Felbab-Brown, "The Obama Administration's New Counternarcotics Strategy."

9. The UNODC publishes yearly reports about the opium trade. They also sponsor reports by consultants that provide valuable glimpses into opium's role as an economic and political agent. Some of the best sources for in-depth analysis of the contemporary opium trade are Jonathon Goodhand, David MacDonald, David Mansfield, and Richard Scott.

10. For insight into opium's role in funding Taliban resistance, see Peters, *Seeds of Terror.* Others have immersed themselves in the drug trade. For these pseudoanthropological memoirs, see Salmon, *Poppy*, and Hafvenstein, *Opium Season.*

11. Frydl, *The Drug Wars in America*, 25.

12. Walker, "Drug Control and the Issue of Culture," 372.

13. Abraham and van Schendel, "Introduction: The Making of Illicitness," 19.

14. Gootenberg, *Andean Cocaine.*

15. I have opted to focus on state formation rather than state building. As Jonathan Goodhand explains, state building implies the "conscious, planned, and often externally driven attempt to establish an apparatus of control." Focusing on state formation, on the other hand, reveals a nonlinear process occurring in "fits and starts," not the gradual diffusion of power outward. See Goodhand, *Bandits, Borderlands, and Opium Wars*, 7.

16. See Scott, *Seeing Like a State*, 78.

17. Olivier Roy, defines a *qawm* as a "communal group, whose sociological basis may vary. It may be a clan (in tribal zones), a village, an ethnic group, an extended family, a professional group." See Roy, *Islam and Resistance in Afghanistan*, 242.

18. Abraham and van Schendel, "Introduction: The Making of Illicitness," 6.

19. See Hopkins and Marsden, *Fragments of the Afghan Frontier*, 219. The authors note that the frontier was often characterized as a series of fragments, preventing unification of a cohesive whole. They explain that this fragmentation is also an important component of the frontier's heterogeneity, however, and serves to bind groups as well as pull them apart. The idea stems from Gyan Pandey's work, *Routine Violence*, in which he calls for historians to recognize the state's constructions of "minorities" and how this is only a fragment of history. Presenting the state as one component of a much larger historical mosaic presents a more complete picture of the history of which the state and "minorities" are both intertwined and equally influential (42). Hopkins and Marsden thus posit that these fragmented groups should be placed alongside states as part of the historical composite.

20. McCoy, *The Politics of Heroin*. Alfred McCoy's *Politics of Heroin* is generally considered the main source for the history of opium during the Cold War. McCoy's thesis centers on the role of US-funded covert wars using the illicit narcotics trade to fight communism. McCoy explains the dramatic rise of opium production in Afghanistan during the Afghan-Soviet War as a result of Pakistan's Inter-Service Intelligence logistical support, CIA covert protection, and the financial services of Pakistani

banks. McCoy's argument that opium was a consequence of the political chaos of the 1970s fails to consider how opium, particularly opium policies, contributed to the fragmentation and eventual downfall of the Afghan state in the first place.

21. Haq's *Drugs in South Asia* is one of the few works to emphasize a broader historical lens to examine the history of drugs in South Asia. He argues that the opium industry in Pakistan and Afghanistan were products of the colonial heritage of opium production in South Asia. More specifically, Haq contends that Pakistan's opium problem resulted from the state's failed attempts to create licit sources of opium for its own population. Unlike McCoy or MacDonald, Haq presents the current opium problem in the region as a consequence of the failed political will of the governments of Pakistan and Afghanistan.

22. MacDonald's *Drugs in Afghanistan* deals primarily with contemporary issues of drug production, trade, and use in Afghanistan. In historicizing the drug trade, however, MacDonald perpetuates the misconception that during the period from 1930 to 1970, aside from brief mentions of the prohibitions of opium in 1945 and 1956, opium was a dormant commodity, an isolated global issue, and a nonfactor in shaping the growth of opium production during the early 1970s. He argues that the "catalyst for the expansion of opium cultivation and production in Afghanistan was the new bans and stricter drug control laws imposed in neighboring Iran, Pakistan, and India at the end of the 1970s" (60).

23. See Allan, "Opium Production in Afghanistan and Pakistan," 141. Consequently, Allan notes, this was also the beginning of the ideological resistance to the West, as many Afghans were shocked by Westerners' behavior, rejecting them and the West as sources of perversion and moral corruption.

24. See Asad, *The Politics and Economics of Drug Production on the Pakistan-Afghanistan Border*. Asad finds that the opium industry emerged along the border of Pakistan and Afghanistan in the wake of the Pakistan government's Hudood Ordinance in 1979, a prohibition policy that ostensibly pushed the licit opium industry underground. Asad also argues that the 1979 prohibition of opium in Iran, which had a large indigenous opium industry, created the demand for Afghan opium.

25. See Lamour and Lamberti, *The International Connection*. Lamour and Lamberti's work, like McCoy's, highlighted the depth of the illicit narcotics trade during the 1970s. But unlike McCoy, it acts as an ethnography of the global drug trade during the 1970s and not as a historical monograph.

26. See Haq, "Pak-Afghan Drug Trade," 948. Haq emphasizes the importance of global factors in shaping the opium industry in Afghanistan. He adds that the prohibition of opium in Iran coincided with the prohibition of opium in Turkey, exposing the Afghan-Pakistan industry to markets outside of central and Southwest Asia. Moreover, he argues that the influx of Western hippies into Afghanistan during the late 1960s exposed many Afghans to the potential of opium as a lucrative commercial product, a point reinforced by Nigel Allan.

27. See Gregorian, *The Emergence of Modern Afghanistan*, 343. Under Nadir Shah, the Mushiban ban recognized that the downfall of their predecessors was largely a consequence of their attempts to modernize Afghanistan. As a result, the Mushiban leadership implemented a policy of "gradual modernization."

28. See Newell, "The Prospects of State-Building in Afghanistan," 113. This was most evident in the declaration of Pashto as the national language despite the overwhelming use of Dari (Persian) as the lingua franca.

29. See Rubin, *The Fragmentation of Afghanistan*.

30. See Barfield, "Problems in Establishing Legitimacy in Afghanistan." Both Barfield and Rubin note that the reliance on foreign aid allowed the state to hover above society rather than integrating into society.

31. See Scott, *Seeing Like a State*.

32. See Tilly, *Coercion, Capital, and European States*. Tilly notes that many of the states in Europe used war as a means of justifying state building and "reached directly into communities and households to seize the wherewithal of war" (104). Afghanistan never went to war under Musahiban leadership. The war on drugs and the need to control illicit narcotics underscored the state attempts to build larger and more intrusive institutions of control, however.

33. Tomlins, "Introduction: The Many Legalities of Colonization," 3.

34. Roy, *Islam and Resistance in Afghanistan*, 24.

35. Scott, *Weapons of the Weak*, 29. Scott defines the ordinary forms of peasant resistance as foot dragging, dissimulation, false compliance, pilfering, feigned ignorance, slander, arson, sabotage, etc.

36. See Hopkins and Marsden, *Fragments of the Afghan Frontier*, 2. They discuss in detail how mobility and states' attempts to regulate and confine people's movements have been fundamental to the history of peoples living on Afghanistan's frontier. Not only has mobility been a key characteristic of survival and reactions to political pressures; it has also been important in strategies for capitalizing on economic opportunities. Hopkins and Marsden note that this mobility, one often invisible in national histories, is fundamental to the identity of those living in frontier spaces.

37. An important theme recurring throughout this project is the role of opium as a licit and illicit commodity. Categorizing opium as illegal and the creation and perpetuation of stereotypical tropes of drug users, farmers, and traders as criminals (those that were historically constructed and then projected onto the rest of the world by the West, especially the United States), are primary targets of this work. I adopt the perspectives proposed by Abraham and van Schendel that identifying how opium the commodity became an illegal substance reveals the origins of and conflicts with regulatory authority. See Abraham and van Schendel, "Introduction: The Making of Illicitness," 16–17.

38. Gallant, "Brigandage, Piracy, Capitalism, and State Formation," 25.

39. See Berridge, "Victorian Opium Eating." Berridge notes that drug laws in Victorian England were not about the drugs but rather about class tensions, race, and the pressures on the medical profession. In this vein, drug control, almost universally, is a form of population control, not benevolent goodwill on the part of governments. Thus, analyzing why governments implement drug control laws provides keen insights into deeper social, political, and cultural issues directly or indirectly linked to drug production, use, and trade.

40. Anthropologists dominate the history of Afghanistan. The incredible diversity of central Asian tribes, clans, and ethnic groups, resulting from geographical isolation

(among many other factors) and the limited state encroachment (as explained earlier) has made anthropology an important contribution to the historical fabric.

41. See Migdal, *Strong Societies and Weak States.*

42. See Weiner, "Political Change in Asia, Africa, and the Middle East."

43. See Campos and Gootenberg, "Toward a New Drug History of Latin America," 10.

44. Walker, "Drug Control and the Issue of Culture," 372. Walker notes that in the design of antiopium policies in Asia the US was remarkably ignorant of the issue of culture. Later historians reinforced these notions by discussing too broadly the role of the state.

45. American perceptions regarding opium use were conflicted and by no means uniform. The vilification of drug use began as early as the nineteenth century, and criminalization soon after that. Much of the debate centered on the core causes of drug addiction.

46. McCoy, "From Free Trade to Prohibition," 308–309.

47. Gootenberg, "Introduction: Cocaine," 20.

1. Colonial and Global Engagements

1. C. Latimer, "Prohibition of the Import of Afghan Opium into British India," January 27, 1925, p. 1, Dangerous Drugs and Poisons: Afghan Opium Transit to Japan, 1924–1936, HO 144/22338, UK National Archives, Kew.

2. Buddenberg, "On the Cultural History of Opium," 4–5.

3. Courtwright, *Forces of Habit*, 32.

4. Courtwright, 32–33.

5. Trocki, *Opium, Empire, and the Global Political Economy*, 21–49.

6. Owen, *British Opium Policy in China and India*, 25.

7. Zheng, "The Social Life of Opium," 16–33.

8. McCoy, *The Politics of Heroin*, 5.

9. Courtwright, *Forces of Habit*, 35.

10. McCoy, *The Politics of Heroin*, 5.

11. Owen, *British Opium Policy in China and India*, 283.

12. Trocki, *Opium, Empire, and the Global Political Economy*, 86.

13. Trocki, 87.

14. Courtwright, *Dark Paradise*, 56.

15. Courtwright, 58. Arguably one of the most famous narratives on opium use was Thomas Dequincey's *Confessions of an Opium Eater*, which made famous the trials and tribulations of opium use and addiction.

16. Taylor, *American Diplomacy and the Narcotics Traffic*, 24.

17. Bewley-Taylor, *The United States and International Drug Control*, 18.

18. Taylor, *American Diplomacy and the Narcotics Traffic*, 24. Pressure from the Anti-Opium society forced the British government to launch a royal commission to investigate the impact of the drug trade and the plausibility of curbing or ending the opium trade. Finalized in 1895, the report was overwhelmingly positive for the British

opium trade. As quoted in Taylor, the report "vindicated the Indian government" and quieted "the agitation against the trade."

19. Bewley-Taylor, *The United States and International Drug Control*, 19.

20. For more on the pre-American origins of drug prohibition, see Windle, "How the East Influenced Drug Prohibition," 1185–1199.

21. Kennedy, *The Rise and Fall of the Great Powers*, 317.

22. Tyrell, *Reforming the World*, 149.

23. Bewley-Taylor, *The United States and International Drug Control*, 29.

24. Bewley-Taylor, 19–20.

25. Bewley-Taylor, 21–22.

26. Bewley-Taylor, 24.

27. Courtwright, *Dark Paradise*, 104–109. The act was the first sweeping federal anti-drug law, which criminalized addiction to drugs. It forced many users to stop getting drugs from doctors or other quasi-medical sources, rather, getting them from illegal sources on the street. More important, unlike other nations, which still held drug addiction to be a medical or scientific issue, the Harrison Act seemed to validate the American notion of drug use as a criminal act, a punitive measure to be enforced by police, not doctors. The antiopium crusade gained enough support to win national laws that expanded the scope of policing to regulate what people were allowed to put in their body. See: McCoy, "Coercion and its Unintended Consequences," *200.*

28. Bewley-Taylor, *The United States and International Drug Control*, 27.

29. See Kusevic, "Drug Abuse Control and International Treaties," 36–52.

30. McCoy, "Coercion and Its Unintended Consequences," 202.

31. Bewley-Taylor, *The United States and International Drug Control*, 33. For example, Americans were unrelenting in their belief that opium, aside from its scientific and medical purposes, was a "moral and social evil." Furthermore, the only way to truly stop the drug trade was to stop drug production at its source.

32. Bewley-Taylor, 34.

33. Staanekzai, *Movad Mokder dar Afghanistan*, 13.

34. Buddenberg, "On the Cultural History of Opium," 5. What tradition means, in this sense, is not definitive or precise. AAN (Afghanistan Analysts Network) points out that all evidence suggests Afghanistan's opium trade is fairly recent, either from the Silk Road from China or from Persia. Furthermore, there are no Persian words for opium in Afghanistan; *koknar* and *taryak*, the two most common names for the plant, derive from Turkish and Greek.

35. Honchell, *Pursuing Pleasure, Attaining Oblivion*, 11.

36. MacDonald, *Drugs in Afghanistan*, 137.

37. MacDonald, 139. MacDonald notes that in some cases there were sharp divisions between those who drank alcohol, *araq*, and those who ate *majun* while commiserating. Taken from Zahirud-Din Muhammad Babur, *Babur-Nama*, translated from Turki by Annette S. Beveridge (Lahore: Sang-e-Meel, 2002), 16.

38. Honchell, *Pursuing Pleasure, Attaining Oblivion*, 21–22.

39. Honchell, 27–28. Honchell notes that many of the British historians fed into the narrative of Humayun as an addict, despite virtually no evidence of drug abuse.

40. Honchell, 42.
41. Honchell, 48.
42. Honchell, 47–48.
43. Haq, *Drugs in South Asia*, 18.
44. Clarke, *Hashish*, 41.
45. Clarke, 42.
46. Pennell, *Among the Wild Tribes of the Afghan Frontier*, 239.
47. Alexander, *Narcotics in India and South Asia*, 28.
48. Gregorian, *The Emergence of Modern Afghanistan*, 129.
49. Gregorian, 130. Gregorian notes that Rahman Khan's appeal differed from that of previous rulers. Traditionally, Afghan rulers claim to power derived from the tribal chieftains and the *loya jirga* (grand tribal council), whereby the monarchy was legitimized. The amir noted, however, that kings were "vice-regents of gods," in effect, acting as god on earth.
50. Gregorian, 130.
51. Gregorian, 131–132.
52. Gregorian, 136–137.
53. Gregorian, 140.
54. Gregorian, 130.
55. Gregorian, 144.
56. Staanekzai, *Movad Mokder dar Afghanistan*, 13. Nasrullah Staanekzai claims the use of drugs was discouraged, but he does not explain the extent to which, or even why, that was the case. Unlike Amanullah Khan a decade later, Staanekzai notes that Abdur Rahman discouraged the trade, but gives little evidence as to how this would have manifested itself. On the other hand, under Amanullah, the evidence of the government trying to curb domestic use is much clearer.
57. *Imperial Gazetteer of India*, 19:196–197. Charas and bhang were also prevalent, despite the fact that cannabis grew throughout the region. Afghan opium traders, along with other foreign opium traders, had to pay a duty of two rupee per seer to have their product admitted into the province. See http://dsal.uchicago.edu/reference/gazetteer/pager.html?objectid=DS405.1.I34_V19_202.gif.
58. Hanifi, *Connecting Histories in Afghanistan*, 130.
59. Hanifi, 134.
60. Hanifi, 137.
61. Gregorian, *The Emergence of Modern Afghanistan*, 133.
62. Gregorian, 146.
63. For example, both Iran and Turkey saw burgeoning constitutional movements challenging the authority of the theocratic monarchies. See Gelvin, *The Modern Middle East*.
64. For more, see Barfield, *Afghanistan*.
65. Newell, *The Politics of Afghanistan*, 51.
66. Barfield, *Afghanistan*, 176.
67. Newell, *The Politics of Afghanistan*, 52.
68. Barfield, *Afghanistan*, 180–181.

69. Barfield, 181. Although the war was a great political move, it was a potential bad economic decision. The Afghan state had been subsidized by the British since Abdur Rahman Khan, and now, for the first time in three decades, lost this subsidy.

70. Newell, *The Politics of Afghanistan*, 53.

71. Manela, *The Wilsonian Moment*.

72. For a more substantial analysis of Amanullah's reforms, see Gregorian, *The Emergence of Modern Afghanistan*, 441–458.

73. Nawid, *Religious Response to Social Change in Afghanistan*, 79.

74. Nawid, 81.

75. Newell, *The Politics of Afghanistan*, 53.

76. Gregorian, *The Emergence of Modern Afghanistan*, 248.

77. Nawid, *Religious Response to Social Change in Afghanistan*, 97.

78. Nawid, 98. Nawid points out that the ulema had significant reservations about laws that predetermined punishments. For "a *qazi* should examine the time, location, type and circumstance of the individual crime and apply precepts of the *shari'at* and his personal judgement."

79. Gregorian, *The Emergence of Modern Afghanistan*, 250–251.

80. Gregorian, 248–249.

81. Gregorian lists the crimes and punishments for drug and alcohol use as falling under Article 91. Considering the numerous versions of the criminal code, this is not all too surprising.

82. Staanekzai, *Movad Mokder*, 14 (Articles 125/131).

83. Staanekzai, 14 (Article 131).

84. MacDonald, 142–143. MacDonald notes that in Muslim countries, as in the rest of the world, there is incredible variation in the interpretation of the Quran and the hadith regarding the use of drugs and alcohol.

85. "Translations of Extracts from the Afghan Customs Tariff, Section 1, Article 2 (1925)," FO 402/6, UK National Archives, Kew.

86. Gregorian, *The Emergence of Modern Afghanistan*, 250.

87. Hickman, "Drugs and Race in American Culture," 71–91.

88. In "Drugs and Race in American Culture," Hickman analyzes how much of the discourse on addiction centered not on the drug itself but on the racial character of the people associated with its use. More often than not, the assumption that drug use was so ingrained in Asian cultures led to a depiction of Western addicts of the drug as Chinese, "Orientals," or Arabs rather than as addicts per se.

89. Gavit, *Opium*, 38.

90. Vavilov and Bukinich, *Agricultural Afghanistan*, 584.

91. Gregorian, *The Emergence of Modern Afghanistan*, 253.

92. Staanekzai, *Movad Mokder*, 14 (Article 125).

93. "Translations of Extracts from the Afghan Customs Tariff, Section 1, Article 2 (1925)."

94. Gregorian, *The Emergence of Modern Afghanistan*, 237.

95. Taylor, *American Diplomacy and the Narcotics Traffic*, 73.

96. Taylor, 80.

97. Haq, *Drugs in South Asia*, 72–76.

98. Haq, 74–83.

99. Haq, 84.

100. McAllister, *Drug Diplomacy in the Twentieth Century*, 76. The British agreed to end the opium trade only on the condition that the Chinese get their own house in order. This would push the actual end of the opium trade into the 1930s.

101. C. Latimer, "Prohibition of the Import of Afghan Opium into British India," January 27, 1925, p. 1.

102. Latimer, 3.

103. Latimer, 3.

104. Latimer, 4.

105. R. R. Maconachie, "Memo 358, Export of Opium from Afghanistan," June 13, 1924, Dangerous Drugs and Poisons: Afghan Opium Transit to Japan, 1924–1936, HO 144/22338, UK National Archives, Kew.

106. Latimer, "Prohibition of the Import of Afghan Opium into British India," 4.

107. R. R. Maconachie, "Proposed Prohibition of Imports of Afghan Opium into British India," September 12, 1924, Dangerous Drugs and Poisons: Afghan Opium Transit to Japan, 1924–1936, HO 144/22338, UK Archives, Kew.

108. Maconachie, 2.

109. Maconachie, 2.

110. Maconachie, 3.

111. A. Tottenham, "Notification. Customs," Finance Department (Central Revenue), November 24, 1924, HO 144/22338, UK National Archives, Kew.

112. Haq, *Drugs in South Asia*, 98.

113. Haq, 96.

114. Hanifi, *Connecting Histories in Afghanistan*, 136.

115. Hanifi, 136.

116. Poullada, *Reform and Rebellion in Afghanistan*, 138.

117. Ghani, *A Review of the Political Situation in Central Asia*, 111.

118. Gallant, "Brigandage, Piracy, Capitalism, and State-Formation," 37.

119. Gallant, 38.

2. The Politics of Prohibition

1. Gregorian, *The Emergence of Modern Afghanistan*, 266.

2. It is unclear whether French authorities mistakenly dropped the package, or whether this was an excuse to search Ghulam Nabi. It is also unclear how much French authorities suspected Ghulam Nabi of potential criminal activity.

3. US State Department, Dispatch No. 9692, July 18, 1929, p. 2, Entry A19, Bureau of Narcotics and Dangerous Drugs (BNDD), Subject Files, 1916–1970, Record Group (RG) 170, Records of the Drug Enforcement Agency, Box 151, "Afghan, Vol. 1, 1929–1968"; National Archives II, College Park, MD.

4. Dupree, *Afghanistan*, 449–458. The term Musahiban denotes the lineage name of Nadir Khan (who later changed his name to Nadir Shah) and his five brothers from the line of Muhmmadzai: Aziz, Hashim, Shah Wali, Shah Mahmud, and Ali Khan

(449, 458). For further explanation of the historical origins of this line and its political ambitions, see Barfield, *Afghanistan*, 195–196.

5. For a review of drug prohibition and alternative development programs, see Farrell, "A Global Empirical Review of Crop Eradication," 410.

6. Gregorian, *The Emergence of Modern Afghanistan*, 273.

7. Dupree, *Afghanistan*, 452.

8. Gregorian, *The Emergence of Modern Afghanistan*, 269.

9. Dupree, *Afghanistan*, 454.

10. Gregorian, *The Emergence of Modern Afghanistan*, 275.

11. Barfield, *Afghanistan*, 193.

12. Gregorian, *The Emergence of Modern Afghanistan*, 278.

13. DeQuincey, *Confessions of an Opium Eater*, 42.

14. *Le MATIN* was a US-funded French language daily newspaper that covered domestic and global events and issues.

15. US State Department, Dispatch No. 9692, July 18, 1929, p. 3.

16. US State Department, Dispatch No. 9692, p. 4.

17. Memorandum for Division of Foreign Control, "Narcotics, Afghanistan Minister," Paris, July 24, 1929, RG 170, Records of the Drug Enforcement Agency, Box 151, "Afghan, Vol. 1, 1929–1968"; NACP.

18. Gregorian, *The Emergence of Modern Afghanistan*, 267.

19. R. F. Wigram, "Drug Smuggling by Ex-Afghan Minister in Paris," India Office, No. F3330/714/87, June 30, 1930, Involvement of Afghan Legation in the Seizure of Cocaine in Paris (1931–1936), IOR/L/E/7/1563, British Library.

20. Viceroy, Foreign and Political Department, to Secretary of State for India, "Copy of Telegram, 3117-S," October 15, 1929, Involvement of Afghan Legation in the Seizure of Cocaine in Paris (1931–1936), IOR/L/E/7/1563, British Library.

21. Wigram, "Drug Smuggling," 3.

22. Gallant, "Brigandage, Piracy, Capitalism, and State Formation," 25. In this case, however, we should probably conclude that bandits *almost* helped make the state.

23. Barfield, *Afghanistan*, 196–198.

24. Gregorian, *The Emergence of Modern Afghanistan*, 295.

25. In Pashto, *loya jirgas* means "grand council" or "grand assembly." Essentially a larger *jirga*, a *loya jirgas* is a meeting of local village elders and representatives to discuss important social, political, and religious matters. *Loya jirgas* became essential political meetings between Afghan politicians and tribal and religious elders, often used by Afghan politicians to legitimize their rule among tribal authorities.

26. Gregorian, *The Emergence of Modern Afghanistan*, 304–306.

27. Gregorian, 313.

28. Davenport-Hines, *The Pursuit of Oblivion*, 105.

29. Article 91, Penal Code of 1924–25. The extent of opium addiction in Afghanistan during Amanullah's reign is unknown. Traditionally, Badakhshan was the only province with a high number of opium addicts. Opium trading was relatively small. It is likely that Amanullah included this provision under the auspices of some Western nations or the League of Nations.

30. Dupree, *Afghanistan*, 475–477.

31. Gregorian, *The Emergence of Modern Afghanistan*, 362.

32. Barfield, *Afghanistan*, 198.

33. Gregorian, *The Emergence of Modern Afghanistan*, 375. Gregorian notes that this was the same year that the Soviet Union joined the League of Nations. It was likely that Afghanistan joined because of the USSR's new membership.

34. Gregorian, 376.

35. Skins from lamb that was a popular commodity for trade among nomadic and sedentary Afghans.

36. Franck, "Problems of Economic Development in Afghanistan," 297. Franck notes that both karakul and fruit were chiefly export products. As a result, they were susceptible to fluctuations and irregularities in the global market.

37. Gregorian, *The Emergence of Modern Afghanistan*, 368–369.

38. Gregorian, 366–367.

39. Franck, "Problems of Economic Development in Afghanistan," 298.

40. Gregorian, *The Emergence of Modern Afghanistan*, 370.

41. Gregorian, 378.

42. *Islah*, January 12, 1935. It should be noted that the United States did not establish a permanent mission in Afghanistan until 1943 (Library of Congress).

43. US State Department, *Foreign Relations*, p. 256: Murray to Dreyfus, January 28, 1941, Entry A19, BNDD, Subject Files, 1916–1970, RG 170, Records of the Drug Enforcement Agency, Box 142, "Misc. Narcotic Files," file 0480-172 Afghan; NACP.

44. Gregorian, *The Emergence of Modern Afghanistan*, 373.

45. Berke, "Public Health and Hygiene in Afghanistan," 6.

46. The original Dangerous Drugs Act was passed by the original twelve signatories of the Hague Convention of 1912; by 1934, there were fifty-six member states. The United States was instrumental in making its own Dangerous Drugs Act, otherwise known as the Volstead Act, a key component in the League of Nations.

47. Bureau of Narcotics, US Treasury Department, "Letter from M. Reich, Manager of Martin H Smith Company to Harry Anslinger," December 27, 1934, RG 170; NACP.

48. Davenport-Hines, *The Pursuit of Oblivion*, 259.

49. US State Department, "Letter from LW Robert, Asst. Sec., to Stuart J Fuller, Division of Far Eastern Affairs," 1934, RG 170; NACP.

50. McAllister, *Drug Diplomacy in the Twentieth Century*, 96. As McAllister explains, the Drug Supervisory Body (DSB) was responsible for administering the estimates. The DSB was also responsible for producing estimates for *all* nations, including those that did not ratify the treaty. The various provisions gave the body a fair amount of power in regulating the international trade for licit and illicit narcotics. The convention itself was largely a manifestation of US motivations to control the global drug trade. The various articles of the treaty contained subtle semantics reflecting the United States' desire to have the rest of the world adopt its administrative structure to suppress illicit traffic of narcotics. Article 15, in particular, gave Harry Anslinger and the BNDD immense power to regulate from which countries US pharmaceutical firms could purchase raw materials and to which nations they could export (see pp. 97–98).

51. League of Nations, "Signature by Afghanistan," No. C.L.54.1937.XI, Geneva, March 23, 1937, RG 170; NACP.

52. W. K. Fraser-Taylor, "Memo No. 86," August 7, 1935, Dangerous Drugs and Poisons: Afghan Opium Transit to Japan, 1924–1936, HO 144/ 22338, UK National Archives, Kew.

53. Kabul Minister to Secretary of State for Foreign Affairs, India Office, July 5, 1932, *Export of Afghan Opium through India*, 1932, Cabinet Office (CO) 825/15/12, UK National Archives, Kew.

54. Telegram from secretary of state to government of India, Foreign and Political Department, September 16, 1932, P.Z. 5438/32, *Export of Afghan Opium through India*, 1932, CO 825/15/12, UK National Archives, Kew.

55. Federal Bureau of Narcotics, "Engert to Sec. of State," No. 300, November 30, 1943, RG 170; NACP.

56. US State Department, "Afghan Opium Exports, 1937–1941," No. 392, February 9, 1944, RG 170; NACP.

57. US State Department, "Attention: Bureau of Narcotics," July 30, 1936, RG 170; NACP.

58. Department of Pensions and National Health, Government of Canada, "Personal Letter to Harry Anslinger," August 3, 1939, RG 170; NACP.

59. Personal Letter, "Harry Anslinger to Col. Clem Sharman," August 16, 1939, RG 170; NACP.

60. Dupree, *Afghanistan*, 480.

61. Gregorian, *The Emergence of Modern Afghanistan*, 390.

62. *Iqtesad Journal*, August–September 1944, Library of Congress.

63. *Iqtesad Journal*, December 43–January 44, Library of Congress.

64. *Iqtesad Journal*, January–February 1944, Library of Congress.

65. *Iqtesad Journal*, August–September 1944, Library of Congress.

66. US State Department, confidential memo from Charles Thayer to secretary of state, "Opium Traffic in Afghanistan," No. 251, August 9, 1943, RG 170; NACP.

67. US State Department, confidential memo from Charles Thayer to secretary of state, "Opium Traffic in Afghanistan."

68. *Iqtesad Journal*, October–November 1944, Library of Congress.

69. Afghan American Trading Company, "Letter to Treasury Department," December 18, 1941, RG 170; NACP.

70. Courtwright, *Forces of Habit*, 77.

71. Note attached to letter from Afghan American Trading Company, December 18, 1941, author unknown, RG 170; NACP.

72. Harry Anslinger, letter to Afghan American Trading Company, December 23, 1941, RG 170; NACP.

73. Harry Anslinger, letter to Fred Stock, Special Advisor, Health Supplies Section, Division of Purchases, Office of Production Management, December 29, 1941, RG 170; NACP.

74. Wilson, American Commissioner, India,. confidential telegram, No. 4, January 8, 1942, RG 170; NACP.

75. Confidential telegram, Attention, Bureau of Narcotics, from Wilson, American commissioner in India, January 10, 1942, RG 170; NACP.

76. Confidential telegram, FE 890H.114 Narcotics 16, January 20, 1942, RG 170; NACP.

77. William McAllister notes that the United States began purchasing opium from countries such as Afghanistan as a way of generating sympathy for the Allied cause. In the case of Afghanistan, because of its previous relationship with Germany, the purchase of opium could shift the tide in a strategic region of central Asia. McAllister, *Drug Diplomacy in the Twentieth Century*, 148.

78. Bureau of Narcotics, letter from Herbert Gaston, assistant secretary of Treasury to the Division of Far Eastern Affairs, January 21, 1942, RG 170; NACP.

79. It is also unclear what happened to the opium in Afghanistan or whether it was exported elsewhere.

80. Harry Anslinger, letter from HA to Mr. John Goodloe, Executive VP, Defense Supplies Corporation, September 12, 1942, RG 170; NACP.

81. Gregorian, *The Emergence of Modern Afghanistan*, 390–391. In 1941, the Afghan government had proposed signing a treaty with the United States. Although both countries slowly grew closer over the course of the war and engaged in a formal exchange of diplomatic missions in 1943, relations remained tepid at best until after the war.

82. Anslinger, letter from Harry Anslinger to Mr. John Goodloe, September 12, 1942, RG 170; NACP.

83. Defense Supplies Corporation, letter from John Goodloe to Mr. Morris Rosenthal, assistant director, Board of Economic Warfare, September 15, 1942, RG 170; NACP.

84. Defense Supplies Corporation, letter from John Goodloe to Morris Rosenthal, Board of Economic Warfare, September 23, 1942, RG 170; NACP.

85. Royal Afghan Consulate, letter from Muhammad Omar to Harry Anslinger, September 25, 1942, RG 170; NACP.

86. Defense Supplies Corporation, letter from Harry Anslinger to John Goodloe, September 26, 1942, RG 170; NACP.

87. Defense Supplies Corporation, letter from John Goodloe to Harry Anslinger, September 30, 1942, RG 170; NACP.

88. Royal Afghan Consulate, letter from Mohammad Omar to Harry Anslinger, re: Afghan Opium, Ref. # 6440, October 20, 1942, RG 170; NACP.

89. Bureau of Narcotics, letter from Harry Anslinger to Mohammad Omar, Royal Afghan Consulate, New York, October 21, 1942, RG 170; NACP.

90. Royal Afghan Consulate, letter from Mohammad Omar to Harry Anslinger, Bureau of Narcotics, Ref. # 6454, October 22, 1942, RG 170; NACP.

91. Bureau of Narcotics, letter from Harry Anslinger to Mohammad Omar, October 24, 1942, RG 170; NACP.

92. Merck & Co. Inc., receipt of purchase for Mohammad Omar, Afghan American Trading Company, November 17, 1942, RG 170; NACP. The deal was finalized November 17, 1942. Through Merck & Co., the United States purchased two separate shipments of eight tons of opium gum containing 16 percent morphine and three tons with

10.5 percent morphine, to be delivered in six weeks and four months, respectively. The shipments were granted all necessary licenses for both the United States and India, and certified by officials in Karachi to verify the purchase before transport.

93. US State Department, confidential telegram, No. 118, June 9, 1943, RG 170; NACP.

94. The Controller of Enemy Trading in India, "US Watch List Report: Intercepted Letter from Afghan National Bank Karachi to Bank Millie Kabul," June 22, 1943, RG 170; NACP.

95. Merck & Co., letter from J. J. Kerrigan to Harry Anslinger, Bureau of Narcotics, June 15, 1943, RG 170; NACP.

96. McAllister, *Drug Diplomacy in the Twentieth Century*, 148.

97. US State Department, confidential memo from Charles Thayer to secretary of state, "Opium Traffic in Afghanistan," No. 251, August 9, 1943, p. 2, RG 170; NACP.

98. US State Department, confidential memo from Charles Thayer to secretary of state, "Opium Traffic in Afghanistan." As McAllister notes, when the price of illicit narcotics was greater than licit ones, it indicated the strength of the recreational narcotics market, most often illicit. McAllister, *Drug Diplomacy*, 19.

99. US State Department, confidential memo from Charles Thayer to secretary of state, "Opium Traffic in Afghanistan."

100. McCoy, *The Politics of Heroin*, 113.

101. Courtwright, *Forces of Habit*, 77.

102. Gregorian, *The Emergence of Modern Afghanistan*, 374.

103. US State Department, "Attention: Bureau of Narcotics (FE 511.4 A 6/1762)," October 20, 1941, p. 3, RG 170; NACP.

104. US State Department, translation of letter from Ministry of Foreign Affairs, Royal Government of Afghanistan to the Legation of the United States of America, Kabul," December 19, 1942 (original letter dated December 2, 1942), RG 170; NACP.

105. Collins, *Regulations and Prohibitions*, 87–99.

106. US State Department, letter from US Legation, Kabul to Bureau of Narcotics," FE 511.A6/1770, January 1, 1943, RG 170; NACP.

107. US Treasury Department, letter from Herbert Gaston, assistant secretary of the Treasury to George A. Morlock, Division of Far Eastern Affairs, Department of State," January 8, 1943, RG 170; NACP.

108. US State Department, letter to American Legation, Kabul," January 21, 1943, RG 170; NACP.

109. US State Department, American Legation, Kabul, to Secretary of State, March 17, 1943, RG 170; NACP. The list was as follows:

> 20 kg Codeinum Purum, 30 kg Codeinum Phosphoricum, 15 kg Cocainum Hydrochloricum, 15 kg Ethyl Morphin Hydrochlo (Dionin), 1 kg Stovainum, 50 kg Pulvis Opium, 250 kg Pulvis Epicacuanha Cum Opium, 100 kg Tincture Opium C Amphoratum, 50 kg tincture Opium Cum Crocus (Laudinum de Syndenham), 30 kg Pulvis Creta Aromatic Cum Opium, 100×12 Amp. Pantopon 2 cc, 10×250 Amp. Eucodal, and 5 kg Extractus Cannabis Indica

110. US State Department, letter from US Legation, Kabul, to Bureau of Narcotics, 890 H.114 Narcotics, April 13, 1943, RG 170; NACP.

111. Letter, Harry Anslinger to Muhammad Omar Khan, April 16, 1943, RG 170; NACP.

112. US State Department, "Bureau of Narcotics: Memo," FE 5511.4A1/2261, June 1, 1943, RG 170; NACP.

113. As William McAllister notes, the end of the war was perceived by the most ardent antinarcotics advocates (Anslinger, Sharman) as a prime opportunity to push the antinarcotic agenda around the world. The plan was to launch a multifaceted campaign in countries ravaged by war to force compliance and limit excess production. As the Cold War developed, however, the various nations that had previously been united in their attempts to regulate narcotics fell into disunion amidst the chaotic political reshuffling of the Cold War. McAllister, *Drug Diplomacy in the Twentieth Century*, 156–157.

114. "Official Telegram to the Secretary of State," October 10, 1943, RG 170; NACP.

115. Letter to League of Nations, from Légation Royale d'Afghanistan à Londres, 1943, RG 170; NACP.

116. US State Department, "Notification of Afghanistan's Adherence to the Hague Opium Convention of 1912 Received by Netherlands Government," No. 140, May 17, 1944, RG 170; NACP.

117. US State Department, letter from Sec. of State A.A. Berle Jr. to Cornelius Van H. Engert, American minister, Kabul, No. 80, January 29, 1944, RG 170; NACP.

118. Afghan American Trading Company, "Letter to Harry Anslinger," No. X8506, February 11, 1944, RG 170; NACP.

119. Bureau of Narcotics, "Letter to Afghan American Trading Company," February 14, 1944, RG 170; NACP.

120. Afghan American Trading Company, "Letter to Harry Anslinger," No. 8155, January 5, 1944, RG 170; NACP.

121. *Iqtesad Journal*, October–November 1944, Library of Congress.

122. Collins, "Regulations and Prohibitions," 99.

123. US State Department Dispatch No. 459, "Letter from Engert to Ali Mohammed Khan, Min. of Foreign Affairs," September 25, 1944, RG 170; NACP. Engerts's letter emphasized all of the major points suggested by Berle earlier in the year. The letter included eighteen bulleted suggestions for the Afghan government to launch the prohibition.

124. US State Department, letter regarding statement from Council of Ministers, from Ministry of Foreign Affairs, Royal Government of Afghanistan to American Legation, Kabul, No. 549, November 12, 1944, RG 170; NACP.

125. US State Department, "Afghan Crude Opium Stocks," No. 790, July 21, 1945, RG 170; NACP.

126. Hon. Walter Judd, Congressional Record, Appendix, House of Representatives, Tuesday, December 5, 1944 (A4993), RG 170; NACP.

127. US State Department, "Interview of Abdul Hosayn Aziz by Helen Howell Moorhead," June 18, 1945, RG 170; NACP.

128. *Iqtesad Journal*, January–February, 1945, Library of Congress.

129. *Iqtesad Journal*, February–March 1945, Library of Congress.

130. *Iqtesad Journal*, June–July 1945, Library of Congress.

131. US State Department, "Afghan Crude Opium Stocks." RG 170; NACP.

132. US State Department, No. 232, September 18, 1947, RG 170; NACP.

133. US Treasury Department, "To the Officer in Charge of the American Mission, Kabul," No. 350, 1947, RG 170; NACP.

3. The Consequences of Coercion in Badakhshan

This chapter was originally published in a slightly different form as "Drug Control in Afghanistan: Culture, Politics, and Power during the 1958 Prohibition of Opium in Badakhshan," *Journal of Iranian Studies* 48, no. 2 (2015): 223–248.

Epigraph: Taken from Fishstein, *A Little-Bit Poppy-Free and a Little-Bit Eradicated*, 44.

1. Fishstein, *A Little-Bit Poppy-Free and a Little-Bit Eradicated*, 42–45.

2. Mansfield, "Our Friends in the North," 8.

3. Mansfield, 8.

4. For more on the difficulties various governing bodies have faced in legitimizing their rule in Afghanistan, see Barfield, "Problems in Establishing Legitimacy in Afghanistan," 263–293.

5. Although the prohibition was officially announced in November of 1957, I chose to reference the prohibition as being in 1958 since that is the year it went into effect.

6. Abraham and van Schendel, "Introduction: The Making of Illicitness," 4.

7. Though not officially part of the Marshall Plan, Afghanistan received a large increase in US aid and investment following the end of World War II. In total, $5.9 billion dollars in aid was sent to Asia. See US Bureau of the Census, *Statistical Abstract of the United States*, 899–902.

8. Franck, *Afghanistan*, 39.

9. Barfield, *Afghanistan*, 209. This was evidenced by the refusal of the United States to help in the building of the Afghan military following World War II.

10. Dupree, *Afghanistan*, 483.

11. For example, the Afghans had built a comfortable foreign exchange surplus after the war. However, the ever-increasing costs of the Helmand Valley Project pushed most of the surplus into the pockets of the Morrison-Knudsen Company, to the tune of $20 million in 1949. See Dupree, *Afghanistan*, 484.

12. Louis G. Dreyfus Jr., US State Department, "Opium Culture in Afghanistan," 889.53/6-2850, June 28, 1950, Entry A19, Bureau of Narcotics and Dangerous Drugs, Subject Files, 1916–1970, RG 170, Records of the Drug Enforcement Agency, Box 151, "Afghan, Vol. 1, 1929–1968"; NACP.

13. US State Department, "Afghan Desire to Re-open Opium Trade," 889.53/3-2551, June 28, 1950, RG 170, Box 151, "Afghan, Vol. 1, 1929–1968"; NACP.

14. US State Department, "Afghan Desire to Re-open Opium Trade," 889.53/3-2551.

15. Memorandum 0660, October 17, 1952, RG 170; NACP.

16. Bulgaria, Greece, India, Iran, Turkey, Yugoslavia, and the USSR.

17. McAllister, *Drug Diplomacy in the Twentieth Century*, 179–181.

18. Memo No. A-31, October 5, 1954, RG 170; NACP. The United States committed to India, Iran, Turkey, and Yugoslavia as the four countries allowed to continue to produce opium licitly under the 1953 Opium Protocol.

19. Dupree, *Afghanistan*, 499.

20. The Daud government stated that the US denial was based on Afghanistan's failure to join the Baghdad Pact or sign the Mutual Security Agreement, both of which the United States used to bind various Asian nations in military and economic aid systems to counter Sino-Soviet expansion. Pakistan happened to be a part of both. US officials countered that Afghanistan demanded guarantees to defend from Russian invasions, but the Americans were reluctant to give such assurances because Afghanistan was not as important to the Cold War as Pakistan. Dupree, *Afghanistan*, 510–511.

21. Franck, *Afghanistan*, 44.

22. In 1956, Afghanistan received $25 million in arms from the Soviet bloc. The United States refused to arm countries bent on aggression. Given the recent uproar over Pashtunistan, the United States did not want to get involved. Dupree, *Afghanistan*, 522.

23. Foreign Service Dispatch No. 285, "Sale of Afghan Opium," June 15, 1953, RG 170; NACP. The Soviets traded sugar for five tons of Afghan opium, priced at $17.90 per kilogram.

24. Aziz was referring to the bloodless coup launched by Daud in 1953.

25. A. Hamid Aziz, letter to United Nations, May 24, 1955, RG 170; NACP.

26. Letter from Charles Siragusa to Harry J. Anslinger, April 18, 1955, RG 170; NACP.

27. *Request for US Support for Amendment to Protocol of 1953*, June 10, 1955, RG 170; NACP.

28. It is interesting that Anslinger made such remarks. He was involved in the 1945 dialogue over the prohibition of opium, and it was apparent then that Afghanistan had an illicit opium industry. Even Afghan officials admitted that the smuggling of opium existed and that the state could do virtually nothing to stop it. (See comments from Wahab.)

29. For the better part of two centuries, Iran had developed a thriving opium industry. As outlined by Rudi Matthee, opium played a vital role in both the public and private lives of Persians. The Safavids and Qajars derived a considerable portion of revenue from the domestic opium industry. By the end of the nineteenth and beginning of the twentieth centuries, opium became a lucrative export for the state. However, there were severe social consequences for the relative ambivalence toward opium use. By World War II, Iran had one of the largest populations of opium addicts in the world, if not the largest. See Matthee, *The Pursuit of Pleasure*.

30. Gerald McLaughlin and Thomas Quinn's analysis revealed the enduring nature of opium use, its importance to state revenue, and the profound social consequences of widespread opium addiction. The state acknowledged that the domestic opium industry created $18 million in revenue. However, the state also argued that one-half million work hours were lost to addiction daily, 5,000 yearly suicides were attributed to addiction, and 300,000 farmers were known to grow opium. McLaughlin and Quinn got the number of 2.8 million addicts from Donald Wilber, *Iran Past and Present* (Princeton, NJ: Princeton University Press, 1958), 230. See also McLaughlin and Quinn, "Drug Control in Iran, 489.

31. Following the US-aided coup ousting Mohammad Mossadegh in 1953, the shah launched a series of measures to expand the power of the state to ensure that he would

never lose absolute power. The opium prohibition could be taken into account as part of the shah's expansion of legislative and judicial reach to solidify his rule. On the other hand, the mounting public pressure against opium, and alleged issues within his own family, may have compelled him to launch the ban on opium as well. See McLaughlin and Quinn, "Drug Control in Iran," 490–491.

32. McLaughlin and Quinn, 495.

33. US State Department, Memo No. 493, September 21, 1955, RG 170; NACP.

34. United States Mission to the United Nations, "Iranian Views on Afghanistan's Request to Be Recognized as an Opium-Producing Country for Export," Dispatch No. 1089, June 22, 1956, RG 170; NACP.

35. US State Department, American Embassy, Tehran, "Request of Afghanistan to Be an Authorized Opium Exporting State," Dispatch No. 1096, August 3, 1956, p. 2, RG 170; NACP.

36. United Nations, Economic and Social Council, "Commission on Narcotic Drugs, Eleventh Session, Item 6," May 3, 1956, RG 170; NACP.

37. United Nations, Economic and Social Council, Twenty-Second Session, "Item 13," July 24, 1956, RG 170; NACP.

38. Letter from Dr. Abdul Zahir to Mr. L. Atzenwiler, United Nations, February 19, 1956, RG 170; NACP. Dr. Zahir also made sure to decrease the amount of pharmaceuticals requested.

39. Opium Act of 1956 (Aswalname Tariawk 1335), Amendment 1, Arshif-e-Milli (National Archives), Kabul, Afghanistan.

40. Opium Act of 1956, Amendment 2 (note).

41. The Opium Act of 1335, Royal Government of Afghanistan, March 23, 1956, RG 170; NACP. Two versions of this law appeared, one at the Arshaf-e-Milli in Kabul, and another at the National Archives II in the United States. Article 10 did not appear in the Afghan version.

42. Abdul Malik, letter to Central Opium Control Board, March 1956, RG 170; NACP.

43. McAllister, *Drug Diplomacy in the Twentieth Century*, 197.

44. US State Department, Memo No. 493, September 21, 1955.

45. "Bureau of Narcotics Memo," February 9, 1956, RG 170; NACP. The sample was sent in a cloth bag, with the words, "Sample Afghan Almond, hard shell No. 1," printed on the side.

46. Letter to Harry Anslinger, No. 510–56, February 15, 1956, RG 170; NACP.

47. G. E. Yates, director, Division of Narcotic Drugs, European Office of the United Nations, "Afghanistan's Claim to Be Recognized as an Opium Producer," December 21, 1956, RG 170; NACP.

48. Federal Bureau of Narcotics, "Harry Anslinger to Gilbert E. Yates," December 27, 1956, RG 170; NACP.

49. US State Department, "Afghanistan's Request for Assistance in Future Opium Conferences," No. A-114, May 13, 1957, RG 170; NACP.

50. The United States Mission to the United Nations, "Afghanistan's Request to Be Recognized as a State Producing Opium for Export," Dispatch No. 1100, June 24, 1957, RG 170; NACP.

51. US State Department, "Letter to USUN: Afghanistan's Request," No. CA-134, July 3, 1957, RG 170; NACP.

52. Bureau of Narcotics, "Opium Smuggling from Afghanistan into Iran," Dispatch no. 312, October 5, 1957, RG 170; NACP. Ganz also mentioned that in his conversation with the source, he was under the impression that most Afghan elites, including government officials, were participating in the illicit opium trade.

53. Foreign Relations Files, United Nations, "Draft: 1958 UN Report: Afghanistan," 1958, p.2, RG 170; NACP.

54. Shahrani, *The Kirghiz and the Wakhi of Afghanistan*, 79–80.

55. Foreign Relations Files, United Nations, "Draft: 1958 UN Report: Afghanistan," 1958, pp. 3–4,170;

56. Bureau of Narcotics, "Afghanistan," April 4, 1958: 1, RG 170; NACP.

57. "Suppressing Opium," *London Times*, May 10, 1958, RG 170; NACP.

58. Farrell, "A Global Empirical Review of Crop Eradication," 410. Farrell's review of alternative development programs focuses primarily on the expansive use of such programs during the late 1980s and early 1990s. Although the Badakhshan case predates his analysis, there are parallels in the core theoretical objective of drug control in this case.

59. "Suppressing Opium," *London Times*, May 10, 1958, 2.170;

60. Afghanistan Permanent Mission to the United Nations, "Letter to Harry Anslinger from Dr. Abdul H. Tabibi," July 3, 1958, RG 170; NACP.

61. Bureau of Narcotics, "Letter from H. Anslinger to Dr. Abdul H. Tabibi," July 16, 1958, RG 170; NACP.

62. McLaughlin, "Growing Ban Hits One-Crop Region," RG 170; NACP.

63. US State Department, "Letter from A.L. Tennyson to Harry Anslinger," October 16, 1958, RG 170; NACP.

64. US State Department, "Afghan Request for P.L. 480 Aid," October 20, 1958, RG 170; NACP.

65. Bureau of Narcotics, "Letter to Dr. Max Myers, from Asst. Sec. A. Gilmore Flues," October 22, 1958, RG 170; NACP.

66. Bureau of Narcotics, "Letter to Guilford Jameson, Deputy Director ICA, from Harry Anslinger," October 27, 1958, RG 170; NACP.

67. International Cooperation Administration, "Letter to Gilford Flues, from Deputy Director Fitzgerald," November 12, 1958, RG 170; NACP.

68. US State Department, "Letter from Douglas Dillon to A. Guilmore Flues," November 19, 1958, RG 170; NACP.

69. Foreign Relations Files, United Nations, "Draft: 1958 UN Report: Afghanistan," 1958, p. 4, RG 170; NACP.

70. "Notes on a Journey to Badakhshan: July 23–August 6, 1961," *Afghanistan Strategic Intelligence, British Records, 1919–1970*, 4:653, Library of Congress.

71. Virginia Berridge notes that when the British government passed the 1868 Poisons and Pharmaceutical Act restricting certain uses of opium, fear of opium did not stem from the drug itself. In most cases, drug use was common and was considered normal, if not entirely necessary, to survive. Rather, the regulation of certain types of opium stemmed from middle-class fears of the working-class migrant labor groups,

whose members commonly used opium because they did not have access to or could not afford more formalized medical care. See Berridge, "Victorian Opium Eating."

72. Tyrell, *Reforming the World*, 147.

73. World Health Organization, "Technical Report Series, No. 131: Report of a Study Group on the Treatment and Character of Drug Addicts," Geneva, 1957, Section 2, RG 170; NACP.

74. United Nations, "Draft: 1958 UN Report: Afghanistan," 1958, p. 12, RG 170; NACP. The common solution for social addiction was to raise the standard of living, which the five-year plan would ideally address. The UN believed that social addiction to opium was the biggest concern for the long-term opium suppression in Badakhshan, and it placed priority on social policies tied to the opium prohibition. In many ways, the UN was right to conclude that the success of the opium prohibition depended largely on the state's ability to develop economic, social, and political infrastructures in Badakshan, but this would require a much greater effort on the part of the Musahiban government to develop an isolated province inhabited by ethnic minorities.

75. Matthee, *The Pursuit of Pleasure*, 99.

76. Abraham and van Schendel, "Introduction: The Making of Illicitness," 19.

77. Barfield, *The Central Asian Arabs of Afghanistan*, 161.

78. "Notes on a Journey to Badakhshan: July 23–August 6, 1961."

79. Barfield, *Central Asian Arabs*, 160.

80. Rubin, *The Fragmentation of Afghanistan*, 65.

81. Rubin, 69.

82. Noorzoy, "Alternative Economic Systems for Afghanistan," 26.

83. Newell, "Afghanistan," 170.

84. "Memo from Diplomatic Representation in Afghanistan," File, FSA 25/5, July 26, 1972, British ambassador trip to Badakhshan, 1970, FCO 37/569, UK National Archives, Kew.

85. Mansfield, *A State Built on Sand*, 122.

86. Mansfield, 125.

87. Mansfield, 124.

88. Mansfield, 126–127.

89. For more on the impact of eradication on the rural population, see Farrell, "A Global Empirical Review of Drug Crop Eradication," 395–436.

90. Mansfield, *State Built on Sand*, 129. Similar to P.L. 480, passed in 1958, the US government authorized $43 million to support farmers and the ban.

91. Giustozzi, *The Art of Coercion*, 5.

92. Mansfield, "Alternative Development in Afghanistan," 13.

4. East Meets West

1. Cohen, "Alternative Tourism," 14.

2. Clarke, *Hashish*, 41–42.

3. For insight into commodity chains and their relations to international crime and regulation, see Hopkins and Wallerstein, "Commodity Chains," 17–19.

4. Paul Gootenberg has written extensively on this process in Gootenberg, *Andean Cocaine.*

5. Sydney Mintz demonstrates that the links forged between production and consumption of sugar cane carried remarkable social, political, and cultural weight. Particularly for the British, the increasing consumption of sugar was emblematic of the transformation of social life, the confirmation of the superiority of the British Empire, and benefits of global capitalism. See Mintz, *Sweetness and Power.*

6. Magnus, "The Constitution of 1964," 53.

7. Babar, "Afghanistan: 1963–1973," 112.

8. Babar, 104.

9. Babar, 104. Taken from *Da Afghanistan Kalinah/Salnanah* (Yearbook; 1964), Ministry of Information and Culture, Kabul, 57.

10. Two articles in particular stood out. Article 15 both granted the king absolute authority and required him to abstain from politics. Article 24 prevented any member of the royal family, including Daud, from getting involved in politics. Both articles had a major role in alienating Daud from the king and royal family. As a result, Daud became an increasingly active figure in the political conflicts in Kabul, culminating in the coup of 1973. See Babar, "Afghanistan: 1963–1973," 136.

11. Poullada, "The Search for National Unity," 46.

12. See Babar, "Afghanistan: 1963–1973," 139. This is not surprising. Most rural Afghans thought the state to be just as foreign an entity as the American and Russian delegations that largely supported them.

13. Dupree, *Afghanistan*, 589. Many of them were socialists, Marxists, and communists, such as Babrak Karmal and Nur Ahmad Taraki, and played major roles in the coup of 1973, the Saur Revolution in 1978, and the eventual invasion by the Soviets in 1979.

14. Babar, "Afghanistan: 1963–1973," 104.

15. US State Department, "Afghan Millat: Summary," A-221, June 29, 1967, 1, NND 52378, RG 84; NACP.

16. *Afghan Millat*, March 28, 1967. US State Department, "Afghan Millat: Summary," NND 52378, RG 84.

17. US State Department, "Afghan Millat: Summary."

18. Babar, "Afghanistan: 1963–1973," 143. According to Farhang, the primary instigator of the incident was the Hizb-I Demukratik-I Khalq-I Afghanistan (Peoples Party of Afghanistan).

19. Babar, 160. This certainly presents a strange paradox. Typically, tribal authorities were suspicious and actively resisted the state's attempt to modernize rural Afghanistan. Yet by the 1960s, and with the brief glimmer of hope in the democracy movement, some were disgruntled that modernization was not reaching them. This undoubtedly has less to do with tribal groups' aspirations for embracing modernity and more to do with local and regional power dynamics, where money and resources supplied by modernization policies could play a key role.

20. Babar, 160.

21. Babar, 160.

22. Dupree, *Afghanistan*, 620.

23. *Kabul Times*, August 4, 1971, Library of Congress.

24. Babar, "Afghanistan: 1963–1973," 237.

25. *Musavat*, November 16, 1971, Library of Congress.

26. Abrahamian, *Iran between Two Revolutions*, 419–421.

27. For a history of American and Iranian relations, see Bill, *The Eagle and the Lion.*

28. McLaughlin and Quinn, "Drug Control in Iran," 489.

29. Matthee notes that opium was used throughout Iran, rarely limited by class, gender, or ethnicity. See Matthee, *Pursuit of Pleasure.*

30. McLaughlin and Quinn, "Drug Control in Iran," 491. The shah's justification for launching the ban was more than a purely benevolent act to alleviate what was becoming a serious social dilemma; rather, it was likely a step to expand further his control over the population.

31. From Law of October 7, 1955, UN Document E/NL.1956/1, 1956 (Article 2). McLaughlin and Quinn, "Drug Control in Iran," 492.

32. McLaughlin and Quinn, 493 (Article 3)

33. McLaughlin and Quinn, 493. Taken from Law of June 22, 1959: *Act to Amend the Law on Poppy Plantation and the Use of Opium*, UN Document E/NL.1960/1, 1960.

34. McLaughlin and Quinn, "Drug Control in Iran," 494.

35. McLaughlin and Quinn, 495–497. McLaughlin and Quinn attribute this failure to the lack of border control by both the Turkish and Afghan governments. This is problematic because it assumes that border control actually works and that the governments in each case were capable of deterring smuggling. The Afghan government could hardly control its urban populations; how was it going to stop the rural traders? And given the long history of smuggling by Afghan tribes into Iran, their indifference to opium and authority, and the incredibly harsh and vast terrain of the Afghan borders, the Afghan state had very little chance to achieve its aims.

36. McLaughlin and Quinn, 496–497.

37. McLaughlin and Quinn, 497.

38. Charles Siragusa, US State Department, "Letter to Harry Anslinger," May 20, 1960, Entry A19, Federal Bureau of Narcotics and Dangerous Drugs, Subject Files, 1916–1970, RG 170, Records of the Drug Enforcement Agency, Box 151, "Afghan, Vol. 1, 1929–1968"; NACP.

39. Jamshid Cyrus, "A Short History of the United States Military Mission with the Imperial Iranian Gendarmerie," US Military Mission, March 10, 1976, p. 9, US State Department, Bureau of Near Eastern and South Asian Affairs, Office of the Officer in Charge, Iranian Affairs (1966–ca. 1979), Box 4, "GENMISH file"; NACP.

40. Cyrus, "Short History," 17.

41. Cyrus, "Short History," 18.

42. The IIG seized all sorts of illicit goods, everything from opium and hash, to caviar and sturgeon. By 1960, IIG officials along the eastern border were increasingly aware of the growing presence of Afghan opium and Afghan smugglers.

43. John Cusack, "Letter to Harry Anslinger: Afghanistan," Bureau of Narcotics, March 7, 1961, RG 170, Records of DEA, Box 151; NACP.

44. John Cusack, "Letter to Henry Giordano: Afghanistan." Bureau of Narcotics. March 5, 1964, p. 1, RG 170; NACP.

45. Cusack, "Letter to Henry Giordano", p 1,

46. By the late 1960s and early 1970s, the IIG wound up focusing not only on anti-smuggling efforts but also on quelling rebellions and insurrections among tribal groups, particularly Baluchis. Calls for an independent Baluchistan by nationalists was a source of significant violence and government oppression in both Iran and Pakistan.

47. McLaughlin, "The Poppy Is Not an Ordinary Flower," 498–500.

48. "Narcotics in Iran," A-41, February 2, 1971, p. 2, RG 59, General Records of the Department of State, 1763–2002, Office of the Senior Adviser to the Secretary on Narcotics, Country Files, Box 7, "Iran 1972"; NACP.

49. "Traffic in Opium and Cannabis Originating from Afghanistan," No. A-219, July 7, 1970, p. 2, RG 59, General Records of the Department of State, 1763–2002, Office of the Senior Adviser to the Secretary on Narcotics, Country Files, Box 3, "Afghanistan 1972"; NACP. The Turkish trade shifted almost exclusively to morphine base and heroin primarily because of its greater profit potential stemming from its higher potency and decreased size. Afghans had yet to transition to morphine and heroin, largely because the Afghan opium being smuggled into Iran did not have high enough morphine content to make the switch.

50. "Traffic in Opium," 2. The idea that kidnapping was a major tactic for higher-level drug distributors is not necessarily an outlandish idea. For some Pashtuns, kidnapping and ransoms were a primary form of generating profit and a source of great esteem for the individual and tribe.

51. "Traffic in Opium," 3.

52. "Traffic in Opium," 4.

53. "Traffic in Opium," 5. Heroin, although not incredibly lucrative at the time, saw a major price jump from 1969 to 1970. The price for a gram leaped from a low of $3.93 to nearly $15.74.

54. "Supplementary Information on the Narcotics Situation in Iran (C-ER-2-56344)," February 29, 1972, p. 6, RG 59, Box 7, "Iran 1972"; NACP.

55. McLaughlin and Quinn, 511.

56. "Supplementary Information on the Narcotics Situation in Iran (C-ER-2-56344)", p. 6,

57. "Supplementary Information on the Narcotics Situation in Iran (C-ER-2-56344)", p. 6,

58. Central Intelligence Agency, "Narcotics in Iran," *International Narcotics Series No. 13*, June 12, 1972, p. 7, RG 59, Box 7, "Iran 1972"; NACP.

59. Exit interview with Colonel Warren Bovee (Precht, July 24, 1970–74?), RG 59, Box 7, "Iran 1972"; NACP.

60. US State Department, No. 194581, October 1972, RG 59, Box 7, "Iran 1972"; NACP.

61. Central Intelligence Agency, "Narcotics in Iran", p. 6,

62. McAllister, *Drug Diplomacy in the Twentieth Century*, 208.

63. McAllister, 209–211.

64. McAllister, 218

65. Farber, "The Intoxicated State/Illegal Nation," 8.

66. Many travelers to Afghanistan, as well as Iran, Turkey, Nepal, and India believed they were embarking on mystical journeys of the mind and body. The myths of Eastern philosophies and the use of psychotropic substances to achieve higher states of spiritual being prompted a wave of young Western Europeans and Americans to seek enlightenment by getting high. To smoke hash or opium in such "exotic" and "mystical" regions lent to the mythology of South and West Asia as havens for narcotic consumption. Many of these travelers were completely ignorant of the political nuances of drug consumption and trafficking. Their knowledge of local laws, customs, and public behaviors was skewed by simplified notions of Asian drug consumption. In many ways, the travelers' naivete exemplified the orientalism inherent in Western culture, evidenced by their perceived openness to Asian philosophies and culture. See Said, *Orientalism.*

67. Maguire, and Ritter, *Thai Stick*, 27–29.

68. Charpentier, "The Use of Hashish," 484. From the Afghanistan Center at Kabul University.

69. Memo A-20, March 2, 1970, "Trafficking of Drugs in Afghanistan, 1970," FCO 47/ 428, UK National Archives, Kew.

70. Charpentier, "The Use of Hashish," 484.

71. Clarke, *Hashish*, 117.

72. Clarke, 127.

73. Levi, *The Light Garden of the Angel King*, 113.

74. Levi, 156.

75. Gobar, "Drug Abuse in Afghanistan," 2. From the Afghanistan Center at Kabul University.

76. Gobar, 7.

77. David Avery, Consular Department, May 19, 1970, Trafficking of Drugs in Afghanistan 1970, FCO 47/ 428, UK National Archives, Kew.

78. See Clarke, *Hashish*, for a detailed examination of the varying arrays of hash production.

79. Zheng, "The Social Life of Opium," 15.

80. Kopytoff, "The Cultural Biography of Things," 78.

81. Lamour and Lamberti, *Les Grandes Manouevres de l'Opium*, 208.

82. Kamm, "World Is a Carousel."

83. Interview with Amir Rod, professor, Academy of Sciences, Kabul, August 19, 2014. Although I never broached the subject with him, it is certainly important to recognize how much of his answer may have been influenced by the historic legacy of Soviet occupation.

84. US State Department, "Letter to Michael Hornblow," July 26, 1968, RG 59, Department of State, Bureau of Near Eastern and South Asian Affairs, Office of the Country Director for Pakistan, Afghanistan, and Bangladesh (1972–ca. 1979), Records Relating to Afghanistan, 1970–1974, Box 2, "Narcotics 1971"; NACP.

85. Courtwright, *Dark Paradise*, 165.

86. US State Department, "Narcotics and Hippies," May 17, 1971, RG 59, Department of State, Box 2, "Narcotics 1971"; NACP. One of the more intriguing elements of

the discussions between Afghan and American officials was that embassy officials were careful not to criticize Afghan desires to maintain their tradition of hospitality and openness.

87. "Letter from Criminal Division of Kabul Police to Interpol," June 2, 1970, Trafficking of Drugs in Afghanistan, 1970, FCO 47/ 428, UK National Archives, Kew.

88. *Kabul Times*, January 29, 1973. This appeared next to a note of twenty-eight kilograms of hash being confiscated at the house of a local Kabul resident. US State Department, Bureau of Near Eastern and South Asian Affairs, Office of the Country Director for Pakistan, Afghanistan and Bangladesh (1972–ca. 1979), Records Relating to Afghanistan, 1970–1974, RG 59, Box 2, "Narcotics 1971"; NACP.

89. *Kabul Times*, July 4, 1973, RG 59; NACP.

90. *Kabul Times*, December 6, 1973, RG 59; NACP.

91. For more on the Brotherhood, see May and Tender, *The Brotherhood of Eternal Love*, and Schou, *Orange Sunshine*.

92. Clarke, *Hashish*, 116. Clarke notes that the demand for hash oil also spurred a change in pricing schemes between traffickers and farmers.

93. BNDD, "July 1972 Brief: Trafficking and Enforcement", pp. 1–2, files from former BNDD/DEA agent Terry Burke.

94. BNDD, "Enforcement Situation in Kabul as of February 1972," file from Terry Burke.

95. In Thomas Gallant's world historical examination of piracy and brigandage, he demonstrates that these illegal groups and the networks they established were fundamental to the growth of global capitalism, as well as the growth of nation-states. See Gallant, "Brigandage, Piracy, Capitalism, and State Formation," 25–62.

96. Frank, Marichal, and Topik, "Introduction: Commodity Chains," 8. The authors' focus on cocaine, sugar, and other colonial commodities helps gives insight on how these commodities became integral to the expansion of the capitalist system. The focus on the consumption and production of the product, not the national history, allowed for greater insight into the how cultures of consumption and production changed in response to shifting political frameworks.

97. For example, in Colombia, the production and trafficking of cocaine was closely tied to deeply entrenched sociopolitical problems stemming from the maintenance of colonial regimes of power. See Thoumi, *Illegal Drugs*.

98. See the *Afghan Millat* cartoons criticizing the Afghan government presented in figures 4.1–4.3 and 4.5.

5. The Afghan Connection

Epigraphs: Richard M. Nixon, "Remarks about an Intensified Program for Drug Abuse Prevention and Control," 738; "Special Message to the Congress," 746.

1. Courtwright, *Dark Paradise*, 165–170.

2. Weimer, *Seeing Drugs*, 54.

3. See Frydl, *The Drug Wars in America*.

4. Lamour and Lamberti, *The International Connection*, 17–35.

5. McCoy, "Heroin as a Global Commodity," 262.

6. McCoy, "Coercion and Its Unintended Consequences," 205.

7. Frydl, *The Drug Wars in America*, 10.

8. Courtwright, *Dark Paradise*, 166. Courtwright noted that there were in fact two separate epidemics, one during 1967–71 and another during 1974–76. He also notes that the disruption was due in part to the disruption of supply from the French Connection.

9. Courtwright, 168–169.

10. Musto, *The American Disease*, 251–252.

11. Nixon, "Special Message to the Congress," 741.

12. Courtwright, *Dark Paradise*, 171.

13. McAllister, *Drug Diplomacy in the Twentieth Century*, 236–237.

14. McAllister, 237. Many states were skeptical of the fund given its independent status. Most feared that the United States would use the fund as a means of dictating its increasingly controversial vision of global drug suppression.

15. McAllister, 238.

16. Epstein, *Agency of Fear*, 86–89. Edward Epstein points out that the Turkish threat was largely embellished as a way of providing the United States with a more attainable victory in the war on drugs, something that it could not achieve in Southeast Asia.

17. McCoy, *The Politics of Heroin*, 393. Gingeras complicates this number a bit, pointing out that the 80 percent number was a relative arbitrary designation. As the drug war ratcheted up, however, the number became an unquestioned "fact" about the drug trade in Turkey.

18. Gingeras, "Hunt for the 'Sultans of Smack,'" 430. Gingeras notes that Federal Bureau of Narcotics officials tried to arrest major drug kingpins, but corruption and national pride largely deterred any major actions.

19. Gingeras, *Heroin*, 189–190.

20. McCoy, *The Politics of Heroin,* 65.

21. McCoy, 69.

22. Spain, "The United States," 298.

23. Gingeras, *Heroin*, 198.

24. McCoy, *The Politics of Heroin*, 72–73.

25. Spain, "The United States," 299.

26. McCoy, *The Politics of Heroin*, 73.

27. Spain, "The United States," 301.

28. Spain, "The United States," 302.

29. Gingeras, *Heroin*, 202–203.

30. Cusack, "Turkey Lifts the Poppy Ban," 3–7.

31. Windle, "A Very Gradual Suppression," 12–13.

32. Gingeras, "Hunt for the 'Sultans of Smack,'" 432.

33. McCoy, *The Politics of Heroin*, 93.

34. McCoy, 94.

35. All of the major producers signed onto the 1953 Opium Protocol, agreeing to forbid the sale of opium on the global market for legal consumption. Afghanistan, which failed to attend the conference, was not a signatory to the convention. However, it spent

the following years trying to become the eighth licit producer of opium, to no avail (see chapter 3).

36. McCoy, *The Politics of Heroin*, 128.

37. McCoy, 129.

38. McCoy, 129–130.

39. McCoy, 128.

40. Lamour and Lamberti, *The International Connection*, 36.

41. Lamour and Lamberti, 37.

42. Lamour and Lamberti, 39–40.

43. Lamour and Lamberti, 43. Much like the French Connection, the Southeast Asian opium industry operated in a similar manner, whereby rural opium farmers were connected to the global market by large and ingeniously operated criminal organizations. In both Turkey and the Golden Triangle opium production was vital to rural farmers dependent on its revenue for survival. In both instances, the farmers were connected to global markets via international crime syndicates which used their incredible political and economic influence in their local cities (Marseilles and Hong Kong/Bangkok) to ship refined heroin to major consumer countries around the world.

44. McCoy, *The Politics of Heroin*, 395. DEA officials theorized that the US GI epidemic may have served as a consumer test for the Chiu Chao in preparation for launching into the US market.

45. McCoy, 394.

46. McCoy, 395.

47. McCoy, 395.

48. McCoy, "Heroin as a Global Commodity," 262–263.

49. Lamour and Lamberti, *The International Connection*, 46

50. Lamour and Lamberti, 47.

51. McCoy, *The Politics of Heroin*, 396. Lamour and Lamberti also shed light on the intricacies of the Chinese narco-trafficking system. Rarely would they use bank transfers, often paying in cash months in advance or after the transaction, and sometimes in exchange for goods and services. Ultimately, "the result is an unofficial and highly complex financial network, based not only on mutual trust between members of the same community but also on the law of retaliation should that trust be betrayed." Lamour and Lamberti, *The International Connection*, 45.

52. Grayson, *Mexico*, 24. Grayson notes that the United States had reached an agreement to help the Mexicans expand the cultivation of opium. Even American officials went to Mexico and helped farmers convert crops to poppy cultivation.

53. Although Mexico had served as a vital source of opium during the war, it failed to produce high percentages of morphine that would have ensured it would remain a primary supplier of opium. The superior-quality opium from Turkey, Iran, and China was more desirable for pharmaceutical companies because of the high morphine content.

54. Grayson, *Mexico*, 28.

55. McCoy, *The Politics of Heroin*, 397.

56. For further discussion of issues surrounding the "balloon effect" and the challenges of researching the consequences of such interventions, see Farrell and Windle,

"Popping the Ballon Effect," 868–876. See also Greenfield and Paoli, "Research as Due Diligence," 162–163.

57. See Farrell and Windle, "Popping the Ballon Effect." Farrell and Windle are correct that academics often wrongly assume supply-side interventions are *the* cause of crop displacement. We may never know the precise reasons drug traffickers and producers adapt without more adequate research of them as sources. This is remarkably difficult given the illicit nature of the work, lack of sources, and challenges to researchers in adequately and objectively acquiring information. Furthermore, the illicit drugs market continues to grow, as new markets in China, Africa, and Eastern Europe emerge. Furthermore, the illicit market is interwoven with the licit. The current US opioid problem has largely centered on the use of prescription opioids, but the growth of opioid overdose deaths has occurred largely because of the decreasing access to prescription narcotics and the rise of fentanyl as a cutting agent in the heroin supply. To reinforce my point, this market continues to expand, and adapt, to changes from US policy pressures, and also changes to demand in types of drugs. For more on the US opioid problem, see Quinones, *Dreamland.*

58. Farrell, "A Global Empirical Review of Crop Eradication," 395–436.

59. McCoy, *The Politics of Heroin*, 262.

60. Lamour and Lamberti, *The International Connection*, 192.

61. For more on Nixon's foreign policy, see Logevall and Preston, *Nixon in the World.*

62. US State Department, "Illicit Drug Traffic in Pakistan," American Consul, Karachi, February 22, 1971, RG 59, Bureau of Near Eastern and South Asian Affairs, Office of the Country Director for Pakistan, Afghanistan, and Bangladesh (1972–ca. 1979), Records Relating to Afghanistan, Box 2, "Afghanistan 1972"; NACP. Many of the young traffickers were given lenient sentences (if any at all) and were often quick to bribe local officials. As a result, many of the traffickers saw the southern route through Pakistan as preferable because of its weak judicial system.

63. Asad, *The Politics and Economics of Drug Production*, 36.

64. US State Department, "Narcotics: Settled Area Poppy Ban," American Consul, Islamabad, October 24, 1973, No. 206245, Electronic Telegrams, 1973, Central Foreign Policy Files 7/1/1973–12/31/1979, Department of State, RG 59; NACP.

65. Lamour and Lamberti noted that at various border crossings, impromptu bazaars had been established whereby anyone could purchase drugs, as well as guns and other contraband. The presence of government officials generated little concern, as most were either indifferent or complicit in the trade. Lamour and Lamberti, *The International Connection*, 182–185.

66. Asad, *The Politics and Economics of Drug Production*, 30–31. By then, however, opium production and trade had moved almost completely into Afghanistan.

67. Pakistan has a large addict population as well, although until recently it was often neglected as a significant social issue in the country. Part of the reason Pakistan was slow to adopt American measures for strict control of use and trade of opium was that vestiges of the colonial system in the subcontinent were well entrenched in Pakistan. Drug policy in Pakistan after partition was mainly a continuation of the colonial policy stemming from Pakistan's role as a major producer for British India.

68. McLaughlin, "The Poppy Is Not an Ordinary Flower," 750–761.

69. US State Department, "Technical Assistance to Iran—Narcotics," July 15, 1971, RG 59,. Bureau of Near Eastern and South Asian Affairs, Office of the Officer in Charge, Iranian Affairs (1966–ca. 1979), Box 8, "Iran 1971"; NACP.

70. "Supreme Judicial Council Meets on Narcotics Problem," *Kabul Times*, February 11, 1970, RG 59; NACP.

71. "Laws of Afghanistan: Anti-Smuggling Law" (translated into English), Kabul, 1975, Library of Congress.

72. US State Department, "Drug Control: Afghanistan. Oct. 27, 1971," RG 59, Bureau of Near Eastern and South Asian Affairs, Office of the Country Director for Pakistan, Afghanistan and Bangladesh (1972–ca. 1979), Records Relating to Afghanistan, Box 2, "Afghanistan 1972"; NACP.

73. "Anti-Smuggling Squads Strengthened," *Kabul Times*, February 16, 1971, 3, RG 59; NACP.

74. US State Department, "Conversation with His Majesty and Foreign Minister-Narcotics, December 4, 1971," RG 59, "Country Files, 1970–1978: Afghanistan," Office of the Senior Adviser to the Secretary on Narcotics, Records Relating to Afghanistan, Box 2, "Afghanistan 1972"; NACP

75. "Economic Statistics of Afghanistan" (*Ma'lumat-I ihsa'ivi-i Afghanistan*) (1974), 211, Library of Congress.

76. James Hawley, "Successful Opium Bid," State Department, January 29, 1972, RG 84, Records of the Foreign Service Posts of the Department of State, 1788–ca. 1991, Department of State, US Embassy, Afghanistan, Afghanistan Box, Exports of Seized Opium File, NND 52378; NACP.

77. David Cohn, "Mallincrokdt Chemical Works' Opium Shipment Operation," State Department, April 15, 1972, RG 84; NACP.

78. Cohn, "Mallincrockdt," 2.

79. US State Department, "Exports of Seized Opium," April 25, 1972, RG 84; NACP.

80. This is based on the exchange rate in 1350 (1971) of roughly eighty afghans to the dollar. See Fry, *The Afghan Economy*.

81. The author described the police measures as "polis tadawbir sahihi awthawz kardan" (the police to take the correct measures) but placed the notion of correct, "sahih," in bold, implying that the police crackdown on opium smuggling was the right thing to do.

82. *Anis*, August 29, 1971, Library of Congress.

83. US State Department, "Political Summary: Feb. 19–March 8, 1971," March 13, 1971, RG 59, "Country Files, 1970–1978: Afghanistan," Office of the Senior Adviser to the Secretary on Narcotics, Records Relating to Afghanistan, Box 2, "Afghanistan 1971"; NACP.

84. US State Department, "Narcotics Traffic in Gulf," October 1972, RG 59, "Country Files, 1970–1978: Afghanistan," Office of the Senior Adviser to the Secretary on Narcotics, Records Relating to Afghanistan, Box 2, "Afghanistan 1972"; NACP.

85. Valentine, *The Strength of the Pack*, 351.

86. US State Department, "Narcotics Briefing," June 1972, p. 6, RG 59, "Afghanistan 1972"; NACP.

87. US State Department, "Narcotics Briefing," June 1972, p. 4, RG 59; NACP.

88. US State Department, "Narcotics Briefing", p. 5.

89. Roy, *Islam and Resistance in Afghanistan*, 21.

90. "Narcotics—Action Plan and Benchmarks, July 9, 1973," RG 59, "Country Files, 1970–1978: Afghanistan," Office of the Senior Adviser to the Secretary on Narcotics, Records Relating to Afghanistan, Box 2, "Afghanistan 1973"; NACP.

91. Ispahani, *Roads and Rivals*, 4–7.

92. "Statement made by Y.P. Maroofi of Afghanistan before the Third Committee of the Twenty-Seventh Session of the United Nations General Assembly," p. 5, RG 59; "Afghanistan 1972"; NACP.

93. "Problems Concerned with Narcotic Drugs in Afghanistan," September–October 1972, p. 13, RG 59; NACP.

94. One and a half million dollars would come from the UN, $500,000 from the Afghan government, and $450,000 from other sources. Of course, given the overwhelming influence of the United States in the UNFDAC, the UN role as advisor to Afghan narcotics endeavors did little to mask the American influence. During the rules of Zahir Shah and Daud, public support from the United States was still discouraged. As a result, using the UN allowed the United States to exert influence on narcotics matters without creating political issues over the US role.

95. US State Department, "Narcotics—Assistance to Afghanistan: Memorandum to NEA Interagency Narcotics Committee," RG 59, Department of State, Bureau of Near Eastern and South Asian Affairs, Office of the Country Director for Pakistan, Afghanistan and Bangladesh (1972–ca. 1979), Records Relating to Afghanistan (compiled 1972–1974, documenting the period 1960–1974), Box 2, "Narcotics 11.1: Narcotics Action Plan 1972"; NACP.

96. US State Department, "Narcotics—Assistance to Afghanistan," p. 9.

97. US State Department, "Narcotics Control Action Plan for Afghanistan—Analysis of the UN/FAO Report on Narcotics Control in Afghanistan," March 1973, Electronic Telegrams, 1973, Central Foreign Policy Files 7/1/1973–12/31/1979, Department of State, RG 59; NACP.

98. James Sterba, "Famine Relief in Afghanistan Hindered by Inertia and Corruption," *New York Times*, June 21, 1972, RG 59, Department of State, Bureau of Near Eastern and South Asian Affairs, Office of the Country Director for Pakistan, Afghanistan and Bangladesh (1972–ca. 1979), Records Relating to Afghanistan (compiled 1972–1974, documenting the period 1960–1974), Box 2, "Narcotics 11.1: Narcotics Action Plan 1972"; NACP. It may have also been a product of the Afghan government's often overt bias and favoritism for Pashtuns.

99. Barfield, *Afghanistan*, 212.

100. Barfield, 213.

101. US State Department, "Political Summary: July 21–August 12, 1971," RG 59, "Country Files, 1970–1978: Afghanistan," Office of the Senior Adviser to the Secretary on Narcotics, Box 2, "Afghanistan 1971"; NACP.

102. Dupree, "A Note on Afghanistan," 19.

103. Barfield, *Afghanistan*, 214.

104. Barfield, 215.

105. Barfield, 216.

106. "Afghanistan—Narcotics. Sept 1973. Geneva: Confidential 4867," State Department, Electronic Telegrams, 1973, Central Foreign Policy Files, 7/1/1973–12/31/1979, Department of State, RG 59; NACP. One proposal put out by Daud's government was a $500 million development program aimed at building infrastructure in Badakhshan and Nangarhar.

107. "Narcotics—Future Afghan Program, DEA: Confidential, Kabul 7314," Electronic Telegrams, 1973, Central Foreign Policy Files, 7/1/1973–12/31/1979, Department of State, RG 59; NACP.

108. In some cases, the monetary reward system was providing useful intelligence. However, the types of seizures were still minor in comparison to the overall quantity of narcotics smuggled out of Afghanistan every year.

109. "DEA Memo about US Program for Financial Incentive Program. Conf: Kabul 8749," December 1973, Electronic Telegrams, 1973, Central Foreign Policy Files, 7/1/1973–12/31/1979, Department of State, RG 59; NACP.

110. "DEA Memo: 4472," July 1975, Electronic Telegrams, 1975, Central Foreign Policy Files, 7/1/1973–12/31/1979, Department of State, RG 59; NACP.

111. "Special Afghan Enforcement Program. Conf: Kabul 4910," DEA, July 1975, Electronic Telegrams, 1975, Central Foreign Policy Files, 7/1/1973–12/31/1979, Department of State, RG 59; NACP.

112. "Ambassador Vance: Meeting with Deputy Ministry of Interior Safi. Conf: Kabul 7555," December 1974, Electronic Telegrams, 1974, Central Foreign Policy Files, 7/1/1973–12/31/1979, Department of State, RG 59; NACP.

113. See Tilly, *Coercion, Capital, and European States.*

114. Roy, *Islam and Resistance in Afghanistan*, 24.

115. Hopkins and Marsden, *Fragments of the Afghan Frontier*, 175.

116. Hopkins and Marsden, 2.

117. Gallant, "Brigandage, Piracy, Capitalism, and State Formation," 25.

118. Courtwright, *Dark Paradise*, 166.

119. Spain, "The United States," 302.

120. Roy, *Islam and Resistance in Afghanistan*, 24.

6. All Goods Are Dangerous Goods

Epigraph: UNODC, *Afghanistan Opium Survey 2008*, vii.

1. UNODC, *Afghanistan Opium Survey 2011*, 17.

2. UNODC, *Afghanistan Opium Survey 2008*, 37.

3. McCoy (*Politics of Heroin*), Chouvy (*Opium*), and Mansfield (*A State Built on Sand*) all emphasize war as the fundamental component shaping the contemporary Afghan opium industry, but Chouvy does state that "opium production predated the Afghan conflict." See Chouvy, *Opium*, 100.

4. Abraham and van Schendel, "Introduction: The Making of Illicitness," 4.

5. Scott, *Seeing Like a State*, 78. Afghanistan embodied the illegible state Scott describes.

6. Ispahani, *Roads and Rivals*, 4. Ispahani looks at "routes" as an important nexus between security and economic development, two concepts that are often dealt with separately rather than intertwined.

7. Latham, "Introduction: Modernization Theory," 3–4.

8. Dupree, "An Informal Talk with Prime Minster Daud," 18.

9. Ansary, *West of Kabul, East of New York*, 69.

10. Scott, "Tribal and Ethnic Groups in the Helmand Valley," 2.

11. Dupree, *Afghanistan*, 482.

12. Gregorian, *The Emergence of Modern Afghanistan*, 373.

13. Shahrani, "State-Building and Social Fragmentation in Afghanistan," 54.

14. Poullada, *The Kingdom of Afghanistan*, 175.

15. Cullather, "Damming Afghanistan," 520–522.

16. Newell, "The Prospects of State-building in Afghanistan," 113. This was most evident in the declaration of Pashto as the national language despite the overwhelming use of Dari (Persian) as the lingua franca.

17. Barfield, *Afghanistan*, 198.

18. Fry, *The Afghan Economy*, 89.

19. Mitchell, *Rule of Experts*, 169. As Timothy Mitchell notes, the story of development was not only about building state control in these far away regions but was constructed locally, and therefore required the state to navigate local realities as it pursued its own ambitions. The history of the Helmand project is as much about the state's ambitions as it is about the way local communities influenced the state project.

20. Giustozzi and Kalinovsky, *Missionaries of Modernity*, 175.

21. Latham, "Introduction: Modernization Theory," 3–4.

22. Engerman, "West Meets East," 202.

23. USAID, *Retrospective Review of US Assistance to Afghanistan*, 11.

24. Engerman, "West Meets East," 200.

25. USAID, *Retrospective Review of US Assistance to Afghanistan*, 9.

26. Dupree, *Afghanistan*, 483.

27. USAID, *Retrospective Review of US Assistance to Afghanistan*, 10.

28. Cullather, "Damming Afghanistan," 523.

29. Dupree, *Afghanistan*, 483. Dupree also notes that human and bureaucratic errors permeated the project. Many of the Afghan engineers were put in administrative positions, preventing them from fulfilling their engineering duties. And many of the Americans failed to understand Afghan cultural practices (483).

30. It was later renamed the Helmand Arghandab Valley Authority (HAVA). To be consistent, I will refer to it as the HAVA henceforth.

31. Dupree, *Afghanistan*, 484. The importance of the HAVA to the Afghan government was significant: all governors of the Helmand Province were named as president of the HAVA, and were also granted cabinet status in Kabul. Dupree, *Afghanistan*, 484.

32. Cullather, "Damming Afghanistan," 525.

33. Fry, *Afghan Economy*, 200.

34. Dupree, *Afghanistan*, 485.

35. USAID, *Retrospective Review of US Assistance to Afghanistan,* 11.

36. Dupree, *Afghanistan*, 510–511.

37. Dupree, *Afghanistan*, 499.

38. USAID, *Retrospective Review of US Assistance to Afghanistan*, 11.

39. Cullather, "Damming Afghanistan," 528. By the late 1950s, Daud made the "Pashtunistan" issue his primary policy. The schism between Pakistan and Afghanistan ultimately drew lines in the Cold War, as the United States remained steadfast in its support of Pakistan.

40. Scott, "Opium Poppy Cultivation in Central Helmand," 4.

41. Dupree, *Afghanistan*, 501.

42. Cullather, "Damming Afghanistan," 529. The resettlement program also had a subversive effect. Many of the Americans and upper-level Afghan government officials viewed nomads with disdain, particularly the tribal leaders, *maliks*. The resettlement program offered families the opportunity to choose new village leaders, *wakils*, with the hope of undermining the authority of the *maliks*.

43. Cullather, "Damming Afghanistan," 529.

44. Emadi, *State, Revolution, and Superpowers in Afghanistan*, 40–41.

45. Dupree, *Afghanistan*, 504.

46. Cullather, "Damming Afghanistan," 532.

47. Cullather, "Damming Afghanistan," 533. Resettlement subsidies were paid off and most of the land was settled by small private landholders, and it seemed that farmers had begun to reshape the landscape for farming.

48. Giustozzi and Kalinovsky, *Missionaries of Modernity*, 176.

49. Ambassador John Steeves, letter to Mr. Delmas H. Nucker, AID, December 19, 1964, RG 59, Department of State, Bureau of Near Eastern and South Asian Affairs, Office of the Country Director for Pakistan, Afghanistan and Bangladesh (1972–ca. 1979), Records Relating to Afghanistan, Box 1, AGR Agriculture-General (Helmand Valley) 1965 File; NACP.

50. Frank Schmelzer, "Helmand Valley and Aid Request," May 11, 1965, RG 59; NACP.

51. "Talking Paper for Discussions with Amb. Steeves and Mission Director Nucker on US Assistance to the Helmand Valley," May 24, 1965, RG 59; NACP.

52. Cullather, "Damming Afghanistan," 534. This was also connected to the broader issues facing the state. As discussed in chapter 4, the late 1960s and early 1970s were a period of tremendous political activity.

53. Cullather, "Damming Afghanistan," 535.

54. Dupree, "An Informal Talk with Prime Minster Daud," 18.

55. Barfield, *Afghanistan*, 214.

56. Mohammad Daud, "Address to the Nation," *Kabul Times*, August 26, 1973, Library of Congress.

57. Rubin, *The Fragmentation of Afghanistan*, 74. Most of the money was to be spent on a railroad linking Afghanistan with the border port of Bandar Abbas. Iran was not the only oil rich country to interact with Afghanistan, as Saudi Arabia, Kuwait, and Iraq all increased aid to Afghanistan. The oil boom also provided unprecedented amounts of remittances that became an important part of the economy.

58. A good indication of the broader scope of economic aggrandizement in Afghanistan was the increase in surplus balance of payments, from $2.2 million in 1972–73 to $65 million in 1976–77.

59. Rubin, *Fragmentation of Afghanistan*, 75.

60. Dupree, "Afghanistan 1977," 7.

61. "Memo of Conversation: Governor Fazil Rabi Pazhwak and Staff," March 28, 1974, RG 84, Records of the Foreign Service Posts of the Department of State, 1788–ca. 1991, Department of State, U.S. Embassy, Afghanistan, Afghanistan Box, Helmand File, NND 52378; NACP.

62. Toynbee, *Between Oxus and Jumma*, 67.

63. "Trip Report (Helmand Valley): David McCaffey," December 13, 1973, RG 84, Records Relating to Afghanistan; NACP.

64. "Memo of Conversation: Governor Fazil Rabi Pazhwak and Staff," March 28, 1974, RG 84, Records Relating to Afghanistan; NACP.

65. Charles Johnson and Richard Scott, "Trip Report: Helmand Valley," September 29, 1973, RG 84, Records Relating to Afghanistan; NACP.

66. Clapp-Wincek and Baldwin, *The Helmand Valley Project in Afghanistan*, 12.

67. Area of cropland devoted to double cropping increased from 9 percent in 1970 to 23 percent in 1975.

68. Scott, Shairzai, and Farouq, *1975: Farm Economic Survey of the Helmand Valley*, 46.

69. Scott, "Opium Poppy Cultivation," 5.

70. Scott, "Opium Poppy Cultivation," 6. Farmers repaid the loan at harvest time. They also received some of the by-products from the cotton gin in Girishk, such as cottonseed, cooking oil, and soap.

71. Scott, Shairzai, and Farouq, *1975 Farm Economic Survey*, 39. The government, along with the cotton gin in Girishk (built by the British), built a cotton-processing plant in Lashkar Gah to take advantage of the abundance of supply.

72. Scott, Shairzai, and Farouq, *1975 Farm Economic Survey*, 46.

73. Clapp-Wincek and Baldwin, *The Helmand Valley*, 13.

74. Jerry Rann, "Helmand Valley Crop and Insect Survey, July 1973," USAID Kabul, RG 84, Records of the Foreign Service Posts of the Department of State, 1788–ca. 1991, Department of State, U.S. Embassy, Afghanistan, Afghanistan Box, Helmand File, NND 52378; NACP. Labor costs were noted in the years 1971 to 1973.

75. Clapp-Wincek and Baldwin, *The Helmand Valley*, 13.

76. Clapp-Wincek and Baldwin, 15. Clapp-Wincek and Baldwin never identify Pashtuns as being at an advantage over other ethnic minorities, but because the majority of Pashtuns live in the southwest of the country and Pashtun chauvinism within the government was strong under the Mushiban leadership, it is safe to say they are suggesting the Pashtuns were at an advantage over other minority groups under the government's resettlement program.

77. Rann, "Helmand Valley Crop," 8–9.

78. Scott, Shairzai, and Farouq, *1975 Helmand Farm Survey*, 114.

79. G. P. Owens and James Clifton, *Poppies in Afghanistan*, USAID, Kabul, Afghanistan, 1972, RG 84; NACP. Poppies were often harvested a few weeks before wheat.

80. Owens and Clifton, *Poppies in Afghanistan*.

81. Owens and Clifton, *Poppies in Afghanistan*.

82. Bernard Weinraub, "Afghans Use US Aid Project for Opium," *New York Times*, May 26, 1973, RG 84, Records Relating to Afghanistan; NACP.

83. "Poppies in Helmand Valley," July 6, 1973, RG 84, Records Relating to Afghanistan; NACP.

84. "Poppies in Helmand Valley." July 6, 1973.

85. "Poppies in Helmand Valley," July 6, 1973.

86. "Poppies in Helmand Valley," July 6, 1973. What is interesting about these comments is that someone had indeed read the cable and offered critiques in the margins. These "offhand" critiques point to deeper concerns, and even fissures, within the US foreign policy establishment over its operations.

87. "Poppies in Helmand Valley," July 6, 1973," 11.

88. "Poppies in Helmand Valley," July 6, 1973," 10.

89. "Poppies in Helmand Valley," July 6, 1973," 2.

90. "Poppies in Helmand Valley," July 6, 1973," 4.

91. "Poppies in Helmand Valley," July 6, 1973," 10.

92. Barfield, *Afghanistan*, 219.

93. Ispahani, *Roads and Rivals*, 125.

94. Shahrani, *The Kirghiz and the Wakhi of Afghanistan*, 79.

95. Rubin, *Fragmentation of Afghanistan*, 79. Rubin also notes that the demand for products such as opium reinforced the demand for cash.

96. Ispahani, *Roads and Rivals*, 4–7. Ispahani calls such state-driven infrastructure "routes," arguing that they provide more than economic development and integration but the expansion of state power. They can be buttressed by "antiroutes," which limit this mobility.

97. Windle, "A Very Gradual Suppression," 207–209. Windle argues that often academics assume supply-side interventions are the primary cause of crop diversion, something Windle rightly complicates.

98. McCoy, "Heroin as a Global Commodity," 262.

99. McCoy, 262–263.

100. McCoy, 263.

101. "Poppies in Helmand Valley," July 6, 1973," 5. It is unclear whether this cable had a direct impact on American officials' decision to renew development agreements in the Helmand Valley in 1974, but given the importance of combating illicit opium in US foreign policy, it is likely that it did.

102. ASUs were the antismuggling units tasked with cracking down on the growing narcotics trade. See chapter 5.

103. Arnold Schifferdecker, "Confidential Memo: October 3, 1973," RG 59, Department of State, Bureau of Near Eastern and South Asian Affairs, Office of the Country Director for Pakistan, Afghanistan and Bangladesh (1972–ca. 1979), Records Relating to Afghanistan, Daud Government—Narcotics 1973 File, Box 3, NND 36435; NACP.

104. "Afghanistan-Narcotics," State Department, Kabul, September 12, 1973, Geneva 4867, Electronic Telegrams, 1973, Central Foreign Policy Files, 7/1/1973–12/31/1979, Department of State, RG 59; NACP.

105. "Narcotics-Afghanistan," State Department, Kabul, September 27, 1973, Kabul 6991, Electronic Telegrams, 1973, Central Foreign Policy Files, 7/1/1973–12/31/1979; Department of State, RG 59; NACP.

106. William Helseth, "Poppies in the Helmand Valley," February 11, 1974, RG 84, Records Relating to Afghanistan; NACP.

107. Vincent Brown, director, USAID Afghanistan, "Memorandum on Narcotics in the Helmand Valley," USAID, March 9, 1974, RG 84, Records Relating to Afghanistan; NACP.

108. A seer is a unit of measurement common in Afghanistan, usually with a weight of a few ounces.

109. One trader noted that French and Italians came to Herat to buy small quantities of hash and were in the process of consolidating the buys. Brown, "Memorandum on Narcotics."

110. Brown, "Memorandum on Narcotics," 2.

111. "Narcotics: No Poppies in Helmand Valley," State Department, Kabul 3363, June 3, 1974, RG 84, Records Relating to Afghanistan; NACP.

112. Brown, "Memorandum on Narcotics," 2. This escalating police crackdown was a product of US and UN funding of ASUs and an informant rewards system.

113. Brown, "Memorandum on Narcotics," 2. Scott and Denton also discussed the growing demand for hash and opium inside of Afghanistan. According to Baluchi traders who passed through the southwest, opium smoking was on the rise in Farah and Nimroz Provinces.

114. Brown, "Memorandum on Narcotics," 3.

115. There are significant parallels with the Taliban ban on opium production in 2001. As David Mansfield shows, some farmers complied with a Taliban opium ban because it was advantageous both economically and politically. Much like in Helmand in 1974, farmers had to balance the future prospects of the drug trade with political realities of the time. In the case of the Taliban, implementing the ban not only helped some farmers the following growing season but by reducing opium surpluses (although not all), it gave the Taliban much needed international recognition and foreign aid (the foreign aid never quite materialized because of the events of 9/11). For more on the Taliban ban, see chapter 6 in Mansfield, *A State Built on Sand*.

116. As Graham Farrell points out, many crop eradications (as well as crop substitution programs) fail to last, often because states lack the resources, the will, or because of political resistance to the programs. See Farrell, "A Global Empirical Review of Crop Eradication," 427–430.

117. "Poppy Cultivation in Afghanistan," Kabul 3367, May 4, 1976, Electronic Telegrams, 1976, Central Foreign Policy Files, 7/1/1973–12/31/1979, Department of State, RG 59; NACP.

118. "Campaign against Planting of Poppies," State Department, Kabul, 7193, September 28, 1976, Electronic Telegrams, 1976, Central Foreign Policy Files, 7/1/1973–12/31/1979, Department of State, RG 59; NACP (retrieved from the Access to Archival Databases at www.archives.gov, February 21, 2013).

119. Emadi, *Superpowers in Afghanistan*, 78.

120. Barfield, *Afghanistan*, 224.

121. D. J. Holder, "Drug Smuggling from Afghanistan," South Asia Department, February 14, 1976, Drug Trafficking in Afghanistan, 1976, FCO 37/1692, UK National Archives, Kew.

122. Central Intelligence Agency, "International Narcotics Biweekly Review," April 26, 1978, CIA digital archives; NACP.

123. C. K. Woodfield, "Afghanistan: Narcotics Control," South Asia Department, December 29, 1976, Drug Trafficking in Afghanistan, 1976, FCO 37/1692, UK National Archives, Kew.

124. Central Intelligence Agency, "International Narcotics Biweekly Review," April 26, 1978.

125. The United States also exerted tremendous pressure on the Pakistan government to curb opium production in that country.

126. "The NNIC Report 1985–1986: The Supply of Illicit Drugs to the United States from Foreign and Domestic Sources," National Narcotics Intelligence Consumers Committee, AF 01881, June 1987, p. 74. Digital National Security Archive, nsarchive.chadwyck.com (accessed July 18, 2012).

127. "US Task Force Focuses on Narcotics in Southwest Asia," United States Information Service, Testimony, 1986, p. 4. AF01681 Digital National Security Archive, nsarchive .chadwyck.com (accessed July 18, 2012).

128. "The Supply of Drugs to the US Illicit Market from Foreign and Domestic Sources in 1981," National Narcotics Intelligence Committee, AFG1305, 1982, 18, Digital National Security Archive, nsarchive.chadwyck.com (accessed July 18, 2012).

129. "The Supply of Drugs," 24.

130. McCoy, *The Politics of Heroin*, 484.

131. For more, see Remick, *Building Local States.*

132. Rubin, *Fragmentation of Afghanistan*, 213, 263.

133. Rubin, 263. Akhunzada's reduction in opium production was eventually offset by his assassination and subsequent takeover of the valley by Hekmatyar.

134. UNODC, *Afghanistan Opium Survey 2003*, 38.

135. Scott, "Opium Poppy Cultivation in Central Helmand," 22.

136. James Ferguson describes a similar process in Lesotho where the "meaning" of development was always about political control, not the ideas of alleviating poverty and inequality that were supposedly at the heart of modernization theory. See Ferguson, *The Anti-Politics Machine.*

137. Anderson, *Imagined Communities.*

138. Roy, *Islam and Resistance in Afghanistan*, 24.

139. Emadi, *Superpowers*, 90.

140. Barfield, *Afghanistan*, 220.

141. James Scott defines the ordinary forms of peasant resistance as foot dragging, dissimulation, false compliance, pilfering, feigned ignorance, slander, arson, sabotage, etc. See Scott, *Weapons of the Weak*, 29.

142. See Hunt, *Ideology and US Foreign Policy*, and Walker, *National Security and Core Values in American History.*

Epilogue

1. Risen, "Propping Up a Drug Lord."
2. Mansfield, *A State Built on Sand*, 104–106.
3. McCoy, *The Politics of Heroin*, 484–485.
4. Mansfield, *A State Built on Sand*, 107.
5. Mansfield, 122.
6. Goodhand, "Poppy, Politics, and State-Building," 61–62.
7. Giustozzi, "War and Peace Economies," 79.
8. Mansfield, *A State Built on Sand*, 110.
9. Martin and Symansky, "Macroeconomic Impact of the Drug Economy," 26.
10. Goodhand, "Poppy, Politics, and State-Building," 60–61.
11. Department of Defense, *Enhancing Security and Stability in Afghanistan*, 18.
12. SIGAR, *Quarterly Report to the United States Congress*, 182.
13. Goodhand, "Poppy, Politics, and State-Building," 66–67.
14. Goodhand, 67–68.
15. Mansfield, *A State Build on Sand*, 300.
16. SIGAR, *Quarterly Report to the United States Congress*, 187.
17. Goodhand, "Poppy, Politics, and State-Building," 61.
18. Goodhand, 57.
19. Mansfield and Pain, "Alternative Livelihoods," 11.
20. See, Felbab-Brown, Trinkunas, and Hamid, *Militants, Criminals, and Warlords.*

Bibliography

Archival Sources

Arshaf-e Milli Afghanistan (National Archives of Afghanistan), Kabul, Afghanistan

British Library, London

Files of the Economic and Overseas Department Papers

Library of Congress, Washington, DC

Library at the Afghanistan Research and Evaluation Unit (AREU), Kabul, Afghanistan

National Archives II, College Park, MD (NACP)

Record Group 59

Bureau of Near Eastern and South Asian Affairs. Office of the Officer in Charge, Iranian Affairs (1966–ca. 1979). Country Files. Boxes 2, 3, 4, 5, and 7.

Note: Figures 4.1, 4.2, 4.3, 4.4, and 5.1 were found in RG 59.

Office of the Senior Adviser to the Secretary on Narcotics. Country Files. Boxes 2 and 4.

Bureau of Near Eastern and South Asian Affairs. Office of the Country Director for Pakistan, Afghanistan and Bangladesh (1972–ca. 1979). Records Relating to Afghanistan, 1970–1974. Box 2.

Record Group 84

Records of the Foreign Service Posts of the Department of State, 1788–ca. 1991, Department of State. US Embassy, Afghanistan. Afghanistan Box, Helmand File.

G. P. Owens and James Clifton, *Poppies in Afghanistan*, USAID (US Agency for International Development), Kabul, Afghanistan (1972), RG 84.

Record Group (RG) 170

Bureau of Narcotics and Dangerous Drugs (BNND), Subject Files, 1916–1970, Records of the Drug Enforcement Agency (DEA). Boxes 142, 151.

Archive Access Database (AAD): www.aad.archives.gov.

Digital National Security Archive: nsarchive.chadwyck.com.

UK National Archives, at Kew

Files of the Home Office (HO), Series 144

Files of the Foreign Office (FO), Series 402

Files of the Cabinet Office (CO), Series 825

Files of the Foreign and Commonwealth Office (FCO), Series 37

United Nations Archives, New York City

Works Cited

Abraham, Itty, and Willem van Schendel. "Introduction: The Making of Illicitness." In *Illicit Flows and Criminal Things: States, Borders, and the Other Side of Globalization,* edited by Itty Abraham and Willem van Schendel, 1–37. Bloomington: University of Indiana Press, 2005.

Abrahamian, Ervand. *Iran between Two Revolutions.* Princeton, NJ: Princeton University Press, 1982.

Alexander, Horace Gundry. *Narcotics in India and South Asia.* London: B.F. Stevens and Brown, 1930.

Allan, Nigel. "Opium Production in Afghanistan and Pakistan." In *Dangerous Harvest: Drug Plants and the Transformation of Indigenous Landscapes*, edited by Michael Steinberg, Joseph Hobbs, and Kent Mathewson, 133–152. Oxford: Oxford University Press, 2004.

Anderson, Benedict. *Imagined Communities.* London: Verso, 2006.

Ansary, Mir Tamim. *West of Kabul, East of New York.* New York: Farrar, Straus and Giroux, 2002.

Asad, Amir Zada, and Robert Harris. *The Politics and Economics of Drug Production on the Pakistan-Afghanistan Border.* Burlington, VT: Ashgate, 2003.

Babar, Jamil. "Afghanistan: 1963–1973." PhD diss., Near Eastern Studies, University of California, Berkeley, 2005.

Barfield, Thomas. *Afghanistan: A Political and Cultural History.* Princeton, NJ: Princeton University Press, 2010.

——. *The Central Asian Arabs of Afghanistan.* Austin: University of Texas Press, 1981.

——. "Problems in Establishing Legitimacy in Afghanistan." *Iranian Studies* 37, no. 2 (2004): 263–293.

Berke, Zehdi. "Public Health and Hygiene in Afghanistan." *Afghanistan,* July-September 1946.

Berridge, Virginia. "Victorian Opium Eating: Responses to Opiate Use in Nineteenth Century England." *Victorian Studies* 21, no. 4 (1978): 437–461.

Bewley-Taylor, David. *The United States and International Drug Control, 1909–1997.* New York: Pinter, 1999.

Bill, James. *The Eagle and the Lion: The Tragedy of American-Iranian Relations.* New Haven, CT: Yale University Press, 1988.

Bradford, James. "Drug Control in Afghanistan: Culture, Politics, and Power during the 1958 Prohibition of Opium in Badakhshan." *Journal of Iranian Studies* 48, no. 2 (2015): 223–248.

Buddenberg, Doris. "On the Cultural History of Opium and How the Opium Poppy Came to Afghanistan." January 11, 2016. Afghanistan Analysts Network. https://www.afghanistan-analysts.org/wp-admin/post.php.

Campos, Isaac, and Paul Gootenberg. "Toward a New Drug History of Latin America: A Research Frontier at the Center of Debates." *Hispanic American Historical Review* 95, no. 1 (2015): 1–35.

Carpenter, Ted Galen. "How the Drug War in Afghanistan Undermines America's War on Terror." *Foreign Policy Briefing*, no. 84 (November 10, 2004): 1–8.

Charpentier, C. J. "The Use of Haschish and Opium in Afghanistan." *Anthropos*, Bd. 68, H 3/4 (1973): 482–490.

Chouvy, Pierre-Arnaud. "Drugs and the Financing of Terrorism." *Terrorism Monitor* 2, no. 20 (2004): 3–5.

——. *Opium: Uncovering the Politics of the Poppy.* Cambridge, MA: Harvard University Press, 2010.

Clapp-Wincek, Cynthia, and Emily Baldwin. *The Helmand Valley Project in Afghanistan.* Washington, DC: USAID, 1983.

Clarke, Robert Connell. *Hashish.* Los Angeles: Red Eye Press, 1998.

Cohen, Erik. "Alternative Tourism—A Critique." *Tourism Recreation Research* 12, no. 2 (1987): 13–18.

Collins, John. "Regulations and Prohibitions: Anglo-American Relations and International Drug Control, 1939–1964." PhD diss., London School of Economics, 2015.

Courtwright, David. *Dark Paradise.* Cambridge, MA: Harvard University Press, 1982.

——. *Forces of Habit.* Cambridge, MA: Harvard University Press, 2001.

Cullather, Nick. "Damming Afghanistan: Modernization in a Buffer State," in "History and September 11," special issue. *Journal of American History* 89, no. 2 (2002): 512–537.

Cusack, John. "Turkey Lifts the Poppy Ban." *Drug Enforcement* (Fall 1974): 3–7.

Davenport-Hines, Richard. *The Pursuit of Oblivion.* New York: Horton, 2002.

Department of Defense. *Enhancing Security and Stability in Afghanistan,* December 2017.

DeQuincey, Thomas. *Confessions of an Opium Eater.* Electronic Classical Series. University Park: Pennsylvania State University Press, 2004.

Dupree, Louis. *Afghanistan.* Princeton, NJ: Princeton University Press, 1980.

——. "Afghanistan 1977: Does Aid Plus Trade Guarantee Development?" *American Universities Field Staff Reports, South Asia Series* 21, no. 3 (1977): 1–13.

——. "An Informal Talk with Prime Minster Daud." September 1959. *American Universities Field Staff Reports,* South Asia Series 3 (September 1959): 1–4.

——. "A Note on Afghanistan: 1971." *South Asia Series (Afghanistan)* 15, no. 2 (1971): 1–35.

Emadi, Hafizullah. *State, Revolution, and Superpowers in Afghanistan.* New York: Praeger, 1990.

Engerman, David. "West Meets East: The Center for International Studies and Indian Economic Development." In *Staging Growth: Modernization, International History, and the Cold War World*, edited by David Engerman, Nils Gilman, Mark Haefele, and Michael Latham, 199–224. Amherst: University of Massachusetts Press, 2003.

Epstein, Edward. *Agency of Fear: Opiates and Political Power in America.* London: Verso, 1999.

Farber, David. "The Intoxicated State/Illegal Nation: Drugs in the Sixties Counterculture." In *Imagine Nation: The American Counterculture of the 1960s and 70s*, edited by Peter Braunstein and Michael William Doyle, 17–40. New York: Routledge, 2002.

Farrell, Graham. "A Global Empirical Review of Drug Crop Eradication, Crop Substitution, and Alternative Development Policy." *Journal of Drug Issues* 28, no. 2 (1998): 395–436.

Farrell, Graham, and James Windle. "Popping the Balloon Effect: Assessing Drug Law Enforcement in Terms of Displacement, Diffusion, and the Containment Hypothesis." *Substance Use and Misuse* 47, no. 8–9 (2012): 868–876.

Felbab-Brown, Vanda. "The Obama Administration's New Counter-narcotics Strategy in Afghanistan: Its Promises and Potential Pitfalls." Brookings Policy Brief Series, No. 171 (2009): 1–7.

——. *Shooting Up: Counterinsurgency and the War on Drugs.* Washington, DC: Brookings Institution Press, 2009.

Felbab-Brown, Vanda, Harold Trinkunas, and Shadi Hamid. *Militants, Criminals, and Warlords: The Challenge of Local Governance in an Age of Disorder.* Washington, DC: Brookings Institution Press, 2018.

Ferguson, James. *The Anti-Politics Machine: Development, Depoliticization, and Bureaucratic Power in Lesotho.* New York: Cambridge University Press, 1990.

Fishstein, Paul. *A Little-Bit Poppy-Free and a Little-Bit Eradicated: Opium Poppy Cultivation in Balkh and Badakhshan Provinces in 2011–2012.* Kabul: Afghanistan Research and Evaluation Unit, 2013.

Franck, Peter. *Afghanistan: Between East and West.* Washington, DC: National Planning Association, 1960.

——. "Problems of Economic Development in Afghanistan." *Middle East Journal* 3, no. 3 (1949): 421–440.

Frank, Zephyr, Carlos Marichal, and Steven Topik. "Introduction: Commodity Chains in Theory and in Latin American History." In *From Silver to Cocaine: Latin American Commodity Chains and the Building of the World Economy, 1500–2000*, edited by Zephyr

Frank, Carlos Marichal, and Steven Topik, 1–24. Durham, NC: Duke University Press, 2006.

Fry, Maxwell. *The Afghan Economy*. Leiden: E.J. Brill, 1974.

Frydl, Kathleen. *The Drug Wars in America*. Cambridge: Cambridge University Press, 2013.

Gallant, Tony. "Brigandage, Piracy, Capitalism, and State-Formation: Transnational Crime from a Historical World-Systems Perspective." In *States and Illegal Practices*, edited by Josiah Heyman, 25–61. Oxford: Berg, 1999.

Gavit, John Palmer. *Opium*. New York: Brentano's, 1927.

Gelvin, James. *The Modern Middle East*. New York: Oxford University Press, 2015.

Ghani, Abdul. *A Review of the Political Situation in Central Asia*. Lahore: Aziz, 1980.

Gingeras, Ryan. *Heroin, Organized Crime, and the Making of Modern Turkey*. Oxford; Oxford University Press, 2014.

——. "In the Hunt for the 'Sultans of Smack': Dope, Gangsters, and the Construction of the Deep State." *Middle East Journal* 65, no. 3 (2011): 426–441.

Giustozzi, Antonio. *The Art of Coercion: The Primitive Accumulation and Management of Coercive Power*. New York: Columbia University Press, 2011.

——. "War and Peace Economies of Afghanistan's Strongmen." *International Peacekeeping* 14, no. 1 (2011): 75–89.

Giustozzi, Antonio, and Artemy Kalinovsky. *Missionaries of Modernity: Advisory Missions and the Struggle for Hegemony in Afghanistan and Beyond*. London: Hurst, 2016.

Gobar, Asad Hassan. "Drug Abuse in Afghanistan." *Bulletin on Narcotics* (United Nations Office on Drugs and Crime), no. 2 (1976): 1–11.

Goodhand, Jonathan. *Bandits, Borderlands, and Opium Wars: Afghan State-Building Viewed from the Margins*. Copenhagen: Danish Institute for International Studies, 2009.

——. "Poppy, Politics, and State-Building." In *Afghanistan: Transition under Threat*, edited by Geoffrey Hayes and Mark Sedra, 51–86. Canada: Center for International Governance Innovation, 2008.

Gootenberg, Paul. *Andean Cocaine: The Making of a Global Drug*. Durham: University of North Carolina Press, 2008.

——. "Introduction: Cocaine: the Hidden Histories." In *Cocaine: Global Histories*, edited by Paul Gootenberg, 1–20. New York: Routledge, 1990.

Grayson, George. *Mexico: Narco-Violence and a Failed State*? New Brunswick, NJ: Transaction Publishers, 2010.

Greenfield, Victoria, and Letizia Paoli. "Research as Due Diligence: What Can Supply-Side Interventions Accomplish and at What Cost?" *International Journal of Drug Policy*, no. 41 (2017): 162–163.

Gregorian, Vartan. *The Emergence of Modern Afghanistan*. Stanford, CA: Stanford University Press, 1969.

Hafvenstein, Joel. *Opium Season: A Year on the Afghan Frontier*. New York: Lyon's Press, 2009.

Hanifi, Shah Mahmoud. *Connecting Histories in Afghanistan: Market Relations and State Formation on a Colonial Frontier*. Stanford, CA: Stanford University Press, 2011.

Haq, Ikramul. "Pak-Afghan Drug Trade in Historical Perspective." *Asian Survey* 36, no 10. (1996): 945–963.

Haq, M Emdad-ul. *Drugs in South Asia: From the Opium Trade to the Present Day*. New York: St. Martin's Press, 2000.

Hickman, Timothy. "Drugs and Race in American Culture: Orientalism in the Turn-of-the-Century Discourse on Narcotics Addiction." *American Studies* 41, no. 1, (2000): 71–91.

Honchell, Stephanie. *Pursuing Pleasure, Attaining Oblivion: The Roles and Uses of Intoxicants at the Mughal Court*. MA diss., University of Louisville, 2012.

Hopkins, Benjamin, and Magnus Marsden. *Fragments of the Afghan Frontier*. New York: Columbia University Press, 2011.

Hopkins, Terrance, and Immanuel Wallerstein. "Commodity Chains: Construct and Research." In *Commodity Chains and Global Capitalism*, edited by Gary Gereffi and Miguel Koreniewicz, 17–19. Westport, CT: Greenwood Press, 1994.

Hunt, Michael. *Ideology and US Foreign Policy*. New Haven, CT: Yale University Press, 1987.

Imperial Gazetteer of India. Vol. 19. Oxford: Clarendon Press, 1908.

Ispahani, Mahnaz. *Roads and Rivals: The Politics of Access in the Borderlands of Asia*. London: I.B Tauris, 1989.

Kamm, Henry. "World Is a Carousel." *New York Times*, November 17, 1972.

Kennedy, Paul. *The Rise and Fall of the Great Powers: Economic Change and Military Conflict from 1500 to 2000*. London: Fontana, 1989.

Kopytoff, Igor. "The Cultural Biography of Things: Commoditization as Process." In *The Social Life of Things: Commodities in Cultural Perspective*, edited by Arjun Appadurai, 64–94. Cambridge: Cambridge University Press, 1986.

Kusevic, Vladimir. "Drug Abuse Control and International Treaties." *Journal of Drug Issues* 7, no. 1 (1977): 36–52.

Lamour, Catherine, and Michael Lamberti. *Les Grandes Manouevres de l'Opium*. Paris: Seuill, 1972.

——. *The International Connection: Opium from Growers to Pushers*. New York: Pantheon, 1974.

Latham, Michael. "Introduction: Modernization Theory, International History, and the Global Cold War." In *Staging Growth: Modernization, International History, and the Cold War World*, edited by David Engerman, Nils Gilman, Mark Haefele, and Michael Latham, 1–22. Amherst: University of Massachusetts Press, 2003.

Levi, Peter. *The Light Garden of the Angel King*. London: Collins, 1972.

Logevall, Fredrik, and Andrew Preston. *Nixon in the World: American Foreign Relations, 1969–1977*. New York: Oxford University Press, 2008.

MacDonald, David. *Drugs in Afghanistan*. London: Pluto Press, 2007.

Magnus, Ralph. "The Constitution of 1964: A Decade of Political Experimentation." In *Afghanistan in the 1970s*, edited by Louis Dupree and Linnette Albert. New York: Praeger, 1974.

Maguire, Peter, and Mike Ritter. *Thai Stick: Surfers, Scammers, and the Untold Story of the Marijuana Trade*. New York: Columbia University Press, 2014.

Manela, Erez. *The Wilsonian Moment: Self-Determination and the International Origins of Anticolonial Nationalism*. New York: Oxford University Press, 2007.

Mansfield, David. "Access to Labour: The Role of Opium in the Livelihood Strategies of Itinerant Harvesters Working in Helmand Province, Afghanistan." Strategic Study, No. 4: Final Report, June 1999. UNODC (United Nations Office on Drugs and Crime).

——. "Alternative Development in Afghanistan: The Failure of Quid Pro Quo." Paper prepared for the International Conference on Alternative Development in Drug Control and Cooperation, Feldafing, January 7–12, 2002. Pp. 1–18.

——. "Diversity and Dilemma: Understanding Rural Livelihoods and Addressing the Causes of Opium Poppy Cultivation in Nangarhar and Laghman, Eastern Afghanistan." A report for the Project for Alternative Livelihoods in Eastern Afghanistan, 2004.

——. "Our Friends in the North: Contrasting Images of Power and Poppy in the Provinces of Balkh and Badakhshan." Paper draft, April 8, 2014.

——. "The Role of Opium as a Source of Informal Credit in Rural Afghanistan." Kabul: World Bank, 2004.

——. *A State Built on Sand: How Opium Undermined Afghanistan*. New York: Oxford University Press, 2016.

Mansfield, David, and Adam Pain. "Alternative Livelihoods: Substance or Slogan." Afghanistan Research and Evaluation Unit, Briefing Paper (October 2005): 1–14.

Markham, James. "Story of Melanie R." *New York Times*, November 17, 1972.

Martin, Edouard, and Steven Symansky. "Macroeconomic Impact of the Drug Economy and Counter-Narcotics Efforts." In *Afghanistan's Drug Industry: Structure, Functioning, Dynamics, and Implications for Counter-Narcotics Policy*, edited by Doris Buddenburg and William Byrd, 25–46. New York: UNODC (United Nations Office on Drugs and Crime) and World Bank, 2006.

Matthee, Rudi. *The Pursuit of Pleasure*. Princeton, NJ: Princeton University Press, 2005.

May, David, and Stewart Tender. *The Brotherhood of Eternal Love: From Flower Power to Hippie Mafia: The Story of the LSD Counterculture*. London: Cyan Books, 2008.

McAllister, William. *Drug Diplomacy in the Twentieth Century*. New York: Routledge Press, 2000.

McCoy, Alfred. "Coercion and Its Unintended Consequences." *Crime, Law, and Social Change* 33, no. 3 (2000): 191–224.

——. "From Free Trade to Prohibition: A Critical History of the Modern Asian Opium Trade." *Fordham Urban Law Journal* 28, no. 1, article 4 (2000): 307–349.

——. "Heroin as a Global Commodity: A History of Southeast Asia's Opium Trade." In *War on Drugs: Study in the Failure of US Narcotics Policy*, edited by Alfred McCoy and Alan A. Block, 237–279. San Francisco: Westview Press, 1992.

——. *The Politics of Heroin: CIA Complicity in the Global Drug Trade*. Chicago: Lawrence Hill Books, 2003.

McLaughlin, Gerald. "The Poppy Is Not an Ordinary Flower: A Survey of Drug Policy in Iran." *Fordham Law Review* 44 (1976): 702–766.

McLaughlin, Gerald, and Thomas Quinn. "Drug Control in Iran: A Legal and Historical Analysis." *Iowa Law Review* 59, no. 3 (1974): 469–524.

Migdal, Joel. *Strong Societies and Weak States*. Princeton, NJ: Princeton University Press, 1988.

Mintz, Sydney. *Sweetness and Power: The Place of Sugar in Modern History*. New York: Viking, 1985.

Mitchell, Timothy. *Rule of Experts: Egypt, Techno-Politics, Modernity*. Berkeley: University of California Press, 2002.

Musto, David. *The American Disease: The Origins of Narcotic Control*. 3rd ed. New York: Oxford University Press, 1999.

Nawid, Senzil. *Religious Response to Social Change in Afghanistan, 1919–29: King Aman-Allah and the Afghan Ulama*. Costa Mesa, CA: Mazda Publishers, 1999.

Newell, Richard. "Afghanistan: The Dangers of Cold War Generosity." *Middle East Journal* 23, no. 2 (1969): 168–176.

——. *The Politics of Afghanistan*. Ithaca, NY: Cornell University Press, 1972.

——. "The Prospects of State-Building in Afghanistan." In *The State, Religion, and Ethnic Politics: Afghanistan, Iran, and Pakistan*, edited by Ali Banuazzi and Myron Weiner, 104–123. Syracuse, NY: Syracuse University Press, 1986.

Nixon, Richard. "Remarks about an Intensified Program for Drug Abuse Prevention and Control, June 17, 1971." In *Public Papers of the Presidents of the United States, Richard Nixon, 1971*. Washington, DC: United States Government Printing Office, 1972.

——. "Special Message to the Congress on Drug Abuse Prevention and Control, June 17, 1971." In *Public Papers of the Presidents of the United States, Richard Nixon, 1971*. Washington, DC: United States Government Printing Office, 1972.

Noorzoy, M Siddieq. "Alternative Economic Systems for Afghanistan." *International Journal of Middle East Studies* 15, no. 1 (1983): 25–45.

Owen, David Edward. *British Opium Policy in China and India*. New Haven, CT: Yale University Press, 1934.

Owens, G.P., and J. H. Clifton. *Poppies in Afghanistan*. Kabul: USAID, 1972.

Pain, Adam. "Opium Poppy and Informal Credit." Kabul: Afghanistan Research and Evaluation Unit, 2008.

Pandey, Gyan. *Routine Violence: Nations, Fragments, Histories*. Palo Alto, CA: Stanford University Press, 2006.

Pennell, T. L. *Among the Wild Tribes of the Afghan Frontier*. London: Seeley, 1908.

Peters, Gretchen. *Seeds of Terror: How Heroin Is Bankrolling the Taliban and al-Qaeda*. New York: St. Martin's Press, 2009.

Poullada, Leon. *The Kingdom of Afghanistan*. Lincoln, NE: Dageford, 1995.

——. *Reform and Rebellion in Afghanistan, 1919–29: King Amanullah's Failure to Modernize a Tribal Society*. Ithaca, NY: Cornell University Press, 1973.

——. "The Search for National Unity." In *Afghanistan in the 1970s*, edited by Louis Dupree and Linnette Albert. New York: Praeger, 1974.

Quinones, Sam. *Dreamland: The True Tale of America's Opioid Epidemic*. New York: Bloomsbury Press, 2016.

Remick, Elizabeth. *Building Local States: China during the Republican and Post-Mao Eras*. Cambridge, MA: Harvard University Press, 2004.

Risen, James. "Propping Up a Drug Lord, Then Arresting Him." *New York Times*, December 11, 2010.

Roy, Olivier. *Islam and Resistance in Afghanistan*. Cambridge: Cambridge University Press, 1990.

Rubin, Barnett. *The Fragmentation of Afghanistan: State Formation and Collapse in the International System*. New Haven, CT: Yale University Press, 2002.

Rubin, Barnett, and Jake Sherman. *Counter-narcotics to Stabilize Afghanistan: The False Promise of Crop Eradication*. New York: UNDP (United Nations Development Programme), 2008.

Said, Edward. *Orientalism*. New York: Vintage Books, 1979.

Salmon, Gregor. *Poppy: Life, Death, and Addiction Inside Afghanistan's Opium Trade*. Sydney: Ebury Press, 2009.

Schou, Nicholas. *Orange Sunshine: The Brotherhood of Eternal Love and Its Quest to Spread Peace, Love, and Acid to the World*. New York: St. Martin's Griffin, 2011.

Scott, James. *Seeing Like a State: How Certain Schemes to Improve the Human Condition Have Failed*. New Haven, CT: Yale University Press, 1998.

——. *Weapons of the Weak: Everyday Forms of Peasant Resistance*. New Haven, CT: Yale University Press, 1985.

Scott, Richard. "Opium Poppy Cultivation Central Helmand, Afghanistan: A Case Study in Bad Program Management." Paper presented at the Society for Applied Anthropology, March 30, 2007.

Scott, Richard. "Tribal and Ethnic Groups in the Helmand Valley." The Afghanistan Council, the Asia Society. Occasional Paper No. 21 (Spring 1980).

Scott, Richard, Frydoon Shairzai, and Ghulam Farouq. *1975: Farm Economic Survey of the Helmand Valley*. Kabul: USAID (US Agency for International Development), 1975.

Shahrani, M. Nazif. "State-Building and Social Fragmentation in Afghanistan." In *The State, Religion, and Ethnic Politics: Afghanistan, Iran, and Pakistan*, edited by Ali Banuazzi and Myron Weiner, 23–74. Syracuse, NY: Syracuse University Press, 1986.

Shahrani, M. Nazif Mohib. *The Kirghiz and the Wakhi of Afghanistan*. Seattle: University of Washington Press, 1979.

SIGAR (Special Inspector General for Afghanistan Reconstruction). *Quarterly Report to the United States Congress*. April 30, 2018, p. 193. https://www.sigar.mil/pdf/quarterly reports/2018-04-30qr.pdf.

Spain, James. "The United States, Turkey, and the Poppy." *Middle East Journal* 29, no. 3 (1975): 295–309.

Staanekzai, Nasrullah. *Movad Mokder dar Afghanistan* (Drugs in Afghanistan Kabul), 1382 (2003).

Taylor, Arnold H. *American Diplomacy and the Narcotics Traffic, 1909–1939*. Durham, NC: Duke University Press, 1969.

Thoumi, Francisco. *Illegal Drugs, Economy, and Society in the Andes*. Baltimore, MD: Johns Hopkins University Press, 2003.

Tilly, Charles. *Coercion, Capital, and European States, AD 990–1990*. Cambridge, MA: Basil Blackwell, 1990.

Tomlins, Christopher. "Introduction: The Many Legalities of Colonization." In *The Many Legalities of Early America*, edited by Bruce Mann and Christopher Tomlins, 1–23. Chapel Hill: University of North Carolina Press, 2001.

Topik, Steven, Carlos Marichal, and Zephyr Frank. "Introduction: Commodity Chains in Theory and in Latin American History." In *From Silver to Cocaine: Latin American Commodity Chains and the Building of the World Economy, 1500–2000*, edited by Steven Topik, Carlos Marichal, and Zephyr Frank, 1–24. Durham, NC: Duke University Press, 2006.

Toynbee, Arnold. *Between Oxus and Jumma*. London: Oxford University Press, 1963.

Trocki, Carl. *Opium, Empire, and the Global Political Economy: A Study of the Asian Opium Trade, 1750–1950*. New York: Routledge, 1999.

Tyrell, Ian. *Reforming the World: The US Moral Empire*. Princeton, NJ: Princeton University Press, 2010.

UNODC (United Nations Office on Drugs and Crime). "Afghan Opium Crop Cultivation Rises Seven Per Cent in 2014." https://www.unodc.org/unodc/en/frontpage/2014/November/afghan-opium-crop-cultivation-rises-seven-per-cent-in-2014-while-opium-production-could-climb-by-as-much-as-17-per-cent.html. Accessed June 23, 2016.

——. *Afghanistan Opium Survey 2003*. Islamabad: United Nations Office on Drugs and Crime, 2003.

——. *Afghanistan Opium Survey 2008*. New York: United Nations Office on Drugs and Crime, August 2008.

——. *Afghanistan: Opium Survey 2011*. New York: United Nations Publications, October 2011.

——. *Afghanistan: Opium Survey 2011*. New York: United Nations Publications, December 2011.

——. *Afghanistan Opium Survey 2012: Opium Risk Assessment for All Regions*. UN Publications, 2012.

——. "Discussion Paper: Is Poverty Driving the Opium Boom?" March 2008.

——. *The Opium Economy in Afghanistan: An International Problem*. New York: United Nations Publications, 2003.

USAID (US Agency for International Development). *Retrospective Review of US Assistance to Afghanistan: 1950–1979*. Consultant study. Bethesda, MD: Devres, 1988.

U.S. Bureau of the Census. *Statistical Abstract of the United States: 1954* (1955). Table 1075: 899–902.

Valentine, Douglas. *The Strength of the Pack: The Personalities, Politics and Espionage Intrigues That Shaped the DEA*. Chicago: Independent Publishers Group, 2009.

Vavilov, N. I., and D. D. Bukinich. *Agricultural Afghanistan: Supplement no. 33 to the Bulletin of Botany and Plant Breeding*. Leningrad, 1929.

Walker, William. *National Security and Core Values in American History*. New York: Cambridge University Press, 2009.

Walker, William III. "Drug Control and the Issue of Culture in American Foreign Relations." *Diplomatic History* 12, no. 4 (1998): 365–382.

Wallerstein, Immanuel, and Terrance Hopkins. "Commodity Chains: Construct and Research." In *Commodity Chains and Global Capitalism*, edited by Gary Gereffi and M. Koreniewicz, 17–19. Westport, CT: Greenwood Press, 1994.

Weimer, Daniel. *Seeing Drugs: Modernization, Counterinsurgency, and US Narcotics Control in the Third World, 1969–1976*. Kent, OH: Kent University Press, 2011.

Weiner, Myron. "Political Change in Asia, Africa, and the Middle East." In *Understanding Political Development*, edited by Myron Weiner and Samuel Huntington, 33–64. New York: Waverland PR, 1994.

Weinraub, Bernard. "Afghans Use US Aid Project for Opium." *New York Times*, May 26, 1973.

Windle, James. "A Very Gradual Suppression: A History of Turkish Opium Controls, 1933–1974. *European Journal of Criminology* 11, no. 2 (2013): 195–212.

——. "How the East Influenced Drug Prohibition." *International History Review* 35, no. 5 (2013): 1185–1199.

Zheng, Yangwhen. "The Social Life of Opium, 1483–1999." *Modern Asian Studies* 37, no. 1 (2003): 1–39.

Zurich, David. *Errant Journeys: Adventure Travel in a Modern Age.* Austin: University of Texas Press, 1995.

Index

1912 Hague Convention, 56–58, 70–84
1925 Geneva Narcotics Convention, 24, 58
1931 Narcotics Convention (international), 57–58, 60–61, 70–71, 76
1944/1945 Opium Prohibition (Afghanistan), 46–47, 74–84, 86, 90, 98, 163
1953 Opium Protocol (UN), 86, 87, 91–93, 98, 102, 239n18, 248n35
1956 Opium Act (Afghanistan), 96–99
1956 UN Commission on Narcotic Drugs, 94–96
1957/1958 Opium Prohibition (Afghanistan), 86–88, 102–115, 117, 146, 163
1961 Single Convention (international), 131–132
1969 Anti-Smuggling Law (Afghanistan), 163–165, 176
1969 Comprehensive Drug Abuse Prevention and Control Act (US), 149–150
1970 Controlled Substances Act (US), 145
1973/1974 prohibition (Afghanistan), 202–208, 210–211

Abdur Rahman, Amir Khan (Iron Amir), 17, 26–30, 41–42, 229n49
Abraham, Itty, 4–5, 89, 110, 181, 226n37
Abul Fazl, 25
addiction
  of Americans, 132, 145–146, 149–150, 161
  in Badakhshan, 69, 109, 242n74
  cultural perceptions of, 26, 34, 80, 108–109, 227n45, 230n88
  to heroin, 138–139, 145–146, 149–150, 152, 155, 157, 209, 228n27
  in Iran, 93–94, 95, 109, 126, 128, 162, 209, 239n29, 239n30
  in Pakistan, 209, 250n67
  punishment for, 33, 228n27
  social, 109, 242n74
  treatment of, 150
Afghan American Trading Company, 63, 65–66, 67, 78, 235n92
Afghan Millat (newspaper), 121, 122fig, 123fig, 134–135, 135fig, 137fig, 143

Afghan Opium Company (Shirkat-i-Taryak), 59, 62, 81
Akhunzada, Mullah Nasim, 209, 216
alcohol, 28, 32, 33, 228n37, 230n81, 230n84
Alexander, Horace, 26
al-khamr, 33
Allan, Nigel, 225n23
alternatives to opium production, 217
  in Badakhshan, 85–86, 103–104
  in Helmand Valley, 15, 182, 184
Amanullah Khan, 17–18, 30–34, 41–43, 44, 47–51
Ancient world, 18–19
Anglo-Afghan Treaty (Treaty of Rawalpindi), 31, 39
Anis (newspaper), 166–167, 167fig
Ansary, Tamim, 185
Anslinger, Harry
  on 1953 protocol, 93, 99
  on Afghan failure to follow guidelines, 99–100
  aid to Badakhshan and, 105, 106, 107
  arranges opium purchases, 65–66, 67, 78
  opposes opium purchases, 92
  power of, 233n50
Anti-Opium Society, 22, 227n18
Armour, Norman, 49–50
Asad, Amir Zada, 225n24
ASUs (antismuggling units), 148, 174–175, 176, 202
Avuncular period, 92
Aziz, Abdul Hosayn, 81
Aziz, A. Hamid, 92–93

babas, 26
Babur, Zahiruddin Muhammad, 25
Badakhshan, 85–115
  1957/1958 Opium Prohibition, 86–88, 102–115, 117, 146, 163
  addiction in, 69, 109, 242n74
  alternatives to opium production in, 85–86, 103–104
  exports from, 40, 62, 63, 67, 81
  high morphine content of opium from, 62, 91
  impact of ban, 103–106
  opium production in, 85–86, 89, 103–108, 115
  targeting of for drug control, 87–89, 102–103
Baldwin, Emily, 256n76
Balkh, 218
balloon effect, 159, 200–201
Bank-i-Milli, 53, 59, 62, 63, 67
bans. *See* prohibition
Barfield, Thomas, 110, 230n69
Bayhan, Kudret, 153
Berle, Adolf A., 75–78
Berridge, Virginia, 226n39, 241n71
Bewley-Taylor, David, 23, 24, 228n31
bhang, 1, 26, 28, 33, 35, 229n57
BNDD (Bureau of Narcotics and Dangerous Drugs), 128, 140, 150, 157, 169–170, 233n50. *See also* DEA; Federal Bureau of Narcotics
Brent, Charles H., 22, 35
British Empire
  pre-WWI, 16–20, 23, 28, 31, 35–43, 227n18, 241n71
  interwar years, 50–51, 58–59, 231n100
Brotherhood of Eternal Love, 139–140
Bureau of Narcotics. *See* BNDD; DEA; Federal Bureau of Narcotics
Burke, Terry, 169

Campos, Isaac, 13
cannabis, 16, 23–24, 107, 139
cash crops, 15, 182, 194–197
  opium as, 197, 200
charse (hashish), from Afghanistan
  colonial era trading in, 17, 18, 28, 41
  exporting of to Iran, 118, 129
  globalization of trade in, 116–117, 118–119, 139–141, 144
  historical use of, 1, 26
  interwar trading in, 16, 33, 35
  professionalization of trade in, 140–142, 143
  tourists and, 132–138, 141–142
China
  British Empire and, 18–19, 20, 35–36, 231n100
  Qing dynasty, opium during, 134, 154
  trafficking system of, 249n51
  US and, 22
Chiu Chau syndicate, 156–157, 249n44
Chouvy, Pierre-Arnaud, 253n3
CIA, 149, 155, 214
civil laws, 27–28
Clapp-Wincek, Cynthia, 256n76
cocaine, 23–24, 45, 51

coercion, 111, 113–114, 147, 176, 206, 221.
  See also prohibition
Cohen, Erik, 116
Cold War
  Afghan-US relations, impact on, 47, 92, 161, 181
  development and, 187–188
  moral crusades of, 92, 146
  war on drugs policy and, 146, 147, 237n113
Collins, John, 72
conflict economy, 216–217
Constable, Peter, 203
corruption and collusion
  in Afghanistan, 121, 124, 167–170, 172, 177, 219, 241n52
  HAVA and, 183, 192, 193–194, 207
  in Iran, 131
cotton growing, 194, 256n70, 256n71
Courtwright, David, 19, 228n27, 248n8
Cullather, Nick, 186
cultural attitudes to opium
  acceptance, 20, 25, 82, 89, 108–109, 142, 241n71
  bridging of gaps, 80, 97
  drug policies in opposition to, 7, 13–14, 89, 109–112, 115
  US, 22–23, 34, 108–109, 227n45, 228n27, 228n31, 230n88

dam projects, 186–187
Daud Khan, Mohammad, and government of
  1953 Opium Protocol, 86, 87, 91–93, 98, 102, 239n18, 248n35
  1956 Opium Act, 96–99
  1957/1958 Opium Prohibition, 86–88, 102–115, 117, 146, 163
  1973/1974 prohibition, 202–208, 210–211
  coup of, 92, 172–173, 192, 243n10
  drug control, decision to undertake, 86–89, 173–175, 183–184, 202
  exports, efforts to achieve, 89–102
  foreign policy of, 92, 173–175, 189–190, 192–193
  HAVA and, 189–190, 192–194
  resignation of, 119
  security forces under, 168–169
  US relations during, 89–102, 105–107, 109, 113, 173–175, 183, 239n20
DEA (Drug Enforcement Agency)
  ASUs, founding of, 174–175, 202
  drug lords as informants for, 214
  globalization of drug trade and, 160
  on hashish trafficking, 140
  Helmand Valley and, 198
  interdiction by, 219
  new infrastructure of, 150
  on soldier epidemic, 249n44
  Turkey, cooperation with, 153
  See also BNDD; Federal Bureau of Narcotics
Decade of Democracy, 118, 124
Defense Supplies Corporation (DSC), 66–67
demand strategies, 150
Denton, Frank, 204
Department of Defense (DOD), 219
De Quincey, Thomas, 49, 227n15
development
  dependence on foreign aid, 111
  failure of, 15, 89, 107–108, 200, 211–212
  modernization theory and, 182, 187, 212–213, 259n136
  as spur to drug trade, 200
  as underlying need, 171–172
  World War II, impact of on, 61, 79
  See also Helmand Valley; modernization
Dimukrasi-yi Naw (Democracy Now), 120
double cropping, 194, 195–196, 206, 256n67
droughts, 172, 192, 201
drug control efforts
  in Afghanistan: as aid to state formation, 34, 45, 111, 114, 148–149, 176, 178; in Badakhshan, 102–115; contradictory effects of, 110–112, 114–115, 178–179; co-opting of, 205–207, 211, 212, 258n115; domestic use, control of, 17, 33–34, 42; foreign pressure, as result of, 6, 46–47, 88, 89, 97–98, 112–114, 143–144, 146–148, 161, 163, 183, 204–205; in Helmand Valley, 183–184, 202–208, 210–211; indifference to, 99–100, 127, 132–133, 136, 144, 169–170, 203–204, 250n65; interwar years, 45, 56–58, 60–61; Nixon's War on Drugs and, 160–179; protocol adherence as challenge for, 91–102, 117, 142–144, 148–149, 160–161, 164–165, 168–171, 176–177, 202–203, 208, 215–219; by Taliban, 112–115; during WWII, 45–47, 61, 65, 74–84
  by France, 91, 99, 152

drug control efforts (*continued*)
by Iran, 117, 118, 125–131, 143, 150, 163, 168, 239n31, 244n30
by Mexico, 150, 158–160, 175–176
by Pakistan, 127, 150, 225n24
securitization of by US, 217
by Turkey, 127, 128, 150, 153–154, 157–158, 163, 178, 200–201, 225n26
See also specific law/measure (by year)
Drug Supervisory Body (DSB), 233n50
Dupree, Louis, 172, 190, 254n29

East India Company (EIC), 19
Ecevit, Bulent, 153
Egypt, 93
Eliot, Theodore, 174, 193
Emdad-ul Haq, M., 37
Epstein, Edward, 248n16
ethnic groups. *See* Badakhshan; Pashtuns
exporting of drugs. *See* illicit exporting of drugs; licit exporting of drugs

famines, 172, 201
faqirs, 26
farmers. *See* rural population
Farrell, Graham, 104, 159, 250n57
Federal Bureau of Narcotics, 71, 72–73, 105–107, 151–152. *See also* Anslinger, Harry; BNDD; DEA
Ferguson, James, 259n136
Flues, A. Gilmore, 106–107
foreign aid
to Afghanistan: from Britain, 230n69; dependence on, 6–7, 10–11, 13–14, 28, 54, 111–112, 113, 143, 146, 192–193, 217; from Germany, 55, 61, 65, 168–169, 186; from Soviet Union, 189–190, 239n22; from US, 74–75, 83, 87, 89–90, 91, 105–108, 111–112, 143, 162, 165–166, 171–175, 188, 191, 192, 202, 203, 209, 217
to Iran, 126–131, 161, 163
to Pakistan, 92, 127–128, 161, 162, 255n39, 259n125
to Turkey, 153
fragmentation, 7–8, 89, 149, 193, 224n19
France
drug control efforts of, 91, 99, 152
illicit operations in, 151–154
smuggling into, 44–45

French Connection, 151–154
frontiers, 224n19
Frydl, Kathleen, 4
Fundamental Law (1923), 31–32

Gallant, Thomas, 43, 51, 247n95
Gaston, Herbert, 65
Gavit, J.P., 16
gendarmerie
in Afghanistan, 148, 161, 162, 164–165, 170
in Iran, 125–131, 168
See also police
Geneva Conferences, 24, 37, 41
Geneva Narcotics Convention (1925), 24, 58
GENMISH (US Military Mission to IIG), 126–131, 162
Germany
aid to Afghanistan, 55, 61, 65, 168–169, 186
exporting of drugs by, 70
trade with Afghanistan, 38, 46, 59
Ghani, Abdul, 42
Ghilzai Pashtuns, 190
Ghulam Nabi, Ala, 44–45, 49–51, 53
Ginsberg, Allen, 132
Giustozzi, Antonio, 191
Gobar, Asad Hassan, 133–134
Golden Triangle, 154–158, 249n43
Goodhand, Jonathan, 224n15
Gootenberg, Paul, 5, 13, 14–15
Government Opium Company. *See* Afghan Opium Company
Gregorian, Vartan, 29, 225n27, 229n49, 235n81
Guerini family, 152

Habibullah, 30–31, 185–186
Hague Conferences, 23–24
Hague Convention (1912), 56–58, 70–84
Haidar, Sheik, 26
Hanifi, Shah Mahmoud, 29
Haq, Ikramul, 225n26
Haq, M Emdad-ul, 225n21
Harrison Narcotics Act (1914), 23–24, 228n27
Hashim Khan, Muhammad, and government of, 53–58, 61–63, 65–69, 74–84, 92
hashish. *See* charse
hash oil, 140
Hastings, Warren, 19
Hekmatyar, Gilbudin, 209

Helmand Valley
ban on opium in, 183–184, 202–208, 210–211
co-opting of opium ban in, 205–207, 211, 212
opium production, emergence of, 15, 175, 178–179, 180–185, 196–202, 210, 212–213; re-emergence after ban, 207–209
project background and challenges, 90, 185–194, 254n29
state decline and, 15, 178–179, 183–184
US relations, impact on, 183, 190–191, 193, 202–203, 204–205
heroin
addiction to, 138–139, 145–146, 149–150, 152, 155, 157, 209
Afghan production of, 209, 216, 217
French production of, 151–154
as medicine, 21, 52–53, 56–57
Mexican production of, 158–159
Nixon's war on, 145, 147–163, 175–179
smuggling of, 44–45, 49–51, 127, 138–139, 140–141, 157–159
Southeast Asian production of, 156–158
Hickman, Timothy, 230n88
"hippie mafia," 139–140
hippies. *See* tourists
historic role of drugs, 24–27
Hong Kong, 156–157
Hopkins, Benjamin, 224n19, 226n36
Humayun, Nasiruddin Muhammad, 25, 228n39

IIG (Imperial Iranian Gendarmerie), 126–131, 244n42, 245n46
illicit exporting of drugs
by Afghanistan: pre-WWI, 18, 29, 37–41, 42–43; continued expansion of today, 215–218; interwar years, 44–46, 49–51, 50–51, 54, 58–61; to Iran, 88, 101, 118, 126–131, 168; professionalization of, 140–142, 143; tourism and, 132–138, 141–142, 161, 225n26, 246n66; trafficking routes, 142fig; to US, 90–91, 99, 132, 139; worldwide, 1–2, 101, 118–119, 139–140, 144, 163–164, 168, 175, 177–179, 200–201; during WWII, 69, 74, 81, 82–83
by Southeast Asia, 150, 154–158, 201, 249n43
by Turkey, 128, 139, 147, 151–154, 244n35, 245n49, 248n16, 249n43
illicit *vs.* licit, 181, 226n37
importing of pharmaceutical drugs. *See* pharmaceutical drug trading
India
British colonial period, 16–17, 19–20, 28, 36–43, 51, 58, 64
neutrality of, 188
infrastructure development, 200
interdiction, 219
International Dangerous Drug Act, 57, 233n46
Iran
addiction in, 93–94, 95, 109, 126, 128, 162, 209, 239n29, 239n30
Afghan opium trade, opposition to, 93–95
drug control efforts by, 117, 118, 125–131, 143, 150, 163, 168, 239n31, 244n30
licit production in, 162, 239n18, 239n29, 239n30
smuggling into, 88, 95, 101, 118, 126–131, 139, 143, 146, 148, 162, 168
US and, 90, 92, 125–131, 140, 161, 163
Iron Amir. *see* Abdur Rahman, Amir Khan
Islamic State, 221
Ispahani, Mahnaz, 254n6, 257n96
Itimadi, Nur Ahmad, 123–124

James, Charles, 203
Japan, 58, 59, 186
Johnson administration, 191
Judd, Walter, 80–81
Judd Resolution, 72, 79
Juma Khan, Hajji, 214–215

Kabul Times (newspaper), 166–167
Kalakani, Habibullah, 48–49
Kalinovsky, Artemy, 191
karakul, 54, 61, 233n36
Karavan (newspaper), 135–136, 136fig, 143
Karmal, Babrak, 121
Karzai, Hamid, 216–217
Katawazi, Colonel, 160, 161
Keeley, Leslie, 34
Kennedy administration, 191

Kerrigan, J.J., 64, 67, 68
Kesey, Ken, 132
Khaliq, Abdul, 53
Khrushchev, Nikita, 189

land redistribution, 190, 191
Lashkar Gah, 185, 193, 204, 256n71
Latimer, C., 38–39
League of Nations, 24, 45, 54, 56–57, 73–75, 233n46
Leary, Timothy, 132, 139–140
legal system (Afghan), 27–28, 31–34
Levi, Peter, 133
licit exporting of drugs
  by Afghanistan: pre-WWI, 10–11, 17, 28, 34–35, 41, 42; interwar years, 54, 58–62; during WWII, 46, 61–69, 73–74, 79–81, 235n77, 235n92; postwar, 91–93, 166
  by Germany, 70
  by Turkey, 19, 63, 70, 239n18
loya jirgas, 52, 232n25
LSD, 139–140

MacDonald, David, 225n22, 228n37
Maconachie, R.R., 39–40
Mahmud (Shah), 89, 92, 186
Maiwandal, Mohammad, 123–124
majun, 25
Malik, Abdul, 97–98
Mallinckrodt Chemical Works, 68, 166
Mansfield, David, 2, 86, 112, 113–114, 114–115, 218, 220, 253n3, 258n115
market agriculture, 15, 182, 194–197
Markham, James, 136, 138
Maroofi, Y.P., 171
Marsden, Magnus, 224n19, 226n36
Martin H. Smith Pharmaceutical Company, 56–57
mast, 26
Matthee, Rudi, 239n29
McCoy, Alfred, 155, 224n20, 253n3
McGovern, George, 149
McLaughlin, Gerald, 239n30
medicine, growth of opium as, 21, 53. *See also* pharmaceutical drug trading
Merck Pharmaceuticals, 64, 66–67, 68, 235n92
Meshad, Iran, 130
methadone maintenance, 150
Mexico
  drug control efforts by, 150, 158–160, 175–176
  legal cultivation in, 249n52, 249n53
  supply shift from, 177
  supply shift to, 147, 158–160, 201
migrant workers, 103, 104
minorities, constructions of, 224n19
Mintz, Sydney, 243n5
Mitchell, Timothy, 254n19
modernization (Afghan)
  pre-WWI, 31–32
  health care, development of, 45, 52–53, 55–58, 70–74
  interwar, 10, 45, 48, 51–58, 186, 187, 225n27
  postwar, 192, 243n19; opposition to, 118, 120–125, 143–144
modernization theory, 182, 187, 212–213, 259n136
Mohammad, Faiz, 174
Montford reforms, 36–37
Morley-Minto reforms, 36
morphine
  in Badakhshan opium, 62, 91
  emergence of as medicine, 21, 52–53
  for nonmedical use, 36
  opium trade and, 63–64, 65, 66–67, 77–78, 91
  seizures of, 141
  Turkish, 151–152, 153, 245n49, 249n53
Morrison-Knudsen Company (MKA), 90, 186, 188–189, 190, 211, 238n11
Mughal dynasty, 25
mujahideen, 209
Musahiban dynasty, 231n4
  foreign aid, dependence on, 6–7, 10–11
  modernization by, 51–58, 186–187, 225n27
  See also Daud Khan; Hashim Khan; Mahmud; Nadir Shah

Nadir Shah, and government of, 45, 47, 52–53, 186, 225n27, 231n4
Nangarhar, 218
Nasrullah, 31
naswar (tobacco snuff), 138
nationalism, 31, 53
Nawid, Senzil, 230n78
Nehru, Jawarhul, 186, 188
Netherlands, 72–73
Newell, Richard, 111
New York Times, 136, 138. *See also* Weinraub, Bernard

Nixon's War on Drugs, 145–179
in Afghanistan, 160–179
aid and resources provided, 146, 147, 151, 153
methods of action, 147, 148, 149–150, 153, 157, 158
motivations for, 145–146, 149–150, 161
regional targets, 151–160
nomads, 190, 255n42
Northwest Frontier Province (NWFP), 28, 37–38

Omar, Muhammad, 65–66, 67, 71, 78
opioid crisis (current US), 250n57
Osman, Ismail, 203

Pahlavi, Muhammad Reza Shah, and government of, 125–131, 239n31, 244n30
Pain, Adam, 220
Pakistan
addiction in, 209, 250n67
drug control efforts by, 127, 150, 225n24
opposition to Afghan exports, 95
production in, 162, 198, 208–209, 225n21, 250n67
smuggling into, 14, 127, 146, 148, 162, 188, 209, 250n62
US and, 90, 92, 100, 127–128, 161, 162, 255n39, 259n125
Pandey, Gyan, 224n19
Pashtuns
as beyond government reach, 162
HAVA and, 182, 187, 190, 212
hegemony of, 13, 89, 104, 110, 190, 195, 212, 226n28, 254n16, 256n76
kidnapping by, 245n50
policies to placate, 10, 49, 87, 88, 89, 108, 110, 187, 190, 212, 252n98
patent medicines, 21
Patna factory, 36
Pazhwak, Fazil Rabi, 193, 203–204, 205
Peace Corps, 199
peasants. *See* rural population
Penal Code (1924–25), 32–34
Pennel, T.L., 26
pharmaceutical drugs trading (Afghan)
exporting of opium for, 46, 59–69, 73–74, 79–81, 91–92, 166, 235n77, 235n92
importing of, 45, 55–58, 70–74, 78, 95–96
police (Afghan), 130–131, 161, 162, 164–165, 167, 168–170, 173, 176–177. *See also* gendarmerie
Poullada, Leon, 120
prices
of illicit hashish, 134, 205fig
of illicit opium, 129–130, 134, 198, 204, 205–206, 205fig
of licit opium, 64–65, 66–67, 69
private opium companies, 62–63, 69
production of drugs
in Afghanistan: in Badakhshan, 85–86, 89, 103–108, 115; current levels, 1–2; economic dependence on, 85–86, 89, 103–106, 142, 203, 218–219, 249n43; in Helmand Valley, 15, 175, 178–179, 180–185, 196–202, 207–209, 210, 212–213; standardization issues, 67–69
alternatives to, 15, 85–86, 103–104, 182, 184, 217
of heroin, 151–154, 156–159, 209, 216, 217
in Iran, 162, 239n18, 239n29, 239n30
in Pakistan, 162, 198, 208–209, 225n21, 250n67
in Southeast Asia, 150, 154–158, 201, 249n43
in Turkey, 19, 63, 139, 151–154, 198, 239n18, 249n43
prohibition
Afghan adoption of, 6, 11, 14, 46–47
by Britain, 39–42, 43
contradictory impacts of, 14, 15, 207, 210–211
in Helmand Valley, 182, 184
in Iran, 94, 98, 127, 143, 225n24, 225n26, 244n30
in Pakistan, 162, 225n24
in Turkey, 127, 128, 153–154, 163, 200–201, 225n26
US as proponent of, 6, 17, 22–24, 228n31
See also 1945 Opium Prohibition; 1958 Opium Prohibition; 1973/1974 prohibition

qawm, 12, 149, 170, 176–177, 184, 211–212, 224n17
qazis, 32, 33, 230n78
Quinn, Thomas, 239n30

Rahman Khan. *See* Abdur Rahman, Amir Khan
Raskine, Joseph, 50
Rawalpindi, Treaty of (Anglo-Afghan Treaty), 31, 39
resettlement, 190, 191, 195, 255n42, 255n47
road building, 200
Robert, L.W., 57
Rod, Mir, 138
Roosevelt, Theodore, 22
Roy, Olivier, 170, 177, 178, 212, 224n17
rural population (Afghan)
  attempts to limit interactions with, 6–7, 10–11, 12, 13–14
  corruption among, 170
  disconnect with state, 110, 112–115, 120–122, 124, 173, 192–193, 212, 243n12
  HAVA's impact on, 190, 191, 193–196
  opium production by: Badakhshan, 85–86, 89, 103–106; continued expansion of, 215–217; Helmand Valley, 15, 175, 178–179, 180–185, 196–202, 207–209, 210, 212–213
  regulation of, increase in, 149, 177, 182, 190, 211, 226n32, 226n36
  resistance methods of, 259n141
  state reluctance to disrupt, 203–204
Russia/Soviet Union
  addicted agents from, 138
  Afghanistan, relations with, 31, 58, 59, 62, 92, 112, 174, 192, 239n22
  invasion of Afghanistan, 181, 208–210, 215–216
  US, Afghanistan, and, 90, 107

Scott, James, 259n141
Scott, Richard, 204, 210
Sea Customs Act (1878), 40
Shafiq, Musa, 165–166
Shanghai Opium Commission, 23, 35–36
sharia law, 27–28, 33, 48, 52, 162
Sharman, Clem, 60
Shirkat-e-Saderat-e-Taryak (the Opium Exporting Company), 63
Shirkat-e-Sahami-e-Taryak (The Opium Joint-Stock Company), 63
Shirkat-i-Taryak (Afghan Opium Company), 59, 62, 81
Siyyum-i Aqrab tragedy, 121–122
smugglers, characteristics of, 128–129
smuggling, definition, 164. *See also* illicit exporting of drugs
snuff, 33, 138
social addiction, 109, 242n74
soldiers, drug use by, 132, 139, 145, 149, 156–157, 249n44
Southeast Asia, 150, 154–158, 201, 249n43
Soviet Union. *See* Russia/Soviet Union
Staanekzai, Nasrullah, 33, 229n56
State Department (US)
  Federal Bureau of Narcotics and, 71, 72–73
  Iran and, 94, 95
  postwar relations with Afghanistan, 82, 83, 91, 100, 101, 105–107, 198–199, 205
  during World War II, 64, 67–68, 71, 72–73, 75–77
state formation (Afghan)
  drug control as aid to, 34, 45, 111, 114, 148–149, 176, 178
  drug control as obstacle to, 2, 7, 216–221
  pre-WWI, 27–34
  regression/loss of legitimacy, 117–118, 120–125, 142–144, 149, 172, 178–179, 192, 208–212, 215–221
  state building *vs.*, 224n15
  trading of drugs as aid to, 2, 6, 29–30, 41
Steeves, John, 191
student protests, 120, 121, 123–124, 172
Sufis, 26
supply, global shifts in, 147, 154, 158, 159–160, 176, 177–178, 200–201
supply-side interventions, 147, 150–161, 257n97

Taliban, 112–115, 214, 216, 217, 221, 258n115
taxation
  Afghan, 17, 27, 28, 29, 33, 35, 42
  British Empire, 16, 20, 36, 38
  India (colonial), 36, 37, 39fig
Taylor, Arnold, 22
Technical Cooperation Administration (TCA), 189
Third Anglo-Afghan war, 31
Tilly, Charles, 226n32
tobacco, 33, 138
tourists, 116–117, 118–119, 132–138, 141–142, 161, 225n26, 246n66
Toynbee, Arnold, 193
tribal laws, 27–28

Trocki, Carl, 19, 20
Turkey
  Afghanistan and, 95, 128
  drug control efforts by, 127, 128, 150, 153–154, 157–158, 163, 178, 200–201, 225n26
  foreign aid to, 153
  Iran and, 94, 126, 127, 163, 225n26
  opium exports from: illicit, 128, 139, 147, 151–154, 244n35, 245n49, 248n16, 249n43; licit, 19, 63, 70, 239n18
  production in, 19, 63, 139, 151–154, 198, 239n18, 249n43
  tourists in, 132, 246n66

ulema, 230n78
UN (United Nations)
  Afghan appeals to, 94–96, 99–101
  assistance to Badakhshan, 104–105, 107, 242n74
  Commission on Narcotic Drugs, 94–96
  funding of Afghan drug control, 202
  payments to opium warlords, 209
  UNFAO (Food and Agricultural Organization), 171
  UNFDAC (UN Fund for Drug Abuse Control), 151, 157, 174–175, 252n94
unemployment, 104, 172, 208
United Kingdom. *See* British Empire
United States
  Afghanistan and: Afghan tactics for relations, 47, 109, 124; during Daud governments, 89–102, 105–107, 109, 113, 173–175, 183, 239n20; foreign aid, 87, 89–90, 91, 105–108, 111–112, 143, 162, 165–166, 171–175, 188, 202, 203, 209, 219; during WWII, 74–75, 79, 82; Helmand Valley and, 183, 190–191, 193, 202–203, 204–205; interwar years, 45–47, 54–55, 56–57; invasion (2001), 216–217; Nixon's War on Drugs, 160–179; pre-WWI, 13–14, 15; recent interactions, 214–221; US agents in Afghanistan, 140–141, 148, 169; US concerns about drug trade, 138–141, 161–162; during WWII, 61–84, 235n81
  discourses on drugs, 22–23, 34, 108–109
  drug users in/from, 132–139, 141–142, 143, 145–146, 149–150, 156–157, 158, 161, 250n57
  illicit drug trade, encouragement of, 155
  Iran and, 90, 92, 125–131, 140
  Pakistan and, 90, 92, 100, 127–128, 161, 162, 255n39, 259n125
  securitization of drug control, 217
USAID, 183, 191, 194, 195–196, 198, 199, 204
USSR. *See* Russia/Soviet Union

Van Schendel, Willem, 4–5, 89, 110, 181, 226n37
Volstead Act, 233n46

Wahab Haider, Abdul, 90–91
Walker, William, 227n44
warlords, 209, 214–217, 218
Weimer, David, 146
Weinraub, Bernard, 198, 199–200, 201, 202
West Germany, 168, 169
wheat growing, 15, 182, 194–197
Windle, James, 250n57, 257n97
World War II, Afghan trade during
  illicit exports, 69, 74, 81, 82–83
  licit exports during, 46, 61–69, 73–74, 79–81
  pharmaceutical drug importing, 70–74, 78

Yusuf, Muhammad, 119–121, 191

Zabuli, Abdul Majod, 189
Zahir, Abdul, 95–96, 123–124, 165, 166
Zahir Shah, Mohammad, 53, 54–55, 118, 119–120, 121, 133, 176
Zeitlein, Arnold, 136
Zia ul-Haq, 162
Zurich, David, 116

www.ingramcontent.com/pod-product-compliance
Lightning Source LLC
Chambersburg PA
CBHW031411270326
41929CB00010BA/1413

* 9 7 8 1 5 0 1 7 3 9 7 6 7 *